AUSTRALIAN Signpost MATHS

3

Alan McSeveny Rachel McSeveny Diane McSeveny-Foster

Pearson Australia
(a division of Pearson Australia Group Pty Ltd)
459–471 Church St, Level 1, Building B, Richmond, Victoria, 3121
PO Box 23360, Melbourne, Victoria 8012
www.pearson.com.au

First published 2024 by Pearson Australia
2028 2027 2026 2025
10 9 8 7 6 5 4 3 2 1

Publishers: Sophie Matta and Kerry Nagle
Project Manager: Michelle Thomas
Production Editor: Laura Rentsch
Development Editor: Rachel Elliott
Designer: Anne Donald
Proofreader: Laura Rentsch
Rights & Permissions Editor: Alice McBroom
Cover Design: Jennifer Johnston
Cover Art: Michael Barter
Illustrator: Michael Barter
Publishing Services: Jit-Pin Chong
Printed in Malaysia by Vivar

ISBN 978 0 6557 0877 3
Pearson Australia Group Pty Ltd ABN 40 004 245 943

Attributions
We would like to thank the following for permission to reproduce copyright material.

Shutterstock: Antpkr, p. 131 (bowl); Chachamp, p. 110 (mug); Ddisq, p. 144; Wu Hsoung, p. 112 (analogue watch); Kues, p. 145; Dany Kurniawan, p. 110 (fish tank); LaMony Betty, pp. 84, 104, 110 (bottle); Iablonskyi Mykola, p. 104 (thermos); MZinchenko, p. 29 (flag); Nayoka, p. 33 (wooden car); TitoOnz, p. 135 (earth); TrotzOlga, p. 110 (dish); Sandsun, p. 79 (swimming pool); Peter Vanco, p. 84 (bin); Duangphorn Wiriya: p. 15 (tent); Wonderful Future World, p. 83 (jug and glasses); Ziviani, p. 112 (digital watch).

123rf.com: Coprid, p. 84 (storage box); Ilterriorm, p. 116 (SUV); Ivanspasic, p. 84, (measuring cup); Kung37, pp. 84, 104 (watering can); Learchitecto, p. 135 (soccer ball); Mychadre77, p. 116 (sea star); Nyvltart, p. 131 (paint tin); Realiia, pp. 84, 104 (container); Serezniy, p. 110 (lunchbox); Shootingtheworld, p. 171; Tap10, pp. 84, 104 (esky).

Unsplash: Eugene Tkachenko, p. 132.

Acknowledgement of Country
Pearson respects and honours Aboriginal and Torres Strait Islander Elders past, present and future. We acknowledge the stories, traditions and living cultures of the Traditional Custodians of the lands on which our company is located and where we conduct our business. Pearson is committed to honouring Australian Aboriginal and Torres Strait Islander peoples' unique cultural and spiritual relationships to the land, waters and seas and their rich contribution to society.

Aboriginal and Torres Strait Islander peoples are advised that this text may contain images, voices and names of deceased persons.

What is Australian Signpost Maths?

Australian Signpost Maths is a mathematics program providing direction and support for teaching and learning. The series covers the content and skills presented in the Australian Curriculum (v9) Mathematics F–10.

Student Books

A Student Book and an online Teacher Resource are provided for Foundation.

For Years 1 to 6, a Student Book, an online Teacher Resource and a Mentals Book are provided for each year level. The online Teacher Resources provide a wealth of support for teachers.

Mentals Books

The content has been carefully sequenced within each year level and across the F–6 series to take into account students' expected mathematical development. However, from the rich and varied material provided, teachers can develop individual learning programs to meet the needs of each student.

Teacher Resource

The Student Books are designed to support explicit teaching methods. Many group activities are provided in Activity, Investigation and Fun spots within the Student Books and the online Teacher Resource.

To maximise the benefits of the program, the Student Book, the online Teacher Resource and the Mentals Book should be used together.

Structure of Australian Signpost Maths

In the Year 3 to 6 books, the worksheet pages cover all three elements: Number sense and algebra, Measurement and geometry, and Statistics and probability. These are presented in five chapters:

- Number and algebra
- Operations and algebra
- Measurement
- Space
- Statistics and probability.

This gives teachers flexibility in programming. The contents cross-reference allows teachers to quickly find the pages where each concept has been covered.

Within the program, explicit teaching, critical and creative thinking, language development and identification and treatment of weaknesses are given high priority.

Identification and addressing areas of need

Five progress tests are designed to identify each student's areas of need, and the follow-up program after each of the tests is designed to address these needs. A reference to the relevant worksheet page is given for each test question. A remediation record page is used to track the student's progress.

These testing resources can be found in the online Teacher Resource.

Parallel progress retests are provided for further testing after remediation has taken place.

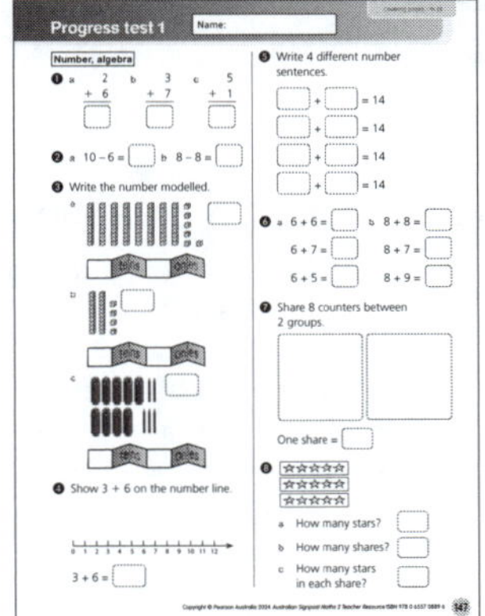

Progress test 1 Name:

Number, algebra

1. a 2 + 6 = ☐ b 3 + 7 = ☐ c 5 + 1 = ☐
2. a 10 – 6 = ☐ b 8 – 8 = ☐
3. Write the number modelled.
   a tens ones
   b tens ones
   c tens ones
4. Show 3 + 6 on the number line.
   3 + 6 = ☐
5. Write 4 different number sentences.
   ☐ + ☐ = 14
   ☐ + ☐ = 14
   ☐ + ☐ = 14
   ☐ + ☐ = 14
6. a 6 + 6 = ☐ 6 + 7 = ☐ 6 + 5 = ☐ b 8 + 8 = ☐ 8 + 7 = ☐ 8 + 9 = ☐
7. Share 8 counters between 2 groups.
   One share = ☐
8. a How many stars? ☐
   b How many shares? ☐
   c How many stars in each share? ☐

147

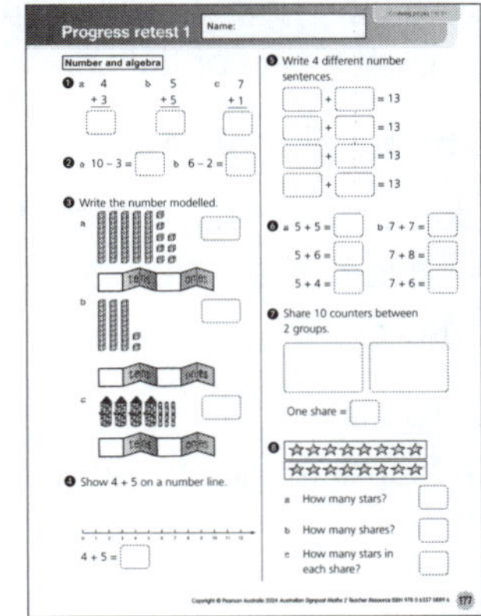

Progress retest 1 Name:

Number and algebra

1. a 4 + 3 = ☐ b 5 + 5 = ☐ c 7 + 1 = ☐
2. a 10 – 3 = ☐ b 6 – 2 = ☐
3. Write the number modelled.
   a tens ones
   b tens ones
   c tens ones
4. Show 4 + 5 on a number line.
   4 + 5 = ☐
5. Write 4 different number sentences.
   ☐ + ☐ = 13
   ☐ + ☐ = 13
   ☐ + ☐ = 13
   ☐ + ☐ = 13
6. a 5 + 5 = ☐ 5 + 6 = ☐ 5 + 4 = ☐ b 7 + 7 = ☐ 7 + 8 = ☐ 7 + 6 = ☐
7. Share 10 counters between 2 groups.
   One share = ☐
8. a How many stars? ☐
   b How many shares? ☐
   c How many stars in each share? ☐

177

Special features of Australian Signpost Maths

- **The traffic light icons**
  These are found on the top right of each worksheet page in the Student Books. They allow students to assess their own progress and give feedback to the teacher.
  - ☐ **Green:** I found this work easy.
  - ☐ **Orange:** I found some work on the page difficult.
  - ☐ **Red:** I don't understand the work on this page.

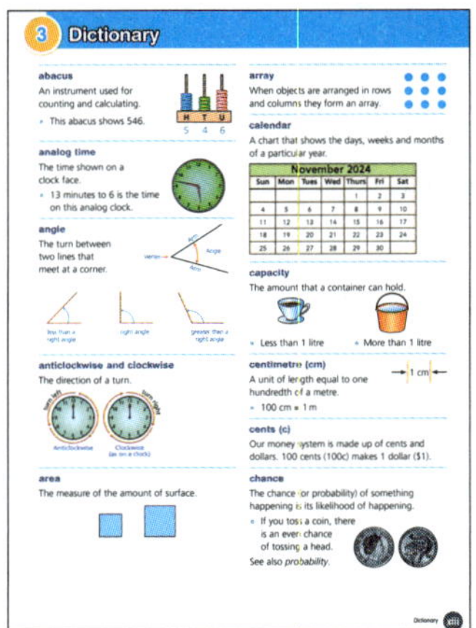

Dictionary

- **Dictionary**
  Terms used in the Student Book and terms that should be understood at this level are recorded here to provide a reference for students and teachers. The dictionary can be found on pages xiii–xxi of this book.

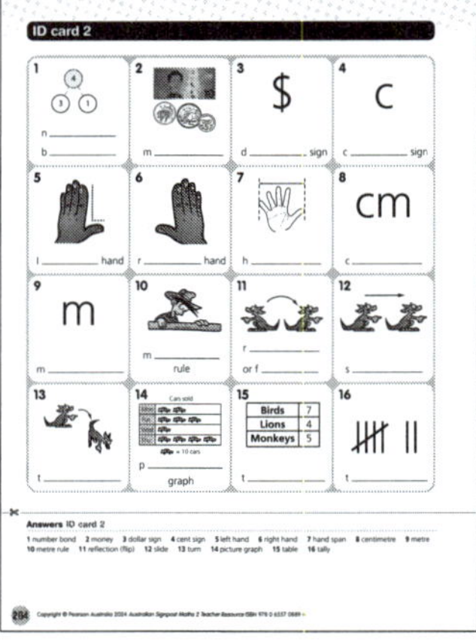

ID card 2

- **ID cards (Years 1 to 6)**
  These cards review the language of Mathematics by asking students to identify common terms, shapes and symbols. They are designed to be reused and are found in the online Teacher Resource and in the front of the Mentals Books.

- **Progress tests**
  These allow the teacher to identify each student's strengths and needs. Cross-references for each question direct teachers and students to the pages where that work is introduced. Tables are provided to record the follow-up that takes place and parallel tests are provided for retesting. These tests can be found in the online Teacher Resource.

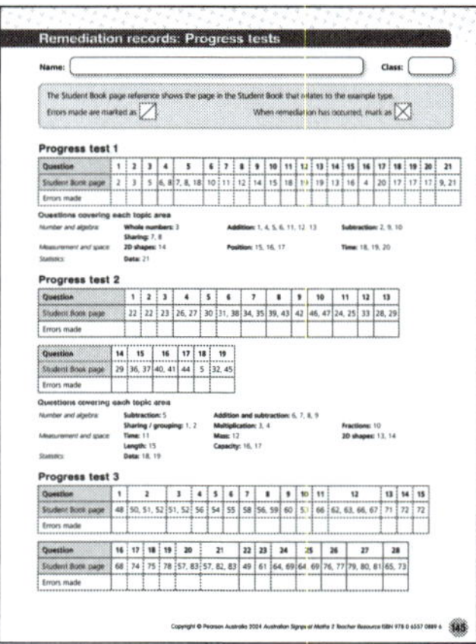

Remediation records: Progress tests

- **Year 3 Consolidation booklet**
  This 32 page booklet is found in the online Teacher Resource. It is designed to reinforce work completed in class and provides practice of important skills and addition and subtraction facts. The booklet can be used when there is limited supervision or when a student finishes classwork early.

AUSTRALIAN Signpost 3 MATHS

Consolidation booklet

Name:

Class:

- **Answers**
  These are supplied in the Student Book and the online Teacher Resource.

- **Blackline masters (BLM)**
  References are made to the blackline masters in the Teacher Resource suggestions provided for each student work page.

- **Differentiation**
  Each student book work page has a Teacher Resource page to support it. Cross-references direct the teacher to pages where the concept is introduced and developed. These references may be from the Student Book for the previous year, the current year or the next year.

- **Extra support pages**
  Addition and subtraction facts are reinforced in Extra Support 1. In Years 3 and 4, the algorithm strategy pages extend the fast workers. In Years 5 and 6, they act as consolidation.

- **Cartoons**
  Cartoons are used to motivate and instruct.

Australian Signpost Maths icons

Signpost icons are used throughout the book as cues to the essential nature of exercises and activities, and as a guide to ways of engaging with them. These icons often indicate alternative or more concrete approaches to dealing with concepts.

This icon highlights **important rules and concepts** occurring throughout the book. It often appears with worked examples.

Activities provide **applications and enrichment**. These activities usually involve the use of concrete materials and partner or group work.

These enjoyable activities are used to **motivate and involve** students in mathematical pursuits. They usually involve games and puzzles.

Investigations allow students to **explore and discover** maths concepts.

These activities involve the use of computers or other technology.

Structure of the Australian Curriculum, F–6 (v9)

Numeracy elements

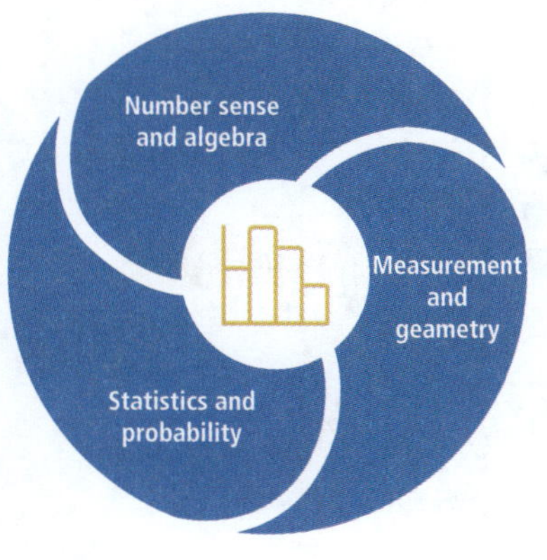

Curriculum content is organised under 6 interrelated strands: Number, Algebra, Measurement, Space, Statistics and Probability.

Sub-elements for Number sense and algebra

- Number and place value
- Counting processes
- Additive strategies
- Multiplicative strategies
- Interpreting fractions
- Number patterns and algebraic thinking
- Understanding money

Sub-elements for Measurement and geometry

- Understanding units of measurement
- Understanding geometric properties
- Positioning and locating
- Measuring time

Sub-elements for Statistics and probability

- Understanding chance
- Interpreting and representing data

The Curriculum strives to develop in students proficiency in Mathematics, highlighting Understanding, Fluency, Reasoning and Problem solving.

Mathematics content of the Australian Curriculum

- It is important that you download the **GENERAL CAPABILITIES** document from 'Downloads' in the top navigation bar of the website homepage. It contains the tables that list the progression level expectations for each Year, F to 10. It also provides the content of all progression levels.
- The LEARNING AREAS download gives a summary of Content descriptions and Elaborations. CROSS-CURRICULUM PRIORITIES can also be found there.

Content and curriculum overview

Suggested program
This weekly program aligns with the Mentals Book, e.g. Mentals Book, Unit 9 covers work taught in Weeks 7 and 8 of this book.

Number and algebra

Page	Unit	Title	Content: Counting, number	Place value	Rounding	Fractions	Decimals	Patterns, algebra	Suggested program	Term
1	1:01	Counting	●					●	Week 3	Term 1
2	1:02	Counting	●					●		
3	1:03	Numbers to 1000	●	●					Week 4	
4	1:04	Numbers to 1000	●	●						
5	1:05	Numbers to 1000		●						
6	1:06	Rounding to the nearest 10			●				Week 10	
7	1:07	Rounding to the nearest 100			●					
8	1:08	Numbers to 1000		●	●					
9	1:09	Fractions of a collection				●			Week 11	Term 2
10	1:10	Fractions of a whole				●				
11	1:11	Numbers to 10 000		●					Week 14	
12	1:12	Numbers to 10 000	●	●						
13	1:13	Fractions				●			Week 15	
14	1:14	Fractions				●				
15	1:15	What's the rule?						●	Week 18	
16	1:16	Making patterns						●		
17	1:17	Numbers to 10 000	●	●				●	Week 21	Term 3
18	1:18	Place value to 10 000		●	●					
19	1:19	Comparing fractions				●			Week 22	
20	1:20	Using fractions				●				
21	1:21	Numbers to 10 000	●	●					Week 26	
22	1:22	Numbers to 10 000		●						
23	1:23	Expanded notation	●	●						
24	1:24	Tenths and fifths				●	●		Week 33	Term 4
25	1:25	Place value using tenths		●		●	●			
26	1:26	Place value using tenths		●		●	●	●		
27	1:27	Numbers over 10 000		●					Week 34	
28	1:28	Numbers over 10 000	●	●						
29	1:29	Larger numbers	●	●						

The teacher will decide when testing occurs. The Progress Tests and Re-tests are found in the online Teacher Resource. The first two units of the Mentals Book review the previous year and could be completed in Weeks 1 and 2.

Operations and algebra

Page	Unit	Title	Content	Addition	Subtraction	Multiplication	Division	Mental strategies	Number patterns	Money	Problem solving	Suggested program	Term
30	2:01	Australian money								●		Week 5	Term 1
31	2:02	Money		●						●			
32	2:03	Addition and subtraction		●	●				●				
33	2:04	Number facts, x 2				●						Week 6	
34	2:05	Number facts, x 5, x 10				●							
35	2:06	Multiplication facts				●							
36	2:07	2, 5 and 10 times tables				●			●			Week 7	
37	2:08	Patterns in + and –		●	●			●	●				
38	2:09	Relating addition and subtraction		●	●							Week 8	
39	2:10	Problem solving		●	●	●		●			●		
40	2:11	Shopping								●		Week 9	
41	2:12	Money		●						●			
42	2:13	Addition to 99		●				●				Week 12	Term 2
43	2:14	Jump strategy		●	●			●					
44	2:15	Jump strategy		●	●			●					
45	2:16	Mental strategies		●				●				Week 13	
46	2:17	Problem solving		●	●	●	●				●		
47	2:18	Number facts, x 3				●						Week 16	
48	2:19	Times tables				●			●				
49	2:20	Multiplication facts				●						Week 17	
50	2:21	Number facts, x 4				●							
51	2:22	3 and 4 times tables				●			●			Week 19	
52	2:23	Number facts, multiplication				●							
53	2:24	Sharing and grouping					●					Week 23	Term 3
54	2:25	Modelling division					●						
55	2:26	Relating x and ÷				●	●				●	Week 24	
56	2:27	Linking x and ÷				●	●						
57	2:28	÷ facts from x facts				●	●					Week 25	
58	2:29	x and ÷ tables				●	●						
59	2:30	Inverse operations, x and ÷				●	●						
60	2:31	Addition to 99, no trading		●						●	●	Week 27	
61	2:32	Subtraction, no trading			●						●		
62	2:33	Addition to 99 with trading		●						●	●	Week 28	
63	2:34	Addition with trading		●							●		
64	2:35	Addition with 2-digit numbers		●									
65	2:36	Addition, trading for 100		●								Week 29	
66	2:37	Addition to 999 with one trade		●						●			
67	2:38	Addition, two trades		●							●	Week 30	
68	2:39	Subtraction with trading to 99			●					●		Week 31	Term 4
69	2:40	Subtraction with trading			●								
70	2:41	Subtraction with trading			●							Week 32	
71	2:42	Checking subtraction by addition		●	●						●		
72	2:43	Addition strategies		●				●				Week 35	
73	2:44	Subtraction strategies			●			●					
74	2:45	Using mental strategies		●	●			●			●		
75	2:46	Change from $2		●	●					●		Week 36	
76	2:47	Problem solving		●		●	●			●	●		

Suggested program
This weekly program aligns with the Mentals Book, e.g. Mentals Book, Unit 9 covers work taught in Weeks 7 and 8 of this book.

The teacher will decide when testing occurs. The Progress Tests and Re-tests are found in the online Teacher Resource.

Measurement

Page	Unit	Title	Content: Length	Area	Volume	Capacity	Mass	Telling the time	Duration	Problem solving	Suggested program	Term
77	3:01	Revision of length	●								Week 7	Term 1
78	3:02	The metre	●									
79	3:03	Using the metre	●									
80	3:04	Clocks						●			Week 8	
81	3:05	Analog time						●				
82	3:06	Analog and digital time						●				
83	3:07	Capacity review			●	●					Week 9	
84	3:08	Estimating the litre				●						
85	3:09	The litre			●	●						
86	3:10	Centimetres	●								Week 11	Term 2
87	3:11	Measuring with centimetres	●									
88	3:12	Recording length	●								Week 12	
89	3:13	Perimeter	●									
90	3:14	Analog and digital time						●			Week 15	
91	3:15	Analog time						●				
92	3:16	Analog and digital time						●				
93	3:17	The kilogram					●				Week 16	
94	3:18	Comparing masses					●					
95	3:19	Using the kilogram					●					
96	3:20	Area		●							Week 21	Term 3
97	3:21	Area		●							Week 22	
98	3:22	The calendar							●			
99	3:23	The calendar							●			
100	3:24	The gram					●				Week 24	
101	3:25	Using grams					●					
102	3:26	Mass problem solving					●			●		
103	3:27	The millilitre			●	●					Week 25	
104	3:28	Capacity problem solving				●				●		
105	3:29	The millimetre	●								Week 26	
106	3:30	Using a ruler	●									
107	3:31	Length problem solving	●							●	Week 31	Term 4
108	3:32	Area problems		●						●		
109	3:33	Area using square centimetres		●								
110	3:34	Standard metric units	●			●	●				Week 37	
111	3:35	Personal benchmarks	●		●	●	●			●		
112	3:36	The stopwatch							●			

Suggested program
This weekly program aligns with the Mentals Book, e.g. Mentals Book, Unit 9 covers work taught in Weeks 7 and 8 of this book.

- 'Money' can be found in Chapter 2.
- 'Angles' can be found in Chapter 4.

The teacher will decide when testing occurs. The Progress Tests and Re-tests are found in the online Teacher Resource.

Page	Unit	Title	Content	2D space	Angles, lines	Symmetry, turning	3D objects	Position, directions	**Suggested program** This weekly program aligns with the Mentals Book, e.g. Mentals Book, Unit 9 covers work taught in Weeks 7 and 8 of this book.	
Space										
113	4:01	Properties of 3D objects					●		Week 4	Term 1
114	4:02	Symmetry		●		●				
115	4:03	Properties of 3D objects					●		Week 5	
116	4:04	Symmetry around us				●				
117	4:05	Parallel and perpendicular lines			●				Week 6	
118	4:06	Regular and irregular shapes		●	●					
119	4:07	Position and giving directions						●	Week 13	Term 2
120	4:08	Giving directions						●		
121	4:09	Shapes revision		●					Week 17	
122	4:10	Properties of 2D shapes		●					Week 18	
123	4:11	Investigating angles			●					
124	4:12	Angles			●					
125	4:13	Trapeziums and parallelograms		●	●				Week 19	
126	4:14	Features of 2D shapes		●						
127	4:15	Right angles			●				Week 21	Term 3
128	4:16	Angles			●					
129	4:17	Describing position						●	Week 23	
130	4:18	Pathways between places						●		
131	4:19	Prisms and cylinders					●		Week 27	
132	4:20	Pyramids					●			
133	4:21	Creating maps						●	Week 33	Term 4
134	4:22	Mazes						●		
135	4:23	Spheres					●		Week 34	
136	4:24	3D objects					●			
137	4:25	The net of a cube					●		Week 35	
138	4:26	3D models					●			

The teacher will decide when testing occurs. The Progress Tests and Re-tests are found in the online Teacher Resource.

Statistics and probability

Page	Unit	Title	Content	Collecting data	Surveys	Creating data displays	Analysing data displays	Chance language	Chance experiments	Suggested program This weekly program aligns with the Mentals Book, e.g. Mentals Book, Unit 9 covers work taught in Weeks 7 and 8 of this book.	
139	5:01	Chance words						●		Week 3	Term 1
140	5:02	Chance						●			
141	5:03	Chance						●			
142	5:04	Tables		●	●	●	●			Week 13	Term 2
143	5:05	Tables and graphs		●	●	●	●			Week 14	
144	5:06	Picture graphs		●		●	●				
145	5:07	Making graphs		●	●	●	●				
146	5:08	Chance						●	●	Week 17	
147	5:09	Possible outcomes						●	●		
148	5:10	Chance						●	●	Week 19	
149	5:11	Reading tables and graphs					●			Week 20	
150	5:12	Reading picture graphs					●				
151	5:13	Dicey graphs		●	●				●	Week 28	Term 3
152	5:14	Class investigation		●	●						
153	5:15	Predicting outcomes		●		●	●	●	●	Week 29	
154	5:16	Ordering events						●			
155	5:17	Drawing graphs		●		●	●				
156	5:18	Surveys		●	●					Week 32	Term 4
157	5:19	Carry out your own survey		●	●						
158	5:20	Researching data					●			Week 36	
159	5:21	Dot plots		●		●	●				

The teacher will decide when testing occurs. The Progress Tests and Re-tests are found in the online Teacher Resource.

Extra Support pages

Page			
160	1 Addition and subtraction facts	2 Addition facts to 20	3 Subtraction facts to 20
163	4 Know your addition facts	5 Addition problems to 99	6 Addition to 999
166	7 Writing the addition algorithm	8 Addition of money	9 Addition to 9999
169	10 Addition to 9999	11 Subtraction, no trading to 999	12 Subtraction, one trade to 999
172	13 Subtraction, one trade to 999	14 Subtraction, two trades to 999	15 Subtraction of money

Suggested program	Term 1	Term 2	Term 3	Term 4
Number and algebra	1:01 – 1:08	1:09 – 1:16	1:17 – 1:23	1:24 – 1:29
Operations and algebra	2:01 – 2:12	2:13 – 2:22	2:23 – 2:38	2:39 – 2:47
Measurement	3:01 – 3:09	3:10 – 3:19	3:20 – 3:30	3:31 – 3:36
Space	4:01 – 4:06	4:07 – 4:14	4:15 – 4:20	4:21 – 4:26
Statistics and probability	5:01 – 5:03	5:04 – 5:12	5:13 – 5:17	5:18 – 5:21
Total number of pages:	38	45	45	31

- See the Teacher Resource for a more detailed suggested program.
- The suggested program aligns with the Mentals Book, Progress Tests and Re-tests.

Contents cross-reference

Number and algebra

1 Whole numbers	Pages
Counting, ordering numbers	1, 2, 3, 4, 12, 17, 21, 23, 28, 29, 31, 36
Place value	3, 4, 5, 8, 11, 12, 17, 18, 21, 22, 23, 25, 26, 27, 28, 29
Fractions	9, 10, 13, 14, 19, 20, 24, 25, 26
Decimals	24, 25, 26
Rounding numbers	6, 7, 8, 18, 66, 165, 171, 172, 173
2 Addition and subtraction	**Pages**
Addition	6, 31, 32, 37, 38, 40, 41, 42, 43, 44, 45, 60, 62, 63, 64, 65, 66, 67, 71, 72, 75, 160, 161, 162, 163, 164, 165, 166, 167, 168, 169, 170, 171, 172, 173
Subtraction / difference	6, 32, 37, 38, 39, 43, 44, 61, 68, 69, 70, 71, 73, 74, 160, 170, 171, 172, 173, 174, 175
Linking addition and subtraction	32, 38, 160, 162
Strategies (+ and –)	37, 39, 42, 43, 44, 45, 72, 73, 74
Jump strategy	43, 44, 45
Mental strategy (+ and –)	42, 43, 44, 45, 60, 61, 62, 63, 64, 65, 66, 67, 68, 69, 70, 71, 164, 165, 166, 167, 168, 169, 170, 171, 172, 173, 174, 175
Problem solving (+ and –)	29, 37, 39, 46, 60, 61, 62, 63, 65, 67, 71, 74, 76, 164, 166, 167, 169, 170, 174
Money	2, 27, 29, 30, 31, 40, 41, 60, 61, 62, 63, 66, 68, 75, 76, 167, 168, 169, 174
3 Multiplication and division	**Pages**
Multiplication	33, 34, 35, 36, 47, 48, 49, 50, 51, 52, 55, 56, 57, 58, 59
Division (sharing and grouping)	53, 54, 55, 56, 57, 58, 59
Multiplication and division (linking)	54, 55, 56, 57, 58, 59
Doubling and halving	33, 34, 59
Problem solving (x and ÷)	39, 46, 55, 76
4 Algebra	**Pages**
Patterns	1, 2, 15, 16, 17, 26, 32, 36, 37, 48, 51, 52, 58, 113
Addition and subtraction facts to 20	32, 37, 38, 160, 161, 162, 163
Multiplication and division facts (x 2, x 10, 2 x, ÷ 2)	33, 34, 35, 36, 47, 48, 49, 50, 51, 52, 55, 56, 57, 58, 59
5 Tools used in problems	**Pages**
Number lines	1, 2, 6, 7, 24, 26, 32, 38, 43, 44, 45, 46, 57, 162

Measurement and space

1	Measurement	Pages
	Length	38, 77, 78, 79, 86, 87, 88, 89, 105, 106, 107, 110, 111
	Area	96, 97, 108, 109
	Capacity and volume	83, 84, 85, 93, 103, 104, 110, 111, 138
	Mass (weight)	93, 94, 95, 100, 101, 102, 110, 111
	Time (duration)	98, 99, 112
	Clocks	80, 81, 82, 90, 91, 92
	Problem solving with measurement	102, 104, 107, 108, 111
2	**Space**	**Pages**
	2D shapes	114, 118, 121, 122, 125, 126
	Angles, parallel and perpendicular lines	117, 118, 123, 124, 125, 127, 128
	Symmetry	114, 116
	3D objects	113, 115, 131, 132, 135, 136, 137, 138
	Position	119, 129, 133
	Directions, giving directions	119, 120, 130, 134

Statistics and probability

1	Data	Pages
	Collecting data and recording data	142, 143, 144, 145, 151, 152, 155, 156, 157, 158, 159
	Analysing data displays	142, 143, 144, 145, 149, 150, 151, 152, 155, 156, 158, 159
	Chance and the language of chance	139, 140, 141, 146, 147, 148, 153, 154
	Chance experiments	146, 147, 148, 151, 153

3 Dictionary

abacus

An instrument used for counting and calculating.

- This abacus shows 546.

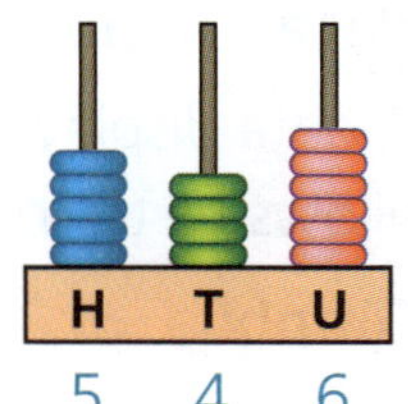

analog time

The time shown on a clock face.

- 13 minutes to 6 is the time on this analog clock.

angle

The turn between two lines that meet at a corner.

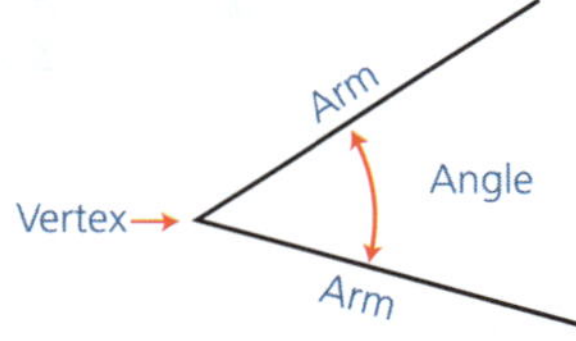

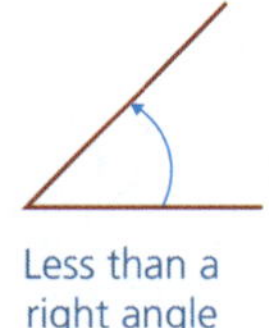

Less than a right angle

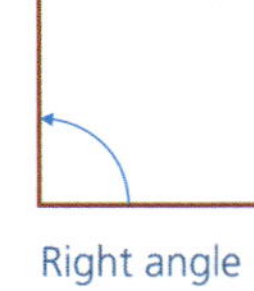

Right angle

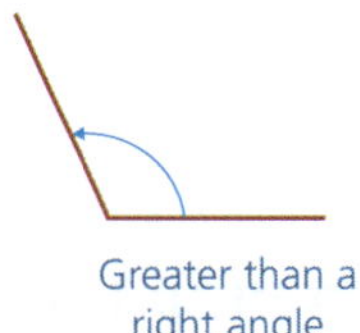

Greater than a right angle

anticlockwise and clockwise

The direction of a turn.

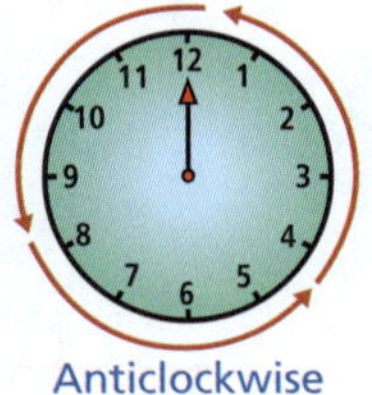

Anticlockwise

Clockwise (as on a clock)

area

The measure of the amount of surface.

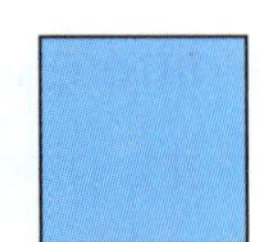

array

When objects are arranged in rows and columns they form an array.

calendar

A chart that shows the days, weeks and months of a particular year.

November 2024						
Sun	**Mon**	**Tues**	**Wed**	**Thurs**	**Fri**	**Sat**
				1	2	3
4	5	6	7	8	9	10
11	12	13	14	15	16	17
18	19	20	21	22	23	24
25	26	27	28	29	30	

capacity

The amount that a container can hold.

- Less than 1 litre

- More than 1 litre

centimetre (cm)

A unit of length equal to one hundredth of a metre.

- 100 cm = 1 m

cents (c)

Our money system is made up of cents and dollars. 100 cents (100c) makes 1 dollar ($1).

chance

The chance (or probability) of something happening is its likelihood of happening.

- If you toss a coin, there is an even chance of tossing a head.

See also *probability*.

clockwise

See *anticlockwise*.

column graph

Groups are compared using the lengths of columns or bars. The graph can be vertical or horizontal.

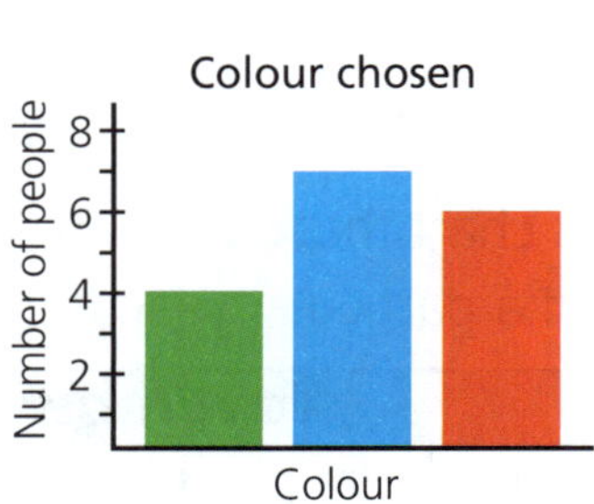

cone

See *3D objects*.

corner (vertex)

A corner is where sides or edges meet at a point.

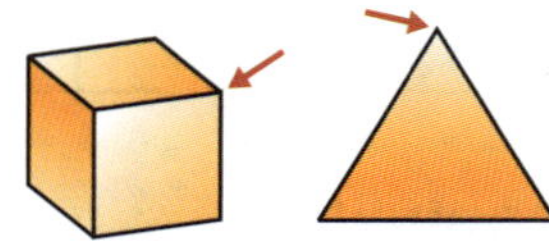

cross-section

The shape formed when an object is cut.

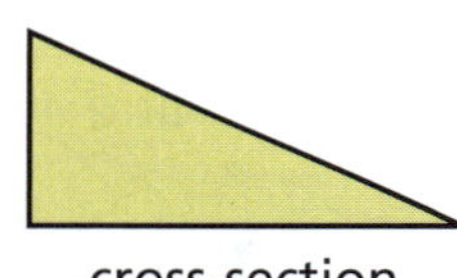
cross-section

cube

See *3D objects*.

curved surface

A curved surface on a 3D object is not flat. It allows an object to roll. A cylinder and cone each have one curved surface.

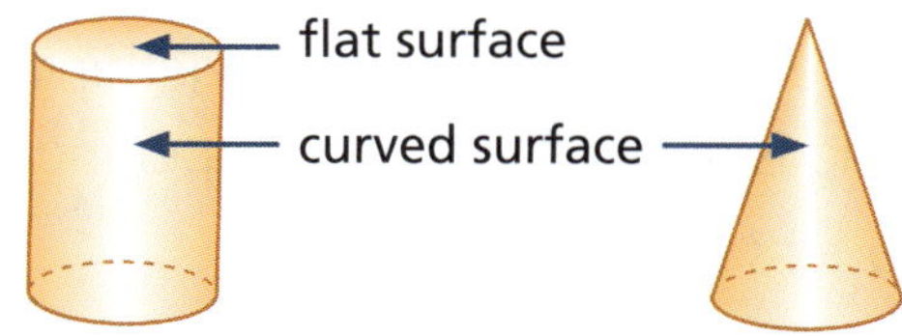

cylinder

See *3D objects*.

data display

A data display shows categories of objects and allows us to compare them.

Graph:

Table:

Dogs	Cats
4	2

date

The date shows the day, the month and the year. For example, 30.5.23 means the 30th day of the 5th month (May) in the year 2023.

decimal notation

The decimal point separates the whole number from the fraction.

0·7 means 7 tenths.

6·5 means 6 ones and 5 tenths.

decimal point

difference

How many more?

The difference between 16 and 13 is 3.

For smaller numbers, line up each group in a row to find the difference.

For larger numbers, place the numbers on a number line to find the difference.

digital time

Time expressed using digits.

- This digital clock shows 24 minutes past 10.

digits

Symbols used to write a number.

- 6 Six is a 1-digit number.
- 47 Forty-seven is a 2-digit number.

division (÷)

Breaking up groups into equal parts.

- 6 ÷ 3

a Sharing
2 each

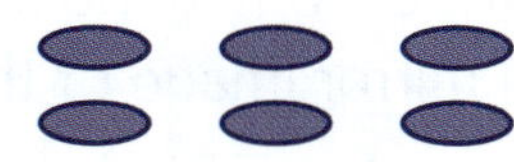

b Grouping
2 groups

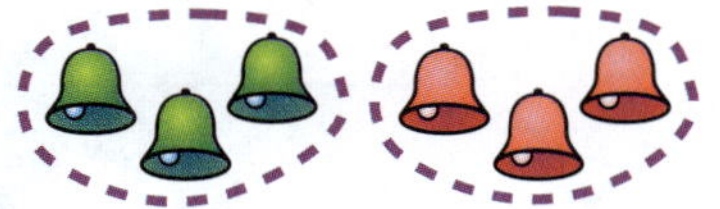

edge

Two faces of a 3D object meet at an edge.

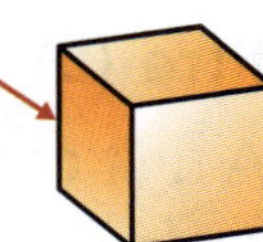

even number

Any number that is a multiple of two and can be grouped in twos. They end in 0, 2, 4, 6 or 8.

- 16, 300, 4394

The other counting numbers are **odd**.

expanded notation

A way of writing numerals to show the place value of each digit.

- 137 = (1 × 100) + (3 × 10) + 7
  = 100 + 30 + 7

face

A flat surface of a three-dimensional object.

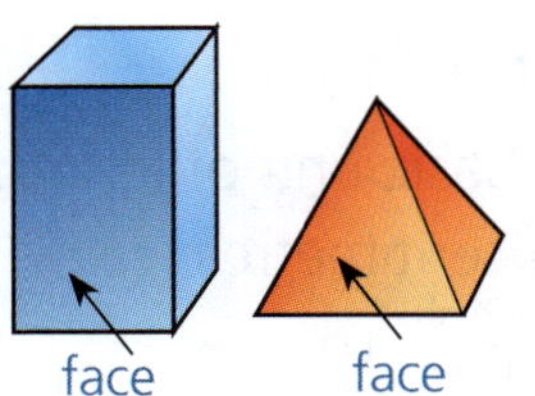

flat surface

A cylinder has 2 flat surfaces, one on both ends, and one curved surface.

A cube has 6 flat surfaces.

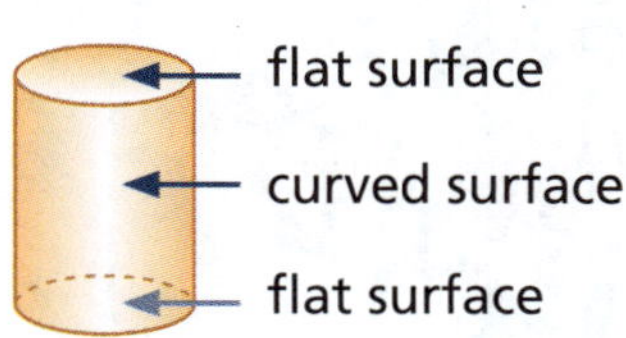

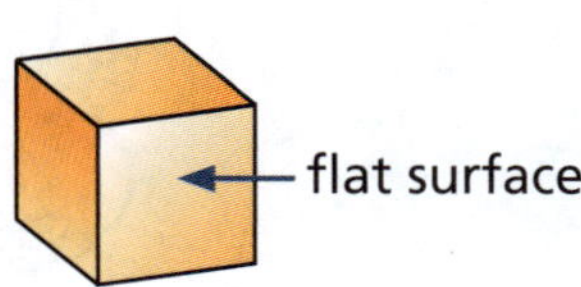

fraction

Any part of a whole, group or object.

- 2 out of 6 shaded

- $\frac{1}{4}$ is shaded

gram (g)

A unit of mass used to measure how heavy something is.

- 1 kilogram = 1000 grams

graph

A diagram or drawing used to record a collection of data.

- Column graph

  Groups are compared using the lengths of columns or bars.
  The graph can be vertical or horizontal.

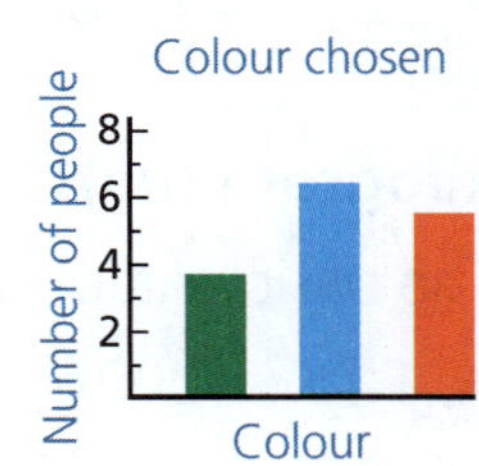

- Picture graph

  A picture is used as a unit to show how many.

heft

To compare masses by lifting them with your hands.

The big one feels heavier.

hexagon

See *2D shapes*.

inverse operations

Adding 8 is the opposite (the inverse) of subtracting 8.

- 100 + 8 – 8 = 100

Multiplying by 2 is the opposite (the inverse) of dividing by 2.

- 4 × 2 ÷ 2 = 4

jump strategy

Adding or subtracting numbers, jumping by tens or ones.

- 52 – 14 = 38

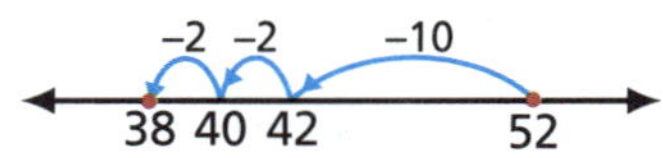

kilogram (kg)

The basic unit of mass, equal to 1000 grams.

- 1 kg = 1000 g

left and right

- Left

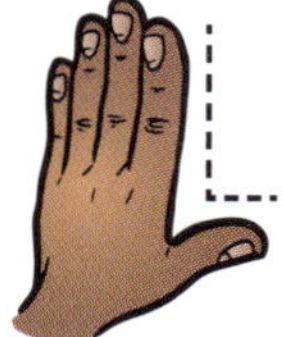

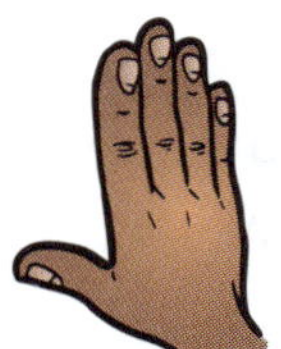

- Right

line

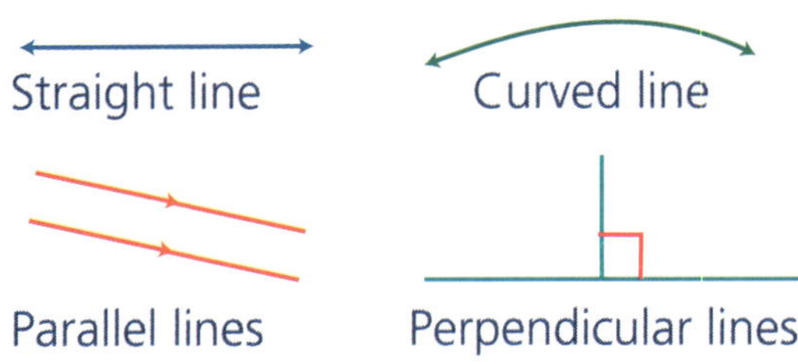

line of symmetry

A line that divides something in half so that each half is a mirror image of the other part.

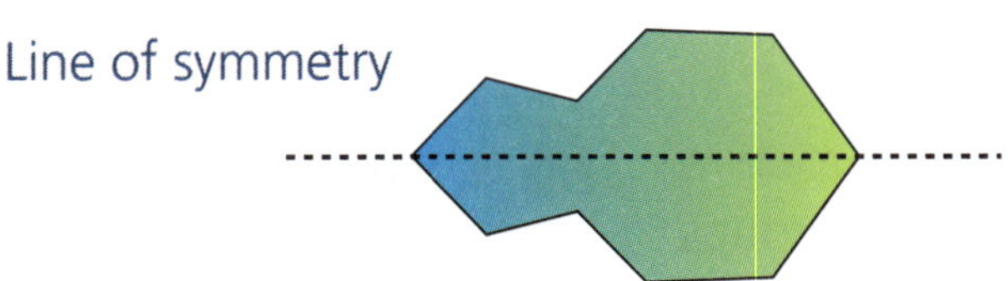

litre (L)

A unit of capacity (or volume) used for the measurement of liquids.

- 1 L = 1000 mL

map or plan

A picture of an area viewed from above.

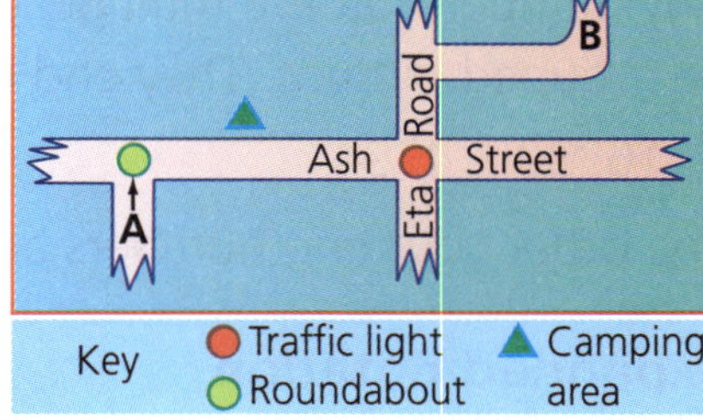

mass

The amount of matter in an object, a measure of how heavy it is.

metre (m)

The basic unit of length, equal to 100 centimetres.

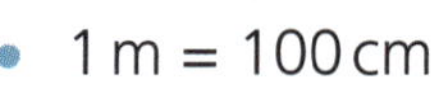

- 1 m = 100 cm

millilitre (mL)

A unit of capacity (or volume) equal to one thousandth of a litre.

- 1000 mL = 1 L

millimetre (mm)

A unit of length equal to one tenth of a centimetre, or one thousandth of a metre.

- 10 mm = 1 cm
- 1000 mm = 1 m

money

multiplication (×)

Combining equal groups.

- 3 × 5 = 15

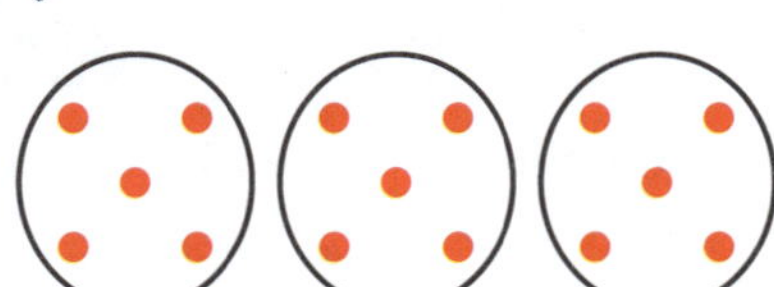

net

A flat shape that can be folded to make a three-dimensional object.

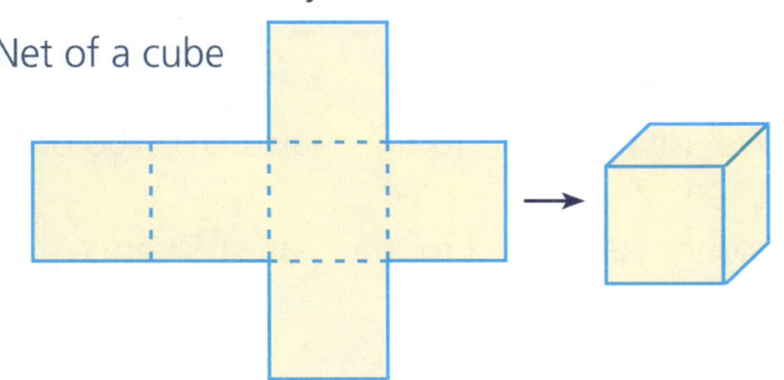

number bonds

These show how a number can be broken up into parts (e.g. the top number, 4, can be broken up into 3 and 1).

number line

A line on which numbers are marked.

Number lines can be used to show operations.

- 2 + 2 + 2 = 6 (0 1 2 3 4 5 6 7)

numeral expander

Breaks up a number into hundreds, tens and ones.

- 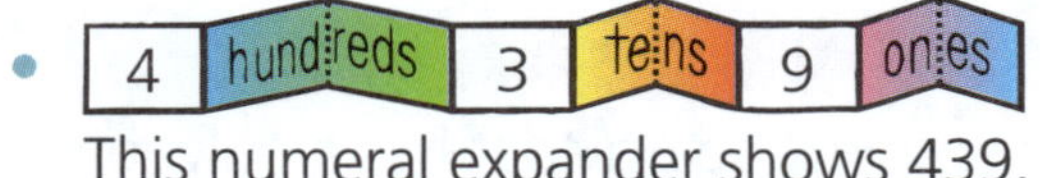

  This numeral expander shows 439.

perimeter

The distance around the outside of a shape; the boundary.

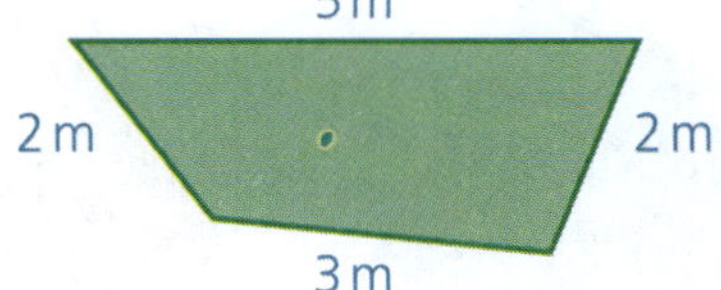

- Perimeter = 2 m + 3 m + 2 m + 5 m
  = 12 m

place-value blocks

These are used to represent numbers.

ones block

tens block

hundreds block

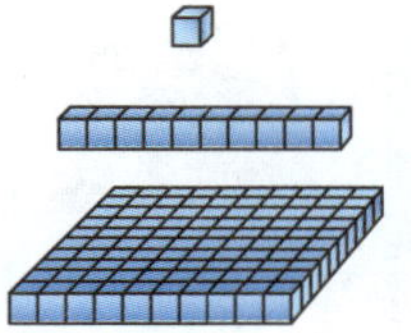

42 shown as:

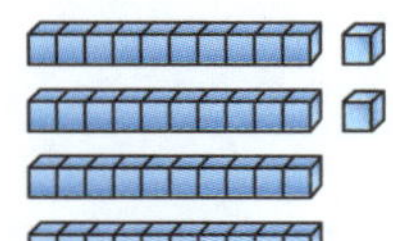

113 shown as:

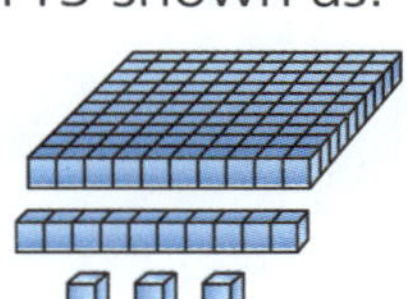

prism

A three-dimensional object with a uniform cross-section. The ends are identical shapes and all other faces are rectangles. Prisms are named by the shape of their ends.

Triangular prism

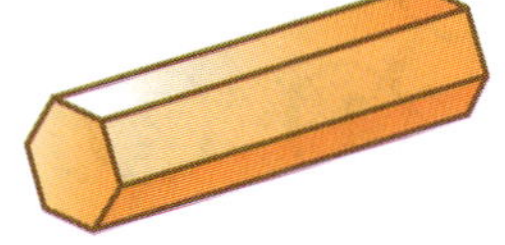

Hexagonal prism

probability

The probability (or chance) of something happening is its likelihood of happening.

- **Chance language**

  possible, impossible, certain, more likely, less likely, least likely, outcome, event

pyramid

A three-dimensional object that has a polygon for a base and triangles for all other faces. Pyramids are named by the shape of their base.

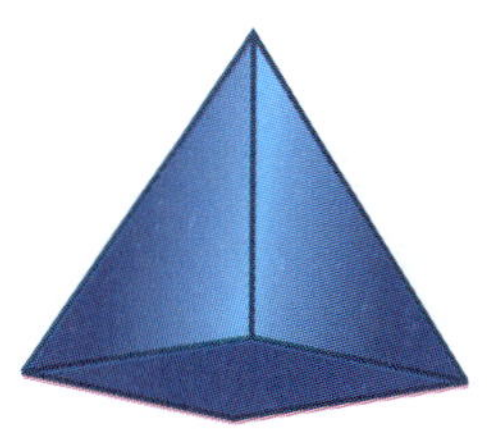

Square pyramid

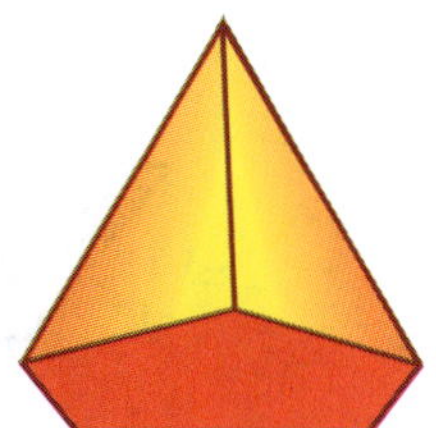

Pentagonal pyramid

quadrilateral

A two-dimensional shape with four straight sides.

quarter of a whole or collection

One of four equal parts.

One quarter of the rectangle is coloured.

One quarter of the collection is coloured.

A quarter of 8 is 2. Another way to say this is 8 divided by 4 is 2. That is $8 \div 4 = 2$.

Three quarters of the rectangle is coloured.

Three quarters of the collection is coloured.

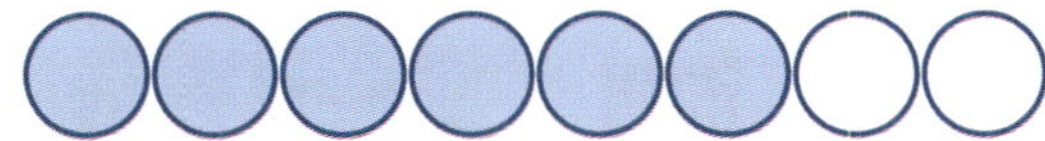

rectangle

See *2D shapes*.

regular and irregular shapes

Regular shapes have all sides and all angles equal. Irregular shapes do not.

Regular shape

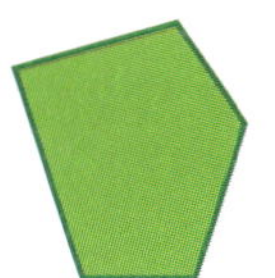

Irregular shape

right and left

- Left

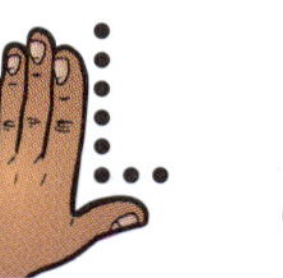

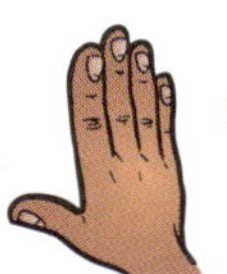

- Right

rounding

We usually round to the nearest 10, 100 or 1000, ...

Money is rounded to the nearest 5 cents.

- 18 rounds to 20.

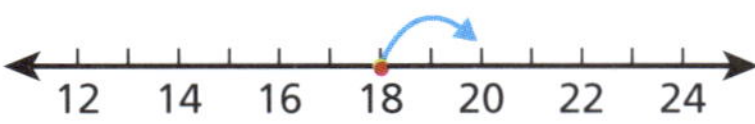

skip counting

Counting on, adding the same number each time.

- 5, 10, 15, 20, 25, … is skip counting by 5.

sphere

See *3D objects*.

split strategy

Adding numbers by splitting them into their parts.

- 36 + 52 = 30 + 6 + 50 + 2
  = (30 + 50) + (6 + 2)
  = 80 + 8
  = 88

square

See *2D shapes*.

square centimetre (cm^2)

A unit for measuring area that is equal to a square with sides of 1 cm.

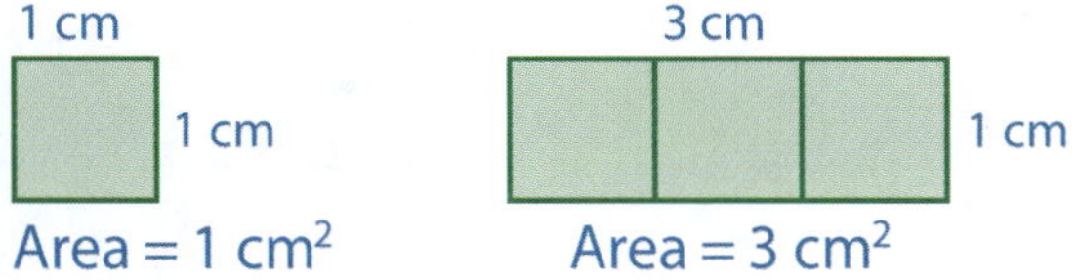

Area = 1 cm^2 Area = 3 cm^2

survey

A list of questions used to discover information.

symmetry

If a figure has a line of symmetry, it can be folded so that the two halves exactly overlap.

Each half is a mirror image of the other.

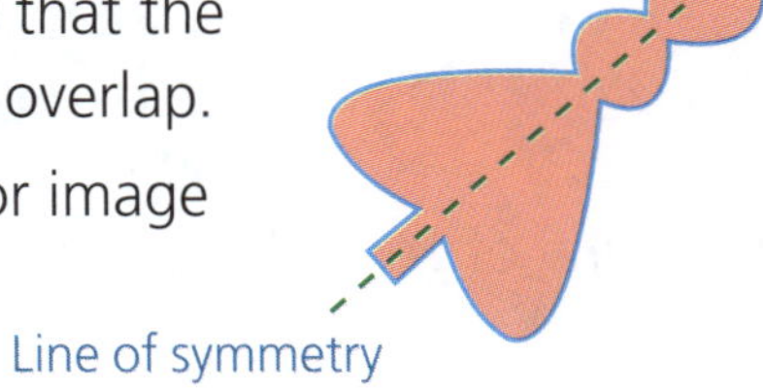

Line of symmetry

table

A simple way to display information in rows and columns.

Birds	12
Lions	2
Monkeys	6

tally

To keep count by making a mark for each item. To make counting easy, the marks are drawn in groups of five, with each fifth mark crossed over the other four marks.

- 𝍸 𝍸 𝍸 ||| = 18

time words

Days			
Sunday	Monday	Tuesday	Wednesday
Thursday	Friday	Saturday	

Months			
January	February	March	April
May	June	July	August
September	October	November	December

Seasons			
Summer	Autumn	Winter	Spring

- clocks

analog clock   digital clock

3 o'clock

- o'clock

When the minute hand (long hand) is pointing to 12, the time is an "o'clock" time. The hour hand (short hand) points to the hour. The hour hand above is pointing to the 3, so it is 3 o'clock.

half past 3

- half past

When the minute (long) hand is pointing to the 6, the time is "half past". The hour (short) hand on this clock points halfway between the 3 and the 4, so it is half past 3.

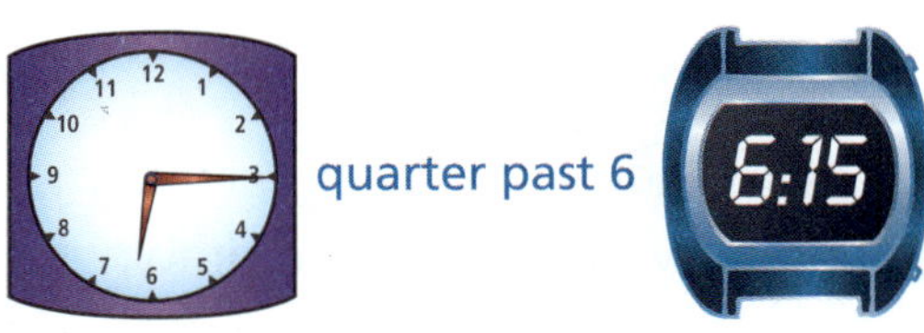

- quarter past

When the minute (long) hand is pointing to the 3, then the time is "quarter past". The hour (short) hand on this clock is a quarter of the way from 6 to 7, so it is a quarter past 6.

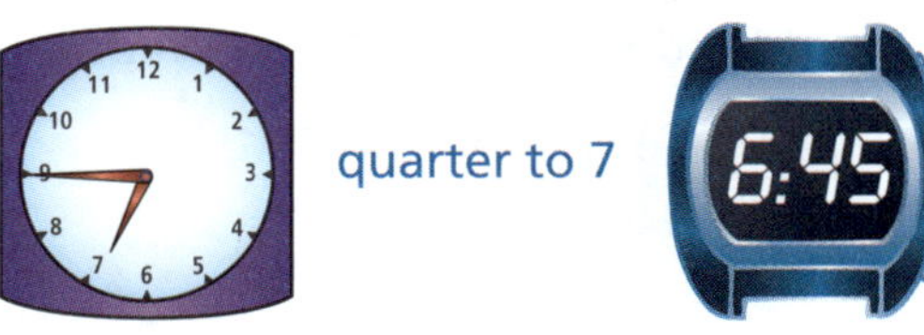

- quarter to

When the minute (long) hand is pointing to the 9, then the time is "quarter to" the next hour. The hour (short) hand on this clock is a quarter of the way from the next number 7, so it is a quarter to 7.

- The number of days in each month:

How to know the number of days in each month.

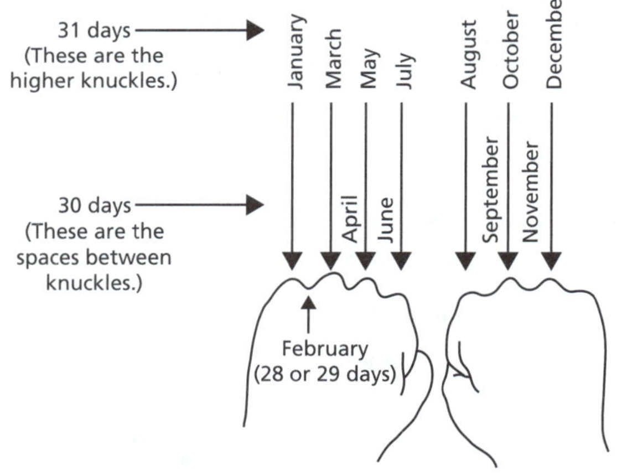

30 days has September, April, June and November. All the rest have 31, except February alone, which has 28 days clear and 29 days each leap year.

timeline

Shows a sequence of events in time.

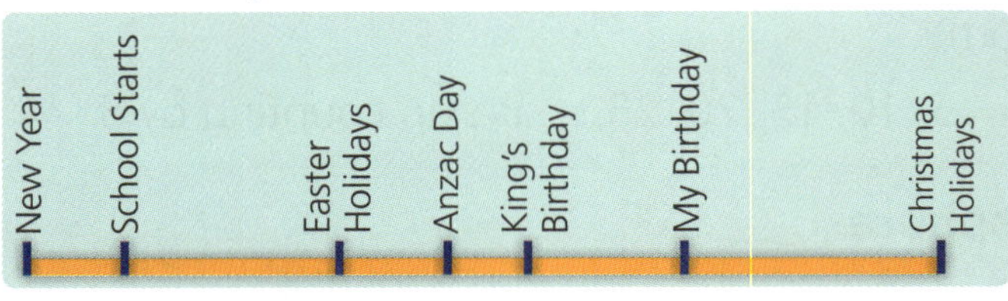

turn

Moving a shape in a clockwise or anticlockwise direction.

- quarter turn
- half turn
- three quarter turn
- full turn

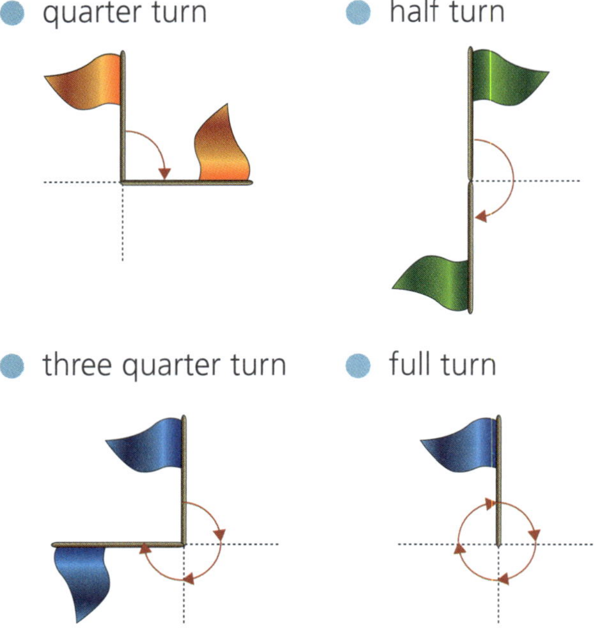

vertex

A point at which two or more lines meet to form a corner on a plane shape or object.

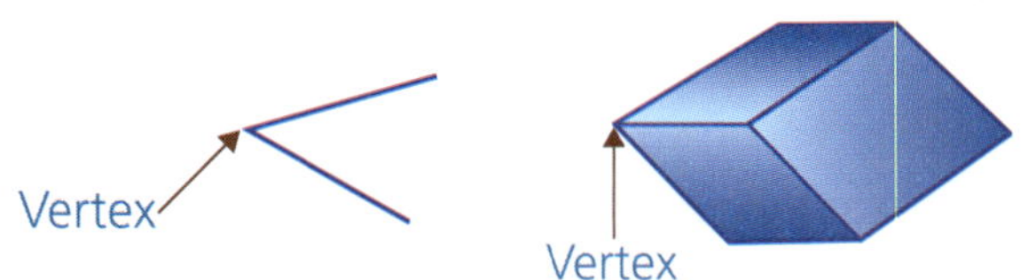

The plural of *vertex* is *vertices*.

volume

The amount of space an object takes up.

year

There are 365 days in a year and 366 days in a leap year (which is every 4th year). There are 12 months in a year.

2D (two-dimensional) shapes

Flat shapes are two-dimensional.
They have length and width.

circle
1 curved side

triangle
3 sides
3 corners

square
4 equal sides
4 corners

rectangle
2 equal long sides
2 equal short sides,
like a stretched square

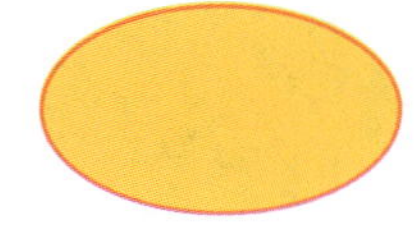

oval
1 curved side, like
a squashed circle

pentagon
5 sides
5 corners

hexagon
6 sides
6 corners

octagon
8 sides
8 corners

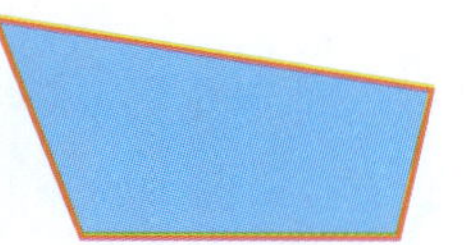

quadrilaterals
4 sides
4 corners

parallelogram
two sets of parallel lines
opposite sides equal

trapezium
one set of
parallel lines

rhombus
all sides equal
(a diamond)

kite
two pairs of
equal sides

All of the blue shapes are quadrilaterals.

3D (three-dimensional) objects

Solid objects are three-dimensional.
They have length, width and height.

sphere

A sphere is curved and round.

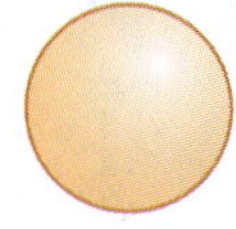

cube

A cube has 6 identical faces,
8 vertices and 12 straight edges.

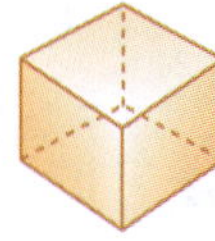

cylinder

A cylinder has 2 circular flat surfaces
and 1 curved surface.

cone

A cone has 1 circular flat surface
and 1 curved surface.

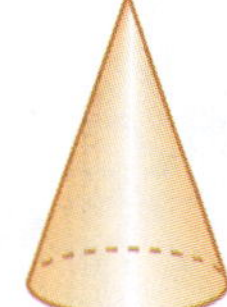

pyramid

A pyramid has triangular
faces joined around a base.

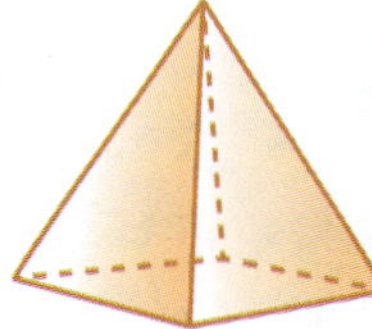

prism

A prism has rectangular faces
joining two identical bases.

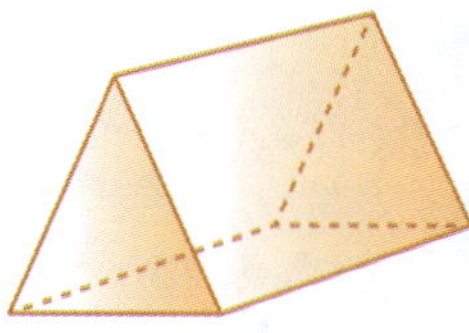

Counting

Even numbers end in 0, 2, 4, 6 or 8.
Odd numbers end in 1, 3, 5, 7 or 9.

1 Use the hundred chart to answer the questions.

a Count by 2s. Colour these numbers yellow.

b Starting at 100, count backwards by 10s.
Draw a cross on these numbers.

c Circle every second even number up to 80.
What do you notice?

Hundred chart

1	2	3	4	5	6	7	8	9	10
11	12	13	14	15	16	17	18	19	20
21	22	23	24	25	26	27	28	29	30
31	32	33	34	35	36	37	38	39	40
41	42	43	44	45	46	47	48	49	50
51	52	53	54	55	56	57	58	59	60
61	62	63	64	65	66	67	68	69	70
71	72	73	74	75	76	77	78	79	80
81	82	83	84	85	86	87	88	89	90
91	92	93	94	95	96	97	98	99	100

d Count by 8s and tick the first 10 numbers you count. Write them below.

2 When we count by 2s from zero, the numbers end in ____.

3 When we count by 5s from zero, the numbers end in ____.

4 When we count by 10s from zero, the numbers end in ____.

5 Continue each pattern. Check your answers with a calculator.

a 223, 233, 243, ____, ____, ____, ____, ____

b 815, 810, 805, ____, ____, ____, ____, ____

c 126, 124, 122, ____, ____, ____, ____, ____

d 1000, 900, 800, ____, ____, ____, ____, ____

6 Show your answers to Questions 5**a** and 5**b** on the number lines.

a

223 233 243

The rule is ____.

b

805 810 815

The rule is ____.

 • *AUSTRALIAN SIGNPOST MATHS 3* • ISBN 9780655708773

1:02 Counting

Five 20c coins make $1.
Ten 10c coins make $1.
Twenty 5c coins make $1.

Understanding number relationships helps us count better.

1 a Count on from 76 to 94 by 2s.

b Count backwards from 1000 by 100s.

c Count on from 645 to 690 by 5s.

d Count backwards from 500 to 400 by 10s.

2 Write the missing numbers.

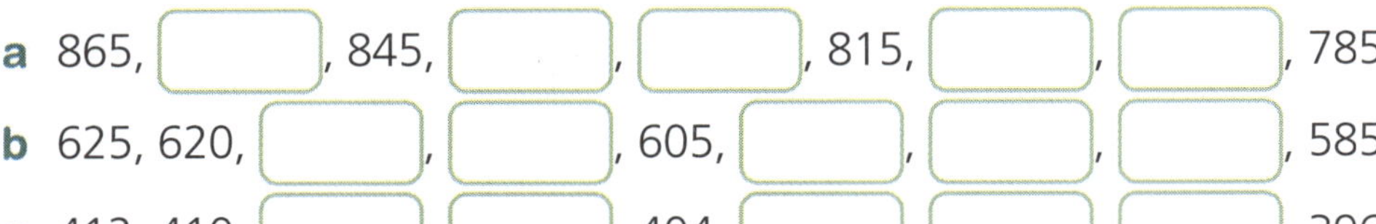

a 865, ___, 845, ___, ___, 815, ___, ___, 785

b 625, 620, ___, ___, 605, ___, ___, ___, 585

c 412, 410, ___, ___, 404, ___, ___, ___, 396

3 Count by 2s and write the first 20 numbers you count. Circle every second number and discuss the pattern.

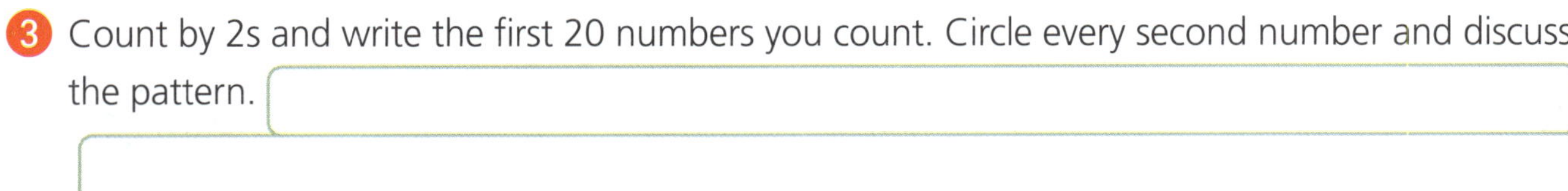

4 Count by 5s and write the first 20 numbers you count. Circle every second number and discuss the pattern.

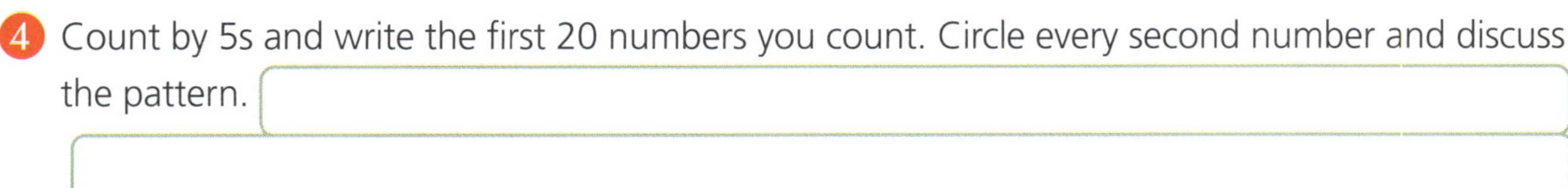

5 If you have to count 300 ten-cent coins, what is the best counting strategy to make sure you count them correctly?

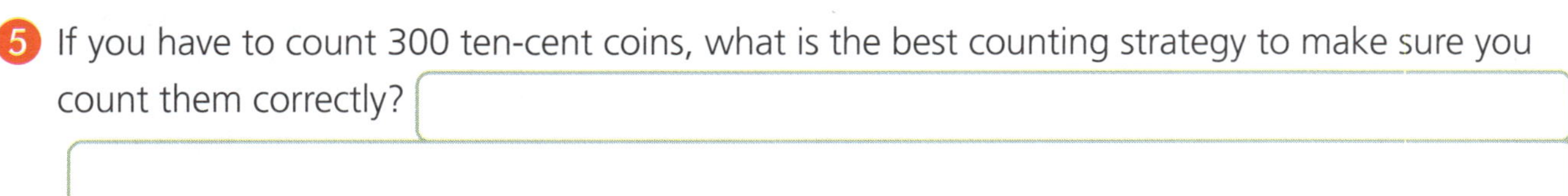

6 Show your answers to Questions 1**a** and 1**b** on the number line.

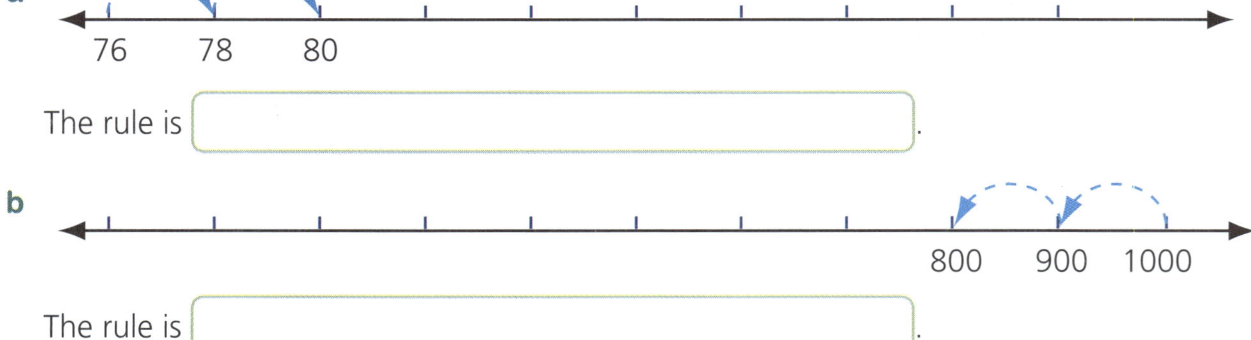

a The rule is ___.

b The rule is ___.

c Try to do Question 1**c** on your own number line.

 • *AUSTRALIAN SIGNPOST MATHS 3* • ISBN 9780655708773

1:03 Numbers to 1000

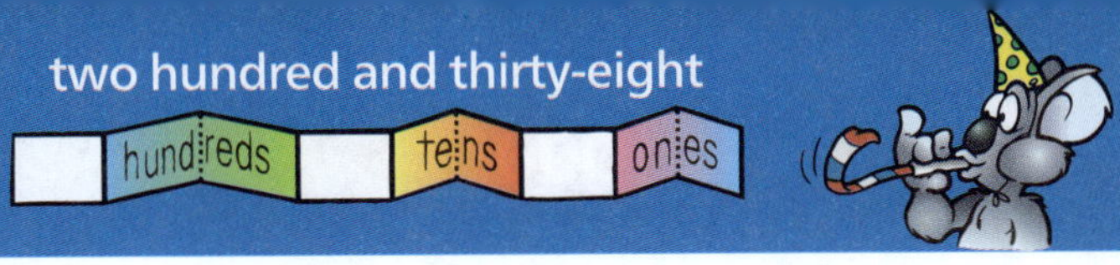

two hundred and thirty-eight

hundreds tens ones

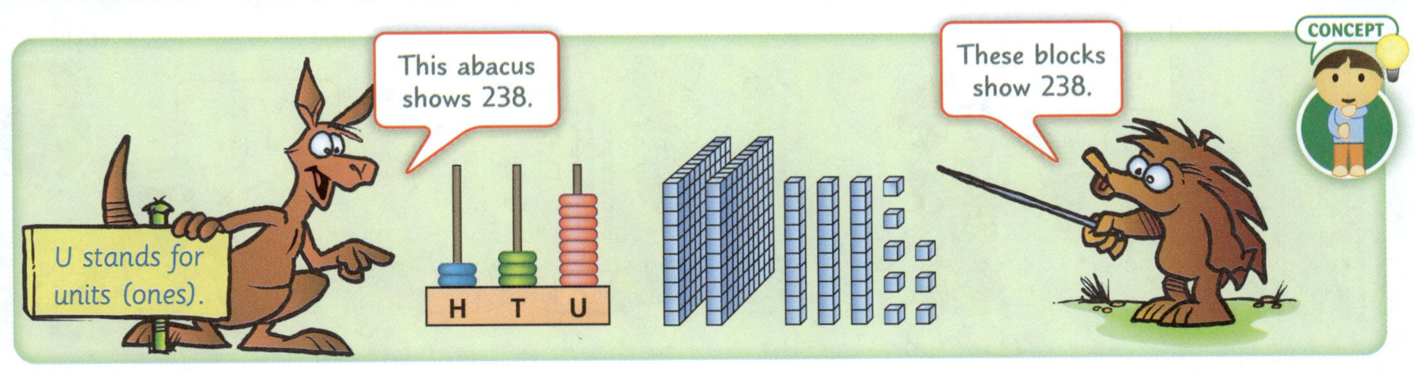

1 Write the number shown by the place-value blocks or abacus.

a 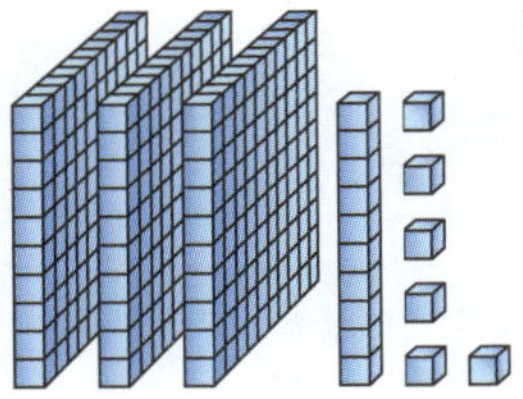 b 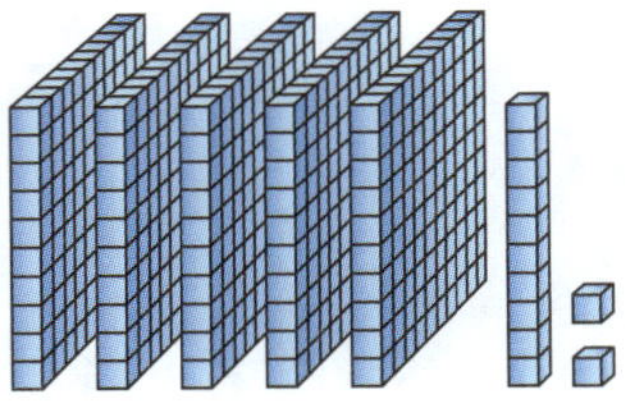 c 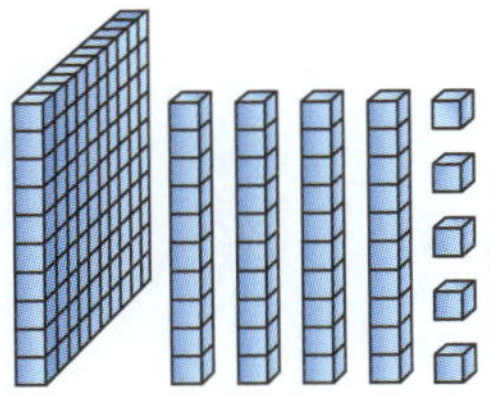 d

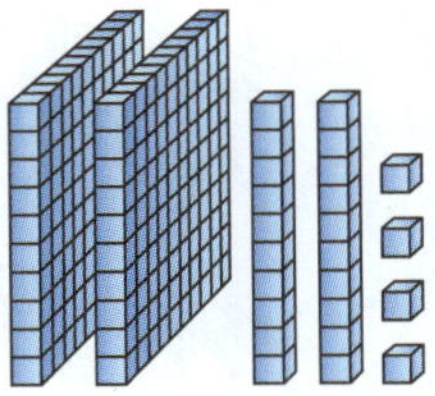

e 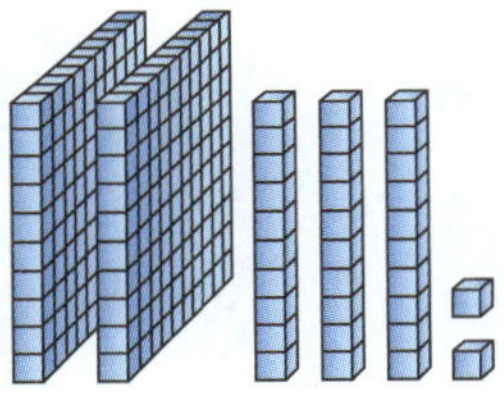 f 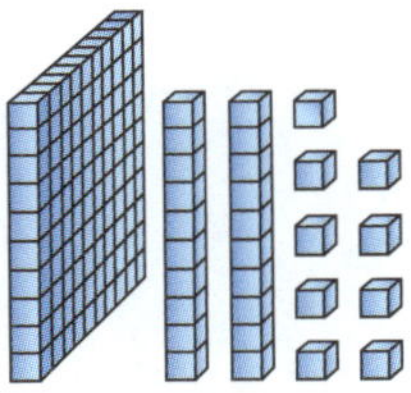 g 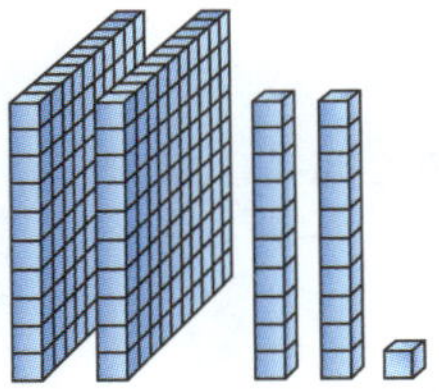 h

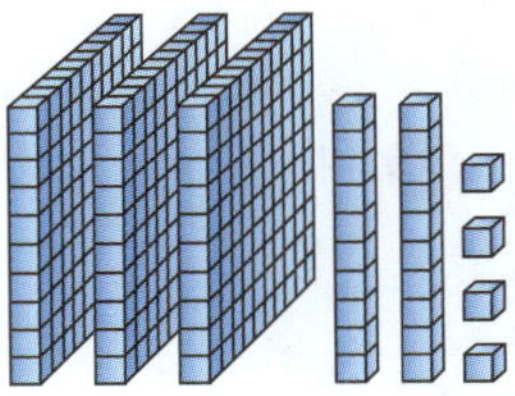

i 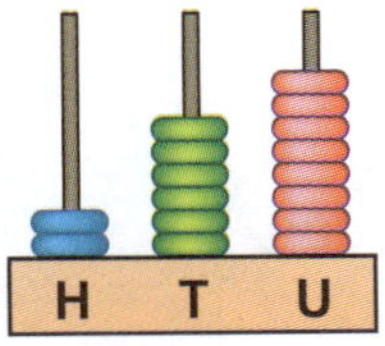 j 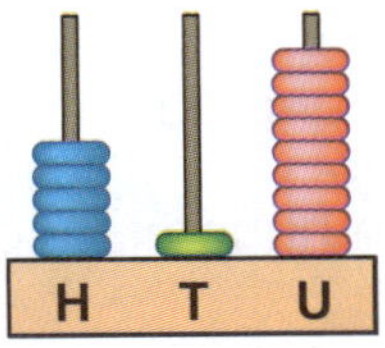 k 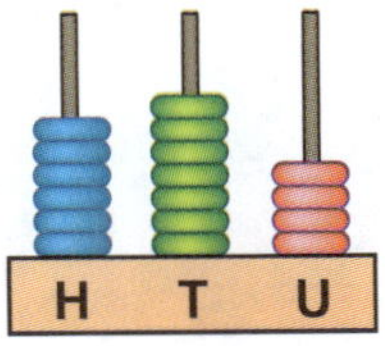 l

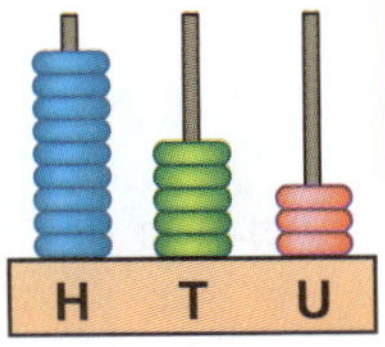

H T U

The abacus was invented thousands of years ago.

2 Which number is larger?

a 169 or 346 ___ b 723 or 481 ___ c 962 or 503 ___

d 375 or 634 ___ e 257 or 572 ___ f 491 or 914 ___

3 Write these in order from smallest to largest.

a 137, 653, 446 ___, ___, ___ b 974, 237, 491 ___, ___, ___

c 819, 106, 567 ___, ___, ___ d 683, 749, 250 ___, ___, ___

 • *AUSTRALIAN SIGNPOST MATHS 3* • ISBN 9780655708773

1:04 Numbers to 1000

Order from smallest (1) to largest (5).
380, 38, 308, 803, 83

1. Write the numeral, fill in the numeral expander and write the number in words.

a hundreds tens ones

b hundreds tens ones

2. How many digits are in each numeral?

a 39 **b** 256 **c** 970 **d** 56 **e** 498
f 13 **g** 7 **h** 520 **i** 1000 **j** 777

3. Write these numbers as numerals.

a two hundred and sixty
b one hundred and fifty-two
c nine hundred and forty
d seven hundred and eighteen
e six hundred and seventy-nine
f five hundred and thirty-four
g eight hundred and sixty-eight
h three hundred and six

4. Write the numbers before and after.

a ___, 999, ___ **b** ___, 863, ___ **c** ___, 659, ___
d ___, 306, ___ **e** ___, 499, ___ **f** ___, 709, ___

ACTIVITY

- Use place-value blocks to model these numbers.
  - 216
  - 525
  - 848
  - 634
  - 967
  - 388
  - 793
  - 364
  - 190
  - 572
  - 451
  - 1000

 • *AUSTRALIAN SIGNPOST MATHS 3* • ISBN 9780655708773

Numbers to 1000

247 = 2 hundreds, 4 tens and 7 ones
= 2 hundreds and 47 ones
= 24 tens and 7 ones

CONCEPT

720 is the same as
7 hundreds and 2 tens
or 72 tens or 720 ones.

1 Complete the numeral expanders.

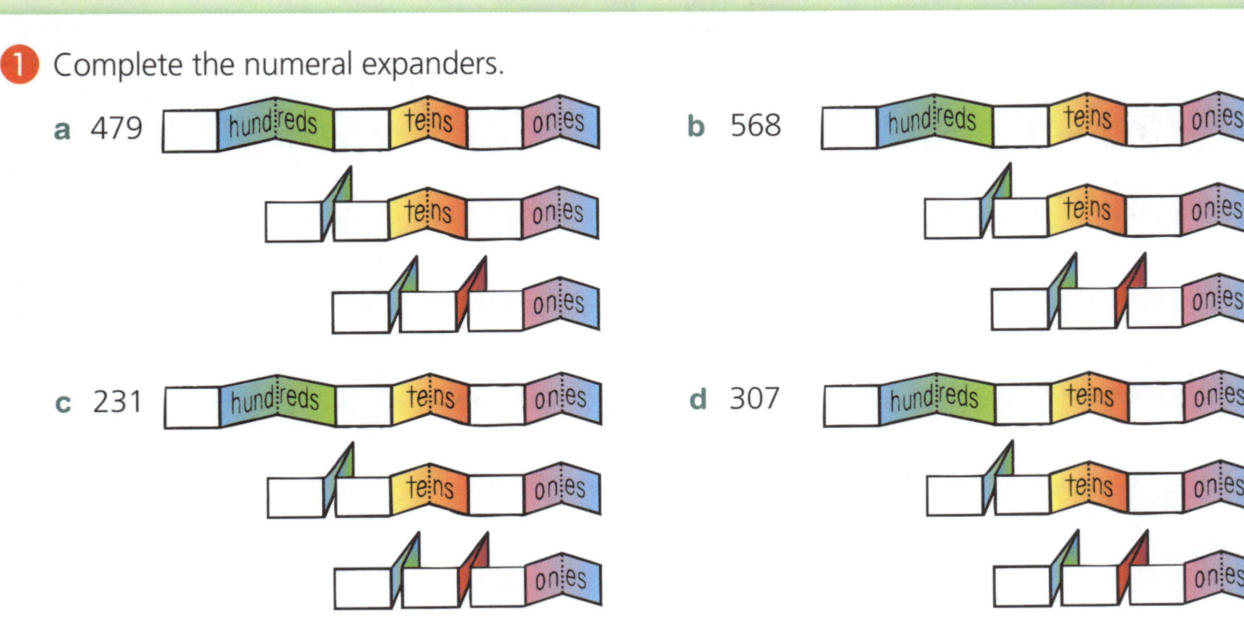

2 Write each number as a numeral.

a six hundred and thirty-two

b eight hundred and seventeen

c four hundred and twenty-nine

d seven hundred and sixty-three

e two hundred and thirty-eight

f five hundred and sixty-two

g nine hundred and forty

h three hundred and fifty-one

3 Write each number in words.

a 106

b 607

c 310

d 841

ACTIVITY

- Use concrete materials to show the numbers in Question 3. Explain your answer to a partner.

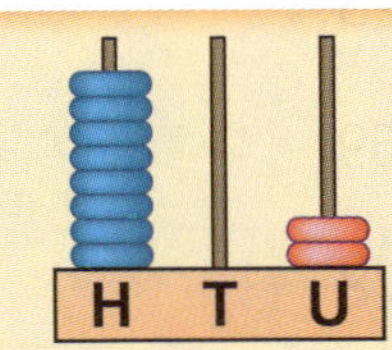

1:06 Rounding to the nearest 10

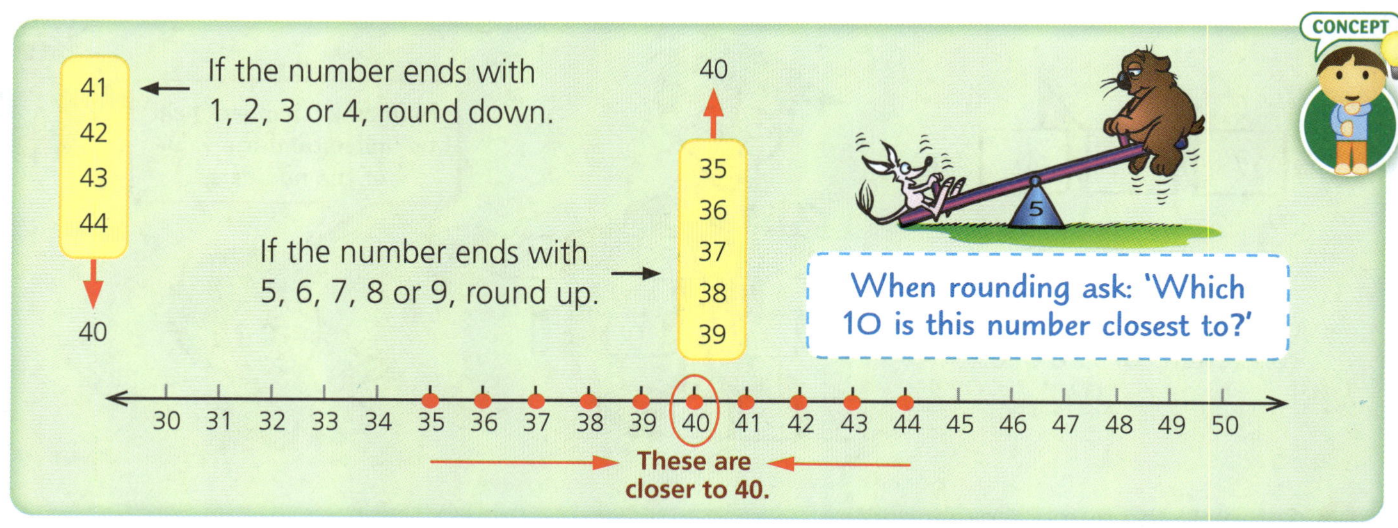

1 a Is 12 closer to 10 or 20? ☐ b Is 77 closer to 70 or 80? ☐

c Is 21 closer to 20 or 30? ☐ d Is 89 closer to 80 or 90? ☐

e Is 33 closer to 30 or 40? ☐ f Is 106 closer to 100 or 110? ☐

2 Round to the nearest 10.

a 24 ☐ b 36 ☐ c 63 ☐ d 47 ☐

e 92 ☐ f 74 ☐ g 59 ☐ h 81 ☐

i 103 ☐ j 115 ☐ k 123 ☐ l 127 ☐

3 a Circle the numbers that round to 60.

57 58 67 68 64

61 69 62 65 52 56

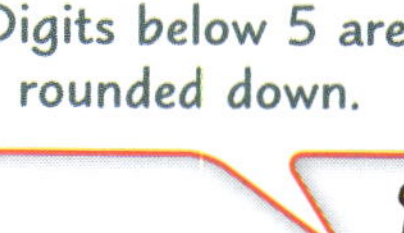

b Circle the numbers that round to 190.

199 187 186 197 194 183

193 185 189 188 191

4 Round off each number to the nearest 10. (77 + 41 becomes 80 + 40. 92 – 38 becomes 90 – 40.)

a 56 + 23 ☐ b 42 – 17 ☐ c 133 – 26 ☐

d 72 + 69 ☐ e 118 – 34 ☐ f 241 – 55 ☐

g 54 + 78 ☐ h 665 – 46 ☐ i 447 – 118 ☐

Rounding to the nearest 100

closer to 100 | closer to 200
100 150 200

150 rounds up to 200.

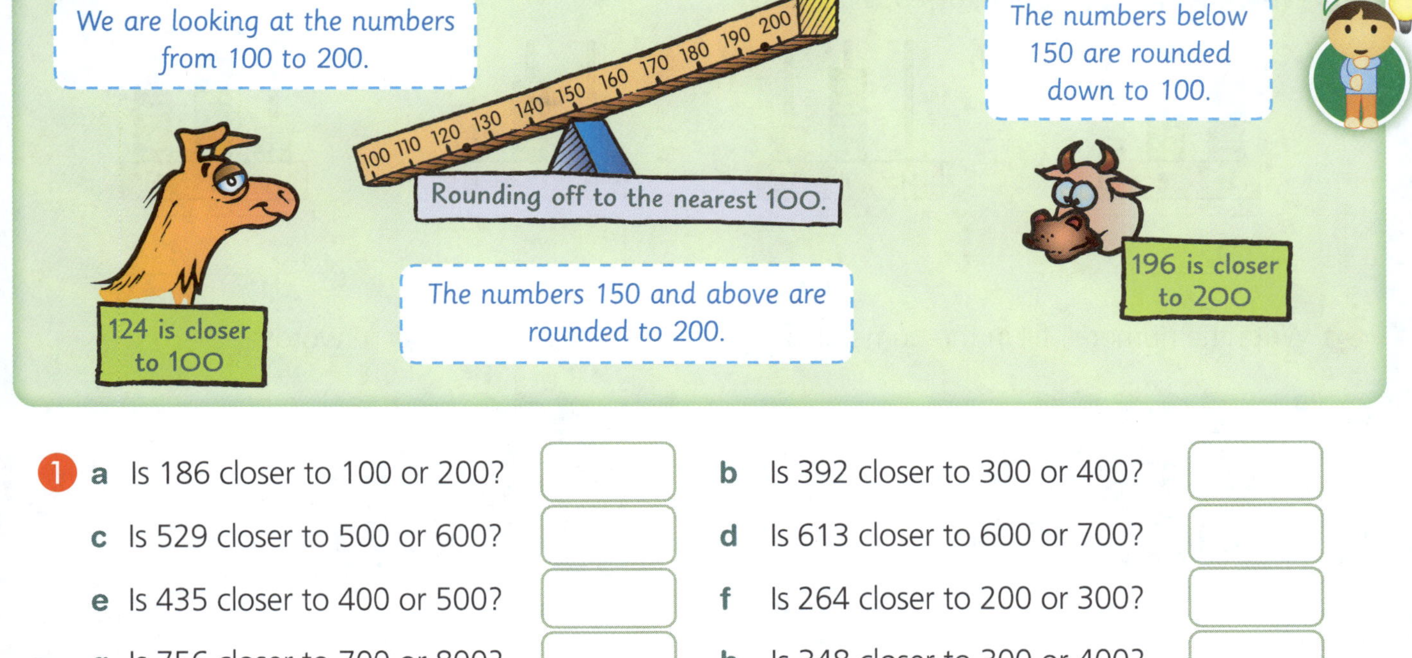

1 **a** Is 186 closer to 100 or 200? ______ **b** Is 392 closer to 300 or 400? ______

c Is 529 closer to 500 or 600? ______ **d** Is 613 closer to 600 or 700? ______

e Is 435 closer to 400 or 500? ______ **f** Is 264 closer to 200 or 300? ______

g Is 756 closer to 700 or 800? ______ **h** Is 348 closer to 300 or 400? ______

2 Round these numbers to the nearest hundred.

a 127 ______	**b** 386 ______	**c** 535 ______	**d** 479 ______
e 216 ______	**f** 794 ______	**g** 890 ______	**h** 607 ______
i 173 ______	**j** 456 ______	**k** 375 ______	**l** 928 ______
m 409 ______	**n** 249 ______	**o** 652 ______	**p** 580 ______

To round to hundreds, look at the 10s digit.

3 **a** Circle the numbers that round to 200.

264	163	296	220	186
217	237	125	143	205

b Circle the numbers that round to 500.

569	467	416	456	575
483	590	532	439	521

4 Answer true or false for each statement.

a 974 rounds off to 900. ______ **b** 426 rounds off to 500. ______

c 396 rounds off to 400. ______ **d** 399 rounds off to 400. ______

e 37 tens is less than 371. ______ **f** 3 hundred is more than 305. ______

g 679 is less than 68 tens. ______ **h** 409 is more than 4 hundred. ______

Number hunt

- Search through newspapers, magazines and catalogues to find 3-digit numerals.
- Group together similar examples, such as crowd attendances, prices or years.
- Discuss how these different examples are written and read differently.

1:08 Numbers to 1000

Order from smallest (1) to largest (3).

421 ☐
42 tens ☐
4 hundreds ☐

1 Write the number shown by each abacus.

a 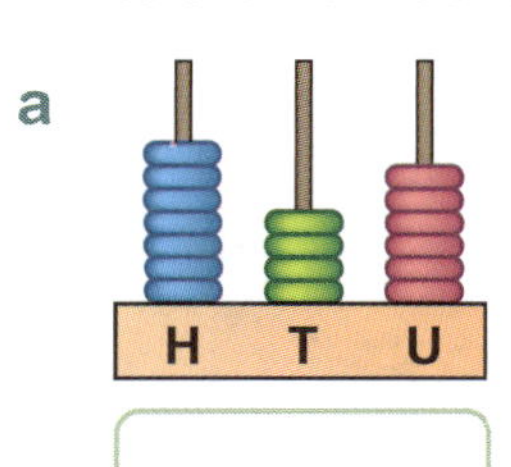

b H T U

c H T U

d H T U

2 Write the numeral, fill in the numeral expander and write the number in words.

a 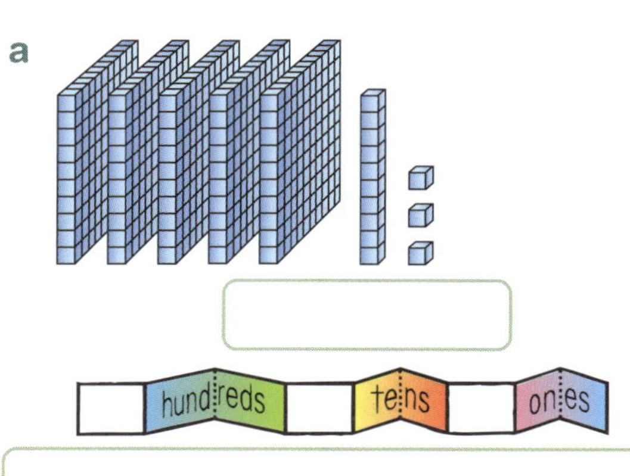

hundreds tens ones

b

hundreds tens ones

3 Complete the numeral expanders.

a 375 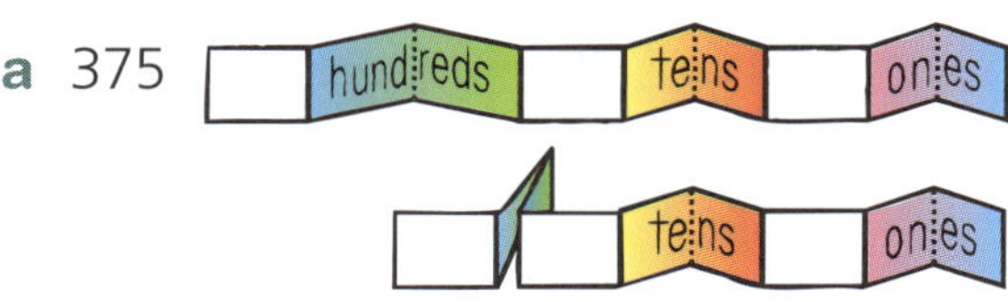

b 198 hundreds tens ones

tens ones

4 Round each number to the nearest hundred.

a	378	b	842	c	296
d	419	e	675	f	324
g	906	h	547	i	752

Higher or lower

FUN SPOT

- One player records a secret 3-digit number and says the boundaries for the number, such as 'between 200 and 300'.
- Other players mark the boundaries on number lines.
- Players take turns to guess the number. After each guess, the holder of the number says whether the secret number is **higher** or **lower** than the guess.
- Players mark this clue for the guess (**higher** or **lower**) on their number lines.
- The game continues until someone guesses the secret number exactly.

235

The secret number is higher.

 • *AUSTRALIAN SIGNPOST MATHS 3* • ISBN 9780655708773

1:09 Fractions of a collection

Two out of three are coloured. $\frac{2}{3}$

1

Group	Number coloured	Total in group	Fraction coloured
			$\frac{4}{5}$

2

a 

fraction coloured ☐ fraction not coloured ☐

b 

fraction coloured ☐ fraction not coloured ☐

c 

fraction coloured ☐ fraction not coloured ☐

d 

fraction coloured ☐ fraction not coloured ☐

e 

fraction coloured ☐ fraction not coloured ☐

f 

fraction coloured ☐ fraction not coloured ☐

3 Colour part of each group to match the fraction.

a  $\frac{4}{6}$

b 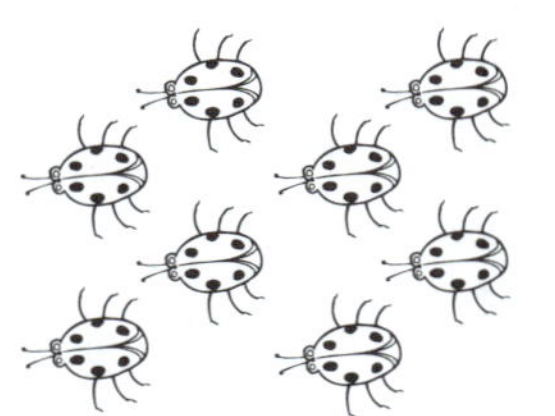 $\frac{7}{8}$

c 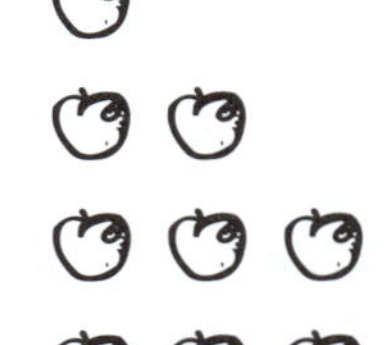 $\frac{8}{10}$

d  $\frac{3}{3}$

e  $\frac{2}{5}$

f $\frac{5}{6}$

- Collect examples of the use of fractions (online, in newspapers and in magazines). Copy as many examples as you can. Paste these onto a large sheet of paper to make a fractions chart.

 ISBN 9780655708773

1:10 Fractions of a whole

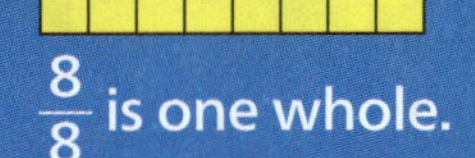
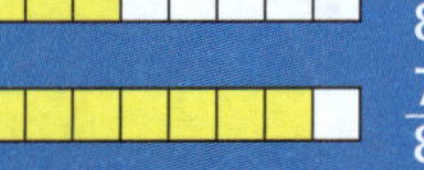

The **d**enominator is written **d**own on the bottom.

1. How much of each shape has been coloured?

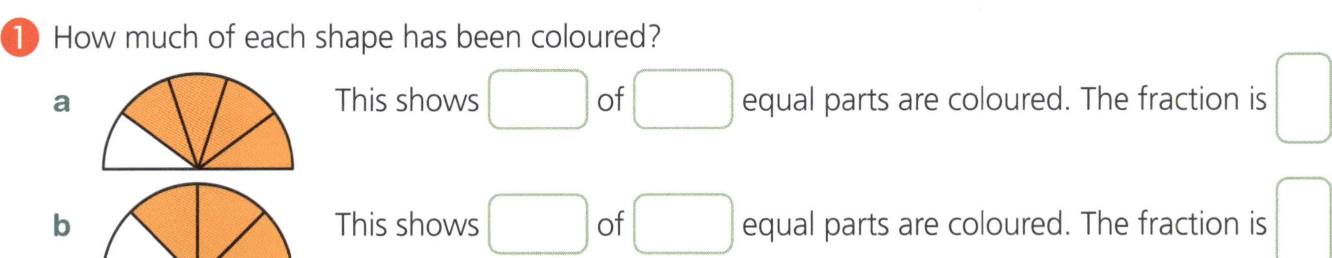

a This shows ☐ of ☐ equal parts are coloured. The fraction is ☐.

b This shows ☐ of ☐ equal parts are coloured. The fraction is ☐.

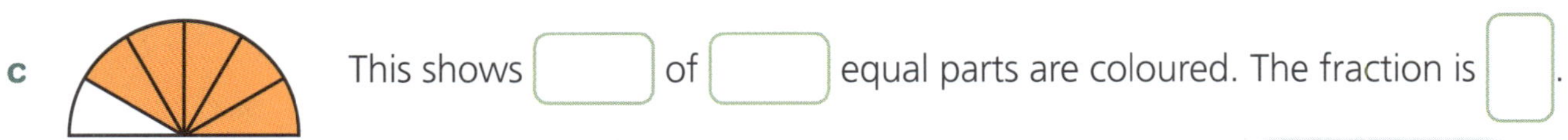

c This shows ☐ of ☐ equal parts are coloured. The fraction is ☐.

2. How much of each shape has been coloured?

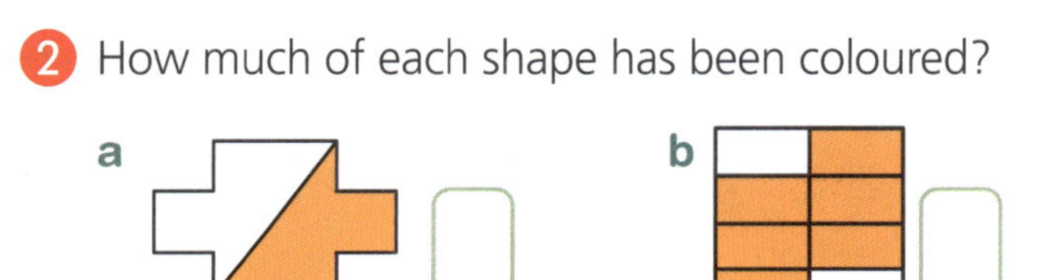

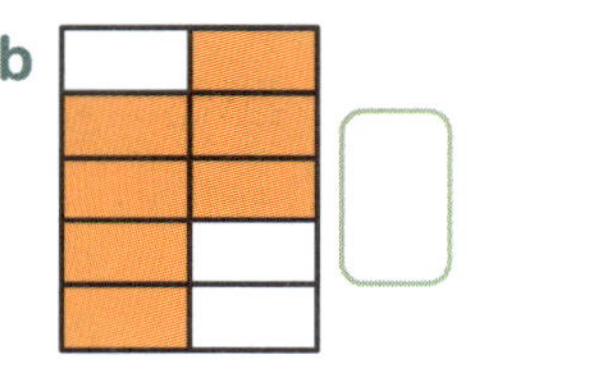

3. Colour part of each shape to match the fraction.

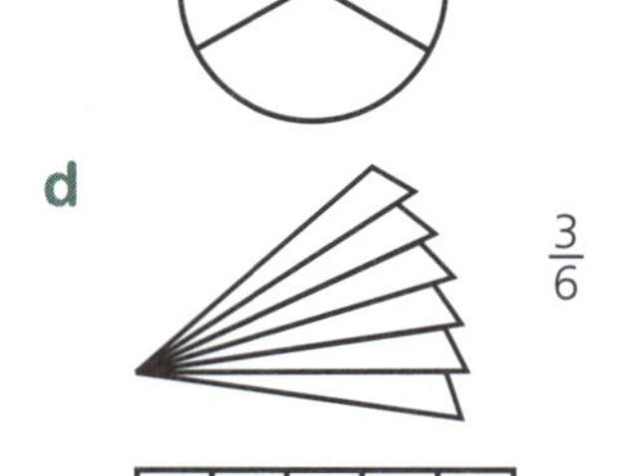

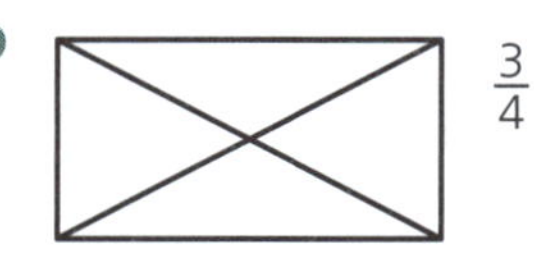

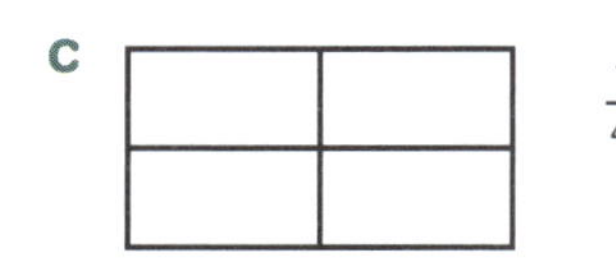
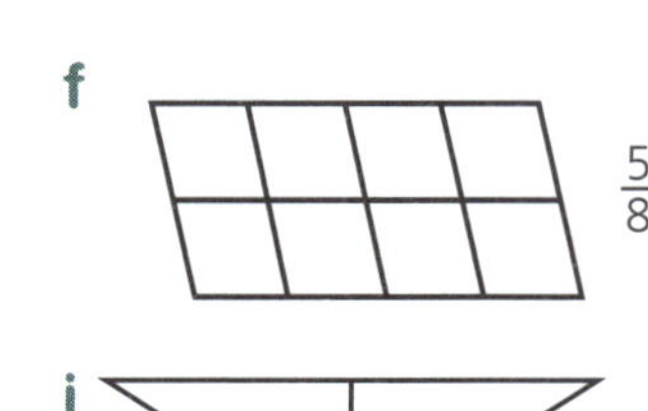

Challenge

Which is greater, one-sixth or one-eighth?

☐ is greater than ☐

1:11 Numbers to 10 000

Order from smallest (1) to largest (3).

100	
10 000	
1000	

1. Write the numeral, fill in the numeral expander and write the number in words.

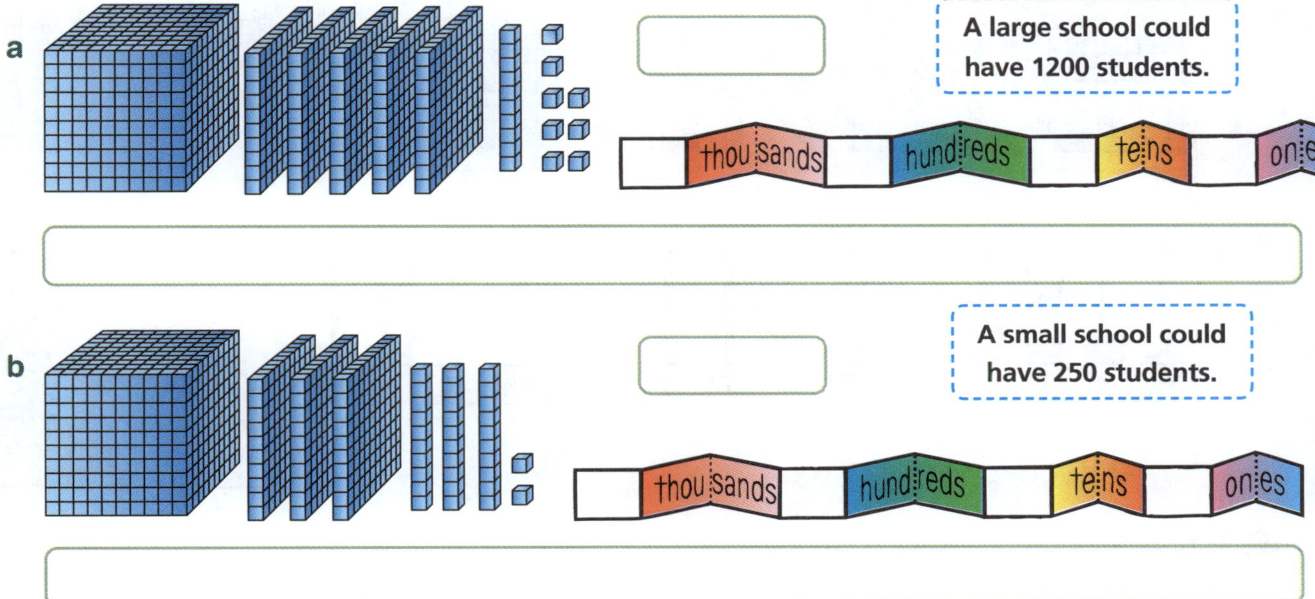

2. How many digits are in each numeral?

a 39	b 1307	c 9	d 85
e 1000	f 99	g 2469	h 1325

Digit game

FUN SPOT

Thousands	Hundreds	Tens	Ones
6	4	3	0

- Each player uses 4 numeral cards to make a number on a place-value chart.
- Players get one numeral card at a time. Before they can see the next card, they must put the card they have onto the place-value chart

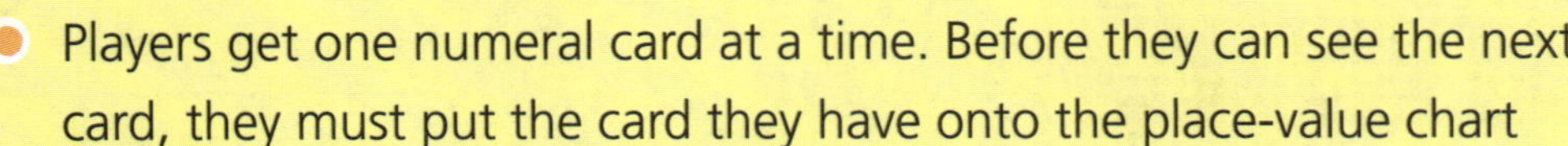

- The player with the largest number at the end wins.

 • *AUSTRALIAN SIGNPOST MATHS 3* • ISBN 9780655708773

1:12 Numbers to 10 000

Why would we use 'U' for 'units' instead of 'O' for 'ones'?

CONCEPT

1 Write the number shown as a numeral.

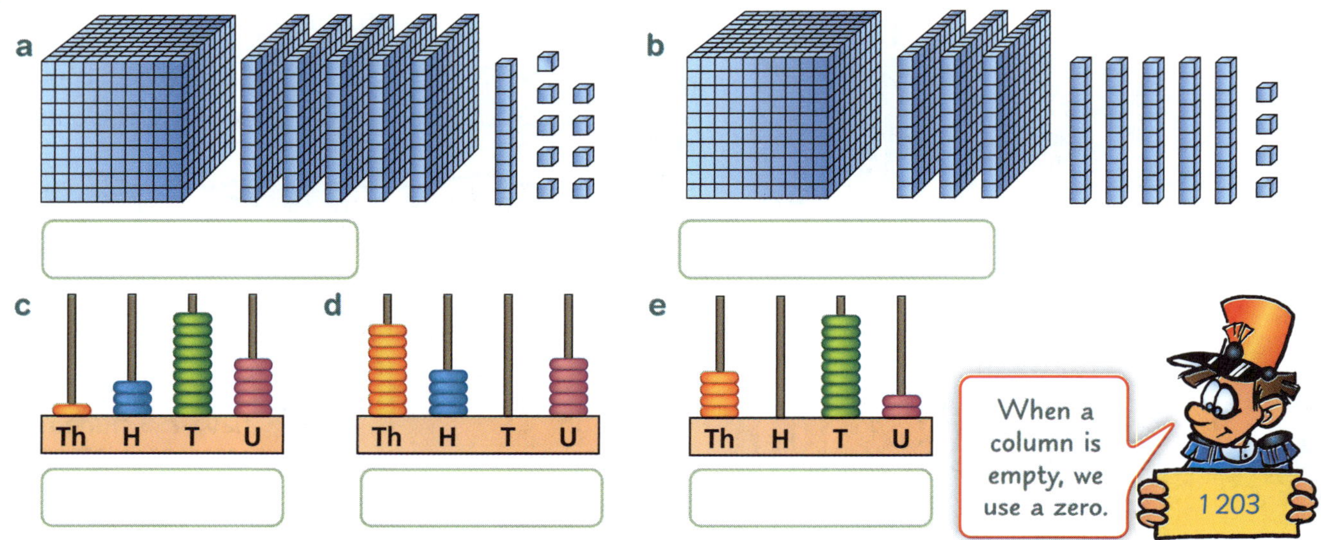

2 Write the numeral for each number.

a five thousand, eight hundred and thirty-seven

b six thousand, nine hundred and two

c four thousand, one hundred and eighty-nine

3 Circle the larger number.

a 1365 or 2547
b 3128 or 4263
c 5409 or 4149
d 2157 or 2010
e 4312 or 4196
f 7256 or 10 000

Comparing numbers

1 Compare the digits in the largest column.

2 If these are the same, compare digits in the next column on the right.

INVESTIGATION

This is **one thousand, one hundred and eleven**

100 is ten

1000 is ten

1111 is 11 hundreds and 11.

 ISBN 9780655708773

Fractions

Draw lines to make thirds.

1 What fraction of each shape is coloured?

a 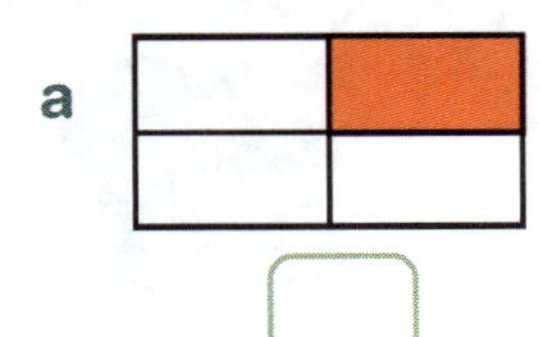 b 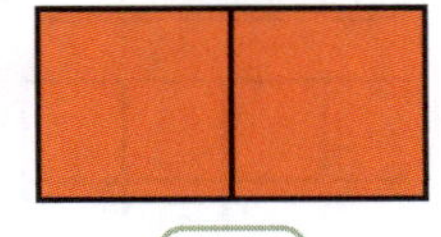 c 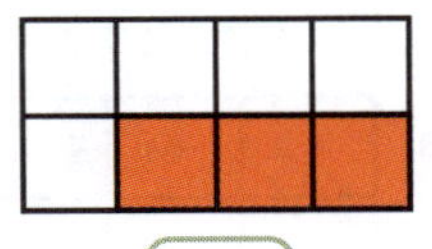 d 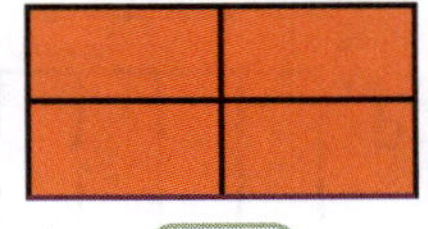

e 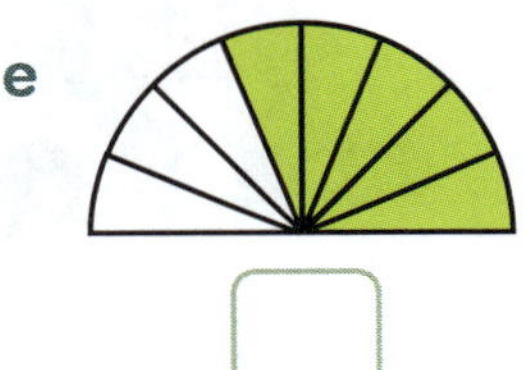 f  g 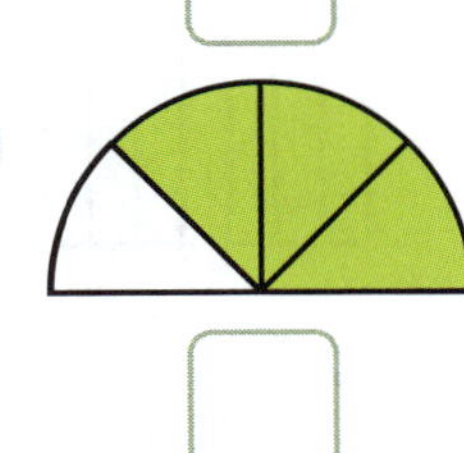 h 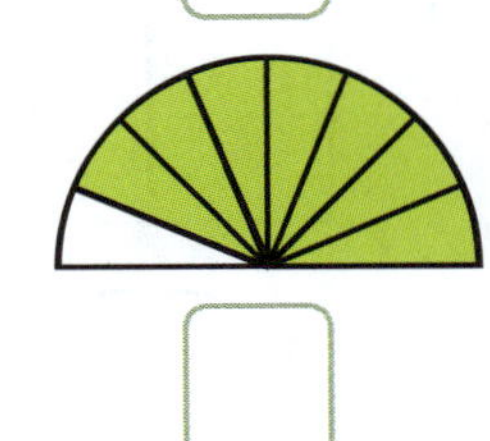

2 Colour each shape to match the fraction.

a  $\frac{3}{8}$ b 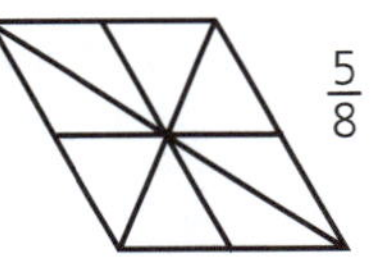 $\frac{5}{8}$ c 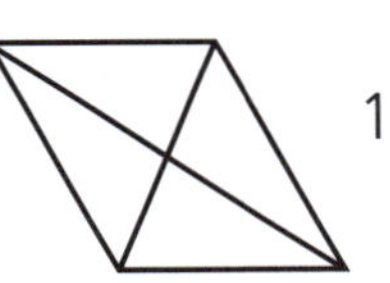 1 d 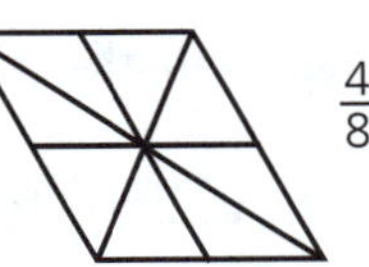 $\frac{4}{8}$

e  $\frac{1}{8}$ f 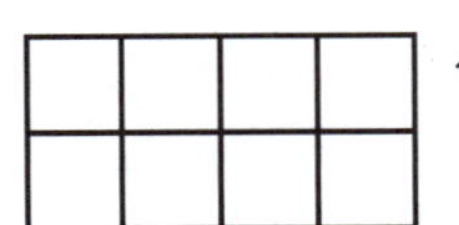 1 g 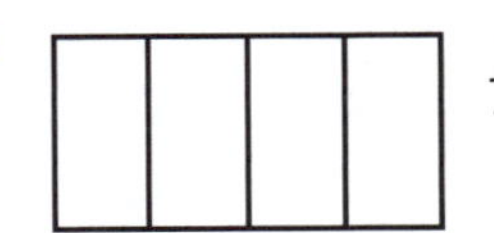 $\frac{2}{4}$ h 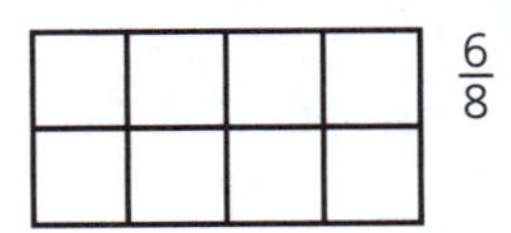 $\frac{6}{8}$

INVESTIGATION

- Show how you would share these cakes equally among the guests.

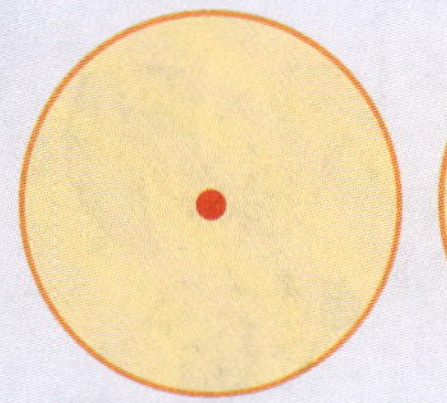

3 guests

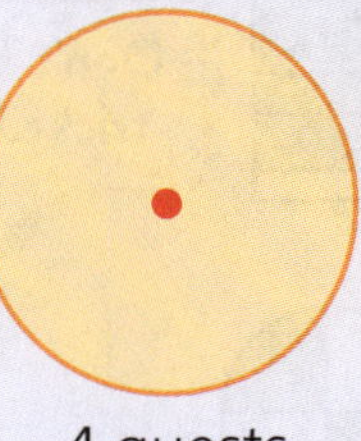

4 guests

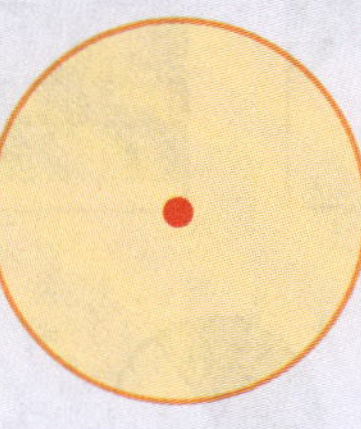

6 guests

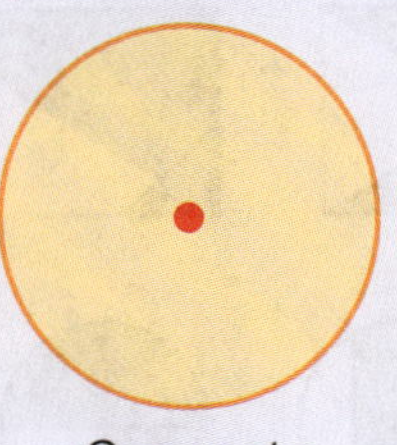

8 guests

Circle *smaller* or *larger*.

The more guests there are, the *smaller / larger* the pieces will be.

 • *AUSTRALIAN SIGNPOST MATHS 3* • ISBN 9780655708773

1:14 Fractions

Colour $\frac{3}{10}$ green.

Colour $\frac{7}{10}$ yellow.

How many eighths of this rectangle make one half?

1. Colour part of each shape to match the fraction.

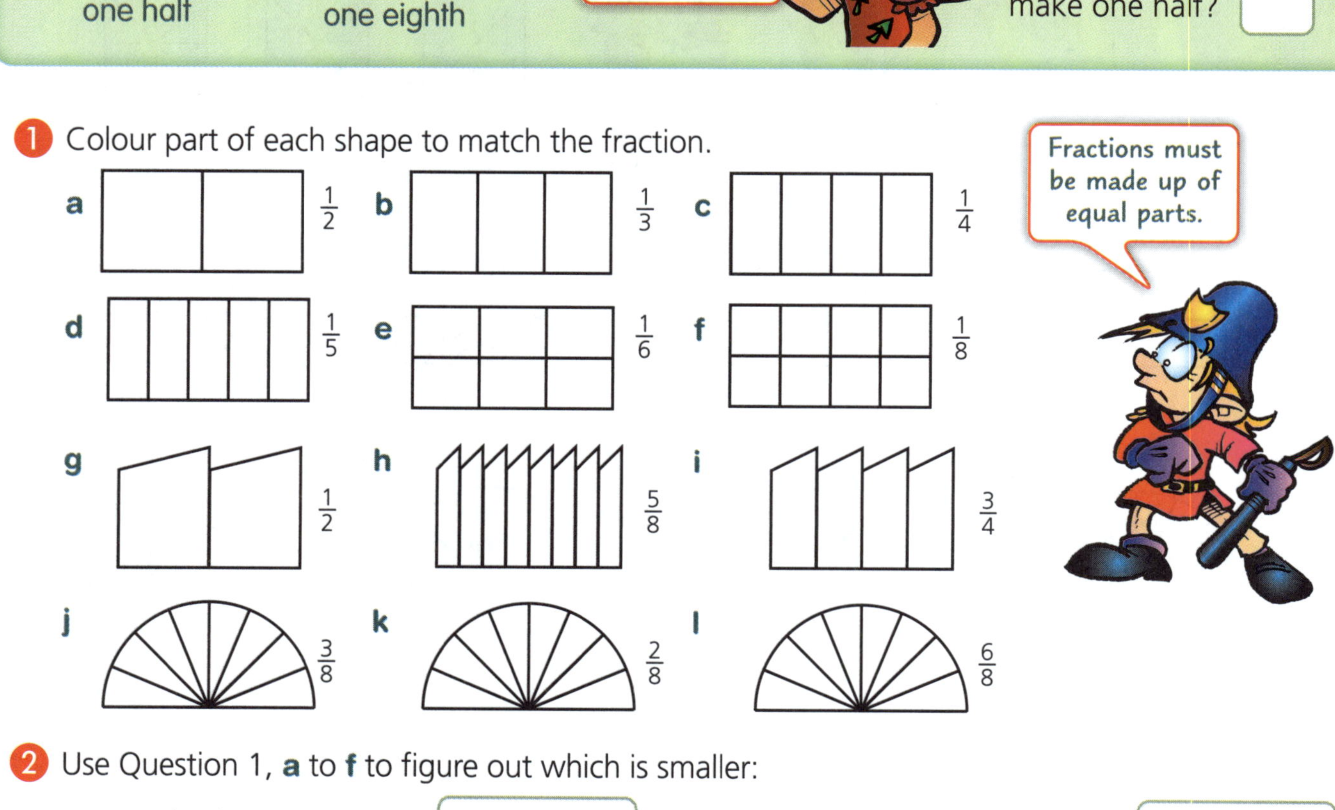

2. Use Question 1, **a** to **f** to figure out which is smaller:

   a one-third or one-quarter

   b one-sixth or one-eighth

3. Draw lines to make:

   a halves

   b fifths

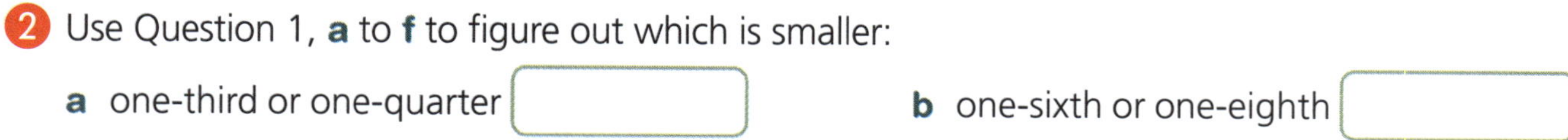

4. Circle the diagram that shows $\frac{3}{4}$.

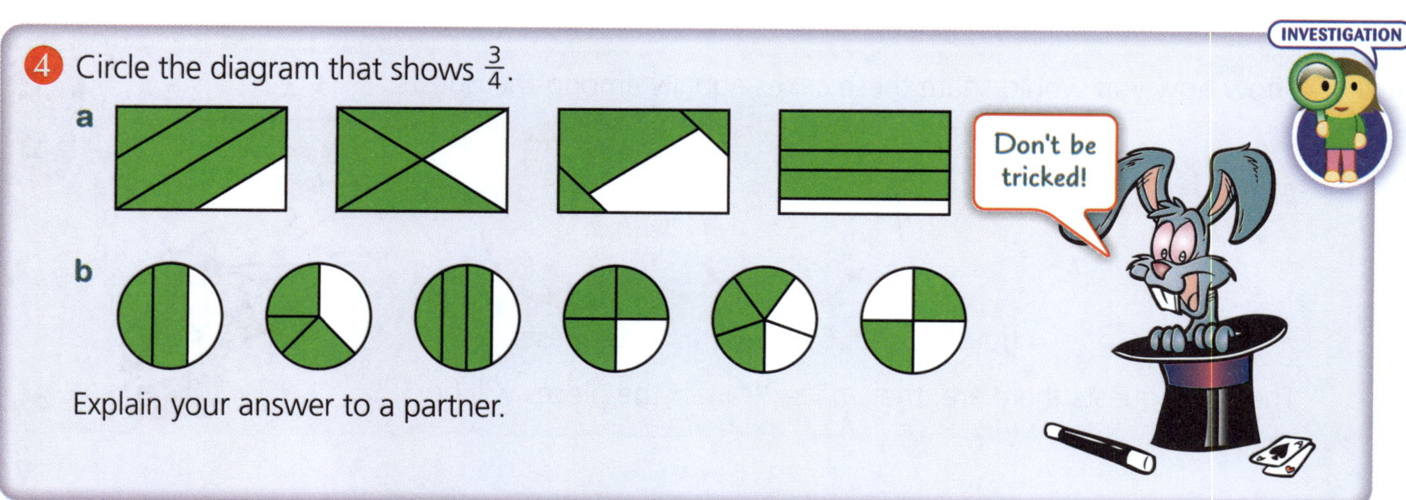

Explain your answer to a partner.

 • *AUSTRALIAN SIGNPOST MATHS 3* • ISBN 9780655708773

What's the rule?

11, 11 + 3, 14 + 3, 17 + 3, ...
11, 14, 17, 20, ...

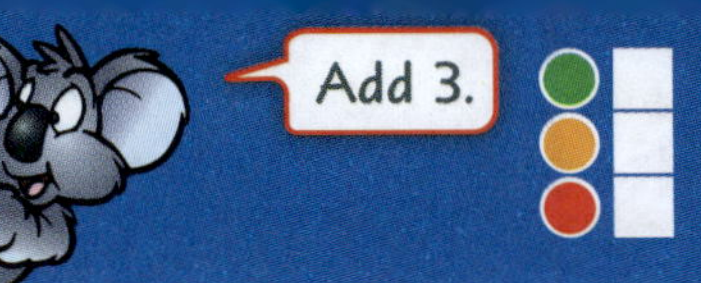

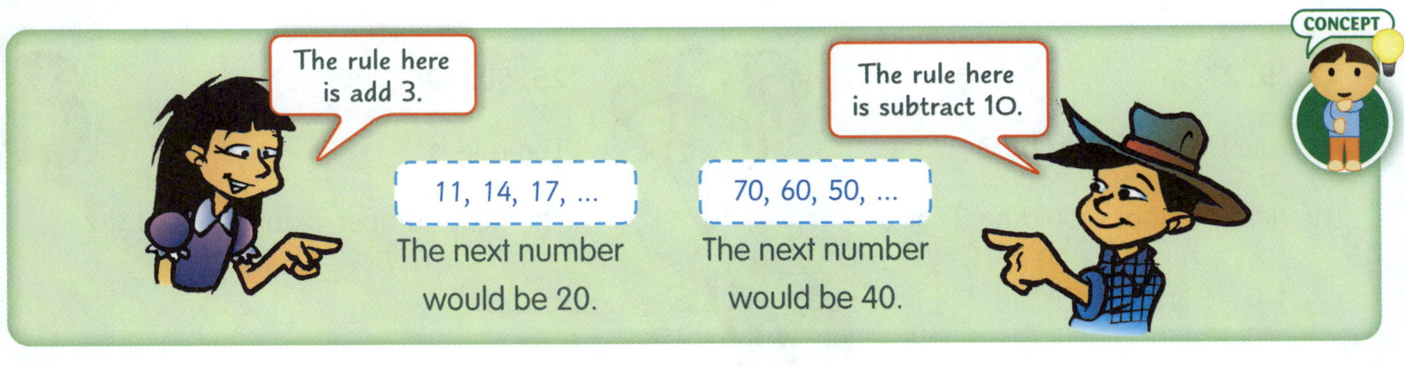

1 Write the next number in each pattern.

a 1, 3, 5, … ☐ **b** 7, 10, 13, … ☐ **c** 10, 20, 30, … ☐
d 20, 16, 12, … ☐ **e** 33, 32, 31, … ☐ **f** 44, 33, 22, … ☐
g 10, 14, 18, … ☐ **h** 75, 70, 65, … ☐ **i** 38, 46, 54, … ☐

2 Write the rule for each pattern in Question 1.

a ☐ **b** ☐ **c** ☐
d ☐ **e** ☐ **f** ☐
g ☐ **h** ☐ **i** ☐

3 Follow the rule to continue each pattern.

a Add 6. 21, ☐, ☐, ☐
b Subtract 1. 41, ☐, ☐, ☐
c Subtract 2. 74, ☐, ☐, ☐
d Add 8. 34, ☐, ☐, ☐
e Add 20. 23, ☐, ☐, ☐
f Subtract 4. 40, ☐, ☐, ☐
g Multiply by 2. 3, ☐, ☐, ☐
h Add 15. 5, ☐, ☐, ☐
i Subtract 10. 63, ☐, ☐, ☐
j Multiply by 2. 1, ☐, ☐, ☐

4 Write the pattern for the number of sides, then write the rule.

a   , …

Pattern: 3, ☐, ☐, ☐, … Rule: ☐

b   , …

Pattern: 10, ☐, ☐, ☐, … Rule: ☐

1:16 Making patterns

Rule: Multiply by 2.
6, 12, 24, 48, 96, …

You could use a calculator.

CONCEPT

1, 3, 9, 27, …

The rule is **multiply by 3**.

The next number would be 27 × 3.

81

They gave me 3 times as many.

25, 50, 100, 200, …

The rule is ______.

The next number would be 200 × 2.

______

1 Multiply each number by 2 to get the next number.

a 1, 2, 4, ___, ___
b 3, 6, 12, ___, ___
c 50, 100, ___, ___
d 10, 20, ___, ___
e 2, ___, ___, ___
f 5, ___, ___, ___
g 6, ___, ___, ___
h 20, ___, ___, ___
i 4, ___, ___, ___
j 7, ___, ___, ___

2 Multiply each number by 3 to get the next number.

To multiply by 3, we can add the number to its double.
18 x 3 = (18 x 2) + 18

a 1, 3, 9, ___, ___
b 2, 6, 18, ___, ___
c 3, ___, ___, ___
d 10, ___, ___, ___
e 4, ___, ___, ___
f 20, ___, ___, ___

3 Multiply each number by 10 to get the next number.

a 1, 10, 100, ___, ___
b 2, 20, 200, ___, ___
c 3, ___, ___, ___
d 10, ___, ___, ___

To multiply by 10, write a zero at the end of the number.
2OO x 1O = 2OOO

FUN SPOT

Make multiplication patterns of your own using a calculator.
Write one of your patterns here.

___, ___, ___, ___, ___, ___, ___

 • *AUSTRALIAN SIGNPOST MATHS 3* • ISBN 9780655708773

1:17 Numbers to 10 000

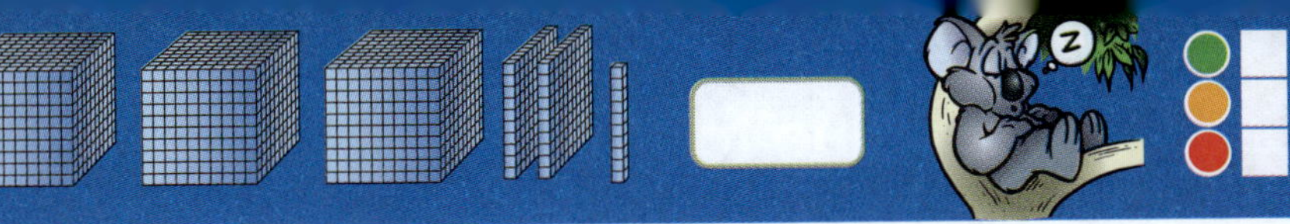

1 Write the number shown as a numeral.

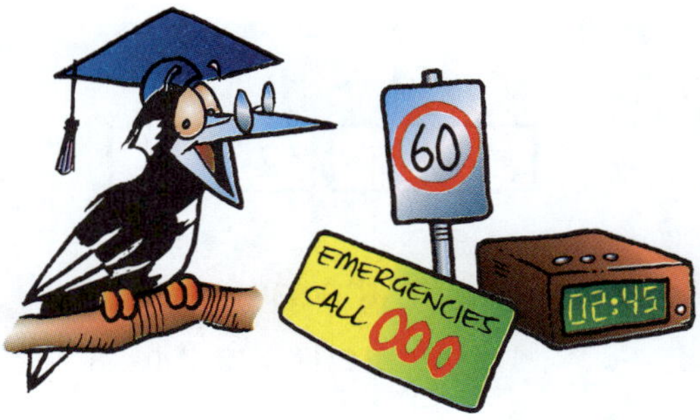

a Th H T U

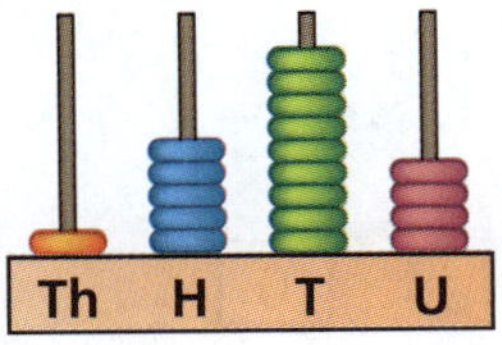

b Th H T U

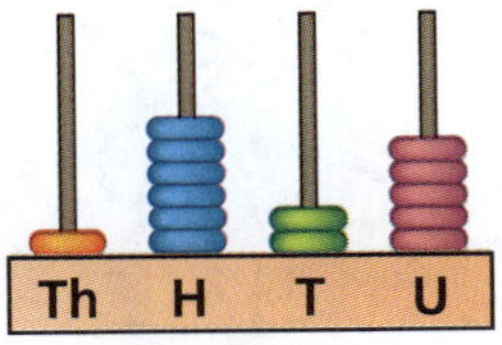

c Th H T U

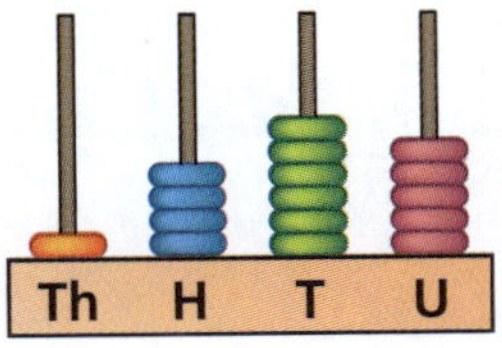

d Th H T U

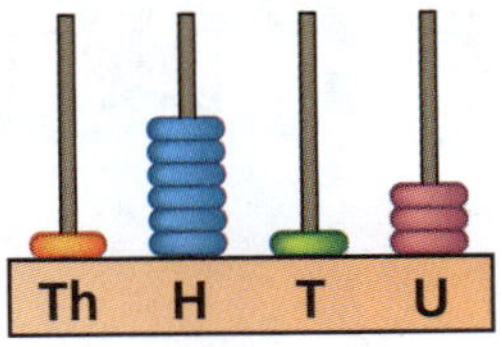

e Th H T U

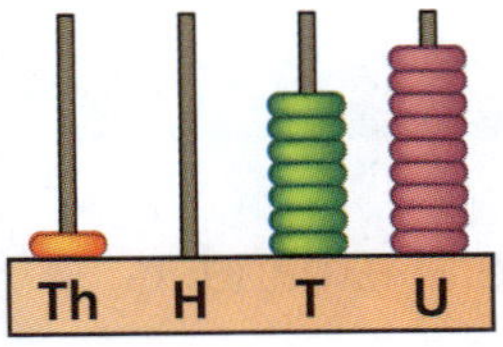

f Th H T U

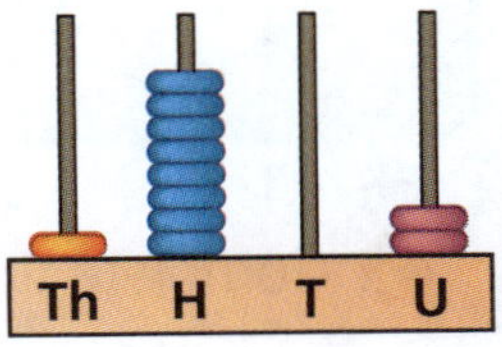

2 Write the numeral, fill in the numeral expander and write the number in words.

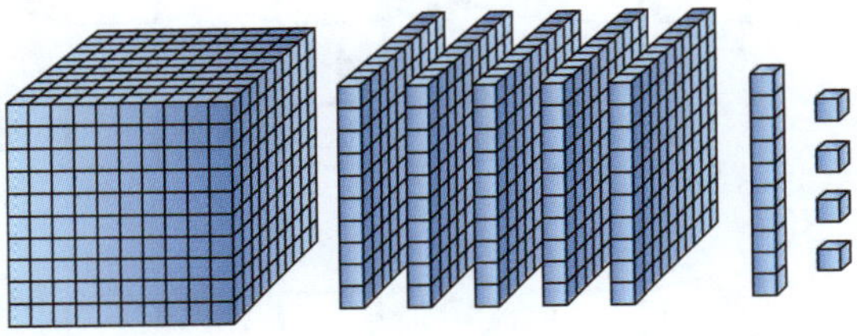

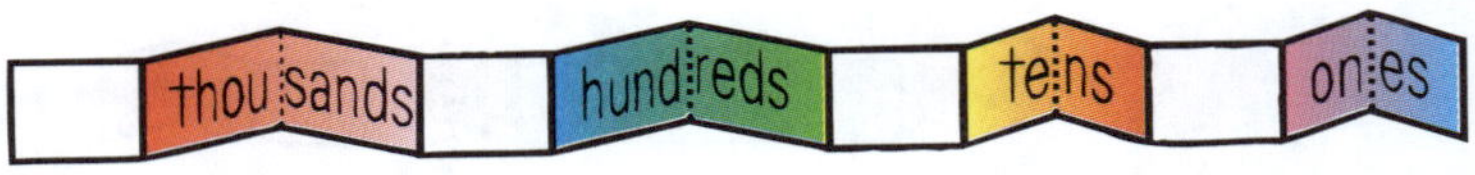

thousands hundreds tens ones

3 How many digits are in each number?

a 147 b 21 c 1945 d 439

e 64 f 2367 g 4003 h 6

4 Continue the number patterns.

a 4340, 4350, 4360, ___, 4380, 4390, ___, 4410, ___, ___

b 7605, 7705, 7805, ___, ___, 8105, 8205, 8305, ___, ___

c 1763, 2763, 3763, ___, ___, 6763, 7763, 8763, ___, ___

5 Write the number after:

a 346 b 679 c 999 d 1316

e 4876 f 3207 g 2649 h 3640

i 2199 j 5010 k 9999 l 1001

1:18 Place value to 10 000

3800 is closer to 4000 than to 3000.
3400 is closer to 3000 than to 4000.

1720 is the same as
17 hundreds and 2 tens
or 172 tens.

1 Complete the numeral expanders.

a 1479

b 3568

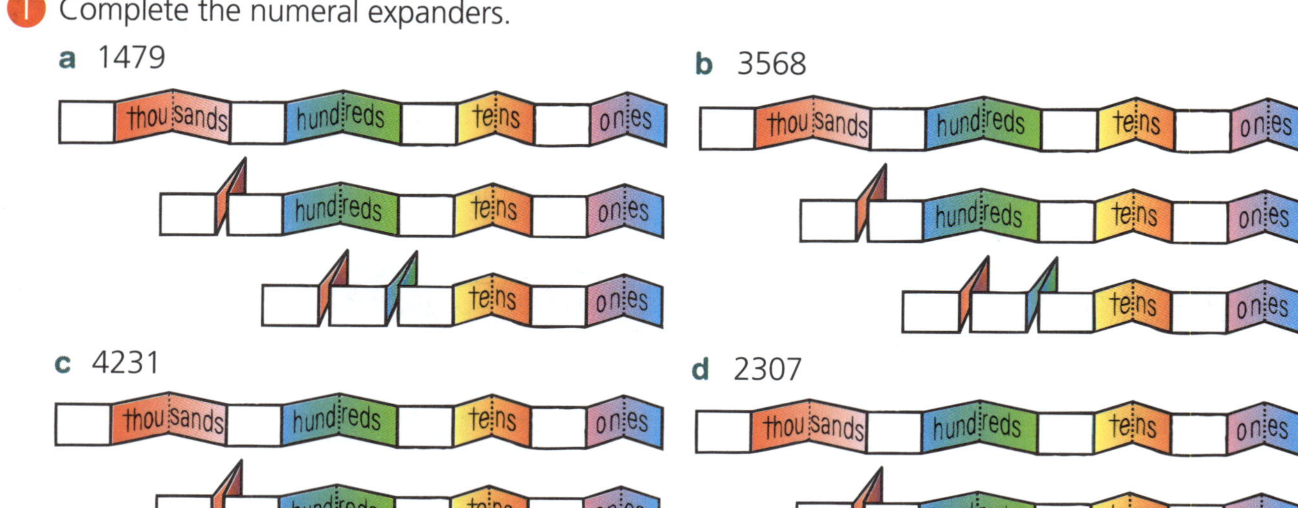

c 4231

d 2307

2 Write the numeral for each number.

a five thousand, seven hundred and sixty-three

b eight thousand, nine hundred and fifty-six

c six thousand, two hundred and seventy-five

d four thousand, six hundred and forty-nine

e nine thousand, five hundred and eighty-two

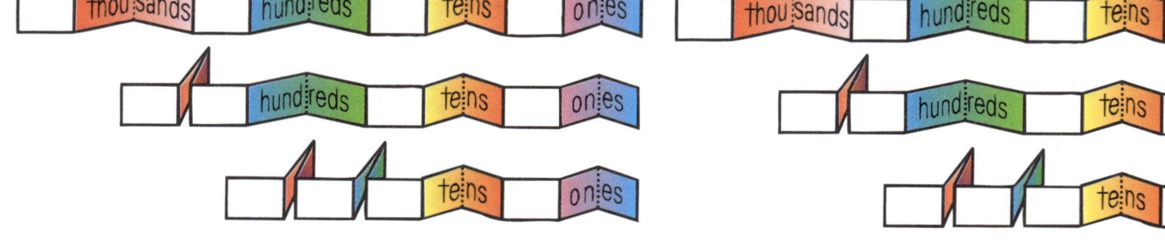

3 Write each number in words.

a 6824

b 2319

4 Round each number to the nearest thousand.

a 4695

b 3126

c 9538

 • *AUSTRALIAN SIGNPOST MATHS 3* • ISBN 9780655708773

1:19 Comparing fractions

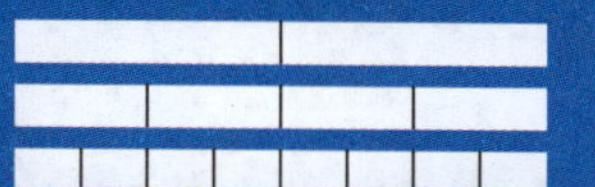

Which is larger: $\frac{3}{4}$ or $\frac{5}{8}$?

1. Write each fraction, then circle the smallest fraction in each row.

a 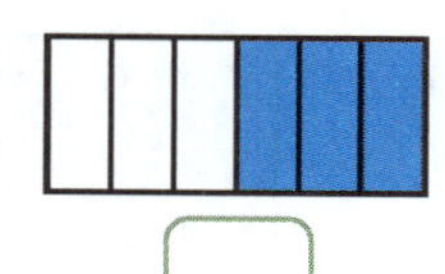

b 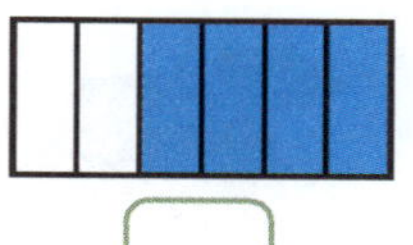

c 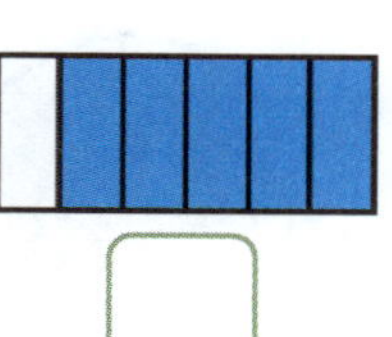

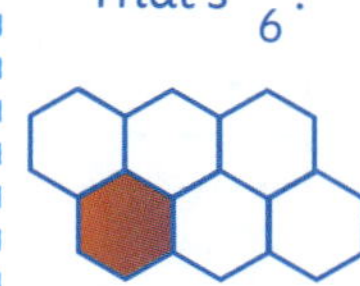

d 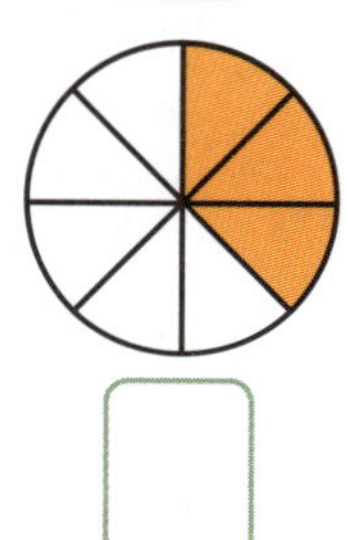

e 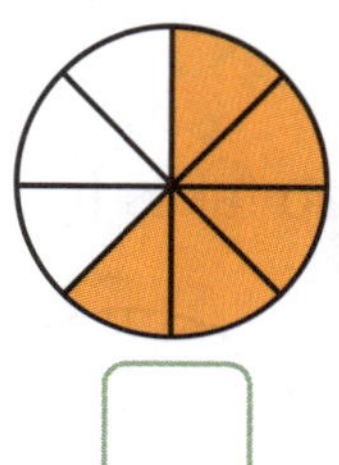

f 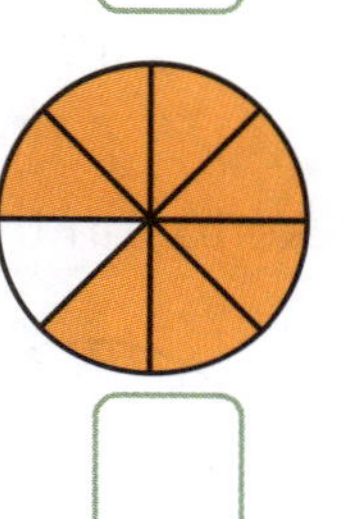

We can compare fractions of shapes if the shapes are the same.

2. Circle the larger fraction in each part.

a 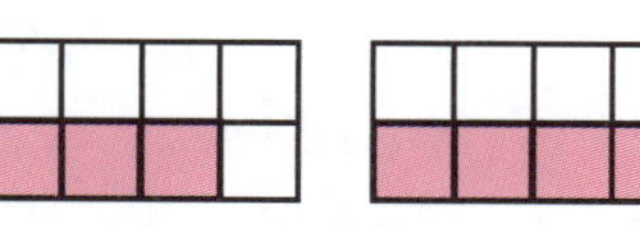
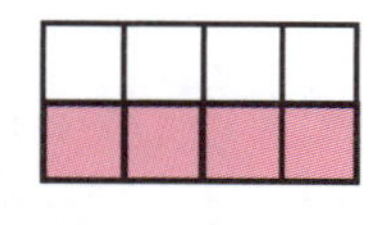

$\frac{3}{8}$ or $\frac{4}{8}$

b 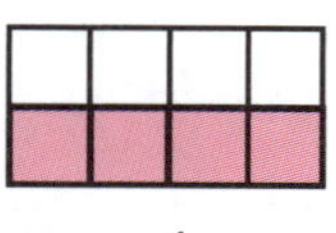
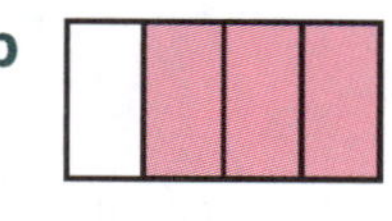

$\frac{3}{4}$ or $\frac{1}{4}$

c 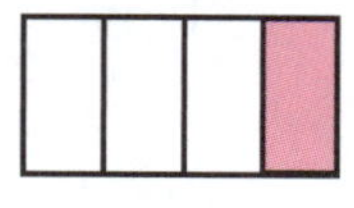
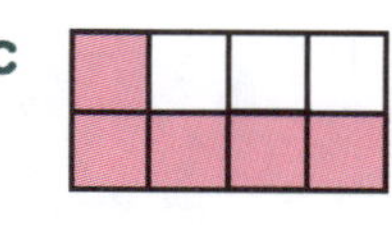
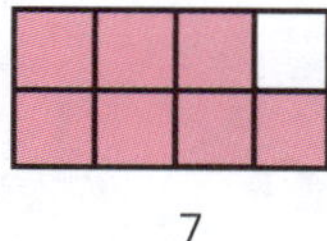

$\frac{5}{8}$ or $\frac{7}{8}$

d 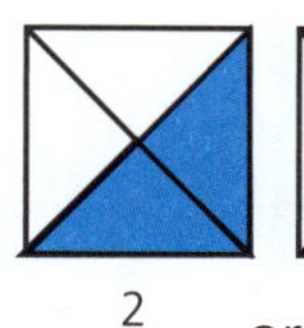

$\frac{2}{4}$ or $\frac{3}{4}$

e 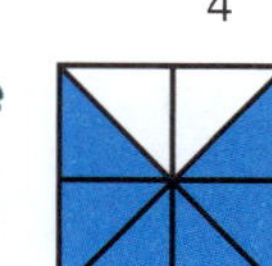
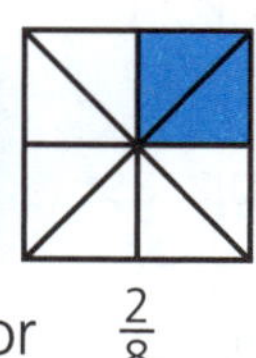

$\frac{6}{8}$ or $\frac{2}{8}$

f 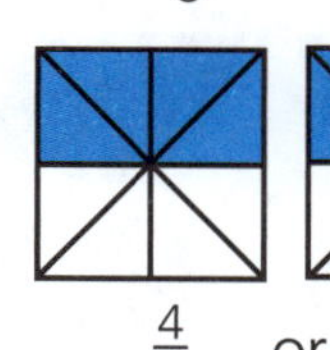

$\frac{4}{8}$ or $\frac{5}{8}$

3. Compare the two fractions using the diagrams on the right. Circle the larger fraction in each case.

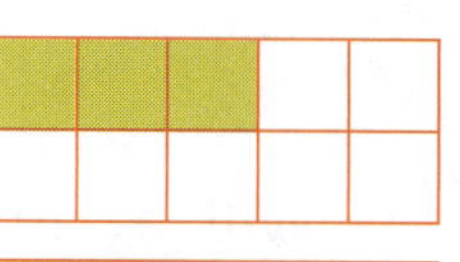

a $\frac{3}{10}$ or $\frac{4}{10}$ b $\frac{9}{10}$ or $\frac{5}{10}$ c $\frac{4}{10}$ or $\frac{1}{2}$ d $\frac{8}{10}$ or $\frac{3}{10}$

e $\frac{1}{2}$ or $\frac{7}{10}$ f $\frac{3}{10}$ or $\frac{1}{2}$ g $\frac{1}{2}$ or $\frac{3}{4}$ h $\frac{3}{10}$ or $\frac{1}{4}$

Using fractions

Five-quarters of a pizza is one and a quarter pizzas.

CONCEPT

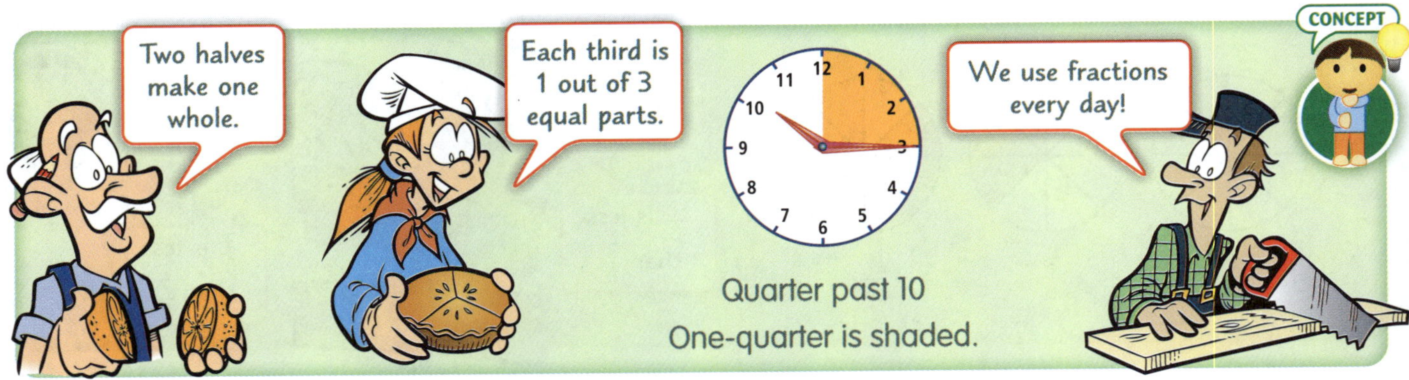

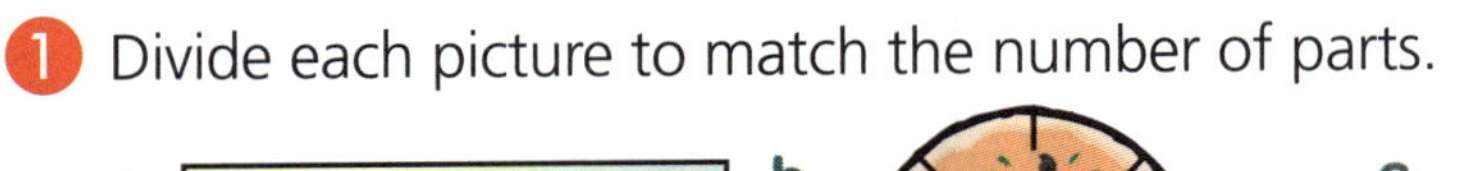

1 Divide each picture to match the number of parts.

a 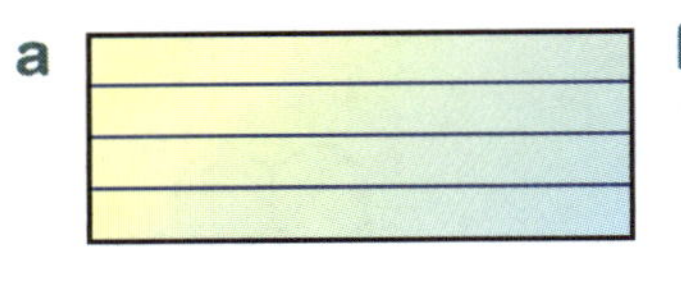 eighths

b 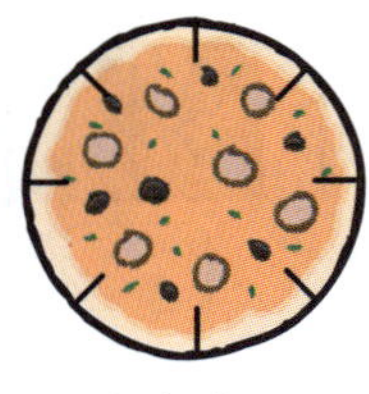 eighths

c  quarters

d  quarters

2 Colour the time it would take to run the laps. One lap takes five minutes.

a 9 laps

b 

3 laps

c 

6 laps

d 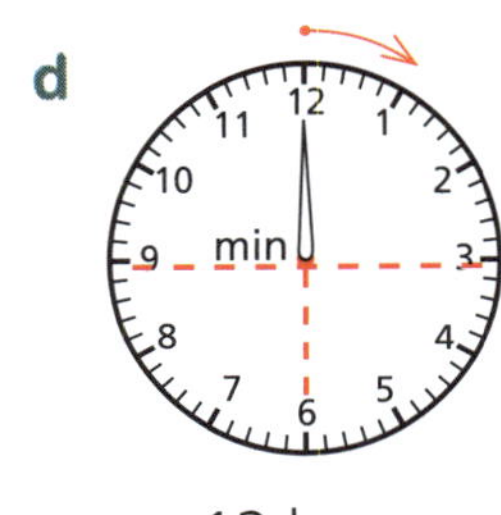

12 laps

3 

Write the number of quarter-pizzas that would be in:

a 1 pizza ☐

b 2 pizzas ☐

c 3 pizzas ☐

d 4 pizzas ☐

e one and a half pizzas ☐

f two and a half pizzas ☐

How many halves are in 3 oranges? ☐

ACTIVITY

- With a partner, write a list of situations where we use fractions.

 • *AUSTRALIAN SIGNPOST MATHS 3* • ISBN 9780655708773

1:21 Numbers to 10 000

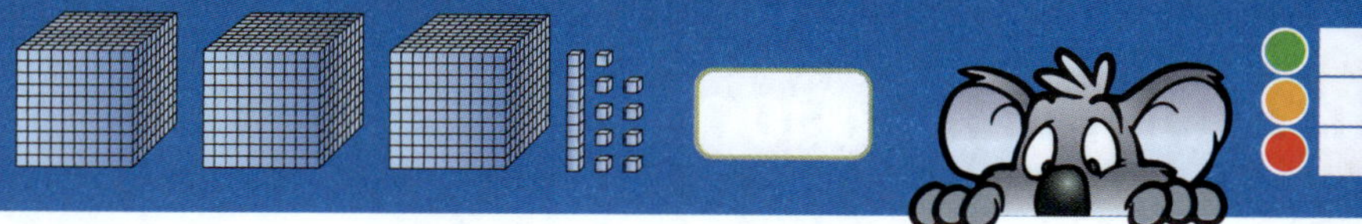

1 Write the number shown as a numeral.

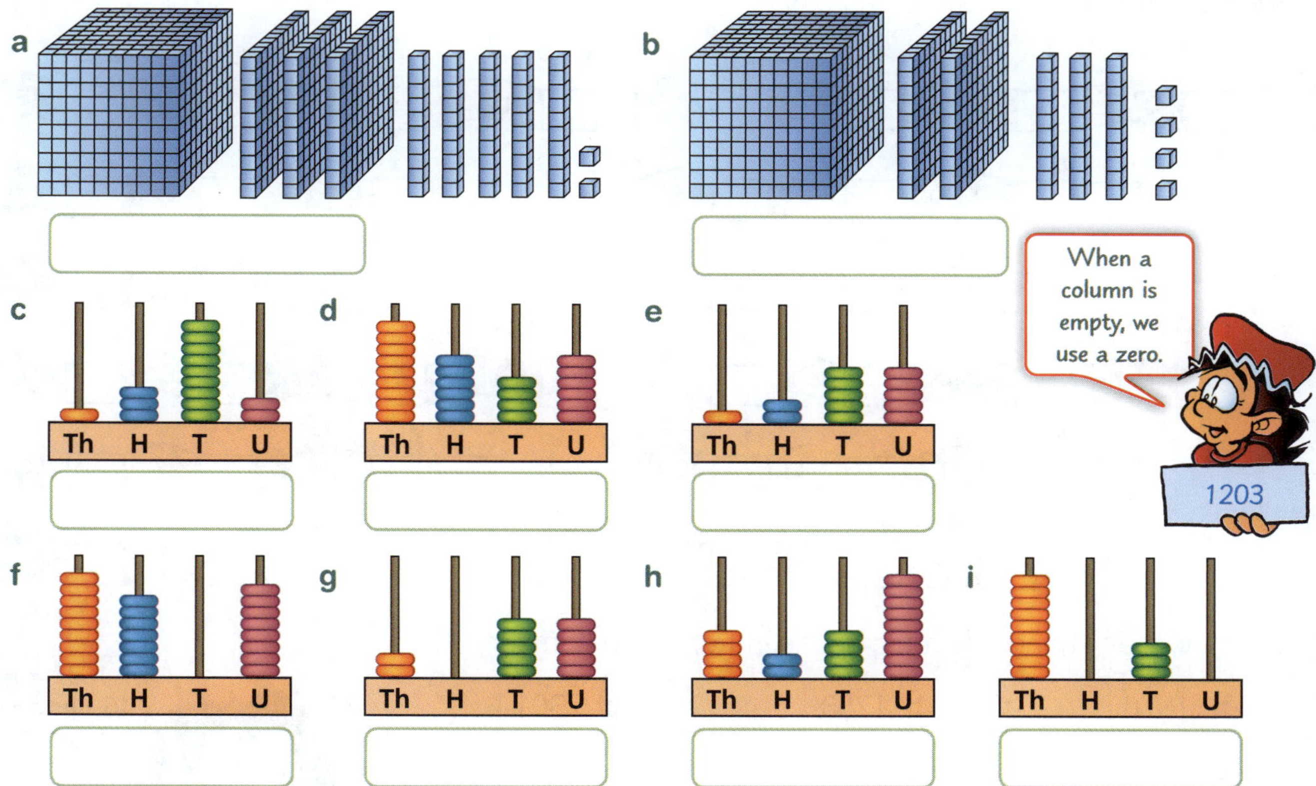

2 Circle the largest number in each group.

a 327, 237, 723 b 569, 669, 965 c 631, 613, 603

d 1246, 1264, 1216 e 2375, 2735, 2753 f 4194, 4094, 4049

3 Write the value of the 6 in each number.

a 3659 b 6125 c 4968

Wipe out a digit

ACTIVITY

- Enter a 4-digit number into a calculator.
- Your partner selects any digit to be **wiped out** – that is, changed to zero.
- Try to wipe out that digit by entering only **one** operation into the calculator. Did it work?
- Take turns with your partner. Score 1 point for each successful wipe out.

1:22 Numbers to 10 000

9076 = 9000 + 70 + 6
9 thousands, 7 tens and 6 ones

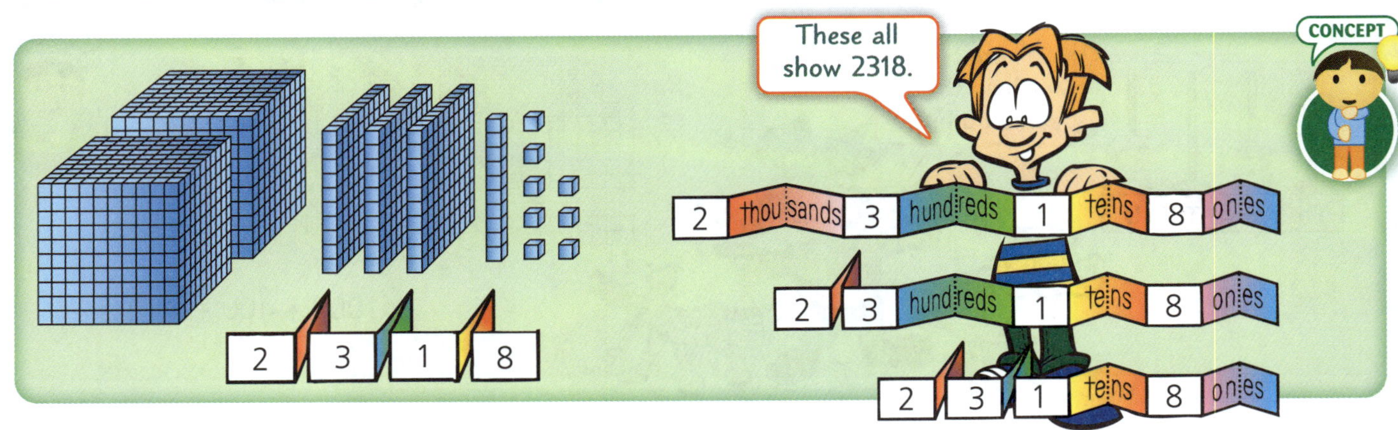

CONCEPT

1 Complete the numeral expanders.

a 1764 b 3795

c 4013 d 9658

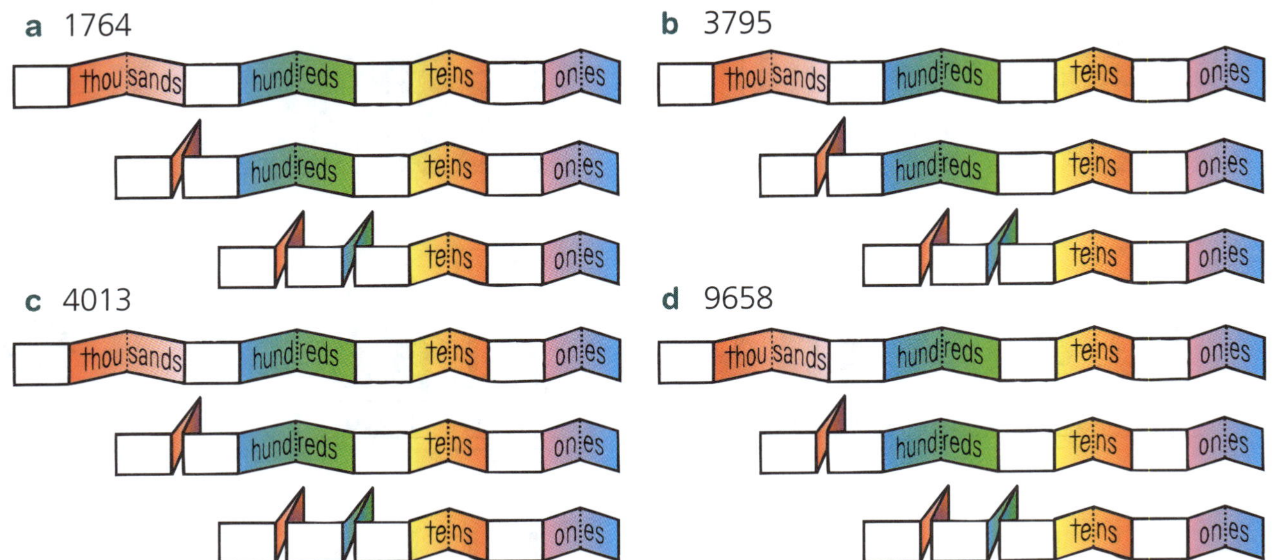

2 How many hundreds could be taken from each number?

a 1576 ☐ b 1253 ☐ c 2301 ☐

d 6192 ☐ e 7471 ☐ f 9368 ☐

3 How many tens could be taken from each number?

a 1742 ☐ b 1624 ☐

c 4906 ☐ d 7264 ☐

4 Write the numeral.

a one thousand, two hundred and ten ☐

b five thousand, six hundred and forty-one ☐

c six thousand, three hundred and one ☐

d two thousand, five hundred and sixteen ☐

5 a 3000 = ☐ tens

= ☐ hundreds

b 700 = ☐ tens

= ☐ hundreds

 • *AUSTRALIAN SIGNPOST MATHS 3* • ISBN 9780655708773

1:23 Expanded notation

CONCEPT

It's expanded notation for 2137.

2000 + 100 + 30 + 7

1 Write the numeral.

a 3000 + 700 + 60 + 9		**b** 4000 + 600 + 30 + 7	
c 2000 + 500 + 80 + 1		**d** 5000 + 400 + 70 + 6	
e 3000 + 900 + 50 + 8		**f** 6000 + 800 + 40 + 3	

2 Write the number in expanded notation.

a 4247		**b** 3169	
c 2675		**d** 5192	

3 Write these numbers in the columns to show the place value.

	Thousands	Hundreds	Tens	Units
a 4378				
b 6249				
c 3821				
d 5873				

That's easy.

4 Write the value of each red digit.

a 2**9**16	**b** **4**037	**c** 627**9**	**d** 56**8**4
e **3**690	**f** 869**5**	**g** 2**6**70	**h** 58**3**6

5 Write the number before.

a 967	**b** 1236	**c** 2191	**d** 4630
e 5729	**f** 6310	**g** 3400	**h** 7020

FUN SPOT

Dicey numbers

- Take turns to roll four dice.
- Record the highest 4-digit number made by the dice.
- State the numbers before and after that number.

6655

1:24 Tenths and fifths

$\frac{\square}{10}$ are yellow. $\frac{\square}{5}$ is blue.

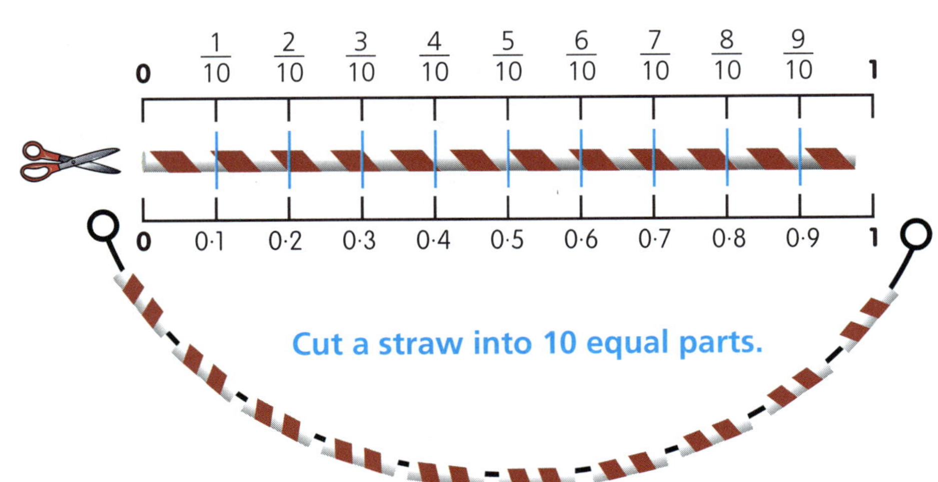

1 Write these decimals as tenths.

a $0{\cdot}3 = \frac{\square}{10}$ b $0{\cdot}5 = \frac{\square}{10}$ c $0{\cdot}9 = \frac{\square}{10}$ d $0{\cdot}7 = \frac{\square}{10}$

1 tenth or 0·1 is 1 of 10 equal parts.

2 Write the decimal for:

a $\frac{2}{10}$ ☐ b $\frac{5}{10}$ ☐ c $\frac{1}{10}$ ☐

d $\frac{8}{10}$ ☐ e $\frac{3}{10}$ ☐ f $\frac{7}{10}$ ☐

g $\frac{4}{10}$ ☐ h $\frac{6}{10}$ ☐ i $\frac{9}{10}$ ☐

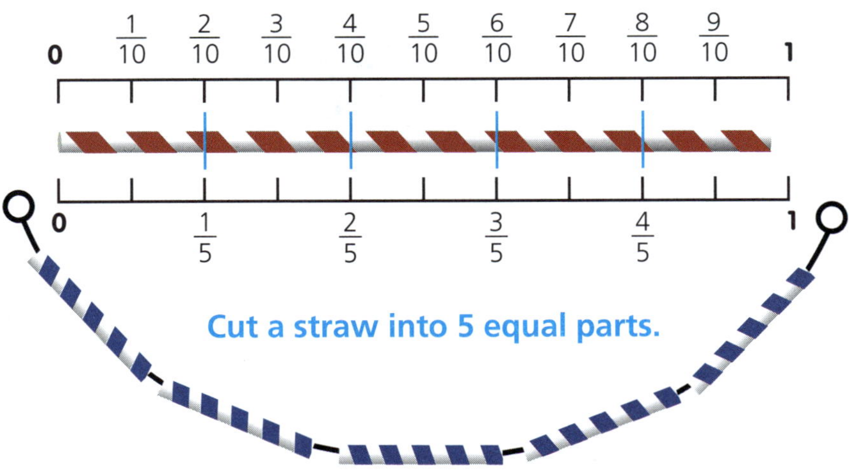

3 Write these as fifths.

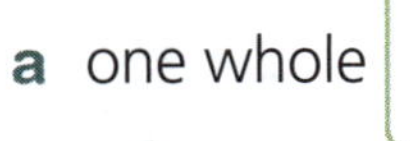

a one whole $\frac{\square}{5}$ b 2 tenths $\frac{\square}{5}$ c 4 tenths $\frac{\square}{5}$

d 8 tenths $\frac{\square}{5}$ e 6 tenths $\frac{\square}{5}$ f 10 tenths $\frac{\square}{5}$

1 fifth is 1 of 5 equal parts.

Place value using tenths

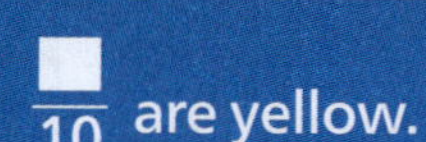

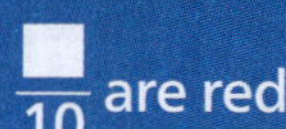

$\frac{\square}{10}$ are yellow. $\frac{\square}{10}$ are red.

CONCEPT

$2\frac{3}{10}$

mixed number
(whole number and a fraction)
2 and 3 tenths

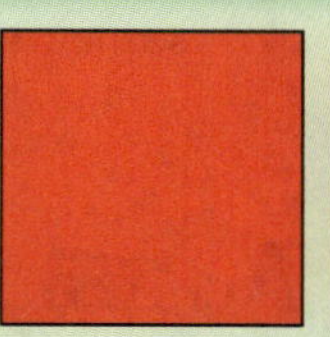

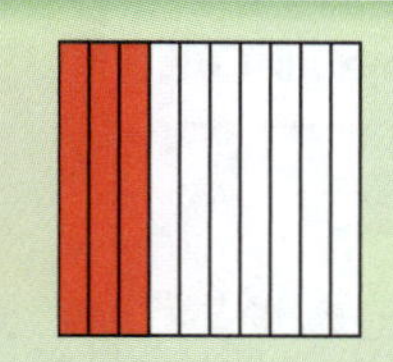

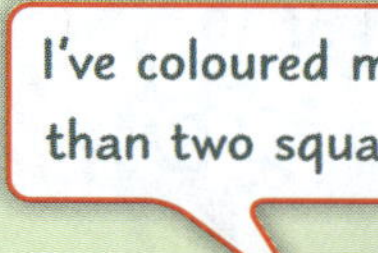

two wholes

three tenths

decimal

2·3

tens	ones		tenths
	2	·	3

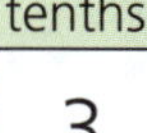

1 Write the decimal for:

a   

tens	ones		tenths
		·	

b 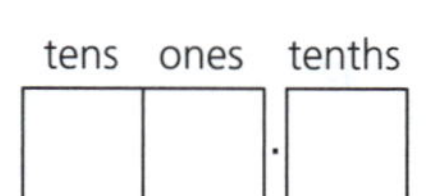  

tens	ones		tenths
		·	

2 Write the decimal for:

a $\frac{1}{10}$ ☐ **b** $\frac{3}{10}$ ☐ **c** $\frac{5}{10}$ ☐

d $\frac{4}{10}$ ☐ **e** $\frac{2}{10}$ ☐ **f** $\frac{8}{10}$ ☐

g $\frac{9}{10}$ ☐ **h** $\frac{7}{10}$ ☐ **i** $\frac{6}{10}$ ☐

three tenths
0·3
↑
decimal point

3 Write the decimal for:

a $1\frac{1}{10}$ ☐ **b** $1\frac{6}{10}$ ☐ **c** $1\frac{2}{10}$ ☐

d $2\frac{3}{10}$ ☐ **e** $2\frac{4}{10}$ ☐ **f** $2\frac{9}{10}$ ☐

g $3\frac{5}{10}$ ☐ **h** $3\frac{8}{10}$ ☐ **i** $3\frac{7}{10}$ ☐

$1\frac{3}{10} = 1{\cdot}3$

$2\frac{6}{10} = 2{\cdot}6$

$3\frac{9}{10} = 3{\cdot}9$

4 Write the fraction (or mixed number) for:

a 0·5 ☐ **b** 0·7 ☐ **c** 0·2 ☐

d 1·4 ☐ **e** 3·1 ☐ **f** 2·8 ☐

g 6·9 ☐ **h** 5·3 ☐ **i** 7·6 ☐

5 Write as a decimal.

a 4 ones and 1 tenth = ☐ **b** 8 ones and 3 tenths = ☐

c 5 ones and 2 tenths = ☐ **d** 3 ones and 4 tenths = ☐

 • *AUSTRALIAN SIGNPOST MATHS 3* • ISBN 9780655708773

1:26 Place value using tenths

1 Write the decimal for:

a $\frac{5}{10}$		**b** $\frac{3}{10}$		**c** $\frac{6}{10}$		**d** $\frac{1}{10}$	
e $\frac{8}{10}$		**f** $\frac{9}{10}$		**g** $\frac{2}{10}$		**h** $\frac{4}{10}$	
i $1\frac{1}{10}$		**j** $1\frac{3}{10}$		**k** $1\frac{9}{10}$		**l** $1\frac{8}{10}$	

2 Match each fraction or mixed number with the correct decimal.

a

$\frac{4}{10}$	0·7
$\frac{9}{10}$	0·4
$\frac{7}{10}$	0·9

b

$\frac{3}{10}$	0·2
$\frac{1}{10}$	0·3
$\frac{2}{10}$	0·1

c

$1\frac{9}{10}$	1·8
$1\frac{8}{10}$	1·9
$1\frac{6}{10}$	1·6

3 Use decimals to write:

a 5 tenths		**b** 3 tenths		**c** 9 tenths		**d** 7 tenths	
e 4 tenths		**f** 8 tenths		**g** 6 tenths		**h** 10 tenths	
i zero point one		**j** zero point eight		**k** zero point five			
l one point nine		**m** one point three		**n** one point zero			

4 Complete the number lines.

a

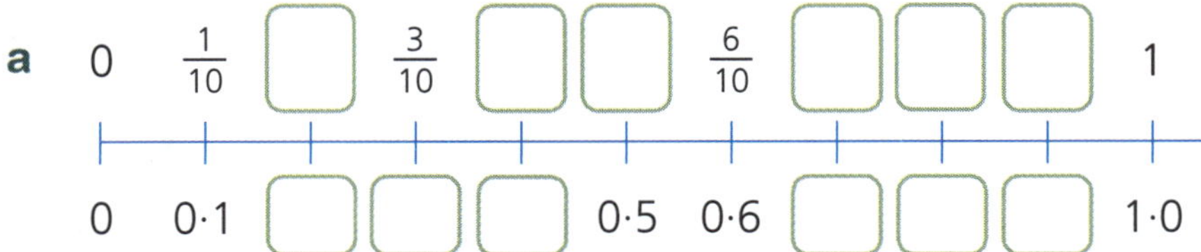

b

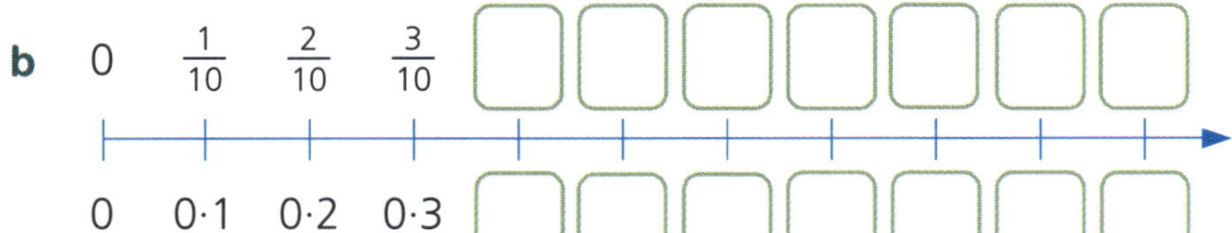

 • *AUSTRALIAN SIGNPOST MATHS 3* • ISBN 9780655708773

1:27 Numbers over 10 000

45 thousand
45 000

123 thousand
123 000

CONCEPT

Thousands	Hundreds, Tens, Ones
75	248
19	783
140	529

75 248

Leave a space to the right of the thousands digit.

75 thousand, 2 hundred and forty-eight
19 thousand, 7 hundred and eighty-three
140 thousand, 5 hundred and twenty-nine

75 248 = 7 ten-thousands, 5 thousands, 2 hundreds, 4 tens and 8 ones
= 70 000 + 5000 + 200 + 40 + 8

1. Write the numeral for:

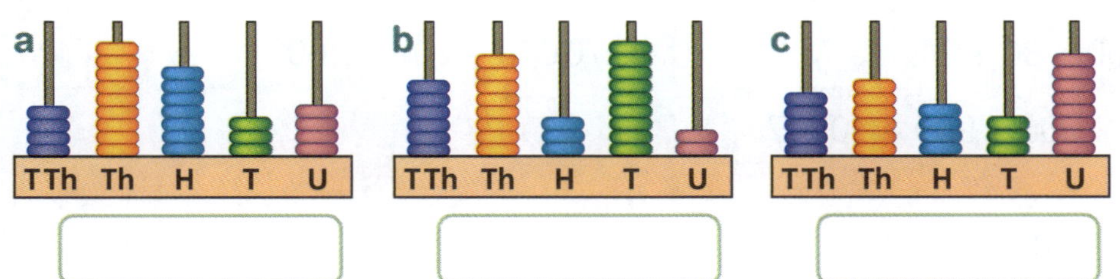

U stands for 'units' or 'ones'.
T Th stands for 'tens of thousands'

2. Read these numbers aloud and then write them in figures on the place-value chart.
   - a twenty-six thousand, three hundred and twenty-four
   - b thirty-five thousand, one hundred and sixty-two
   - c eighty-two thousand, nine hundred and seventy
   - d fifty-two thousand, eight hundred and fourteen
   - e seventy-four thousand, two hundred and sixty

T Thous	Thous	Hund	Tens	Ones

3. Write the numeral for:
   - a 30 000 + 4000 + 500 + 20 + 8
   - b 60 000 + 7000 + 900 + 30 + 4
   - c 50 000 + 8000 + 400 + 60 + 2
   - d 90 000 + 2000 + 700 + 40 + 8
   - e 80 000 + 2000 + 300 + 50 + 9
   - f 40 000 + 8000 + 600 + 70 + 3

4. Write these as 'thousands' and 'hundreds, tens, ones':
   - a The library paid $47 500 for a painting of Perth.
   - b The population of Geelong was 263 280 in 2020.
   - c In 2021 there were 984 000 Aboriginal and Torres Strait Islander people living in Australia.

Thousands	Hundreds, Tens, Ones

1:28 Numbers over 10 000

49 620 = 49 000 + 620
270 539 = 270 000 + 539

1 Write the numeral for:

a 50 000 + 8000 + 400 + 30 + 7 ____
b 50 000 + 400 + 30 + 7 ____
c 80 000 + 1000 + 500 + 20 + 6 ____
d 10 000 + 4000 + 200 + 1 ____
e 30 000 + 5000 + 800 + 30 + 2 ____
f 70 000 + 2000 + 600 ____
g 400 000 + 60 000 + 2000 + 900 + 30 + 7 ____

2 Circle the largest number in each group.

a 34 728, 38 274, 87 352
b 15 906, 90 651, 51 960
c 79 207, 97 207, 97 702
d 75 098, 69 999, 70 789
e 112 403, 87 345, 60 913
f 56 920, 105 206, 49 502

3 Put in order from smallest to largest.

a 50 712, 51 270, 50 752, 9752 ____
b 75 098, 69 999, 70 789, 508 970 ____

4 How many digits are in:

a 76 084 ____
b 4073 ____
c 76 830 ____
d 116 777 ____

5 Complete the numeral expanders for the number 213 605.

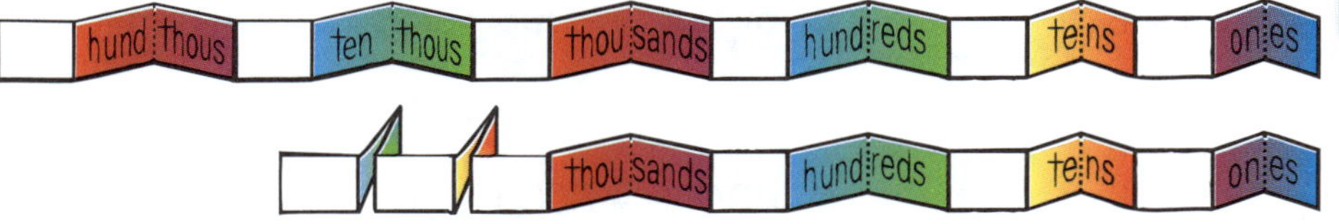

The zero is used as a place holder.

6 Complete.

a 1 hundred = ____ tens
b 1 thousand = ____ hundreds
c 1 ten thousand = ____ thousands
d 1 hundred thousand = ____ ten thousands

Larger numbers

The population of Australia in 2022 was 25 978 935.

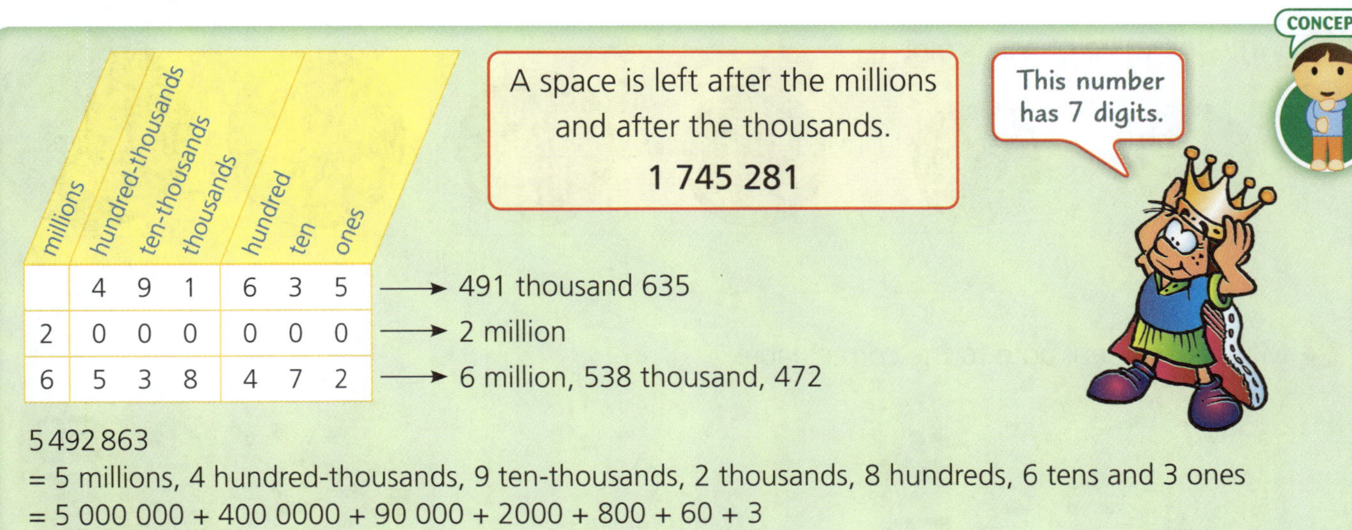

CONCEPT

A space is left after the millions and after the thousands.

1 745 281

This number has 7 digits.

millions	hundred-thousands	ten-thousands	thousands	hundred	ten	ones	
	4	9	1	6	3	5	→ 491 thousand 635
2	0	0	0	0	0	0	→ 2 million
6	5	3	8	4	7	2	→ 6 million, 538 thousand, 472

5 492 863
= 5 millions, 4 hundred-thousands, 9 ten-thousands, 2 thousands, 8 hundreds, 6 tens and 3 ones
= 5 000 000 + 400 0000 + 90 000 + 2000 + 800 + 60 + 3

1 Write the numeral for:

a 8 000 000 + 400 000 + 10 000 + 2000 + 600 + 90 + 3 ______

b 3 000 000 + 700 000 + 20 000 + 9000 + 500 + 40 + 9 ______

c 5 000 000 + 30 000 + 20 + 4 ______ **d** 9 000 000 + 700 + 1 ______

About one million, three hundred Earths could fit inside the sun.

2 Write these as 'millions', 'thousands' and 'hundreds, tens, ones'.

a The area of the Northern Territory is 1 347 791 square kilometres.

b The area of Western Australia is 2 527 013 square kilometres.

c The area of Queensland is 1 729 742 square kilometres.

d The area of South Australia is 984 321 square kilometres.

Millions	Thousands	Hundreds, Tens, Ones

3 Order the area of the Australian states in Question 2 from smallest to largest.

______

4 Complete the numeral expanders for the number 4 368 024.

☐ millions ☐ hund thous ☐ ten thous ☐ thousands ☐ hundreds ☐ tens ☐ ones

☐ millions ☐ ☐ ☐ thousands ☐ hundreds ☐ tens ☐ ones

The artwork 'Blue Poles' by Jackson Pollock was purchased for $1 300 000 in 1973.

5 Joseph sold his house for $2 462 000 and bought another house for $2 000 000. How much more did his first house cost?

______

2:01 Australian money

50c = 20c + 20c + ☐

= 20c + ☐ + ☐ + ☐

1 Write the value of each coin.

☐ ☐ ☐ ☐ ☐ ☐

2 Match each banknote to the correct label.

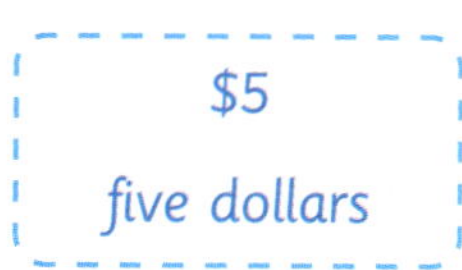

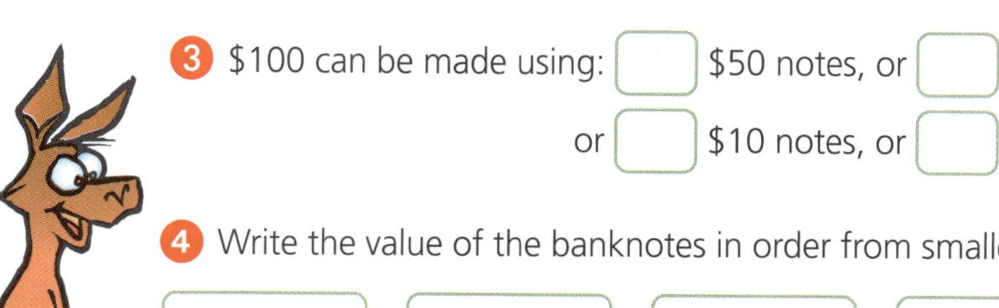

3 $100 can be made using: ☐ $50 notes, or ☐ $20 notes, or ☐ $10 notes, or ☐ $5 notes.

4 Write the value of the banknotes in order from smallest to largest.

☐ ☐ ☐ ☐ ☐

 • *AUSTRALIAN SIGNPOST MATHS 3* • ISBN 9780655708773

Number, Algebra

2:02 Money

Add the notes, starting with the highest note and working to the lowest.

1 Write the total value of each group of banknotes.

a

b

c

d

2 Circle the larger amount.

a

b

c

3 Write the amounts in order from smallest to largest.

Algebra

2:03 Addition and subtraction

16
9 7
This is a number bond diagram.

1 Complete the additions and subtractions. Discuss any patterns you can see.

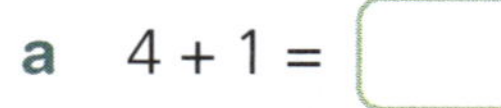

a 4 + 1 = ☐
1 + 4 = ☐
5 − 4 = ☐
5 − 1 = ☐

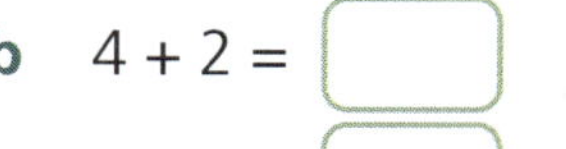

b 4 + 2 = ☐
2 + 4 = ☐
6 − 4 = ☐
6 − 2 = ☐

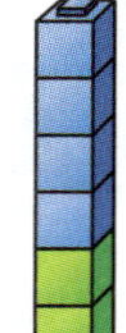

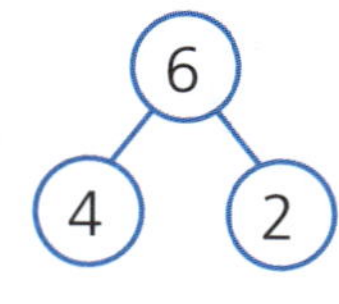

c 1 + 9 = ☐
9 + 1 = ☐
10 − 1 = ☐
10 − 9 = ☐

d 2 + 8 = ☐
8 + 2 = ☐
10 − 2 = ☐
10 − 8 = ☐

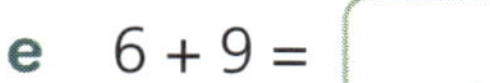

e 6 + 9 = ☐
9 + 6 = ☐
15 − 6 = ☐
15 − 9 = ☐

2 Colour matching pairs the same.
For example: 6 + 7 = 7 + 6
(The 13s are coloured blue.)
Show the answers to these and their partners on the grid.
4 + 8, 9 + 7, 8 + 9, 7 + 8, 5 + 9, 6 + 5, 5 + 7

+	0	1	2	3	4	5	6	7	8	9	10
0											
1											
2						7					
3											
4											
5			7								
6								13			
7							13				
8											
9											
10											

3 Use the number line to complete the number facts. Look for patterns.

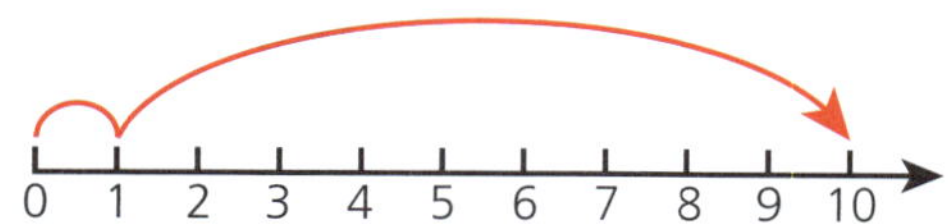

a 1 + 9 = ☐
2 + 8 = ☐
3 + 7 = ☐
4 + 6 = ☐
5 + 5 = ☐
6 + 4 = ☐
7 + 3 = ☐
8 + 2 = ☐
9 + 1 = ☐

b 10 − 9 = ☐
10 − 8 = ☐
10 − 7 = ☐
10 − 6 = ☐
10 − 5 = ☐
10 − 4 = ☐
10 − 3 = ☐
10 − 2 = ☐
10 − 1 = ☐

See *Extra Support 1–4* (Number facts).

 • *AUSTRALIAN SIGNPOST MATHS 3* • ISBN 9780655708773

2:04 Number facts, ×2

$2 \times 6 = 6 \times 2$
Double 6 is the same as 6 twos.

1 Use the number models to complete the multiplications.

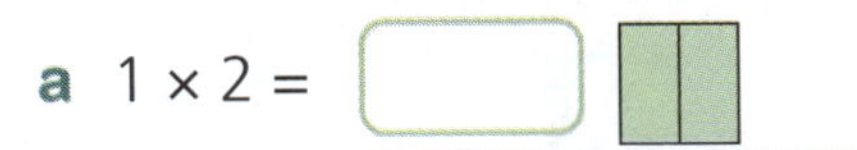

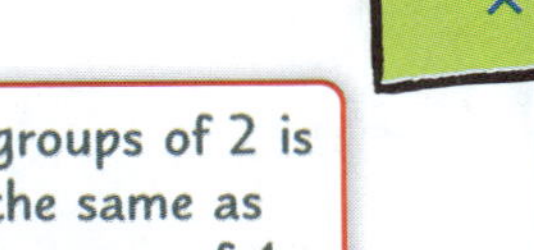

a $1 \times 2 =$ ☐
b $2 \times 2 =$ ☐
c $3 \times 2 =$ ☐
d $4 \times 2 =$ ☐
e $5 \times 2 =$ ☐
f $6 \times 2 =$ ☐
g $7 \times 2 =$ ☐
h $8 \times 2 =$ ☐
i $9 \times 2 =$ ☐
j $10 \times 2 =$ ☐

k $1 \times 4 =$ ☐
l $2 \times 4 =$ ☐
m $3 \times 4 =$ ☐
n $4 \times 4 =$ ☐
o $5 \times 4 =$ ☐

2
a $8 \times 2 =$ ☐, $3 \times 2 =$ ☐, 8×2 plus $3 \times 2 = 11 \times 2 =$ ☐
b $7 \times 2 =$ ☐, $5 \times 2 =$ ☐, 7×2 plus $5 \times 2 = 12 \times 2 =$ ☐
c $4 \times 2 =$ ☐, $9 \times 2 =$ ☐, 4×2 plus $9 \times 2 = 13 \times 2 =$ ☐
d $10 \times 2 =$ ☐, $6 \times 2 =$ ☐, 10×2 minus $6 \times 2 = 4 \times 2 =$ ☐

3

a 6×2 plus $2 = 7 \times 2 =$ ☐
b 7×2 plus $2 = 8 \times 2 =$ ☐
c 10×2 plus $2 = 11 \times 2 =$ ☐
d 11×2 plus $2 = 12 \times 2 =$ ☐

$2 \times 4 = 4 \times 2$

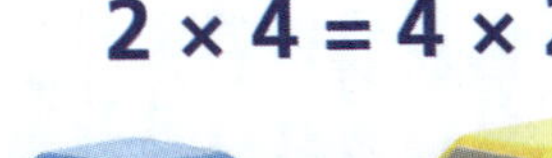

4
a

	3	10	2	1	5	4	7	9	8	6
×2	6	20								

b

	6	4								
×2	12	8	16	4	10	20	2	14	18	6

c

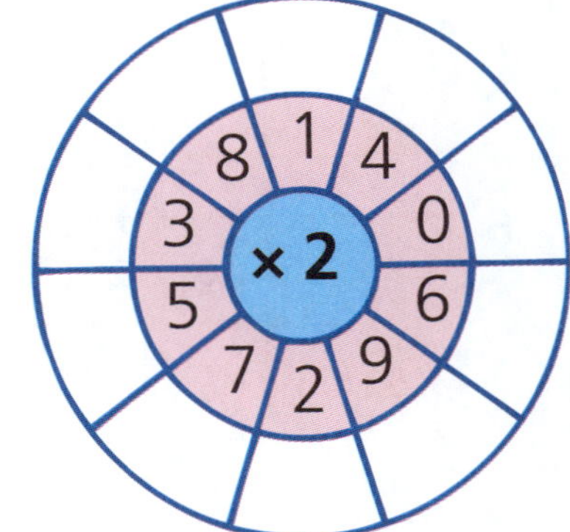

2:05 Number facts, ×5, ×10

10 × 5 = 5 × 10
Ten 5s are the same as five 10s.

1 Use the number models to complete the multiplications.

a 1 × 5 = ☐

b 2 × 5 = ☐

c 3 × 5 = ☐

d 4 × 5 = ☐

e 5 × 5 = ☐

f 6 × 5 = ☐

g 7 × 5 = ☐

h 8 × 5 = ☐

i 9 × 5 = ☐

j 10 × 5 = ☐

k 1 × 10 = ☐

l 2 × 10 = ☐

m 3 × 10 = ☐

n 4 × 10 = ☐

o 5 × 10 = ☐

2 Use the place-value blocks to complete the multiplications.

a

6 groups of 10

10 × 6 = ☐

b

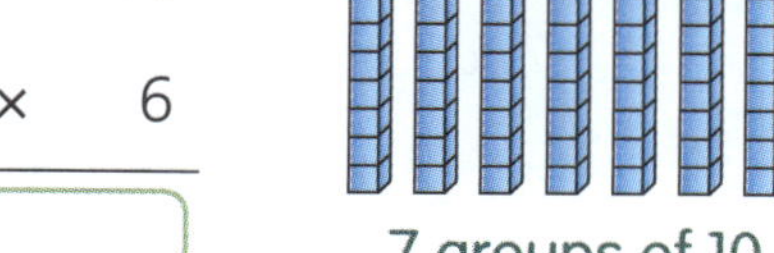

7 groups of 10

10 × 7 = ☐

c

8 groups of 10

10 × 8 = ☐

d

9 groups of 10

10 × 9 = ☐

e

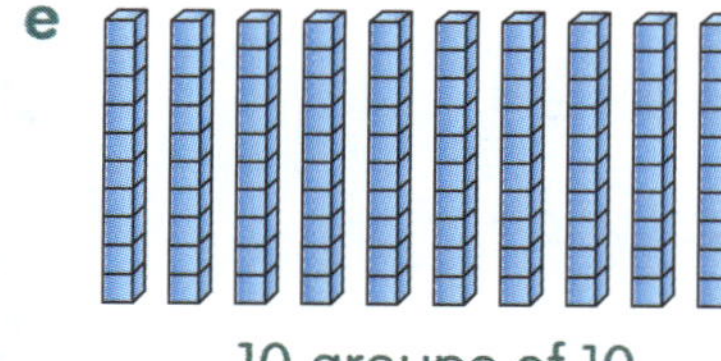

10 groups of 10

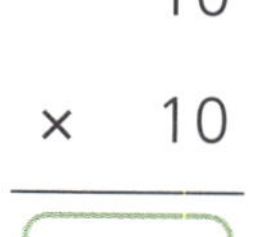

10 × 10 = ☐

3 **a**

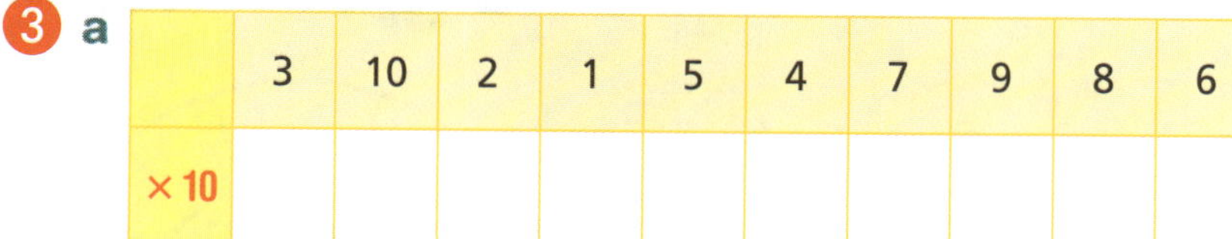

	3	10	2	1	5	4	7	9	8	6
× 10										

b

	3	10	2	1	5	4	7	9	8	6
× 5										

c Is 3 × 5 half of 3 × 10? ☐

d Is 5 × 5 half of 10 × 5? ☐

e Is 9 × 5 half of 9 × 10? ☐

f Does 5 × 10 = 10 × 5? ☐

g Do 7 fives equal 6 fives plus 1 five? ☐

 ISBN 9780655708773

Multiplication facts

$1+1+1+1+1+1=6\times1=6$
$0+0+0+0+0+0=6\times0=0$

- Any number multiplied by 1 always gives that number.
- Any number multiplied by 0 always gives zero.

$5\times0=0$

       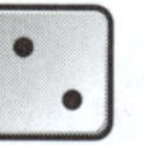  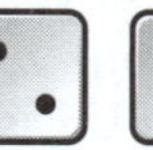  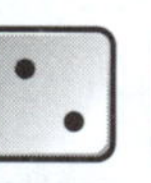 

1 Use the dice to find the answers.

a $6\times2=$ ☐	b $7\times5=$ ☐	c $7\times2=$ ☐	d $8\times10=$ ☐
e $7\times10=$ ☐	f $8\times2=$ ☐	g $5\times5=$ ☐	h $10\times5=$ ☐
i $9\times2=$ ☐	j $6\times5=$ ☐	k $6\times10=$ ☐	l $9\times10=$ ☐
m $8\times5=$ ☐	n $11\times2=$ ☐	o $9\times5=$ ☐	p $11\times5=$ ☐

2 Complete each pair of multiplication facts.

a $2\times1=$ ☐	b $2\times5=$ ☐	c $2\times10=$ ☐
$1\times2=$ ☐	$5\times2=$ ☐	$10\times2=$ ☐
d $1\times5=$ ☐	e $5\times0=$ ☐	f $5\times10=$ ☐
$5\times1=$ ☐	$0\times5=$ ☐	$10\times5=$ ☐

3 Measure the time you take to complete each set of multiplication facts. Record your times.

a	b	c	d
$9\times0=$ ☐	$8\times0=$ ☐	$6\times0=$ ☐	$7\times0=$ ☐
$7\times1=$ ☐	$6\times1=$ ☐	$9\times1=$ ☐	$8\times1=$ ☐
$6\times5=$ ☐	$9\times5=$ ☐	$8\times5=$ ☐	$7\times5=$ ☐
$10\times5=$ ☐	$10\times10=$ ☐	$10\times2=$ ☐	$10\times1=$ ☐
$3\times2=$ ☐	$2\times2=$ ☐	$5\times2=$ ☐	$4\times2=$ ☐
$5\times5=$ ☐	$4\times5=$ ☐	$3\times5=$ ☐	$2\times5=$ ☐
$4\times10=$ ☐	$5\times10=$ ☐	$2\times10=$ ☐	$3\times10=$ ☐
$6\times2=$ ☐	$9\times2=$ ☐	$7\times2=$ ☐	$8\times2=$ ☐
$8\times5=$ ☐	$7\times5=$ ☐	$9\times5=$ ☐	$6\times5=$ ☐
$7\times10=$ ☐	$8\times10=$ ☐	$6\times10=$ ☐	$9\times10=$ ☐
☐ seconds	☐ seconds	☐ seconds	☐ seconds

 • *AUSTRALIAN SIGNPOST MATHS 3* • ISBN 9780655708773

2, 5 and 10 times tables

skip counting by 2

2, 4, 6, 8, 10, 12, …

+2 +2 +2 +2 +2

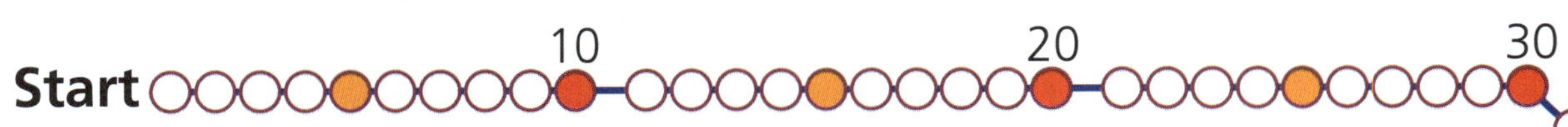

CONCEPT

5, 10, 15, 20, 25, 30, 35, 40, 45, 50

To skip count by 5, add 5.

10, 20, 30, 40, 50, 60, 70, 80, 90, 100

To skip count by 10, add 10.

5 × 2 = 2 × 5

1 Join each question to its answer using a pencil and ruler.

a

	=	
2 × 2		0
4 × 2		2
0 × 2		4
1 × 2		6
3 × 2		8
7 × 2		10
5 × 2		12
10 × 2		14
9 × 2		16
6 × 2		18
8 × 2		20

b

	=	
3 × 2		0
0 × 2		2
5 × 2		4
1 × 2		6
7 × 2		8
2 × 2		10
8 × 2		12
4 × 2		14
6 × 2		16
10 × 2		18
9 × 2		20

c

	=	
1 × 10		0
3 × 10		10
0 × 10		20
5 × 10		30
2 × 10		40
7 × 10		50
4 × 10		60
6 × 10		70
10 × 10		80
9 × 10		90
8 × 10		100

×2 answers end in: 0, 2, 4, 6, or 8.

×10 answers end in: 0.

d

	=	
4 × 10		70
2 × 10		20
7 × 10		40
3 × 10		90
9 × 10		30
1 × 10		60
6 × 10		10
10 × 10		50
5 × 10		80
8 × 10		100
0 × 10		0

e

	=	
1 × 5		50
6 × 5		25
10 × 5		5
5 × 5		30
8 × 5		0
0 × 5		40
2 × 5		15
9 × 5		35
3 × 5		20
7 × 5		10
4 × 5		45

f

	=	
0 × 5		0
6 × 5		15
3 × 5		30
8 × 5		20
4 × 5		25
10 × 5		40
5 × 5		10
2 × 5		50
1 × 5		35
7 × 5		45
9 × 5		5

×5 answers end in: 5, or 0.

20 is:

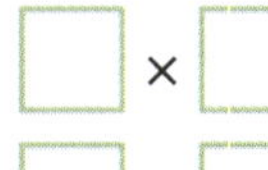

☐ × ☐

☐ × ☐

☐ × ☐

40 50 60 70 80 90 100

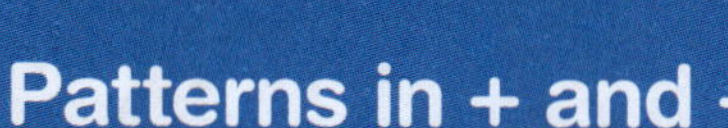

Patterns in + and −

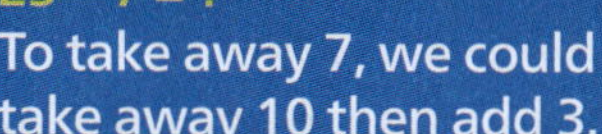

23 − 7 = ?
To take away 7, we could take away 10 then add 3.

INVESTIGATION

1 When we add 9, what happens to the tens and the ones digits?

Example: **37** + 9 = 37 + 10 − 1 = **46**

- The tens digit: ______
- The ones digit: ______

So, to add 9 we can add **10** and then subtract ___.

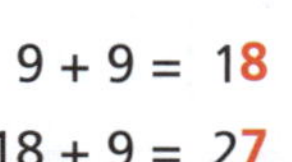

9
9 + 9 = 18
18 + 9 = 27
27 + 9 = 36
36 + 9 = 45
45 + 9 = 54

2 When we subtract 9, what happens to the tens and the ones digits?

Example: **42** − 9 = 42 − 10 + 1 = **33**

- The tens digit: ______
- The ones digit: ______

So, to subtract 9 we can subtract **10** and then add ___.

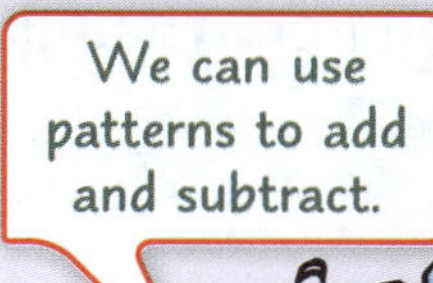

3 Race a partner to complete these. Use the strategy above.

a 7 + 9 = ___ **b** 16 + 9 = ___ **c** 28 + 9 = ___ **d** 42 + 9 = ___

e 17 − 9 = ___ **f** 34 − 9 = ___ **g** 99, 90, 81, ___, ___, ___, ___

4 Discuss and explore strategies for adding or subtracting 8. Race a partner to complete these.

a 6 + 8 = ___ **b** 19 + 8 = ___ **c** 53 + 8 = ___ **d** 75 + 8 = ___

e 23 − 8 = ___ **f** 67 − 8 = ___ **g** 32, 40, 48, ___, ___, ___, ___

52	?
61	

5 Complete the number sentence to find the answer.

a Heather has 23 pins. How many more does she need to have 32?

23 + ___ = 32

b Jack needs 55 cents. He has 40 cents. How much more does he need?

40 + ___ = 55

c 61 nails were lost. Luke found 52. How many are still missing?

52 + ___ = 61

6 Complete the patterns.

a
11 − 4 = 7
21 − 4 = 17
31 − 4 = ___
41 − 4 = ___
51 − 4 = ___

b
14 − 8 = 6
24 − 8 = 16
34 − 8 = ___
44 − 8 = ___
54 − 8 = ___

c
15 − 6 = 9
25 − 6 = 19
35 − 6 = ___
45 − 6 = ___
55 − 6 = ___

 • *AUSTRALIAN SIGNPOST MATHS 3* • ISBN 9780655708773

2:09 Relating addition and subtraction

If 7 – 2 = 5
then
5 + 2 = 7.

CONCEPT

Jenny needed to find the difference in length between these two ribbons.

33 – 15 = ☐ can also be thought of as 15 + ☐ = 33.

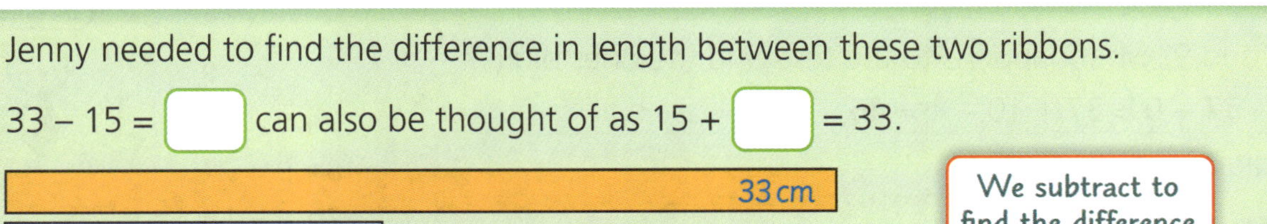

We subtract to find the difference or write 15 + ☐ = 33.

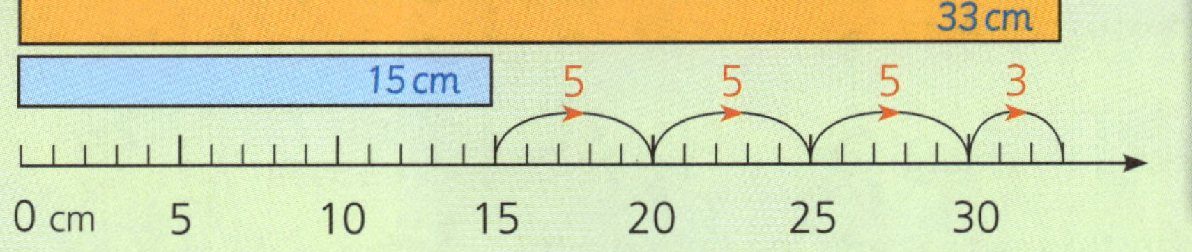

We count on from 15 until we reach 33.

The length difference between the two ribbons is 5 + 5 + 5 + 3 cm = 18 cm.

1 Find the length differences between ribbons.

a

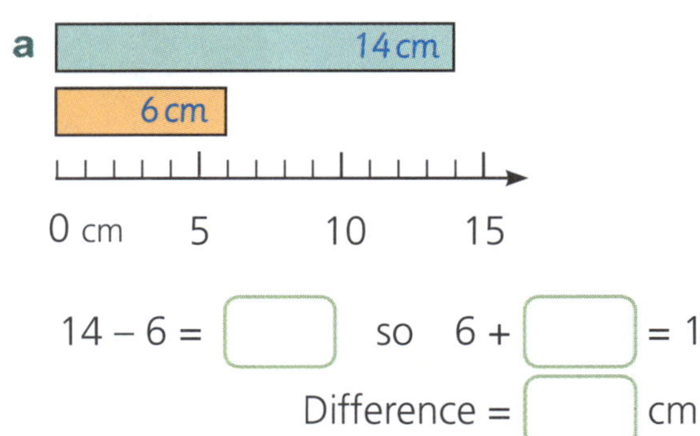

14 – 6 = ☐ so 6 + ☐ = 14

Difference = ☐ cm

b

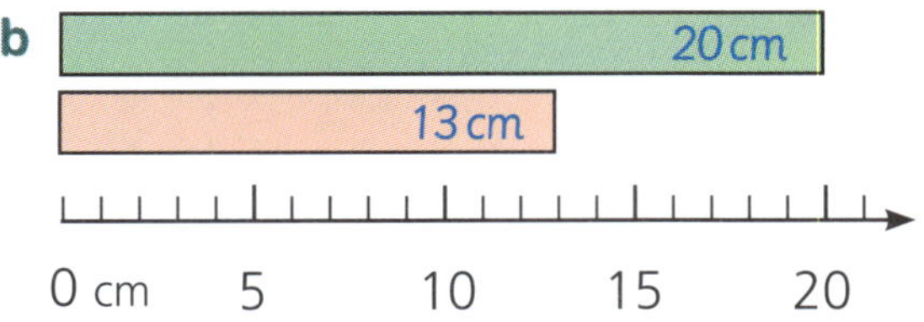

20 – 13 = ☐ so 13 + ☐ = 20

Difference = ☐ cm

c

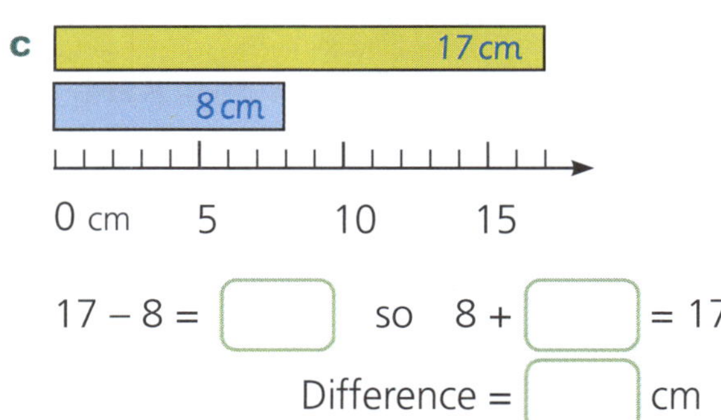

17 – 8 = ☐ so 8 + ☐ = 17

Difference = ☐ cm

d

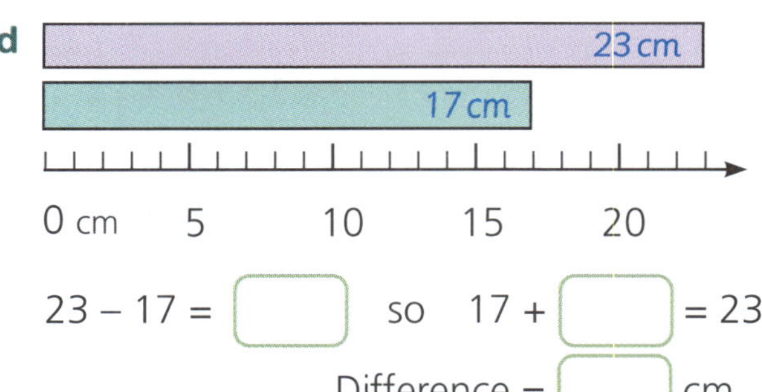

23 – 17 = ☐ so 17 + ☐ = 23

Difference = ☐ cm

e

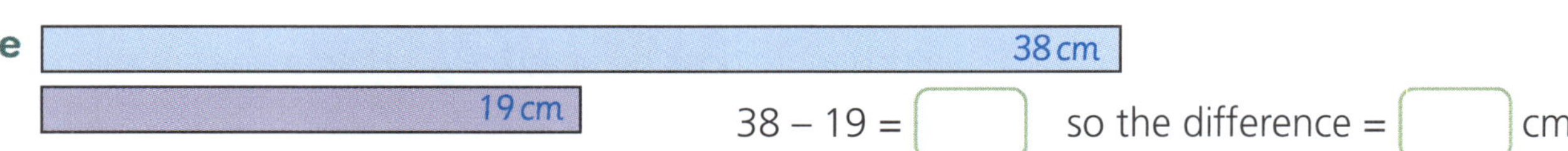

38 – 19 = ☐ so the difference = ☐ cm

f

44 – 16 = ☐ so the difference = ☐ cm

- Compare pieces of paper cut to different centimetre lengths, or draw lines of different lengths.
- Write your own addition and subtraction number sentences to match the lengths.

 • *AUSTRALIAN SIGNPOST MATHS 3* • ISBN 9780655708773

Problem solving

Skip counting by 5
5, 10, 15, 20, 25, 30, 35, 40, 45, 50.

Solve these problems.

1 Davis has 100 bones. He gave his dog 40 of them. How many were left?

Find:

Number sentence: =

Answer:

?	40
100	

Find: How many bones were left?

Number sentence: 100 – 40 =

Answer: There were bones left.

2 Ten pies are needed to fill one tray. Three trays are filled. How many pies are there?

Find:

Number sentence: =

Answer:

3 Corina had 24 apricots. She gave 2 to each friend until no apricots were left. How many friends were given apricots?

Find:

Number sentence: =

Answer:

4 In a library, one shelf holds 24 books. Another shelf holds 55. How many books do these shelves hold altogether?

Find:

Number sentence: =

Answer:

5 At the first stop, 15 people got off the bus. At the second stop, 10 people got off. At the third, 8 got off. How many people got off altogether?

Find:

Number sentence: =

Answer:

6 In a shop, bottles are kept in rows of 5. There are 3 full rows and 2 bottles left over. How many bottles are there altogether?

Find:

Number sentence: =

Answer:

7 How many rows of bottles could you make if you had 45 bottles and you put 5 bottles in each row?

Find:

Number sentence: =

Answer:

8 Discuss ways of solving these problems in your head.

a 1000 – 101 =
b 1000 – 110 =
c 1000 – 410 =
d 1000 – 510 =
e 1000 – 302 =
f 1000 – 802 =
g Could you use place value to find your answers quickly?

 • *AUSTRALIAN SIGNPOST MATHS 3* • ISBN 9780655708773

2:11 Shopping

Can you list all of the coins and notes?

CONCEPT

To make an amount of money, start with the higher value coins or notes.

1 Use coins to make $1.65.

Steps:

Start with $1 and count on.

- Use 50c to make $1.50.
- Use 10c to make $1.60.
- Use 5c to make $1.65.

2 Use coins to make $3.85.

Steps:

Start with $2 and count on.

- Use $1 to make $3.
- Use 50c to make $3.50.
- Use 20c to make $3.70.
- Use 10c to make $3.80.
- Use 5c to make $3.85.

1 Colour the coins you could use to buy each item.

a Exercise Book — 90c

b $1.85

c Mmm... Milk — $2.70

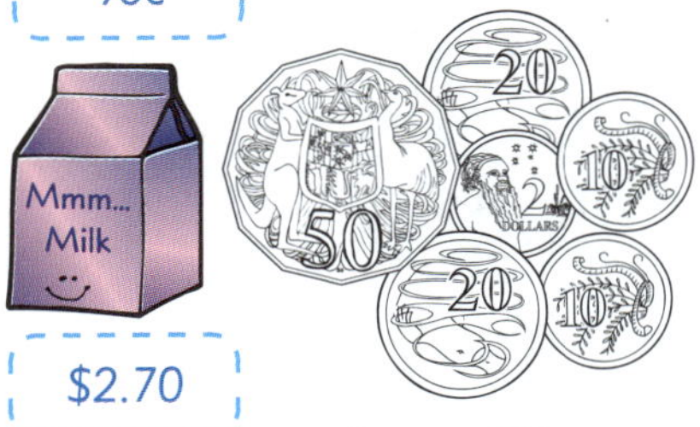

d $3.60

e 12 coloured pencils — $2.95

f $3.20

g $7.70

h $5.30

Make $5 using coins in four different ways.

FUN SPOT

2 Choose coins or notes to make each amount of money.

a $3.80

b $2.95

c $4.35

d $9.10

e $12.70

f $15.50

Money

$2 = 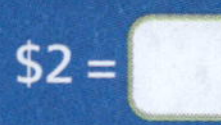 $1 coins $2 =  20c coins

$2 = ☐ 50c coins $2 = ☐ 10c coins

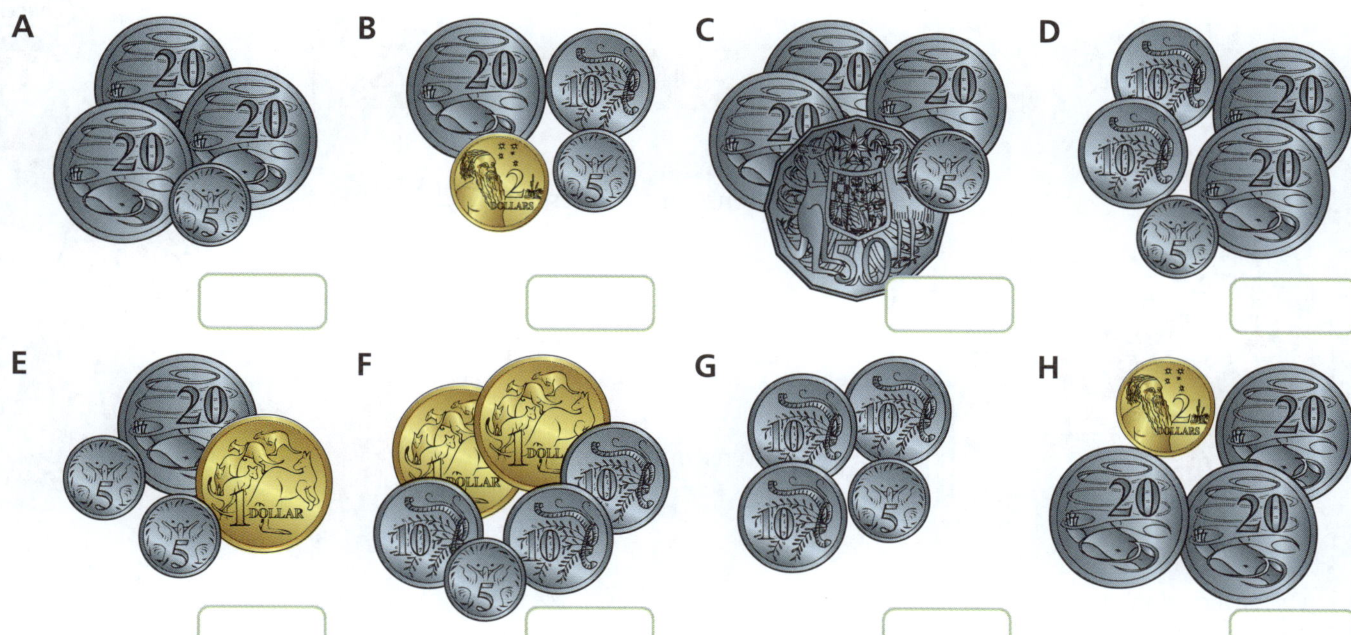

1 Which group of coins is worth:

a the same as A? ☐
b the same as F? ☐
c less than D? ☐
d more than B? ☐

2 Write the total value of the coins in:

a A and D ☐
b E and F ☐
c C and G ☐

3 Which group of banknotes is worth:

a the same as P? ☐
b the same as T? ☐
c less than P? ☐
d more than Q? ☐

M

N

O

P

Q

R

S

T

2:13 Addition to 99

34 + 23
= (30 + 20) + (4 + 3)

Add ones.
Add tens.

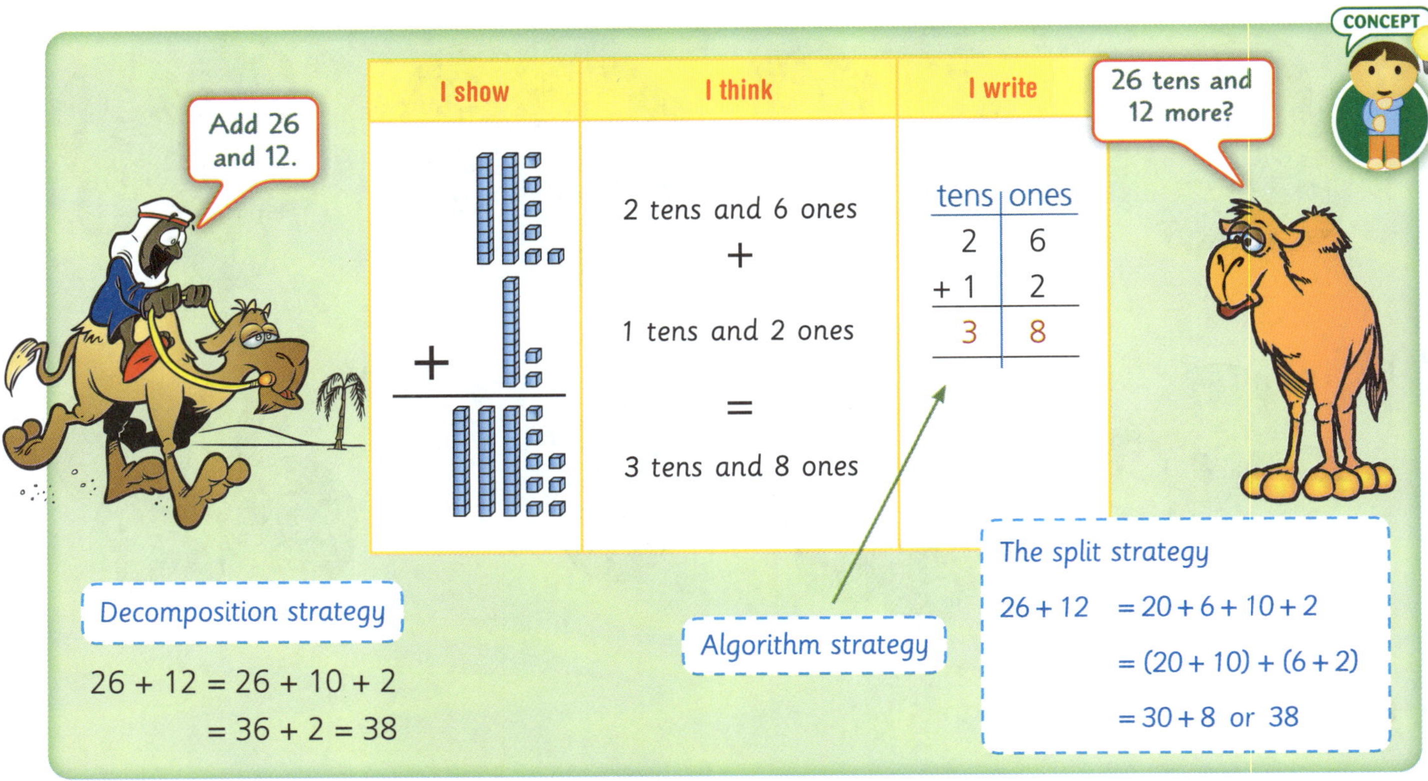

1 Model these problems and write them as number sentences.

a 5 eggs
12 eggs
How many eggs altogether?
☐ + ☐ = ☐

b 13 horses
32 horses
How many horses altogether?
☐ + ☐ = ☐

2 Use the split strategy or place-value blocks to answer these.

a

tens	ones
1	6
+ 1	1

b

tens	ones
2	0
+ 2	3

c

tens	ones
1	4
+ 2	3

d

tens	ones
3	1
+ 2	2

e

tens	ones
3	8
+ 1	0

f

tens	ones
1	7
+ 2	2

g

tens	ones
2	3
+ 2	5

h

tens	ones
1	4
+ 1	5

3 **a** 3 tens and 5 ones
+ 1 ten and 2 ones
____

b 2 tens and 4 ones
+ 2 tens and 5 ones
____

c 1 ten and 3 ones
+ 2 tens and 6 ones
____

4 **a** 36 + 62 ☐ **b** 51 + 37 ☐ **c** 25 + 43 ☐

 ISBN 9780655708773

Jump strategy

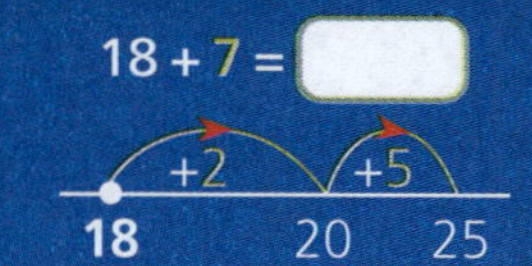

Addition

35 + 19

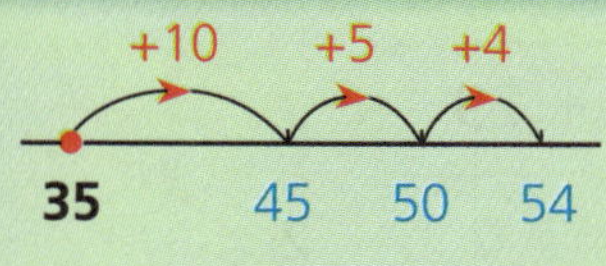

35 + 19 = 35 + 10 + 5 + 4
= 45 + 5 + 4
= 50 + 4 = 54

1 a 27 + 8 ☐

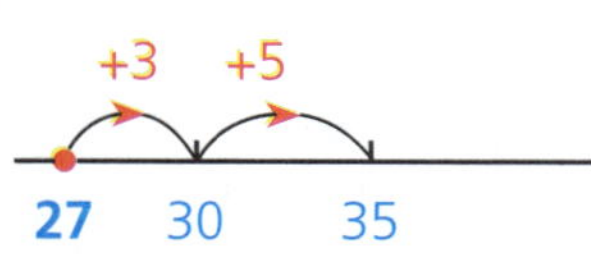

b 16 + 17 ☐

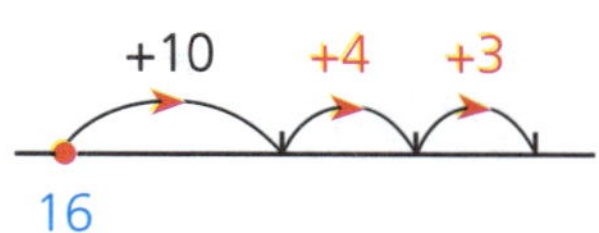

c 36 + 15 ☐

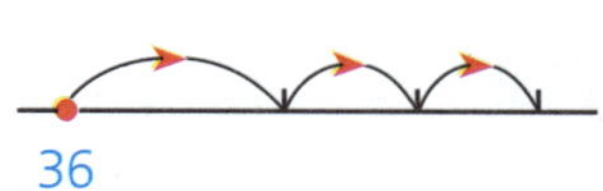

d 74 + 19 ☐

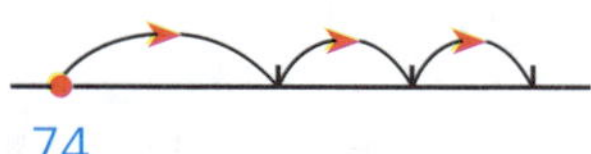

e 58 + 6 ☐

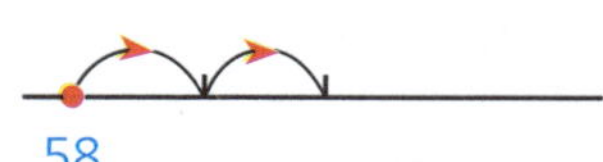

f 45 + 27 ☐

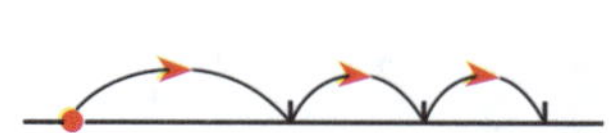

Subtraction

31 – 14

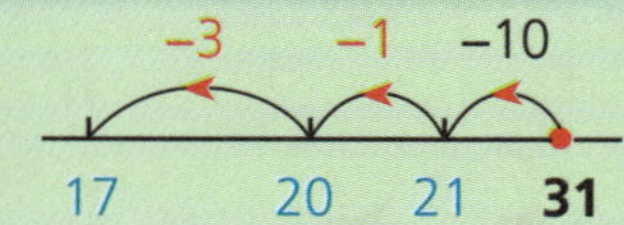

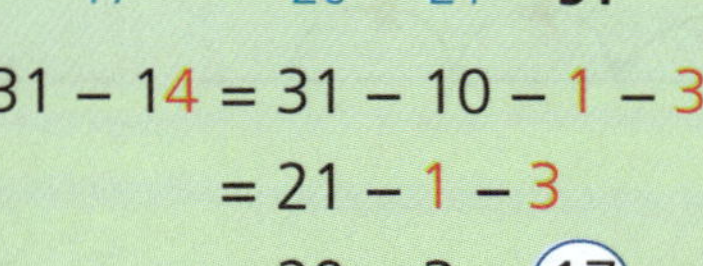

31 – 14 = 31 – 10 – 1 – 3
= 21 – 1 – 3
= 20 – 3 = 17

2 a 33 – 19 ☐

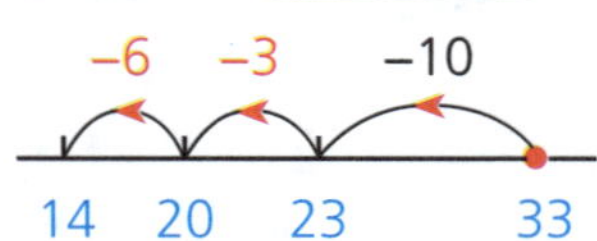

b 36 – 28 ☐

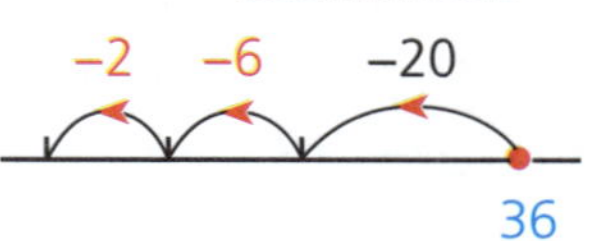

c 41 – 27 ☐

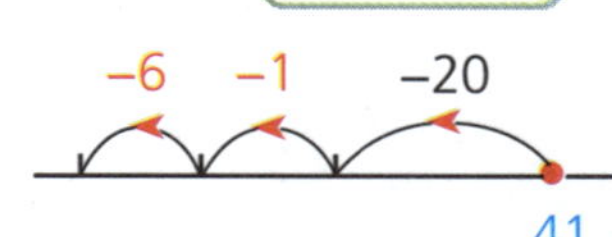

d 42 – 23 ☐

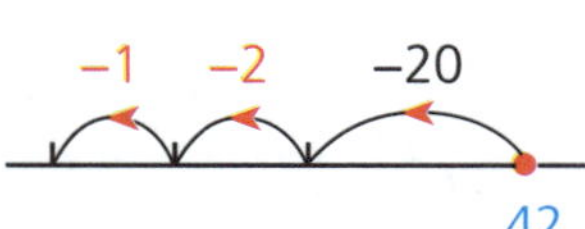

e 75 – 38 ☐

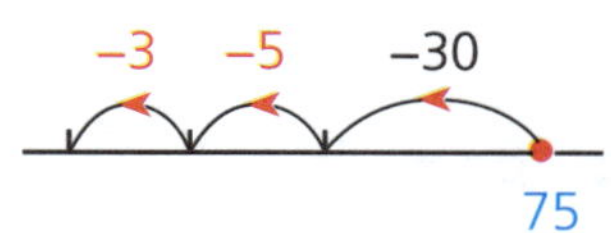

f 93 – 62 ☐

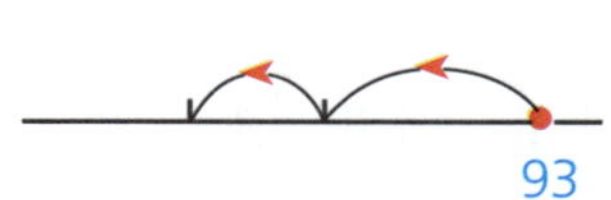

g 44 – 37 ☐

h 62 – 45 ☐

i 57 – 28 ☐

2:15 Jump strategy

57 + 38 =

+30 +3 +5

57 87 90 95

57 38

Addition 43 + 29

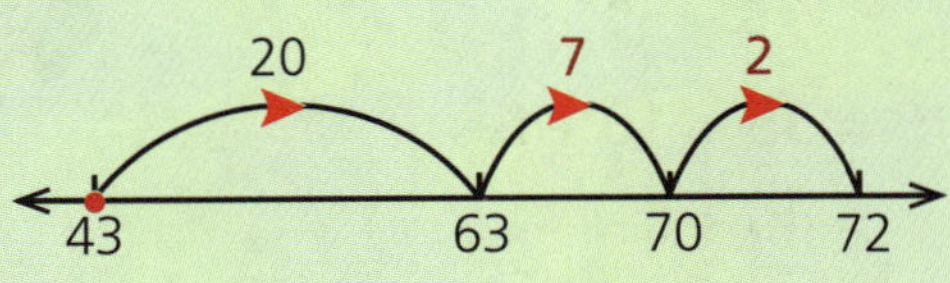

43 + 29 = 43 + 20 + 7 + 2
= 63 + 7 + 2
= 70 + 2 = 72

Subtraction 82 − 27

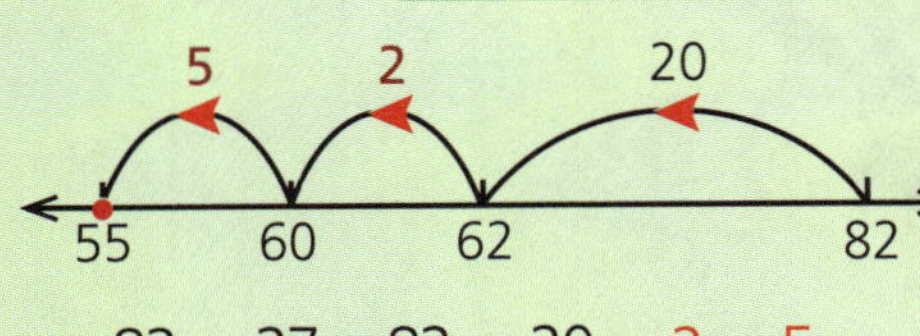

82 − 27 = 82 − 20 − 2 − 5
= 62 − 2 − 5
= 60 − 5 = 55

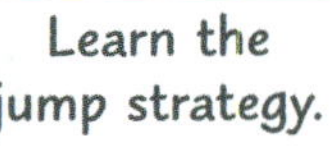

Learn the jump strategy.

1 a 72 + 19

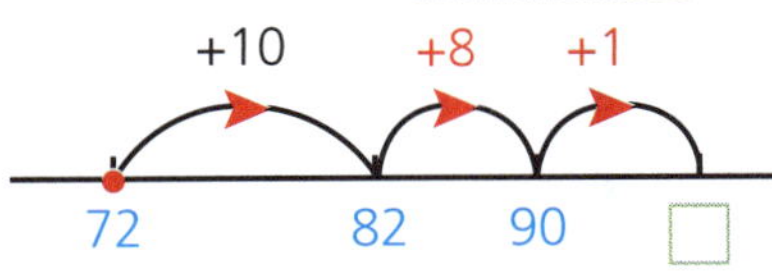

b 35 + 47

+40 +5 +2

35 75 80

c 28 + 35

d 54 + 18

54

e 42 + 36

42 72

f 77 + 15

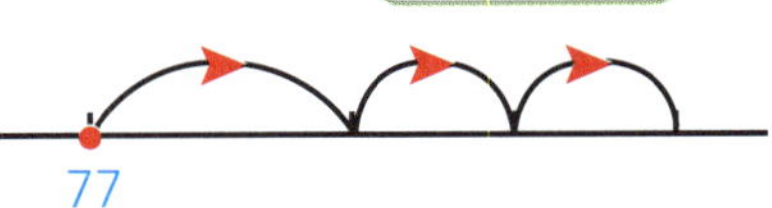

g 66 + 35

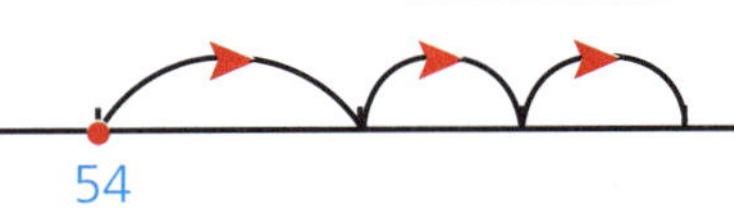

h 35 + 68

Work out the tens, then jump to the 10 above for addition or the 10 below for subtraction.

2 a 92 − 19

b 86 − 48

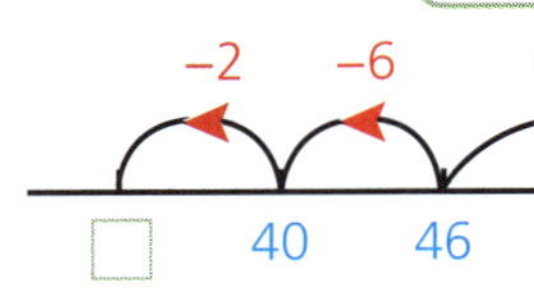

c 42 − 23

−1 −2 −20

42

d 75 − 38

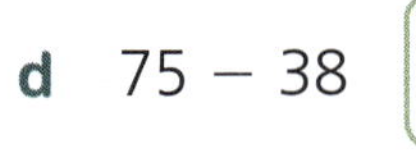

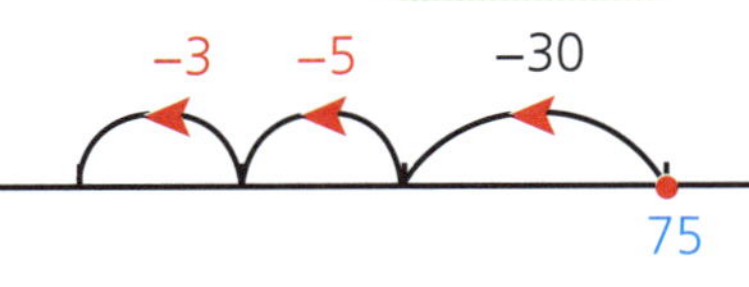

e 93 − 62

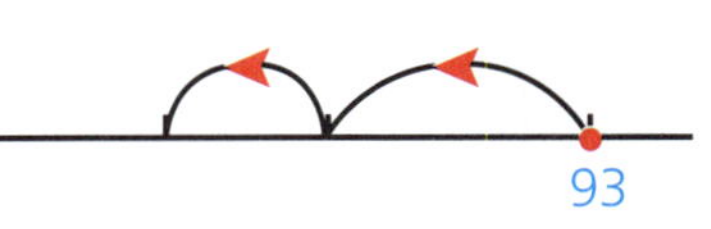

f 44 − 37

g 62 − 45

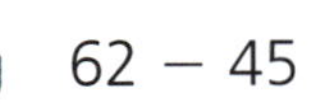

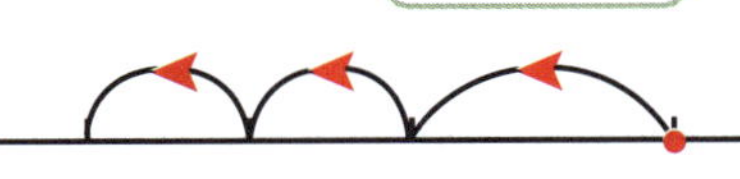

h 87 − 28

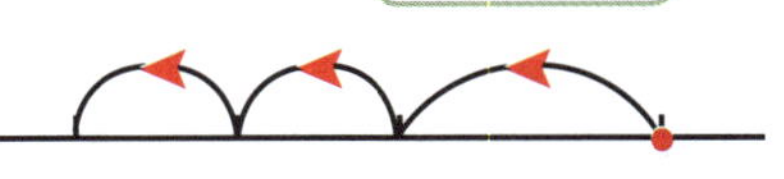

3 a 55 + 28

b 83 − 47

c 78 + 46

 • *AUSTRALIAN SIGNPOST MATHS 3* • ISBN 9780655708773

Mental strategies

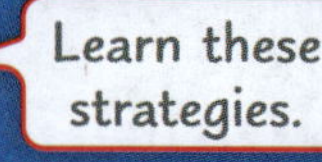

CONCEPT

Different types of questions need different strategies.

A	Using patterns	5 + 4 = 9 so 500 + 400 = 900
B	Changing the order	16 + 8 + 4 = 16 + 4 + 8 = 20 + 8 = 28
C	Bridging to 10s	45 + 8 = 45 + 5 + 3 = 50 + 3 = 53
D	Compensation	63 + 19 = 63 + 20 – 1 = 83 – 1 = 82
E	Split	23 + 35 = 20 + 30 + 3 + 5 = 50 + 8 = 58
F	Jump	58 + 23 (58 +20 78 +2 80 +1 81) 58 + 23 = 81

1 Using patterns

a 500 + 200 = ☐ b 200 + 700 = ☐ c 400 + 300 = ☐ d 200 + 400 = ☐

2 Changing the order

a 16 + 7 + 4 = ☐ b 27 + 4 + 3 = ☐ c 65 + 8 + 5 = ☐ d 28 + 4 + 2 = ☐

3 Bridging to 10s

a 38 + 8 = ☐ b 29 + 4 = ☐ c 37 + 6 = ☐ d 54 + 7 = ☐

4 Compensation

a 37 + 19 = ☐ b 63 + 29 = ☐ c 48 + 19 = ☐ d 25 + 39 = ☐

5 Split

a 32 + 41 = ☐ b 55 + 34 = ☐ c 23 + 16 = ☐

d 14 + 34 = ☐ e 36 + 21 = ☐ f 47 + 33 = ☐

Memorise the addition facts. See Extra Support on pages 160 to 163.

6 Jump

a 67 + 22 = ☐

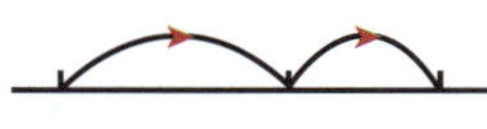

b 53 + 25 = ☐

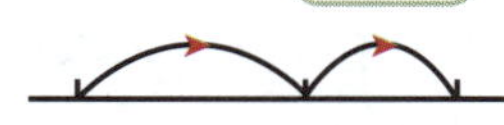

c 27 + 34 = ☐

d 44 + 18 = ☐

INVESTIGATION

7 Complete the additions. Write the strategy you used (from **A** to **F** above).

a 51 + 37 = ☐ ☐ b 36 + 3 + 4 = ☐ ☐ c 44 + 9 = ☐ ☐

d 38 + 7 = ☐ ☐ e 300 + 500 = ☐ ☐ f 39 + 27 = ☐ ☐

Discuss how and why you chose each strategy.

 • *AUSTRALIAN SIGNPOST MATHS 3* • ISBN 9780655708773

2:17 Problem solving

I invited 10 people, you invited 6.
How many will be there?

10	6
?	

Solve these problems.

1 Holly had 43 football cards and bought 25 more. How many altogether?

Find:

Number sentence:

Answer:

Working

My mum caught 37 prawns.
I caught 5 more than she did.
How many did we catch altogether?

Find: How many altogether?

Number sentence: 37 + (37 + 5)

Answer:

Working

2 5 boys shared 45 books equally. How many did each boy have?

Find:

Number sentence:

Answer:

Working

3 A farmer had 96 sheep but sold 28. How many did she have left?

Find:

Number sentence:

Answer:

Working

4 Marnie collected 54 aluminium cans before lunch and 37 in the afternoon. How many cans did she collect?

Find:

Number sentence:

Answer:

Working

5 Lee planted seeds in rows of 5. He planted 6 full rows and had 4 seeds left. How many seeds were there altogether?

Find:

Number sentence:

Answer:

Working

6 Lauren and Justin want to play handball. For a handball court they need two squares next to each other.

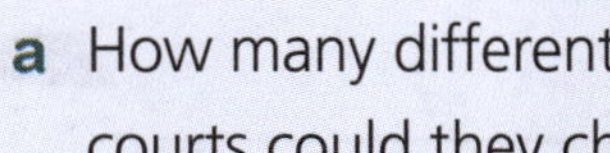

a How many different courts could they choose?

b How many courts could all be used at the same time?

c If they needed three squares in a row to make a court, how many courts could be used at the same time?

 • *AUSTRALIAN SIGNPOST MATHS 3* • ISBN 9780655708773

Number facts, ×3

skip counting by 3

3, 6, 9, 12, 15, 18, …
+3 +3 +3 +3 +3

1 Use the number models to complete the multiplications. Practise counting by 3s.

- **a** 1 × 3 = ☐
- **b** 2 × 3 = ☐
- **c** 3 × 3 = ☐
- **d** 4 × 3 = ☐
- **e** 5 × 3 = ☐
- **f** 6 × 3 = ☐
- **g** 7 × 3 = ☐
- **h** 8 × 3 = ☐
- **i** 9 × 3 = ☐
- **j** 10 × 3 = ☐

Because 3 × 2 = 6, we know that 2 × 3 = 6.
Because 3 × 5 = 15, we know that 5 × 3 = 15.
Because 3 × 10 = 30, we know that 10 × 3 = 30.

4 groups of 3 is the same as 2 groups of 6.

2 Write the answers. Remember that 3 × 1 = 1 × 3.

a 3 × 0 = ☐	**b** 0 × 3 = ☐	**c** 3 × 10 = ☐	**d** 10 × 3 = ☐
e 3 × 2 = ☐	**f** 2 × 3 = ☐	**g** 3 × 1 = ☐	**h** 1 × 3 = ☐
i 3 × 5 = ☐	**j** 5 × 3 = ☐	**k** 8 × 3 = ☐	**l** 4 × 3 = ☐
m 9 × 3 = ☐	**n** 6 × 3 = ☐	**o** 3 × 3 = ☐	**p** 7 × 3 = ☐

3

a 5 × 1 = ☐	**b** 1 × 5 = ☐	**c** 5 × 2 = ☐	**d** 2 × 5 = ☐
e 5 × 0 = ☐	**f** 0 × 5 = ☐	**g** 5 × 10 = ☐	**h** 10 × 5 = ☐
i 2 × 10 = ☐	**j** 10 × 2 = ☐	**k** 5 × 5 = ☐	**l** 10 × 10 = ☐

4 **a** 3 pens in a set
8 sets
How many pens?

$$\begin{array}{r} 3 \\ \times\ 8 \\ \hline \square \end{array}$$

b 3 dollars per person
9 people
How many dollars?

$$\begin{array}{r} \$\ 3 \\ \times\ 9 \\ \hline \$\ \square \end{array}$$

5 Try to complete these tables from memory.

a

	4	7	9	5	8	6
× 3						

b

	4	7	9	5	8	6
× 5						

c

	4	7	9	5	8	6
× 2						

d

	4	7	9	5	8	6
× 10						

 • *AUSTRALIAN SIGNPOST MATHS 3* • ISBN 9780655708773

Times tables

3, 6, 9, 12, 15, 18, 21, 24, 27, 30
To skip count by 3, add 3.

Any number times 1 stays the same.

3 × 1 = 3 10 × 1 = 10

Any number times 0 is equal to 0.

3 × 0 = 3 10 × 0 = 0

1 Join each question to its answer, using a pencil and ruler.

a

	=	
0 × 3		6
1 × 3		3
2 × 3		0
3 × 3		9
4 × 3		15
5 × 3		18
6 × 3		12
7 × 3		27
8 × 3		21
9 × 3		24
10 × 3		30

b

	=	
3 × 3		0
0 × 3		3
5 × 3		6
1 × 3		9
7 × 3		12
2 × 3		15
8 × 3		18
4 × 3		21
6 × 3		24
10 × 3		27
9 × 3		30

c

	=	
1 × 3		9
3 × 3		3
0 × 3		0
5 × 3		21
2 × 3		12
7 × 3		15
4 × 3		6
6 × 3		27
10 × 3		24
9 × 3		18
8 × 3		30

×2 answers end in: 0, 2, 4, 6, or 8.

×10 answers end in: 0.

d

	=	
4 × 2		35
2 × 3		6
7 × 5		8
3 × 10		9
9 × 1		30
4 × 0		40
8 × 5		0
10 × 2		50
5 × 10		20
8 × 0		21
7 × 3		0

e

	=	
1 × 5		18
6 × 3		50
10 × 5		5
5 × 5		24
8 × 3		0
0 × 5		25
2 × 5		27
9 × 3		10
3 × 5		21
7 × 3		12
4 × 3		15

f

	=	
7 × 1		18
6 × 3		7
3 × 5		24
8 × 3		15
4 × 3		10
8 × 5		40
5 × 2		12
6 × 5		21
1 × 0		30
7 × 3		27
9 × 3		0

×5 answers end in: 5 or 0.

30 is

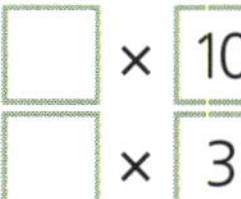

☐ × 10
☐ × 3
☐ × 5

100 90 80

 • *AUSTRALIAN SIGNPOST MATHS 3* • ISBN 9780655708773

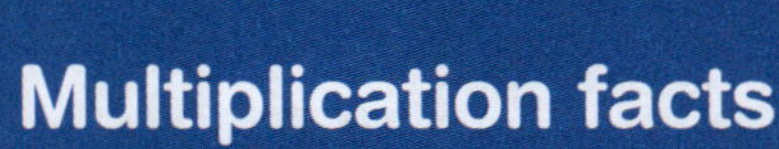

2:20 Multiplication facts

Does it end in 0? ... 10 times table
Does it end in 5 or 0? ... 5 times table
Does it end in 2, 4, 6, 8 or 0? ... 2 times table

1 Complete each pair of multiplication facts.

a 2 × 3 = ☐ 3 × 2 = ☐	**b** 3 × 5 = ☐ 5 × 3 = ☐	**c** 3 × 10 = ☐ 10 × 3 = ☐
d 1 × 3 = ☐ 3 × 1 = ☐	**e** 3 × 0 = ☐ 0 × 3 = ☐	**f** 3 × 6 = ☐ 6 × 3 = ☐

2 Measure the time you take to complete each set of multiplication facts. Write the time.

a	**b**	**c**	**d**
9 × 0 = ☐	3 × 0 = ☐	6 × 0 = ☐	7 × 0 = ☐
7 × 1 = ☐	6 × 1 = ☐	9 × 1 = ☐	3 × 1 = ☐
6 × 3 = ☐	3 × 3 = ☐	8 × 3 = ☐	7 × 3 = ☐
10 × 5 = ☐	10 × 10 = ☐	6 × 3 = ☐	10 × 1 = ☐
3 × 3 = ☐	2 × 3 = ☐	5 × 3 = ☐	4 × 3 = ☐
5 × 5 = ☐	4 × 5 = ☐	3 × 5 = ☐	2 × 5 = ☐
4 × 10 = ☐	5 × 10 = ☐	2 × 10 = ☐	3 × 10 = ☐
4 × 3 = ☐	9 × 3 = ☐	7 × 3 = ☐	8 × 3 = ☐
8 × 3 = ☐	7 × 3 = ☐	9 × 3 = ☐	6 × 3 = ☐
7 × 10 = ☐	8 × 10 = ☐	6 × 10 = ☐	9 × 10 = ☐
☐ seconds	☐ seconds	☐ seconds	☐ seconds

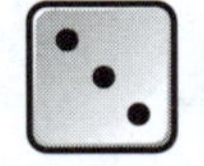             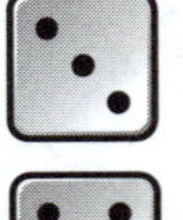

Learn the three times tables.

3 Use the dice to find the answers.

a 2 × 3 = ☐	**b** 7 × 3 = ☐	**c** 1 × 3 = ☐	**d** 4 × 3 = ☐
e 3 × 5 = ☐	**f** 8 × 3 = ☐	**g** 5 × 5 = ☐	**h** 10 × 3 = ☐
i 9 × 3 = ☐	**j** 6 × 5 = ☐	**k** 3 × 3 = ☐	**l** 6 × 3 = ☐
m 8 × 5 = ☐	**n** 5 × 3 = ☐	**o** 9 × 5 = ☐	**p** 11 × 3 = ☐

4 Complete this pattern.

3, 6, 9, ☐, ☐, ☐, ☐, ☐, ☐, ☐.

 • *AUSTRALIAN SIGNPOST MATHS 3* • ISBN 9780655708773

Algebra

2:21 Number facts, ×4

Skip count by 4

4, 8, 12, 16, 20, 24, …

+4 +4 +4 +4 +4

$4 \times 4 = 16$

1 Use the number models to complete the multiplications.

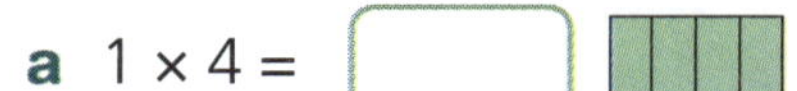

a 1 × 4 = ☐

b 2 × 4 = ☐

c 3 × 4 = ☐

d 4 × 4 = ☐

e 5 × 4 = ☐

f 6 × 4 = ☐

g 7 × 4 = ☐

h 8 × 4 = ☐

i 9 × 4 = ☐

j 10 × 4 = ☐

Learn your × 4 facts.

5 × 4 is the same as 4 × 5.

The answers to × **4** tables are always even (ending in 0, 2, 4, 6 or 8).

2

a 5 × 4 = ☐ **b** 1 × 4 = ☐ **c** 6 × 4 = ☐ **d** 2 × 4 = ☐

e 7 × 4 = ☐ **f** 1 × 4 = ☐ **g** 8 × 4 = ☐ **h** 3 × 4 = ☐

i 9 × 4 = ☐ **j** 1 × 4 = ☐ **k** 10 × 4 = ☐ **l** 4 × 4 = ☐

3

a

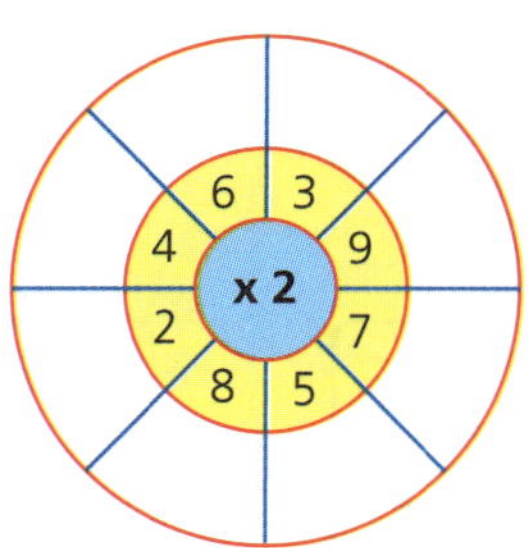

b **c**

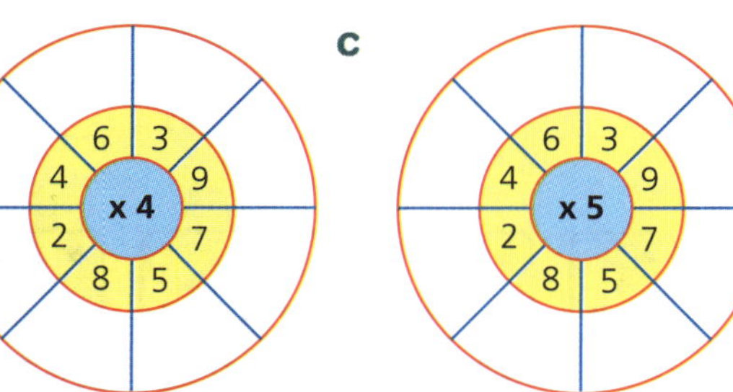

d

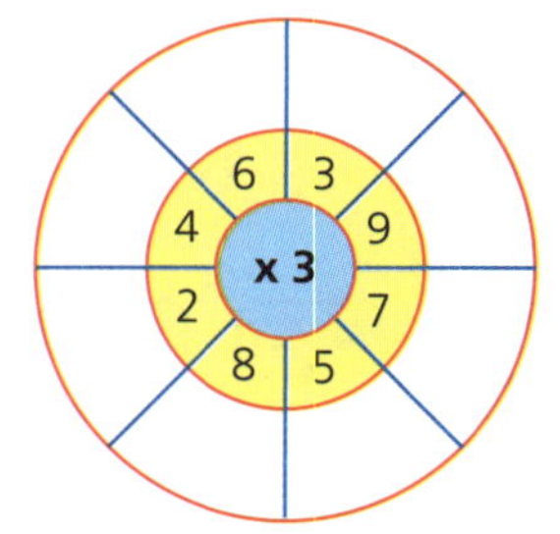

4

a **5 × 4 =** ☐ and **1 × 4 =** ☐ so **6 × 4 =** **20** + **4** = ☐

b **6 × 4 =** ☐ and **1 × 4 =** ☐ so **7 × 4 =** **24** + **4** = ☐

5 Try to complete these tables from memory.

a

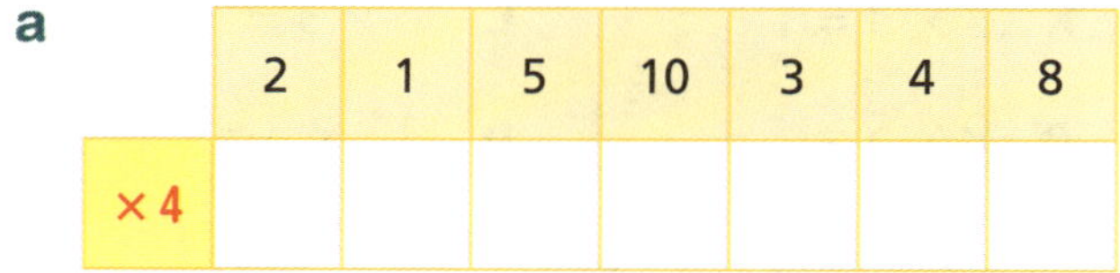

	2	1	5	10	3	4	8
× 4							

b

	4	6	8	5	9	7	3
× 4							

2:22 3 and 4 times tables

2 × 3
means '2 groups of 3'
or '2 rows of 3'.

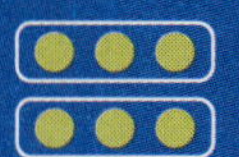

Are you a tables champion?

4 threes is the same as 3 fours.

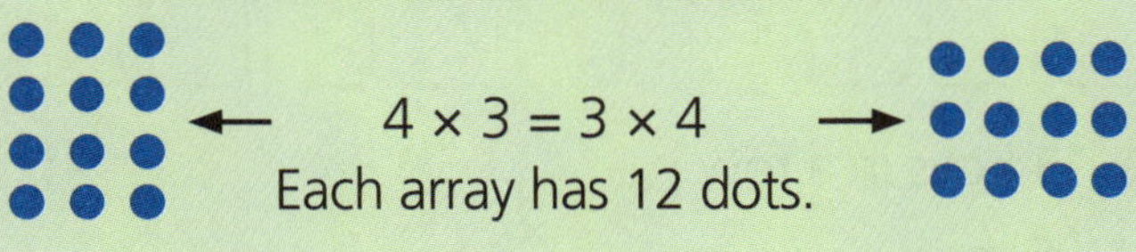

Keep practising until you can recall all the facts on this page instantly.

CONCEPT

1 Join each question to its answer using a pencil and ruler. You could practise your tables facts by rubbing out your answers and doing them again. Challenge your classmates.

a

	=	
3 × 3		0
2 × 3		3
4 × 3		6
0 × 3		9
1 × 3		12
7 × 3		15
5 × 3		18
6 × 3		21
10 × 3		24
8 × 3		27
9 × 3		30

b

	=	
3 × 4		0
2 × 4		4
0 × 4		8
6 × 4		12
1 × 4		16
4 × 4		20
5 × 4		24
9 × 4		28
10 × 4		32
7 × 4		36
8 × 4		40

c

	=	
2 × 10		10
4 × 10		0
1 × 10		60
0 × 10		20
6 × 10		40
3 × 10		50
5 × 10		30
8 × 10		90
7 × 10		100
9 × 10		80
10 × 10		70

d

	=	
2 × 2		0
4 × 2		2
1 × 2		4
0 × 2		6
6 × 2		8
3 × 2		10
5 × 2		12
8 × 2		14
7 × 2		16
9 × 2		18
10 × 2		20

e

	=	
0 × 3		27
9 × 3		24
8 × 3		0
6 × 3		9
3 × 3		18
5 × 3		6
4 × 3		3
7 × 3		15
2 × 3		12
1 × 3		30
10 × 3		21

f

	=	
0 × 4		4
6 × 4		12
1 × 4		0
3 × 4		20
10 × 4		24
4 × 4		40
8 × 4		16
5 × 4		36
9 × 4		32
2 × 4		28
7 × 4		8

g

	=	
1 × 5		0
3 × 5		25
0 × 5		5
5 × 5		15
2 × 5		30
6 × 5		10
4 × 5		45
9 × 5		35
7 × 5		20
10 × 5		40
8 × 5		50

h

	=	
6 × 3		12
4 × 3		28
7 × 4		18
8 × 4		36
5 × 3		27
9 × 4		32
9 × 3		15
5 × 4		21
7 × 3		20
4 × 4		24
8 × 3		16

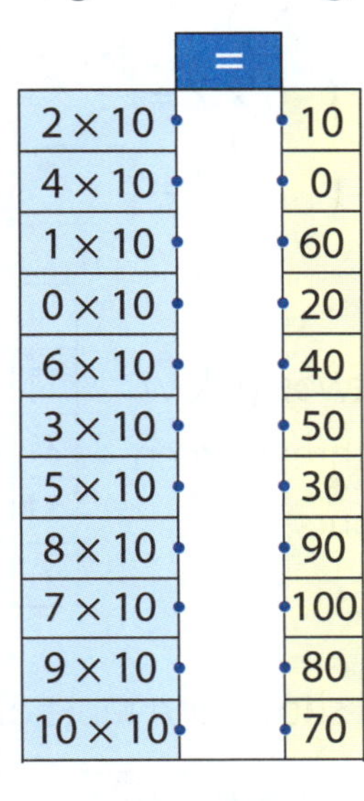

Start 4 10 20 30 40 50

2 Try to complete these tables from memory.

a

	5	3	4	8	6	9	7
× 3							

b

	5	3	4	8	6	9	7
× 4							

 AUSTRALIAN SIGNPOST MATHS 3 • ISBN 9780655708773

Number facts, multiplication

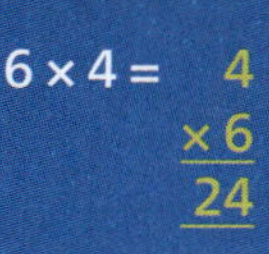

1 Write each problem as a number sentence or a vertical times table, and find the answer.

a 7 rows of 5 hats

☐ × ☐ = ☐

b 4 groups of 10 pens

☐ ☐ ☐ ☐ ☐

c 5 groups of 5 eggs

☐ ☐ ☐ ☐ ☐

d 5 girls in a team
8 teams
How many girls? ☐

e 5 boys in a row
6 rows
How many boys? ☐

2

a 9 × 2 = ☐	**b** 4 × 5 = ☐	**c** 8 × 10 = ☐	**d** 7 × 2 = ☐
e 4 × 1 = ☐	**f** 6 × 2 = ☐	**g** 3 × 10 = ☐	**h** 5 × 2 = ☐
i 3 × 5 = ☐	**j** 3 × 1 = ☐	**k** 7 × 10 = ☐	**l** 8 × 0 = ☐

3 On this 50 chart:

- colour the table of twos yellow
- colour the table of threes green
- circle the table of fours.

1	2	3	4	5	6	7	8	9	10
11	12	13	14	15	16	17	18	19	20
21	22	23	24	25	26	27	28	29	30
31	32	33	34	35	36	37	38	39	40
41	42	43	44	45	46	47	48	49	50

4 This multiplication grid shows the table of 2s. Write in the tables of 3s, 4s and 5s.

×	0	1	2	3	4	5	6	7	8	9	10
0			0								
1			2								
2	0	2	4	6	8	10	12	14	16	18	20
3			6								
4			8								
5			10								
6			12								
7			14								
8			16								
9			18								
10			20								

Each table should be written twice, once across a row and once down a column.
2 × 10 = 10 × 2

2:24

Sharing and grouping

How many koalas could be given 2?

12 ÷ 2 = ☐

1 Use the pictures to find how many in each share.

a 12 are shared by 3 ☐

b 12 are shared by 4 ☐

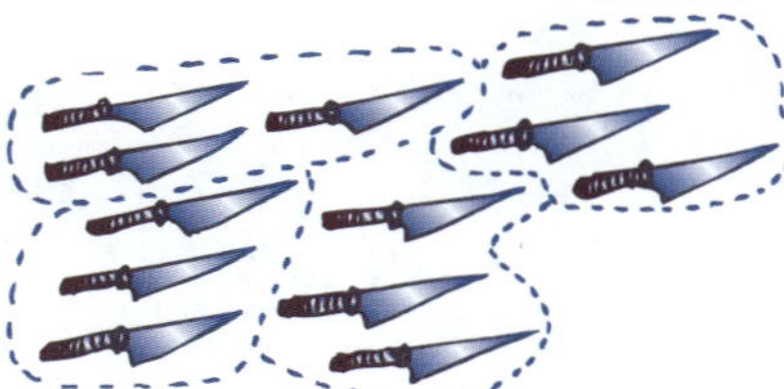

c 18 are shared by 9 ☐

d 9 are shared by 3 ☐

e 16 are shared by 4 ☐

f 28 are shared by 4 ☐

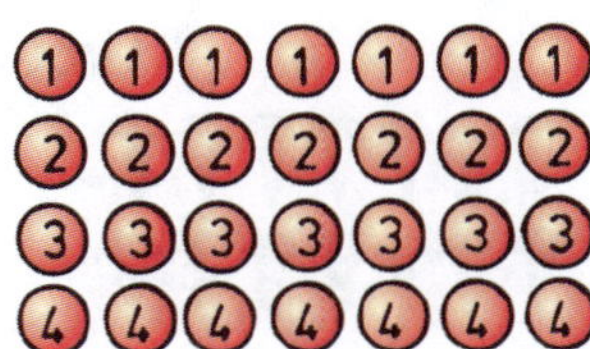

g 14 are shared by 2 ☐

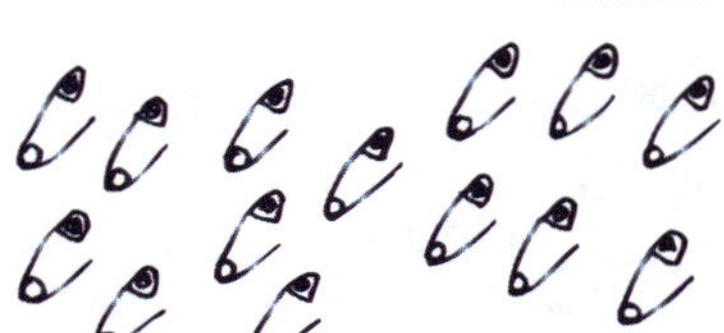

h 24 are shared by 6 ☐

i 15 are shared by 3 ☐

2 Use the pictures to find how many groups there are.

a Groups of 2 ☐

b Groups of 6 ☐

c Groups of 3 ☐

d Groups of 7 ☐

e Groups of 4 ☐

f Groups of 5 ☐

ACTIVITY

Use counters to find how many in each share.

3 12 pieces of toast:

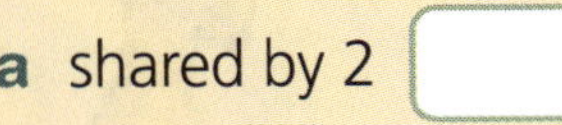

a shared by 2 ☐

b shared by 3 ☐

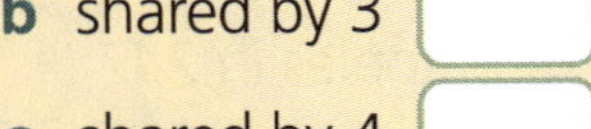

c shared by 4 ☐

4 10 mugs:

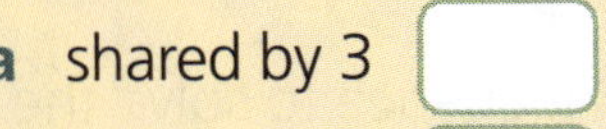

a shared by 3 ☐

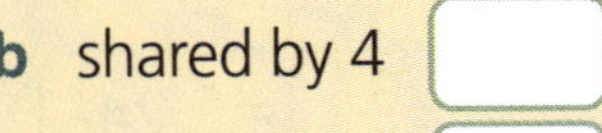

b shared by 4 ☐

c shared by 5 ☐

Discuss what you could do with those left over.

 • *AUSTRALIAN SIGNPOST MATHS 3* • ISBN 9780655708773

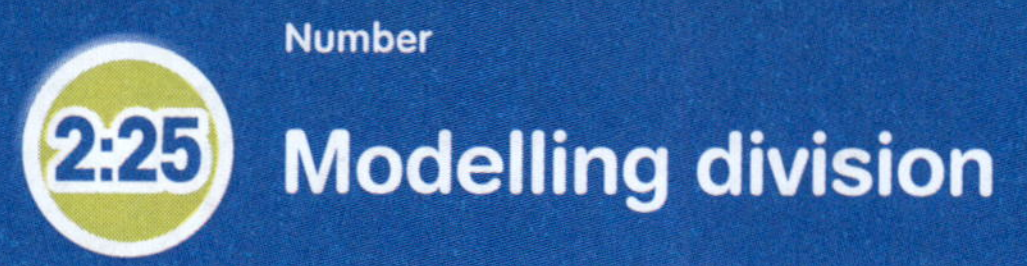

2:25 Modelling division

÷ is the opposite of ×.

5 × 10 = 50
50 ÷ 10 = 5

÷ means **shared among**
means **in groups of**
means **divided by**

15 shared among 3 ...

Groups of 3 in 15 ...

15 ÷ 3 = ☐

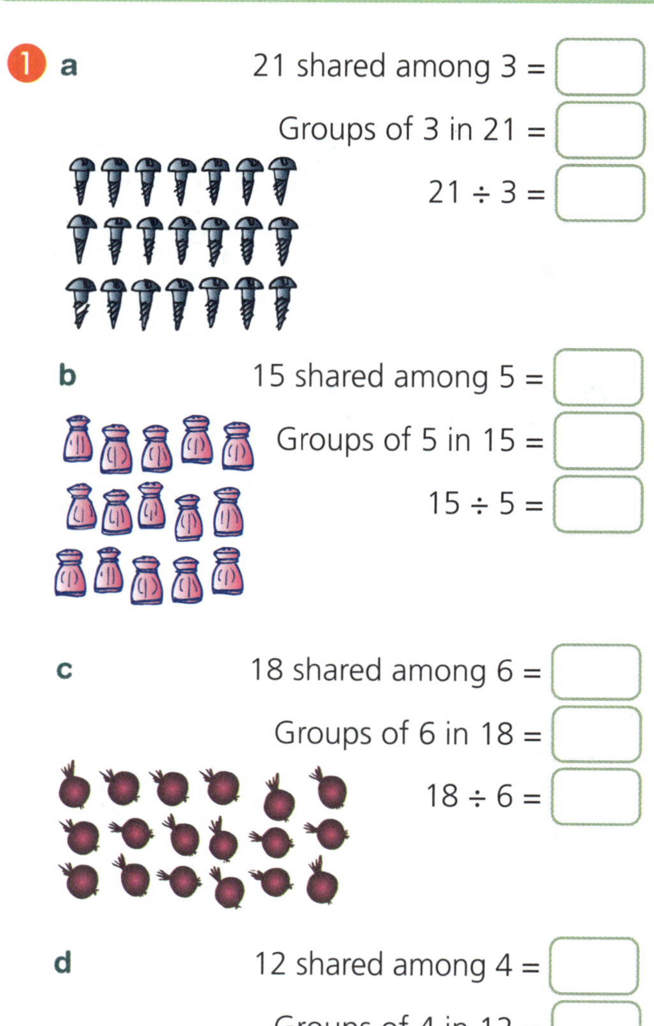

1 **a** 21 shared among 3 = ☐

Groups of 3 in 21 = ☐

21 ÷ 3 = ☐

b 15 shared among 5 = ☐

Groups of 5 in 15 = ☐

15 ÷ 5 = ☐

c 18 shared among 6 = ☐

Groups of 6 in 18 = ☐

18 ÷ 6 = ☐

d 12 shared among 4 = ☐

Groups of 4 in 12 = ☐

12 ÷ 4 = ☐

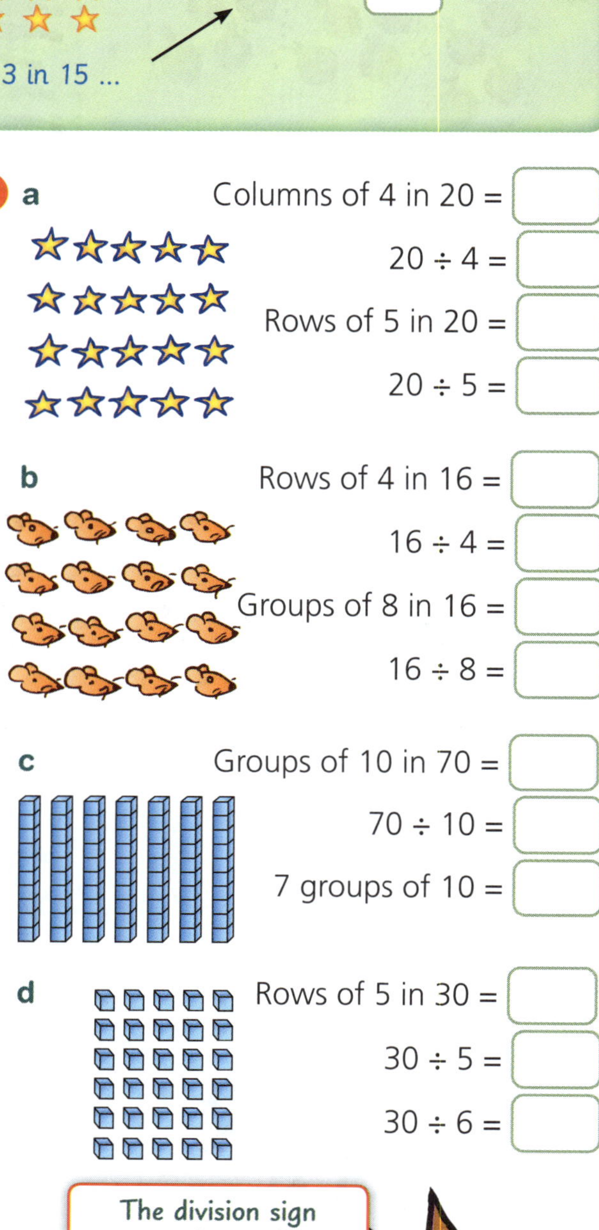

2 **a** Columns of 4 in 20 = ☐

20 ÷ 4 = ☐

Rows of 5 in 20 = ☐

20 ÷ 5 = ☐

b Rows of 4 in 16 = ☐

16 ÷ 4 = ☐

Groups of 8 in 16 = ☐

16 ÷ 8 = ☐

c Groups of 10 in 70 = ☐

70 ÷ 10 = ☐

7 groups of 10 = ☐

d Rows of 5 in 30 = ☐

30 ÷ 5 = ☐

30 ÷ 6 = ☐

3 Use the addition sequence to solve the division problem.

a 8 + 8 + 8 = 24 How many groups of 8 apples in 24? ☐

b 9 + 9 + 9 + 9 = 36 How many rows of 9 buttons in 36? ☐

c 7 + 7 + 7 + 7 = 28 4 boys share 28 pens. One share = ☐

 • *AUSTRALIAN SIGNPOST MATHS 3* • ISBN 9780655708773

Algebra

2:26 Relating × and ÷

4 threes
4 × 3

How many 3s in 12?
Share 12 among 3.
12 ÷ 3

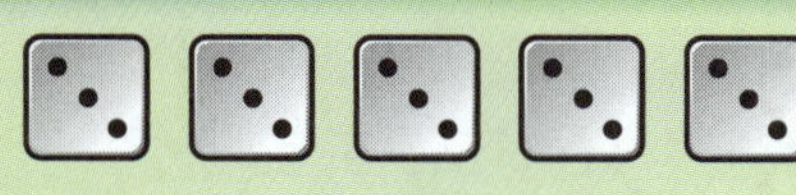

5 groups of 3 make ☐. 5 × 3 = 15

How many groups of 3 in 15? ☐ 15 ÷ 3 = 5

1 Complete each question and write the related number sentences.

a

5 groups of 2 make ☐.

How many 2s in 10? ☐

5 × 2 = ☐ 10 ÷ 2 = ☐

b

6 groups of 3 make ☐.

How many 3s in 18? ☐

6 × 3 = ☐ 18 ÷ 3 = ☐

c

5 × 5 = ☐

25 ÷ 5 = ☐

5 × ☐ = 25

d

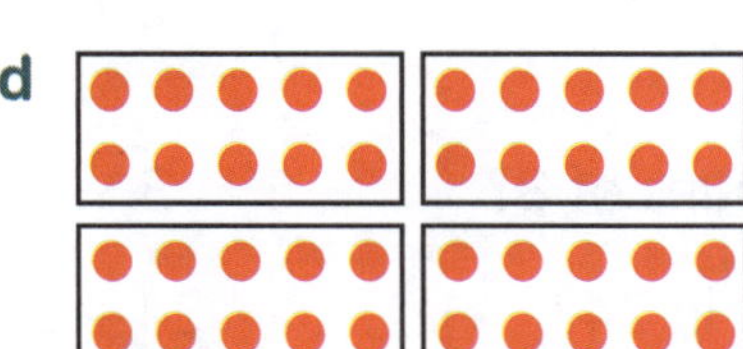

4 × 10 = ☐

40 ÷ 10 = ☐

☐ × 10 = 40

e

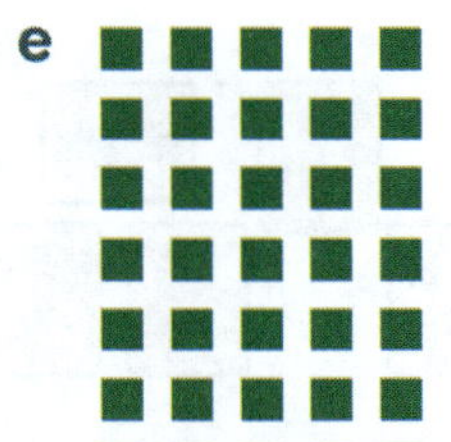

7 × 5 = ☐

35 ÷ 5 = ☐

☐ × 5 = 35

f

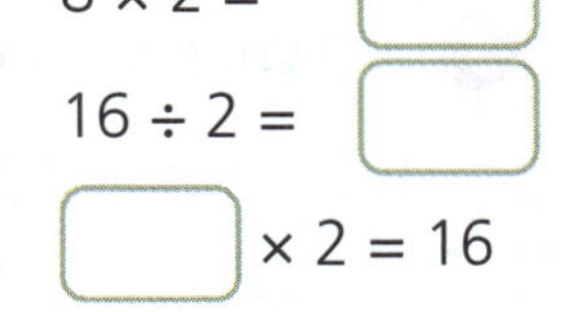

8 × 2 = ☐

16 ÷ 2 = ☐

☐ × 2 = 16

If you share 35 squares among 5 students, how many is each given? ☐

2
- **a** 9 × 3 = 27 so 27 ÷ 3 = ☐
- **b** 6 × 3 = 18 so 18 ÷ 3 = ☐
- **c** 4 × 3 = 12 so 12 ÷ 3 = ☐
- **d** 7 × 3 = 21 so 21 ÷ 3 = ☐
- **e** 5 × 3 = 15 so 15 ÷ 3 = ☐
- **f** 8 × 3 = 24 so 24 ÷ 3 = ☐
- **g** 10 × 3 = 30 so 30 ÷ 3 = ☐

3
- **a** 6 × 5 = 30 so 30 ÷ 5 = ☐
- **b** 7 × 2 = 14 so 14 ÷ 2 = ☐
- **c** 9 × 5 = 45 so 45 ÷ 5 = ☐
- **d** 7 × 10 = 70 so 70 ÷ 10 = ☐
- **e** 7 × 5 = 35 so 35 ÷ 5 = ☐
- **f** 10 × 5 = 50 so 50 ÷ 5 = ☐
- **g** 8 × 5 = 40 so 40 ÷ 5 = ☐

4

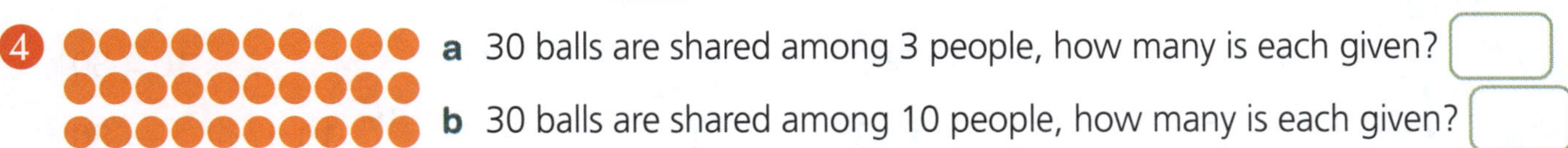

- **a** 30 balls are shared among 3 people, how many is each given? ☐
- **b** 30 balls are shared among 10 people, how many is each given? ☐

Linking × and ÷

5 × 2 = 10, So:
there are 5 twos in 10 and 2 fives in 10.
10 ÷ 2 = 5 and 10 ÷ 5 = 2

CONCEPT

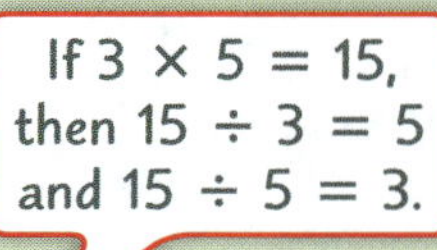

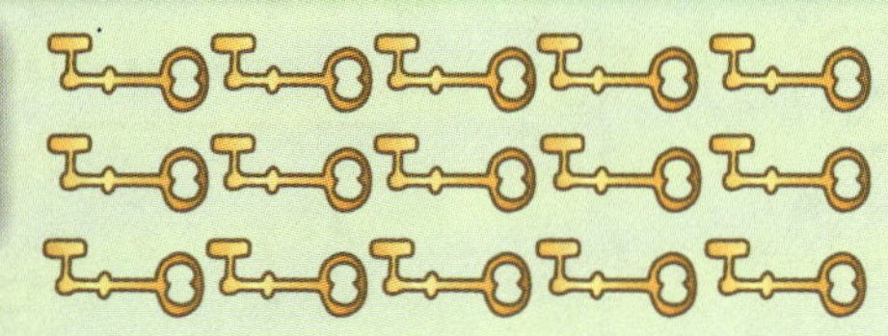

For 15 ÷ 5, ask:
What × 5 = 15?

Grouping: How many groups of 5 keys can be made from 15?
Sharing: 15 keys are shared by 5 people. What is each share?

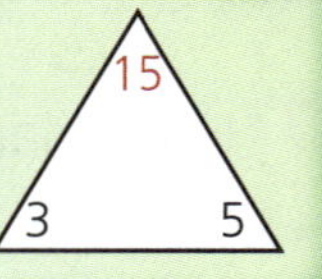

1. a What is 4 groups of 5? ☐ 4 × 5 = ☐
   b How many 5s in 20? ☐ 20 ÷ 5 = ☐
   c Share 20 among 4. ☐ 20 ÷ 4 = ☐

2. a What is 5 groups of 4? ☐ 5 × 4 = ☐
   b How many 4s in 20? ☐ 20 ÷ 4 = ☐
   c Share 20 among 5. ☐ 20 ÷ 5 = ☐

3. a What is 3 groups of 8? ☐ 3 × 8 = ☐
   b How many 8s in 24? ☐ 24 ÷ 8 = ☐
   c Share 24 among 3. ☐ 24 ÷ 3 = ☐

4. a What is 9 groups of 2? ☐ 9 × 2 = ☐
   b How many 2s in 18? ☐ 18 ÷ 2 = ☐
   c Share 18 among 9. ☐ 18 ÷ 9 = ☐

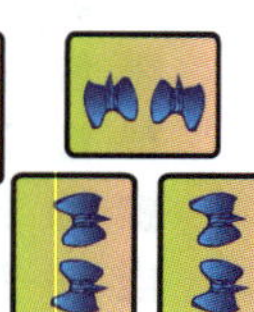

CONCEPT

10 × 5 = 50 → 50 ÷ 5 = 10 and 50 ÷ 10 = 5

For 50 ÷ 5 = ?, ask: ☐ × 5 = 50 and 5 × ☐ = 50

5. Use the first number sentence to complete the others.

   a 5 × 2 = 10
   10 ÷ 2 = ☐
   10 ÷ 5 = ☐

   b 10 × 3 = 30
   30 ÷ 3 = ☐
   30 ÷ 10 = ☐

   c 7 × 2 = 14
   14 ÷ 2 = ☐
   14 ÷ 7 = ☐

   d 9 × 3 = 27
   27 ÷ 3 = ☐
   27 ÷ 9 = ☐

6. Use the first number sentence to complete the others.

   a 12 ÷ 3 = 4
   ☐ × 3 = 12
   3 × ☐ = 12

   b 35 ÷ 5 = 7
   ☐ × 5 = 35
   5 × ☐ = 35

   c 50 ÷ 10 = 5
   ☐ × 10 = 50
   10 × ☐ = 50

   d 80 ÷ 10 = 8
   ☐ × 10 = 80
   10 × ☐ = 80

 ISBN 9780655708773

÷ facts from × facts

To work out 21 ÷ 3 ask:
'How many 3s make 21?'
3 × ? = 21 or 3 × ☐ = 21

To find how many 5s in 15, ask:
What multiplied by 5 gives 15?

Groups of 5 in 15:

Answer: 3

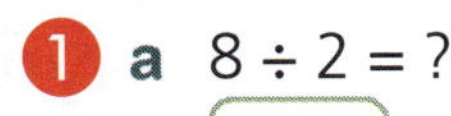

1
- **a** 8 ÷ 2 = ?
  ☐ × 2 = 8
  Answer = ☐
- **b** 50 ÷ 5 = ?
  ☐ × 5 = 50
  Answer = ☐
- **c** 50 ÷ 10 = ?
  ☐ × 10 = 50
  Answer = ☐
- **d** 20 ÷ 5 = ?
  ☐ × 5 = 20
  Answer = ☐
- **e** 45 ÷ 5 = ?
  ☐ × 5 = 45
  Answer = ☐
- **f** 18 ÷ 3 = ?
  ☐ × 3 = 18
  Answer = ☐
- **g** 35 ÷ 5 = ?
  ☐ × 5 = 35
  Answer = ☐
- **h** 80 ÷ 10 = ?
  ☐ × 10 = 80
  Answer = ☐

2 Use the first number sentence to complete the others.
- **a** 2 × 10 = 20
  20 ÷ 10 = ☐
  20 ÷ 2 = ☐
- **b** 6 × 2 = 12
  12 ÷ 2 = ☐
  12 ÷ 6 = ☐
- **c** 5 × 3 = 15
  15 ÷ 3 = ☐
  15 ÷ 5 = ☐
- **d** 8 × 5 = 40
  40 ÷ 5 = ☐
  40 ÷ 8 = ☐

3
- **a** ☐ × 10 = 10
- **b** ☐ × 2 = 20
- **c** ☐ × 10 = 60
- **d** ☐ × 3 = 15
- **e** 5 × ☐ = 5
- **f** 3 × ☐ = 30
- **g** 4 × ☐ = 8
- **h** 2 × ☐ = 16

4
- **a** 10 ÷ 2 = ☐
- **b** 8 ÷ 2 = ☐
- **c** 14 ÷ 2 = ☐
- **d** 12 ÷ 2 = ☐
- **e** 25 ÷ 5 = ☐
- **f** 30 ÷ 5 = ☐
- **g** 40 ÷ 5 = ☐
- **h** 45 ÷ 5 = ☐
- **i** 20 ÷ 10 = ☐
- **j** 80 ÷ 10 = ☐
- **k** 90 ÷ 10 = ☐
- **l** 70 ÷ 10 = ☐

5
- **a** How many groups of 2 are in 10? ☐ 10 ÷ 2 = ☐
- **b** Is there a whole number answer to how many groups of 10 are in 2? ☐
- **c** Is 10 ÷ 2 equal to 2 ÷ 10? ☐

Number line jumps

ACTIVITY

- One person draws a number line starting at zero that shows several equal jumps.
- The other person writes multiplication and division number sentences to match the picture.

This shows 6 × 5 = 30 and 30 ÷ 5 = 6.

0 5 10 15 20 25 30 35 40 45 50

× and ÷ tables

10 ÷ 2 can mean:
'How many 2s are in 10?' or 'How many in each share if 10 is shared by 2?'

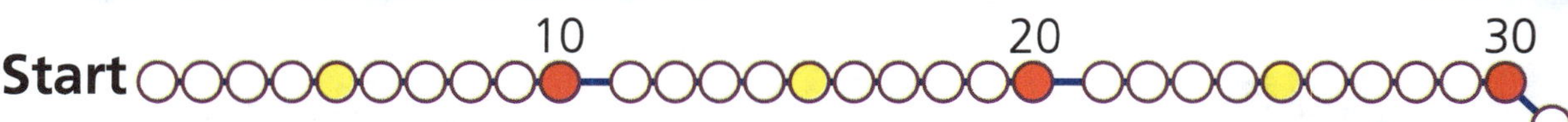

If 4 × 5 = 20 then
- 20 ÷ 5 (How many 5s in 20?) = 4
- 20 ÷ 4 (20 shared by 4) = 5 (each)

Multiplication is the opposite of division.

12 ÷ 3 × 3 = 12

30 ÷ 5 × 5 = 30

1 Join each question to its answer using a pencil and ruler.

a

	=	
2 × 3		0
4 × 3		3
0 × 3		12
1 × 3		6
3 × 3		21
7 × 3		15
5 × 3		9
10 × 3		27
9 × 3		30
6 × 3		24
8 × 3		18

b

	=	
3 × 4		4
0 × 4		20
5 × 4		0
1 × 4		8
7 × 4		32
2 × 4		16
8 × 4		12
4 × 4		28
6 × 4		36
10 × 4		24
9 × 4		40

c

	=	
6 × 10		25
9 × 2		3
5 × 5		40
3 × 1		18
8 × 5		60
9 × 10		14
7 × 2		35
7 × 5		20
8 × 1		90
4 × 5		40
8 × 5		8

×2 answers end in: 0, 2, 4, 6, or 8.

×10 answers end in: 0.

d

	=	
4 ÷ 2		8
60 ÷ 10		3
16 ÷ 2		9
30 ÷ 10		2
18 ÷ 2		6
70 ÷ 10		1
6 ÷ 6		7
50 ÷ 10		4
20 ÷ 2		0
8 ÷ 2		5
0 ÷ 10		10

e

	=	
20 ÷ 5		7
14 ÷ 2		2
10 ÷ 5		10
10 ÷ 1		9
45 ÷ 5		4
0 ÷ 2		0
30 ÷ 5		1
40 ÷ 5		6
5 ÷ 5		5
5 ÷ 1		8
15 ÷ 5		3

f

	=	
18 ÷ 3		0
32 ÷ 4		6
0 ÷ 3		3
8 ÷ 4		8
9 ÷ 3		2
28 ÷ 4		4
27 ÷ 3		10
20 ÷ 4		7
30 ÷ 3		9
16 ÷ 4		1
3 ÷ 3		5

×5 answers end in: 5, or 0.

20 is
☐ × ☐
☐ × ☐
☐ × ☐

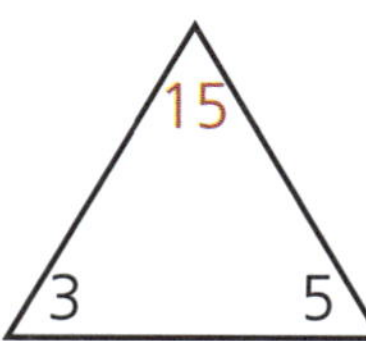

5 × 3 = 15   15 ÷ 5 = 3

3 × 5 = 15   15 ÷ 3 = 5

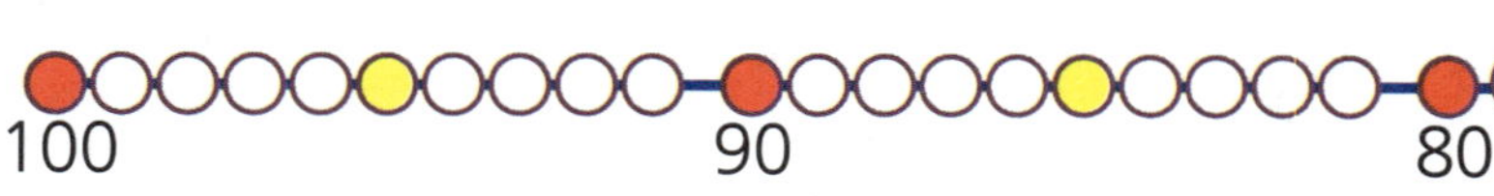

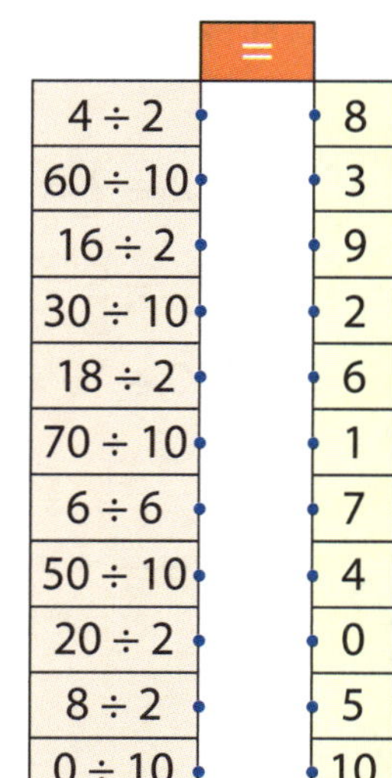

2:30 Inverse operations, × and ÷

CONCEPT

Double 5 = 10
Half 10 = 5
So,
5 × 2 ÷ 2 = 5

12 ÷ 2 = 6
6 × 2 = 12
So,
12 ÷ 2 × 2 = 12

1
- a 20 ÷ 10 × 10 = ☐
- b 10 × 5 ÷ 5 = ☐
- c 3 × 2 ÷ 2 = ☐
- d 30 ÷ 5 × 5 = ☐
- e 8 × 2 ÷ 2 = ☐
- f 60 ÷ 10 × 10 = ☐

2
- a
  - Half 14 = ☐
  - Double 7 = ☐
  - So, 14 ÷ 2 × 2 = ☐
- b
  - 15 ÷ 5 = ☐
  - 3 × 5 = ☐
  - So, 15 ÷ 5 × 5 = ☐
- c
  - 4 × 10 = ☐
  - 40 ÷ 10 = ☐
  - So, 4 × 10 ÷ 10 = ☐
- d
  - 4 × 5 = ☐
  - 20 ÷ 5 = ☐
  - So, 4 × 5 ÷ 5 = ☐
- e
  - 5 × 2 = ☐
  - 10 ÷ 2 = ☐
  - So, 5 × 2 ÷ 2 = ☐
- f
  - 20 ÷ 2 = ☐
  - 10 × 2 = ☐
  - So, 20 ÷ 2 × 2 = ☐

3
- a 6 × 2 ÷ 2 = ☐
- b 10 ÷ 5 × 5 = ☐
- c 30 ÷ 10 × 10 = ☐
- d 4 ÷ 2 × 2 = ☐
- e 8 × 5 ÷ 5 = ☐
- f 50 ÷ 10 × 10 = ☐
- g 9 × 2 ÷ 2 = ☐
- h 7 × 5 ÷ 5 = ☐
- i 45 ÷ 5 × 5 = ☐
- j 6 × 10 ÷ 10 = ☐

Circle parts that undo each other.
5 × 2 ÷ 2

FUN SPOT

Make up your own inverse number sentences.
Example: 8 × 10 ÷ 10 × 3 ÷ 3 × 4 × 2 ÷ 4 ÷ 2 = 8

 • *AUSTRALIAN SIGNPOST MATHS 3* • ISBN 9780655708773

Addition to 99, no trading

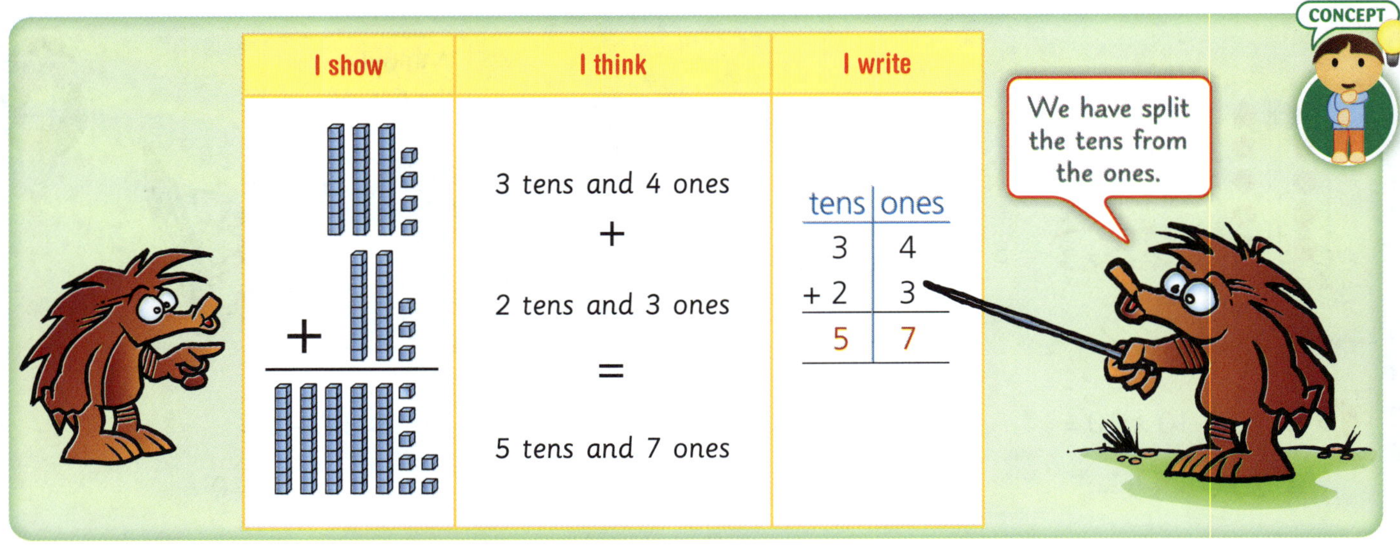

1 Use the split strategy or place-value blocks to answer these.

a

tens	ones
3	2
+ 2	6

b

tens	ones
4	3
+ 3	5

c

tens	ones
3	7
+ 4	0

d

tens	ones
6	4
+ 2	5

e

tens	ones
5	6
+ 4	0

f

tens	ones
4	2
+ 3	5

g

tens	ones
5	3
+ 3	6

h

tens	ones
7	3
+ 2	5

i

tens	ones
$6	6
+ $2	3

j

tens	ones
$7	5
+ $2	2

k

tens	ones
$4	8
+ $3	1

l

tens	ones
$5	4
+ $3	5

2

a 4 tens and 6 ones
+ 4 tens and 2 ones

b 5 tens and 4 ones
+ 3 tens and 3 ones

c 2 tens and 4 ones
+ 5 tens and 5 ones

d 7 tens and 3 ones
+ 1 ten and 6 ones

e 6 tens and 0 ones
+ 2 tens and 9 ones

f 3 tens and 1 one
+ 4 tens and 7 ones

3

a I paid $35 for a shirt and $61 for pants. How much did I spend? ☐

b There are 11 girls and 18 boys in our class. How many are in our class? ☐

c 15 horses and 42 cows are on our farm. How many animals altogether? ☐

d I saved $53. Alana saved $24. How much did we save? ☐

2:32 Subtraction, no trading

37 – 24
= (30 – 20) + (7 – 4)

Subtract tens.
Subtract ones.

1 Model the word problem using place-value blocks. Write a number sentence.

a 36 badges, 4 sold.
How many are left?

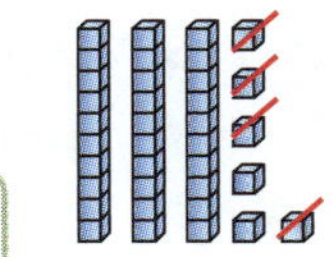

b 55 birds, 23 fly away.
How many remain?

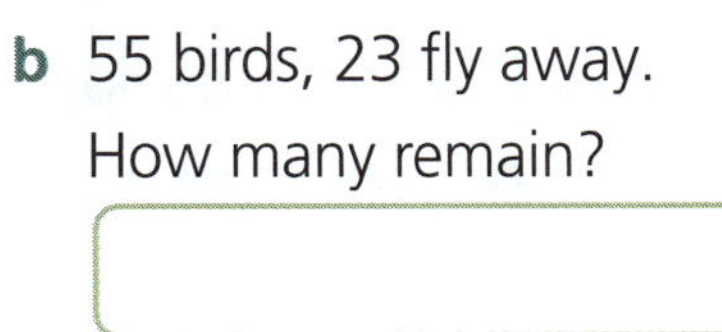

c 47 girls, 5 boys.
How many more girls than boys?

d 68 needed, 34 collected.
How many more to collect?

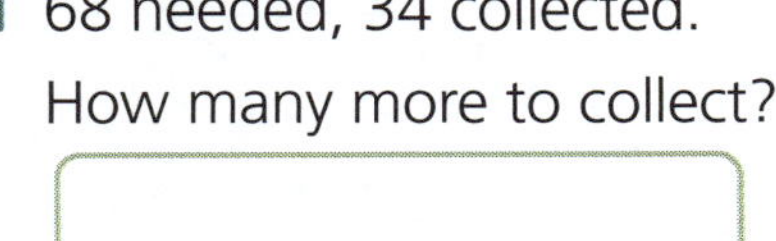

34	?
68	

e 76 books, 42 covered.
How many more to cover?

f 59 grapes, 46 eaten.
How many are left?

2

a

tens	ones
4	9
– 1	3

b

tens	ones
7	5
– 4	4

c

tens	ones
5	7
– 3	4

d

tens	ones
6	9
– 4	2

e

tens	ones
5	6
– 2	1

f

tens	ones
4	8
– 1	4

g

tens	ones
6	7
– 2	5

h

tens	ones
7	4
– 4	0

i

tens	ones
$9	4
– $3	1

j

tens	ones
$6	3
– $2	3

k

tens	ones
$8	5
– $8	1

l

tens	ones
$7	4
– $2	2

3 Use mental strategies to check your answers in Question 2.

2:33 Addition to 99 with trading

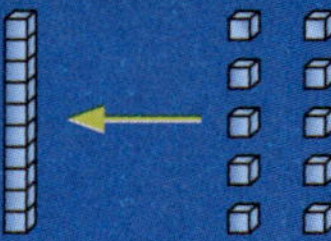

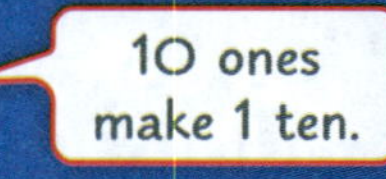

CONCEPT

45 + 27

	tens	ones
	1	
+	4	5
	2	7
	7	2

The 10 ones are shown as 1 ten.

Steps

1 5 ones + 7 ones = **12** ones

2 Trade **10 ones for 1 ten** and write the **2** that is left.

3 (**1** + 4 + 2) tens = 7 tens

or 45 + 27 = 45 + 20 + 5 + 2
= 65 + 5 + 2 = 72

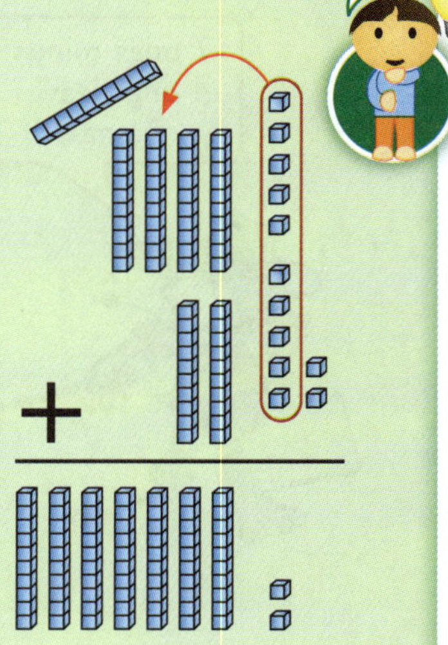

1 Trade ten ones for one ten in each addition. Use mental strategies to check your answers.

	tens	ones
a	2	4
+		7

	tens	ones
b	1	8
+	1	5

	tens	ones
c	3	5
+		6

	tens	ones
d	4	6
+	1	9

	tens	ones
e	1	3
+	5	8

	tens	ones
f	2	7
+	4	7

	tens	ones
g	1	4
+	7	6

	tens	ones
h	4	8
+	3	4

	tens	ones
i	3	6
+	3	6

	tens	ones
j	4	9
+		9

	tens	ones
k	5	6
+	3	8

	tens	ones
l	5	8
+	1	8

	tens	ones
m	$	5
+	$8	9

	tens	ones
n	$5	4
+	$2	9

	tens	ones
o	$2	7
+	$3	3

	tens	ones
p	$6	9
+	$2	8

2 Write a number sentence including the answer for each number story.

a Myah has 4 cats and 29 mice. How many animals has she altogether?

b Mark has 16 canaries and 27 budgies. How many birds does he have?

c Flynn has 65 ants and 28 bees. How many insects has he altogether?

d I have 57 five-cent coins and 26 ten-cent coins. How many do I have?

See Extra Support 5 (Addition problems to 99).

 • *AUSTRALIAN SIGNPOST MATHS 3* • ISBN 9780655708773

Addition with trading

14 ones is the same as 1 ten and 4 ones.

Thirty-eight ducks and twenty-six chickens were in the yard. How many birds were there altogether?

- **Find:** How many birds?
- **Number sentence:** 38 + 26 = ☐
- **Answer:** 64 birds were in the yard.

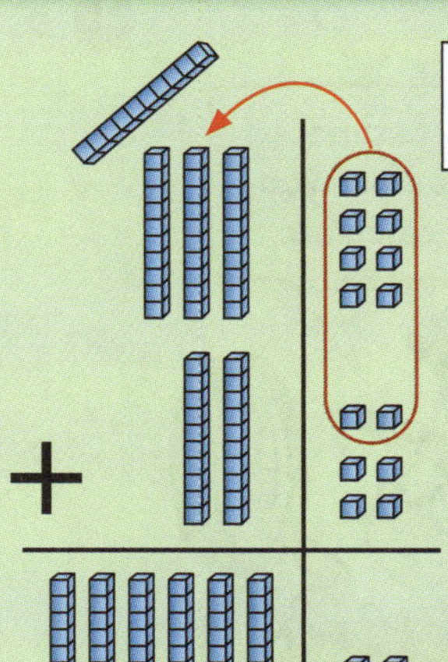

Learn the tables facts on page 160.

tens	ones
1	
3	8
+ 2	6
6	4

8 + 6 = 14
14 = **10** + 4

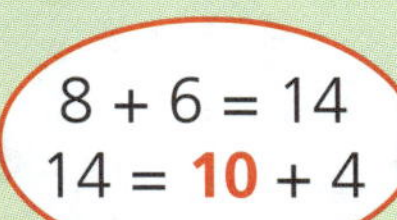
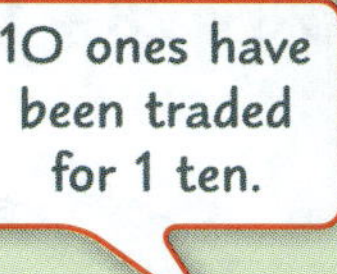

1 Complete the additions and show the trading. Check your answers using a mental strategy.

	a	b	c	d
	tens ones	tens ones	tens ones	tens ones
	1 2	3 3	4 5	2 7
	+ 2 8	+ 3 9	+ 1 6	+ 3 4

	e	f	g	h
	tens ones	tens ones	tens ones	tens ones
	6 5	1 1	3 6	2 4
	+ 2 8	+ 5 9	+ 5 7	+ 2 8

	i	j	k	l
	tens ones	tens ones	tens ones	tens ones
	7 7	6 6	4 5	2 8
	+ 1 7	+ 2 9	+ 3 7	+ 5 4

	m	n	o	p
	tens ones	tens ones	tens ones	tens ones
	\$4 6	\$ 7	\$2 6	\$4 9
	+ \$ 8	+ \$8 9	+ \$6 4	+ \$3 1

2
a How many students are in both classes if there are 27 in class 3P and 26 in class 3N? ☐

b We collected 43 cans on Monday and 37 on Tuesday. How many have we collected? ☐

c I have 35 stamps. Peter has 2 more than me. How many stamps altogether? ☐

d I had 3 cards less than 50. I was given 46 more cards. How many do I have now? ☐

See Extra Support 5 (Addition problems to 99).

2:35 Addition with 2-digit numbers

21
= 20 + 1
= 2 tens + 1 one

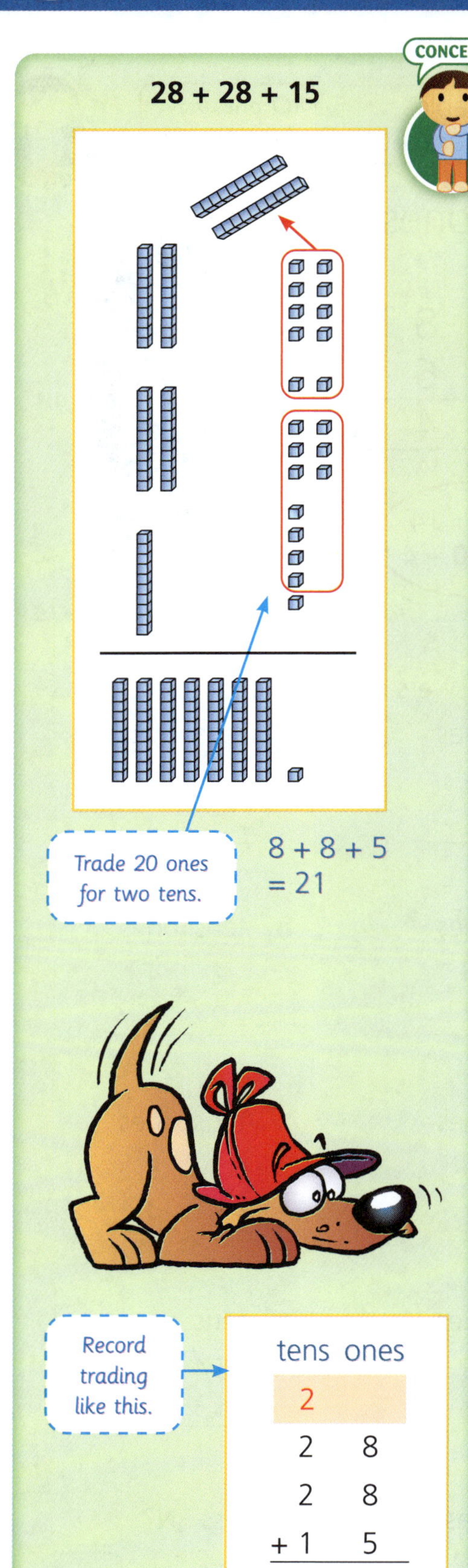

1

a

tens	ones
2	1
	7
+ 4	5

b

tens	ones
1	6
1	2
+ 1	7

c

tens	ones
2	5
3	9
+ 1	9

d

tens	ones
	7
2	1
+ 3	7

e

tens	ones
3	1
2	7
+ 1	5

f

tens	ones
4	5
1	7
+ 1	8

g

tens	ones
2	7
1	7
+ 2	7

h

tens	ones
5	8
	7
+ 2	8

2 Circle the answer.
Adding 3 odd numbers gives an **odd / even** answer.

3

a

tens	ones
2	6
2	4
1	7
+ 1	6

b

tens	ones
3	2
2	3
1	4
+	1

c

tens	ones
2	5
3	7
1	4
+ 1	5

d

tens	ones
1	5
1	5
1	5
+ 1	5

e

tens	ones
1	3
3	7
1	4
+ 1	6

f

tens	ones
5	5
	7
2	9
+	3

 ISBN 9780655708773

2:36 Addition, trading for 100

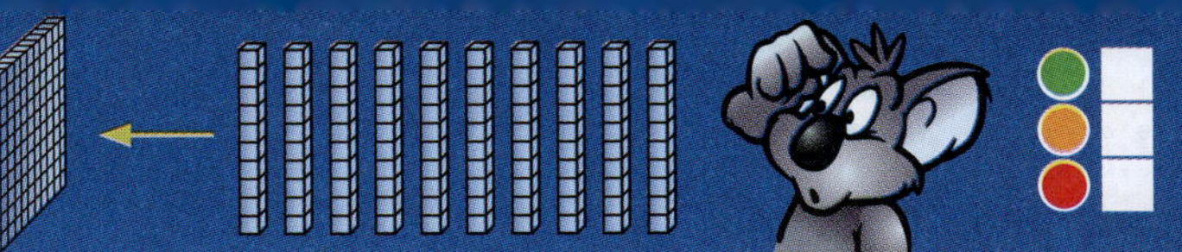

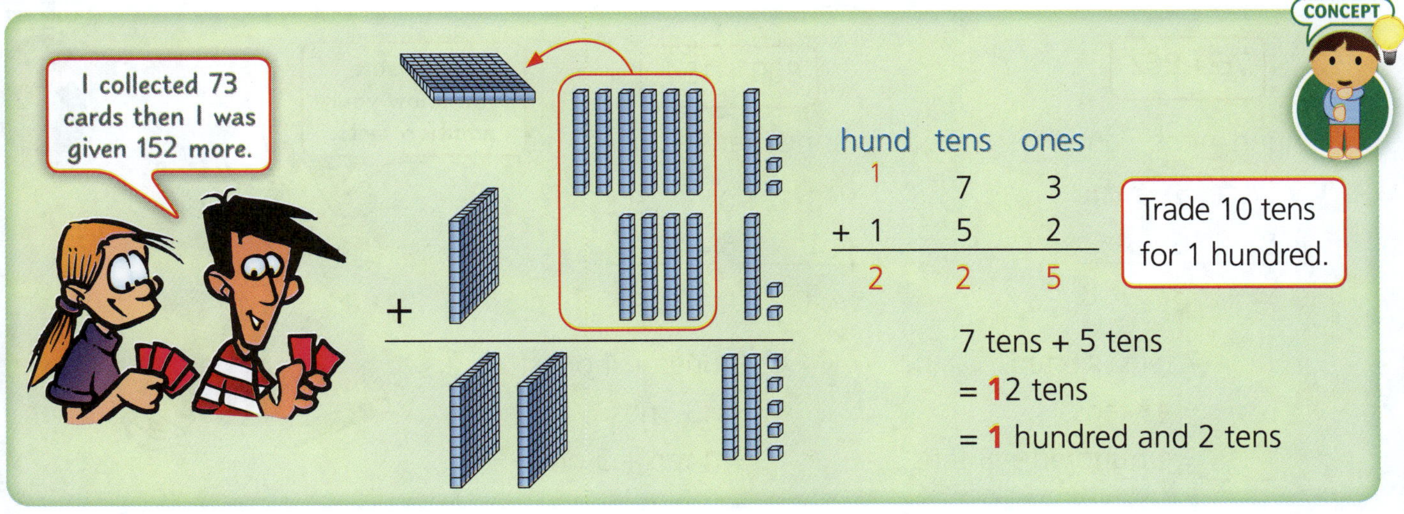

1 Model these problems with place-value blocks. Fill in the answers.

a 62 books, 144 books. ☐ + ☐ = ☐
How many books altogether? ☐

b 173 pens, 251 pens. ☐ + ☐ = ☐
How many pens altogether? ☐

2 Trade 10 tens for 1 hundred in each addition. Use mental strategies to check your answers.

a

	hund	tens	ones
		5	3
+		5	2

b

	hund	tens	ones
		7	6
+	4	3	1

c

	hund	tens	ones
	2	8	2
+		5	4

d

	hund	tens	ones
	1	6	4
+		6	3

e

	hund	tens	ones
		8	0
+	6	3	9

f

	hund	tens	ones
		9	2
+	5	9	6

g

	hund	tens	ones
	2	5	3
+		7	2

h

	hund	tens	ones
		2	9
+	3	9	0

i

	hund	tens	ones
		8	3
+	7	4	5

j

	hund	tens	ones
	6	3	7
+		8	1

k

	hund	tens	ones
	4	8	2
+		6	5

l

	hund	tens	ones
	8	9	4
+		4	3

m

	hund	tens	ones
	2	5	5
+	2	5	4

n

	hund	tens	ones
	1	8	3
+	3	5	4

o

	hund	tens	ones
	7	3	6
+	1	9	2

p

	hund	tens	ones
	5	4	7
+	2	8	0

See *Extra Support 6* (Addition to 999); *Extra Support 7* (Writing the addition algorithm); *Extra Support 8* (Addition of money); *Extra Support 9* and *10* (Addition to 9999).

 • *AUSTRALIAN SIGNPOST MATHS 3* • ISBN 9780655708773

2:37 Addition to 999 with one trade

Trade 10 ones for 1 ten.
Trade 10 tens for 1 hundred.

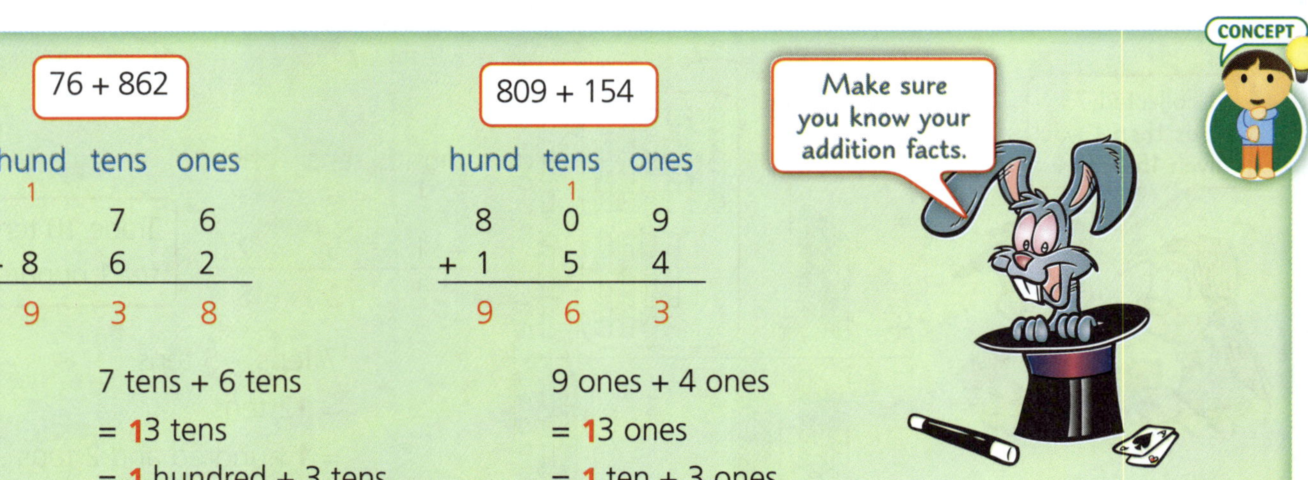

1 Use trading to find the answers. Use mental strategies to check your answers.

a

hund	tens	ones
	6	8
+	9	1

b

hund	tens	ones
	2	7
+ 8	1	5

c

hund	tens	ones
5	4	2
+	7	6

d

hund	tens	ones
1	3	6
+	3	7

e

hund	tens	ones
1	6	0
+ 2	9	9

f

hund	tens	ones
	7	5
+ 4	8	2

g

hund	tens	ones
2	8	2
+ 3	9	2

h

hund	tens	ones
	3	9
+ 4	4	6

i

hund	tens	ones
	8	8
+ 8	9	0

j

hund	tens	ones
3	3	7
+ 2	4	8

k

hund	tens	ones
2	2	2
+ 5	5	8

l

hund	tens	ones
8	1	4
+	5	6

m

hund	tens	ones
1	7	2
+ 4	4	0

n

hund	tens	ones
	7	9
+ 8	1	4

o

hund	tens	ones
3	0	8
+ 1	8	2

p

hund	tens	ones
5	3	6
+	8	3

2 Use trading to find the answers.

a

hund	tens	ones
$ 2	3	5
+$ 2	3	5

b

hund	tens	ones
$	3	5
+$ 7	9	0

c

hund	tens	ones
$ 2	6	0
+$ 6	4	7

d

hund	tens	ones
$ 4	3	7
+$ 3	1	7

3 Test your answers to Questions 1 and 2 by rounding the numbers and adding.

See *Extra Support 6* (Addition to 999); *Extra Support 7* (Writing the addition algorithm); *Extra Support 8* (Addition of money); *Extra Support 9* and *10* (Addition to 9999).

Addition, two trades

Trade 10 ones for one ten.
Trade 10 tens for one hundred.

CONCEPT

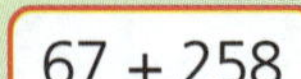

67 + 258

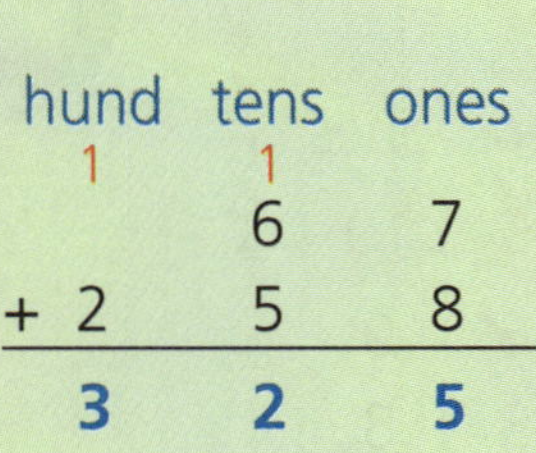

	hund	tens	ones
	1	1	
		6	7
+	2	5	8
	3	**2**	**5**

Steps

1. 7 ones and 8 ones = 15 ones. Write the **5** and trade 10 ones for **1** ten.
2. **1**, 6 and 5 tens = 12 tens. Write the **2** and trade 10 tens for **1** hundred.
3. Add the 100s.

1 Use trading to find the answers. Use mental strategies to check your answers.

a

	hund	tens	ones
		4	9
+		7	9

b

	hund	tens	ones
		3	4
+	7	8	6

c

	hund	tens	ones
	4	6	8
+		3	6

d

	hund	tens	ones
	1	4	5
+		5	5

e

	hund	tens	ones
	1	7	6
+	3	5	6

f

	hund	tens	ones
	2	7	2
+	5	3	8

g

	hund	tens	ones
	5	1	8
+		8	4

h

	hund	tens	ones
	7	3	4
+	1	8	6

i

	hund	tens	ones
	6	2	4
+	1	9	7

j

	hund	tens	ones
	3	7	5
+	2	7	5

k

	hund	tens	ones
	2	8	7
+	3	3	3

l

	hund	tens	ones
	4	7	5
+	2	6	9

m

	hund	tens	ones
	4	4	9
+	3	5	7

n

	hund	tens	ones
	6	7	5
+		7	6

o

	hund	tens	ones
	1	2	6
+	7	7	4

p

	hund	tens	ones
		5	3
+	8	7	9

2
a Alan has 46 birds in one aviary and 178 in the other. How many birds does he have?
b Each packet of coloured paper has 156 sheets. How many sheets are in 2 packets?
c 99 meals were provided today and 98 yesterday. How many meals were provided?
d 286 cows were on one boat and 88 on the other. How many cows were on the boats?

See *Extra Support 6* (Addition to 999); *Extra Support 7* (Writing the addition algorithm); *Extra Support 8* (Addition of money); *Extra Support 9* and *10* (Addition to 9999).

2:39 Subtraction with trading to 99

60 = 5 tens + 10

1 Show how one ten can be traded for 10 ones.

	tens	ones
a	5	0
b	7	0
c	4	0
d	9	0

2 Use the method above or place-value blocks to answer these.

a tens ones: 6 0 – 4

b tens ones: 8 0 – 7

c tens ones: 5 0 – 6

d tens ones: 9 0 – 8

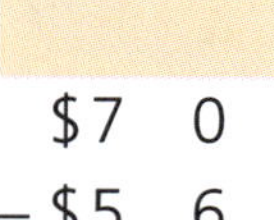

e tens ones: \$7 0 – \$5 6

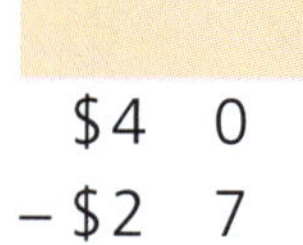

f tens ones: \$4 0 – \$2 7

g tens ones: \$8 0 – \$3 5

h tens ones: \$9 0 – \$4 2

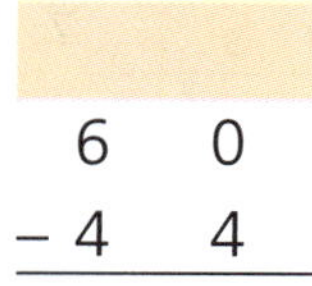

3 **a** tens ones: 6 0 – 4 4

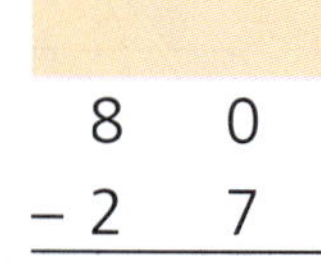

b tens ones: 8 0 – 2 7

c tens ones: 5 0 – 3 6

d tens ones: 9 0 – 7 8

4 Use written algorithms on your own paper to find the answers to these problems.

a \$70 – \$17 ☐ **b** \$80 – \$46 ☐ **c** \$50 – \$28 ☐

See *Extra Support 11–15* (Subtraction with trading to 999 including money).

Subtraction with trading

23 = 2 tens + 3 ones
= 1 ten + 13 ones

Trade 1 ten.

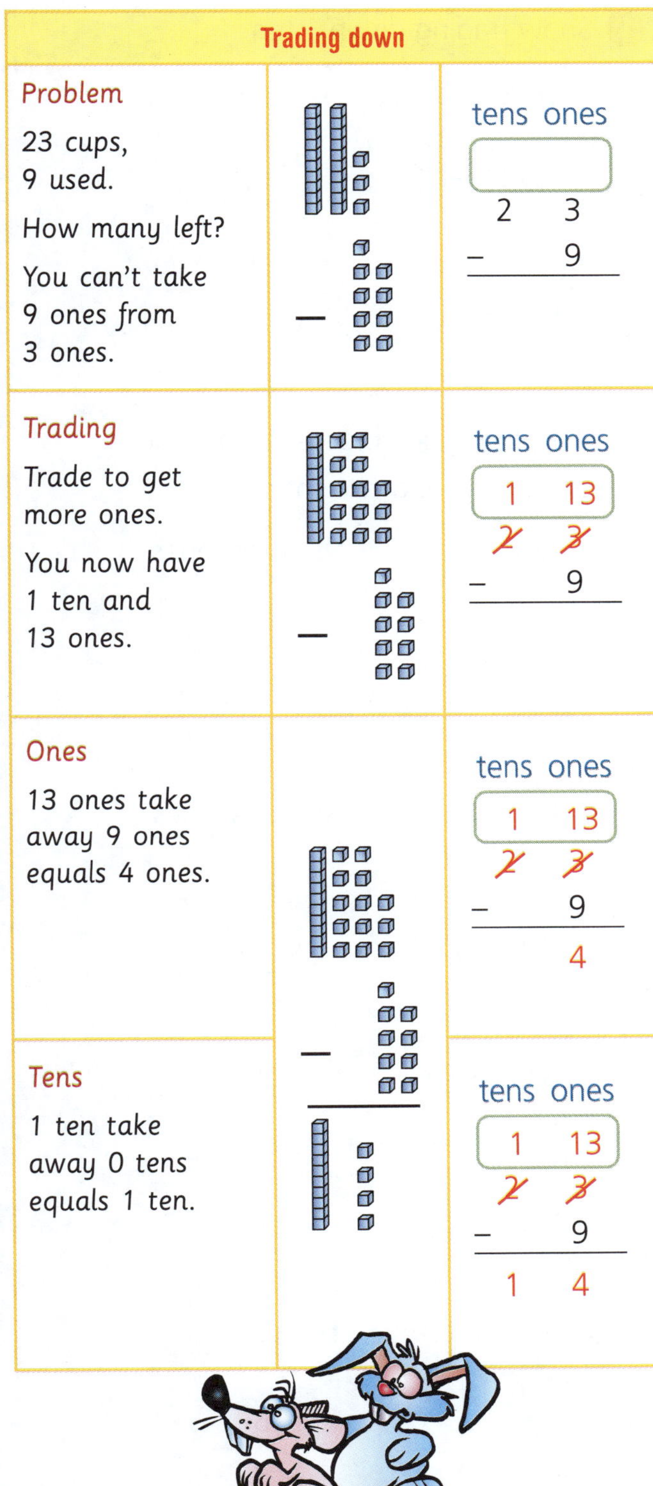

Trading down		
Problem 23 cups, 9 used. How many left? You can't take 9 ones from 3 ones.		tens ones [ ] 2 3 – 9
Trading Trade to get more ones. You now have 1 ten and 13 ones.		tens ones [1 13] ~~2~~ ~~3~~ – 9
Ones 13 ones take away 9 ones equals 4 ones.		tens ones [1 13] ~~2~~ ~~3~~ – 9 4
Tens 1 ten take away 0 tens equals 1 ten.		tens ones [1 13] ~~2~~ ~~3~~ – 9 1 4

1 Show trading down 1 ten.

	tens ones		tens ones
a	[ ] 3 4	**b**	[ ] 5 7
c	[ ] 4 6	**d**	[ ] 7 2
e	[ ] 6 3	**f**	[ ] 8 5

2 Use place-value blocks to do these. Estimate your answer first.

	tens ones		tens ones
a	[ ] 2 4 – 6	**b**	[ ] 2 5 – 9
c	[ ] 3 7 – 8	**d**	[ ] 5 6 – 7
e	[ ] 7 3 – 5	**f**	[ ] 6 1 – 4
g	[ ] 3 5 – 7	**h**	[ ] 4 2 – 5

Make up number stories for Question 2 parts **g** and **h**. Use mental strategies to check your answers.

See *Extra Support 11–15* (Subtraction with trading to 999 including money).

 • *AUSTRALIAN SIGNPOST MATHS 3* • ISBN 9780655708773

Subtraction with trading

34 = 3 tens + 4 ones
= 2 tens + 14 ones

Trade 1 ten.

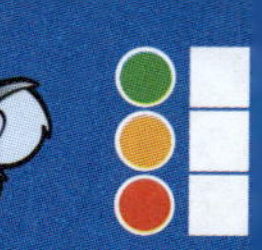

Trading down		
Problem 34 birds, 18 leave. How many stay? You can't take 8 ones from 4 ones.		tens ones 3 4 − 1 8
Trading Trade to get more ones. You now have 2 tens and 14 ones.		tens ones 2 14 ~~3~~ ~~4~~ − 1 8
Ones 14 ones take away 8 ones equals 6 ones.		tens ones 2 14 ~~3~~ ~~4~~ − 1 8 6
Tens 2 tens take away 1 ten equals 1 ten.		tens ones 2 14 ~~3~~ ~~4~~ − 1 8 1 6

Check by adding the answer to the bottom row. This should give the top row.

1 Show trading down 1 ten.

a tens ones

4 5

b tens ones

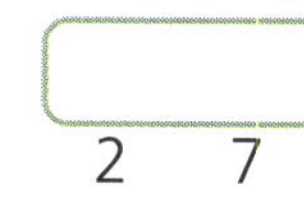

2 7

c tens ones

3 1

d tens ones

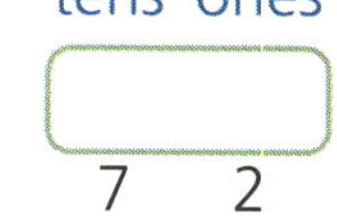

7 2

2 Use place-value blocks to do these. Estimate your answer first.

a tens ones
5 6
− 1 8

b tens ones
8 3
− 2 9

c tens ones
6 2
− 3 4

d tens ones
3 7
− 1 8

e tens ones
4 1
− 2 7

f tens ones

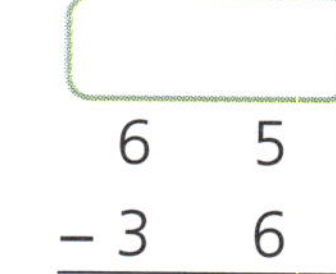

6 5
− 3 6

g tens ones
7 4
− 4 9

h tens ones
9 2
− 3 5

i tens ones

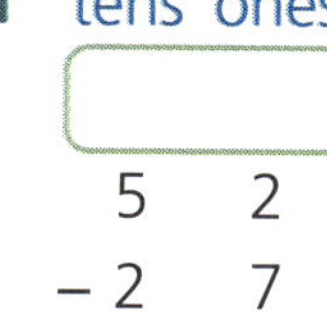

5 2
− 2 7

j tens ones

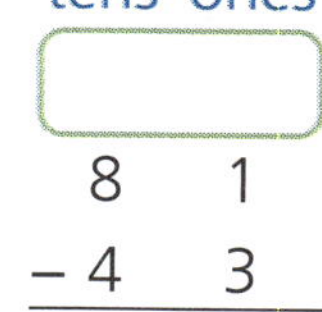

8 1
− 4 3

See *Extra Support 11–15* (Subtraction with trading to 999 including money).

2:42 Checking subtraction by addition

11 − 4 = 7
so
7 + 4 = 11

Diane has 26 books left.

1 Complete each problem and check the answer.

a The teacher had 36 frogs. 14 got away. How many were left?

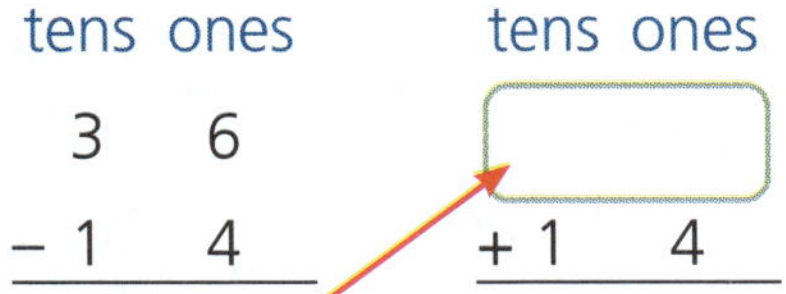

☐ frogs were left.

b James had $87. He spent $42. How much did he have left?

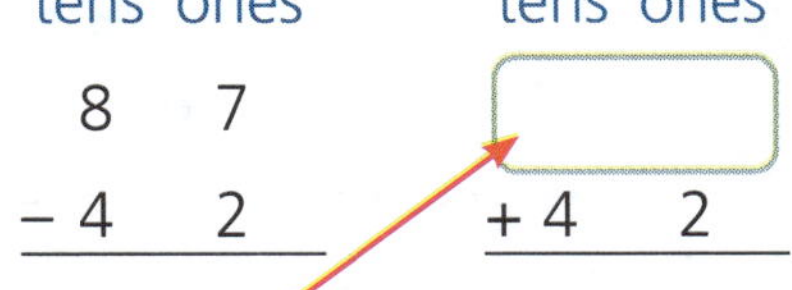

Addition is the inverse of subtraction.

James had $ ☐ left.

c 47 flowers were given to Kaylee. She gave away 9. How many were left?

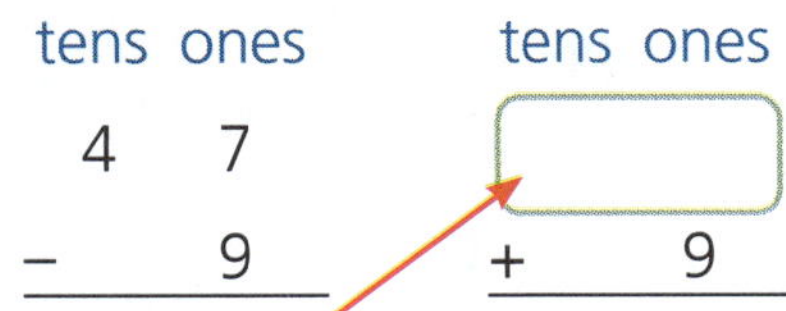

Kaylee had ☐ flowers left.

d The zoo has 24 emus and 8 koalas. How many more emus than koalas?

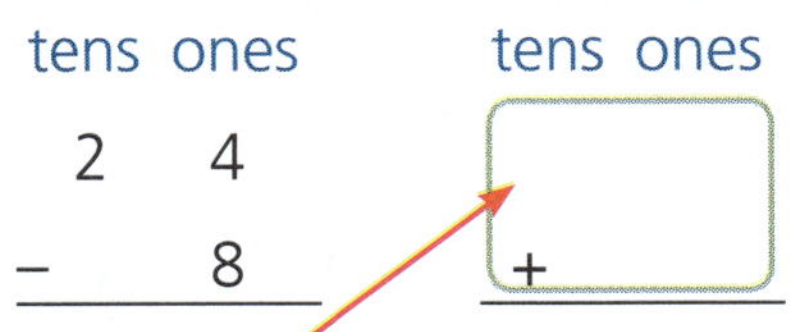

There are ☐ more emus.

To find the distance, you subtract.

2 Find the distance between the places on each sign.

a Blaxland 25 km
Lawson 6 km
Distance = ☐ km

b Mackay 41 km
Clairview 7 km
Distance = ☐ km

c Horsham 8 km
Nhill 36 km
Distance = ☐ km

3 Use the signpost to find these distances:

Place	Distance
Caves	79 km
Gumnut	44 km
Bellus	17 km
Dunnart	5 km

a Dunnart to Bellus ☐
b Dunnart to Caves ☐
c Bellus to Caves ☐
d Gumnut to Caves ☐
e Dunnart to Gumnut ☐
f Bellus to Gumnut ☐

2:43 Addition strategies

Using strategies is like playing with numbers.

CONCEPT

- 7 + 3 = 10, so 27 + 3 = 30.
  2 + 8 = 10, so 152 + 8 = 160.
- 27 **+ 8 + 3** = 27 **+ 3 + 8** = 30 **+ 8** = 38
  345 **+ 6 + 5** = 345 **+ 5 + 6** = 350 + **6** = 356

1 **a** 3 + 7 = 10 so 153 + 7 = ☐ **b** 4 + 6 = 10 so 674 + 6 = ☐

c 252 + 9 + 8 = 252 + 8 + 9 = ☐ **d** 174 + 7 + 6 = 174 + 6 + 7 = ☐

e 28 + 5 + 2 ☐ **f** 79 + 7 + 1 ☐ **g** 56 + 9 + 4 ☐

h 277 + 2 + 3 ☐ **i** 146 + 5 + 4 ☐ **j** 782 + 3 + 8 ☐

CONCEPT

	Question	Bridging to 10	Change the order	Add
A	36 **+ 9**	36 **+ 4 + 5**		40 **+ 5** = 45
B	315 **+ 8**	315 **+ 5 + 3**		320 **+ 3** = 323
C	36 **+ 9** + 13	36 **+ 4 + 5** + 13	40 + 13 **+ 5**	53 **+ 5** = 58
D	508 **+ 4** + 61	508 **+ 2 + 2** + 61	510 + 61 **+ 2**	571 **+ 2** = 573

2 **a** 52 **+ 9** = 52 **+ 8 + 1** = ☐ **b** 877 **+ 8** = 877 **+ 3 + 5** = ☐

c 25 + 8 ☐ **d** 66 + 6 ☐ **e** 87 + 9 ☐ **f** 38 + 6 ☐

g 17 + 7 ☐ **h** 66 + 7 ☐ **i** 25 + 8 ☐ **j** 67 + 7 ☐

k 288 + 5 ☐ **l** 516 + 9 ☐ **m** 873 + 8 ☐ **n** 356 + 9 ☐

o 52 **+ 9** + 13 = 52 **+ 8 + 1** + 13 = 60 + 13 **+ 1** = ☐

p 838 **+ 5** + 41 = 838 **+ 2 + 3** + 41 = 840 + 41 **+ 3** = ☐

q 534 **+ 8** + 23 = 534 **+ 6 + 2** + 23 = 540 + 23 **+ 2** = ☐

Talk about how to use strategies.

Working

 • *AUSTRALIAN SIGNPOST MATHS 3* • ISBN 9780655708773

2:44 Subtraction strategies

15 − 8 = 
(15 + 2) − (8 + 2)
17 − 10 = 7

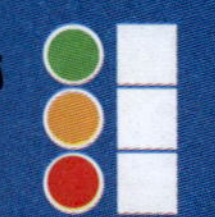

- 43 − 18 = (43 + 2) − (18 + 2) = 45 − 20 = 25
- 781 − 49 = (781 + 1) − (49 + 1) = 782 − 50 = 732

We made the second number easier to take away.

1 a 24 − 9 = (24 + 1) − (9 + 1) = 25 − 10 = ☐

b 61 − 17 = (61 + 3) − (17 + 3) = 64 − 20 = ☐

c 74 − 39 = (74 + 1) − (39 + 1) = 75 − 40 = ☐

d 598 − 39 = (598 + 1) − (39 + 1) = 599 − 40 = ☐

e 962 − 78 = (962 + 2) − (78 + 2) = 964 − 80 = ☐

2 a 73 − 18 = ☐

b 47 − 29 = ☐

c 62 − 37 = ☐

d 288 − 69 = ☐

e 461 − 48 = ☐

CONCEPT

Use patterns • 12 − 8 = 4 so 42 − 8 = 34 • 16 − 9 = 7 so 536 − 9 = 527

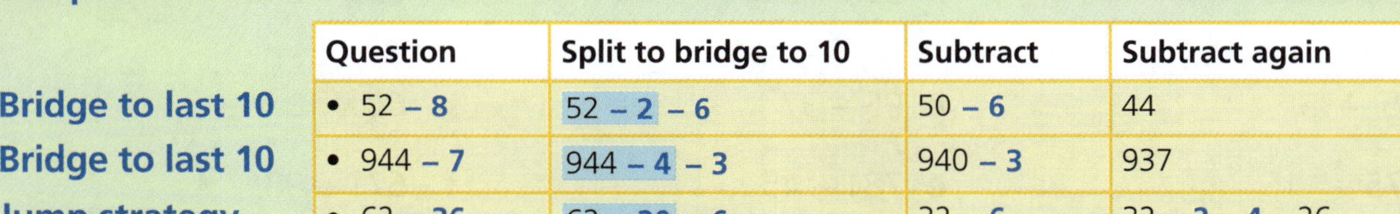

	Question	Split to bridge to 10	Subtract	Subtract again
Bridge to last 10	• 52 − 8	52 − 2 − 6	50 − 6	44
Bridge to last 10	• 944 − 7	944 − 4 − 3	940 − 3	937
Jump strategy	• 62 − 36	62 − 30 − 6	32 − 6	32 − 2 − 4 = 26

3 a 13 − 7 = 6 so 53 − 7 = ☐

b 14 − 6 = 8 so 74 − 6 = ☐

c 14 − 6 = 8 so 754 − 6 = ☐

d 11 − 4 = 7 so 641 − 4 = ☐

e 15 − 8 = 7 so 365 − 8 = ☐

f 16 − 7 = 9 so 526 − 7 = ☐

g 34 − 9 = 34 − 4 − 5 = 30 − 5 = ☐

h 52 − 8 = 52 − 2 − 6 = 50 − 6 = ☐

i 181 − 8 = 181 − 1 − 7 = 180 − 7 = ☐

j 493 − 7 = 493 − 3 − 4 = 490 − 4 = ☐

k 82 − 9 ☐ l 56 − 7 ☐ m 36 − 8 ☐ n 41 − 6 ☐

o 21 − 8 ☐ p 66 − 9 ☐ q 71 − 25 ☐ r 66 − 18 ☐

Working

Using mental strategies

485 + ☐ = 500

CONCEPT

It is often useful to jot down your thinking when solving a problem.

Amy's jottings

485 + 365
15 + 350
(485 + 15 = 500)
500 + 350 = 850
Answer: 850

842 − 361
700 + 140 + 2
−300 −60 −1
400 + 80 + 1 = 481
Answer: 481

John's jottings

Make your own jottings on paper to answer these problems.

1

a 84 + 23 ☐	**b** 98 + 42 ☐	**c** 85 + 35 ☐
d 145 + 35 ☐	**e** 75 + 145 ☐	**f** 162 + 198 ☐
g 445 + 335 ☐	**h** 180 + 325 ☐	**i** 285 + 645 ☐
j 760 + 160 ☐	**k** 518 + 290 ☐	**l** 699 + 248 ☐

2

a 95 − 35 ☐	**b** 95 − 37 ☐	**c** 64 − 18 ☐
d 275 − 115 ☐	**e** 781 − 45 ☐	**f** 671 − 98 ☐
g 915 − 609 ☐	**h** 765 − 445 ☐	**i** 405 − 285 ☐
j 459 − 297 ☐	**k** 865 − 195 ☐	**l** 605 − 315 ☐

Check your answers to Question 2. Add the answer to the number taken away.

3 **a** How many students came to the library last week if 221 came on Monday, 135 on Tuesday, 126 on Wednesday, 85 on Thursday and 231 on Friday? ☐

Number sentence:

b How many visits to the local park occurred last week if there were 380 on Sunday, 27 on Monday, 132 on Tuesday, 180 on Wednesday, 54 on Thursday, 17 on Friday and 151 on Saturday? ☐

Number sentence:

2:46 Change from $2

CONCEPT

To give change, we count on from the price paid.

Example: What is the change from $2 if the cost is 35c?

35c

- Count on from 35c.
- 35c and 5c makes 40c, and 10c makes 50c, and 50c makes $1, and $1 makes $2.
- The change is 5c + 10c + 50c + $1 = **$1.65**.

1 Colour the coins to show the change from $2.

2 Use the coins to count on and find the change.

	Cost	Money given	Coins counted	Total change
a	45c	60c	5c, 10c	15c
b	65c	80c		
c	55c	$1		
d	$1.75	$2		

Coins

3 What is the change from $2 if the item costs:

a 70c? ______ **b** $1.40? ______ **c** 45c? ______ **d** $1.05? ______

2:47 Problem solving

For Questions 2 and 3, you could use trial and error.

1 Daren must pay $5 for each light globe and $2 for each battery.
How much change will he have from $20 if he bought:

a 2 batteries and 2 light globes? ☐ b 3 light globes and 2 batteries? ☐

c 1 battery and 2 light globes? ☐ d 1 light globe and 5 batteries? ☐

2 I was given five of these number cards. 1 2 3 4 5 6
The total of the numbers on my cards was 18. What were my numbers?
The 5 cards were ☐.
Hint: What is the total of all of the cards?

3 I had a collection of stars. Some had 5 points.
Some had 6 points.
I could see 21 points on my star collection.
How many of each type could I have?

5-point star 6-point star

Number of 5-point stars ☐ Number of 6-point stars ☐

4 a How could you throw a total of 24 on this dartboard using 3 darts?
☐ or ☐

b Can I throw a total of 21 on this dartboard using 3 darts? ☐
Explain why or why not. ☐
☐

4 6 8 10 8 6 4

INVESTIGATION

5 Rachel put 20 chairs in front of the stage in 2 rows of 10 chairs, as shown. Use 20 counters to find other ways to arrange the chairs in equal rows. Write your findings.

2 × 10	

Stage

2 × 10

6 List ways that 30 chairs can be arranged in equal rows.

3:01 Revision of length

We can measure length using informal units or compare objects directly.

CONCEPT

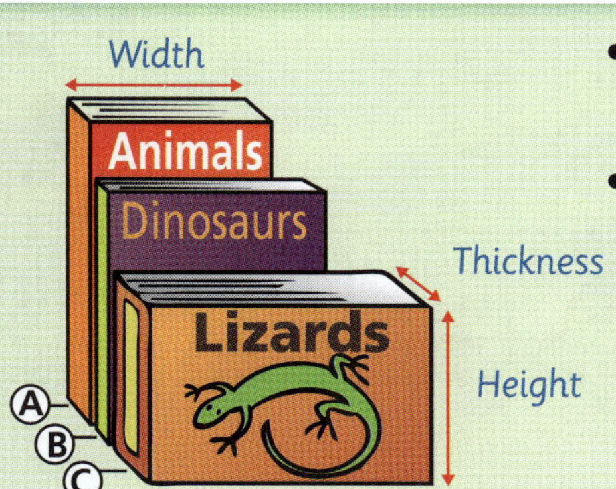

- We can compare the height, width and thickness of books by placing them side by side.
- We can measure using handspans.

This book is 2 handspans wide.

1 Use the labels **A**, **B** and **C** on the picture above to answer these questions.

a Which book is the widest? ☐

b Which book is the thickest? ☐

c Which book is the tallest? ☐

2 List the books **A**, **B** and **C** in order from least to most, according to:

a width ☐

b thickness ☐

c height ☐

ACTIVITY

- Use direct comparison to compare the height, width and thickness of books.
- Compare the lengths of 4 objects. List them in order from shortest to longest.

☐ ☐ ☐ ☐

- Use handspans to measure the length of objects. Mark off each handspan or count the units as you go.
  You can estimate the length first by visualising how many handspans are needed.

Item	Measurement
length of desk	handspans
width of desk	handspans
height of desk	handspans

Item	Measurement
	handspans
	handspans
	handspans

- Explain how you could use handspans to measure objects.

 • *AUSTRALIAN SIGNPOST MATHS 3* • ISBN 9780655708773

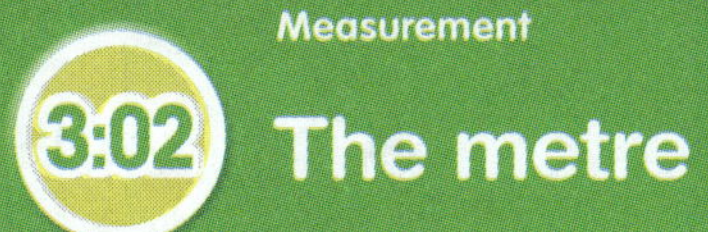

3:02 The metre

Metres are used to measure the length of longer objects.

1 metre

CONCEPT

1 Make a list of objects that are about 1 metre long.

2 Cut a strip of paper that is 1 metre long.
About how many of the items below would it take to match your 1-metre length?

Item		Estimate	Measurement
	How many shoes?		
	How many books?		
	How many handspans?		

3 Match each length with the best answer.

- height of a tree
- width of a door
- length of a shoe
- length of a desk
- width of a path
- height of your teacher

- less than 1 metre
- about 1 metre
- more than 1 metre

3:03 Using the metre

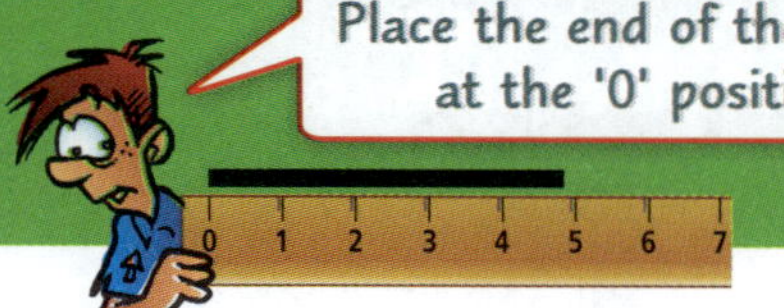

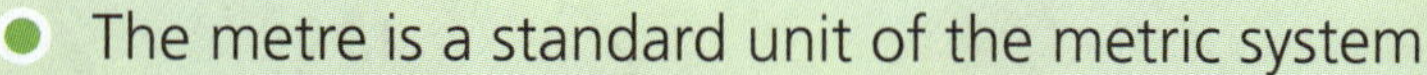

CONCEPT

- The metre is a standard unit of the metric system.
- One metre is usually about the length of your arm span, or two of your steps.
- **m** is short for **metre**.

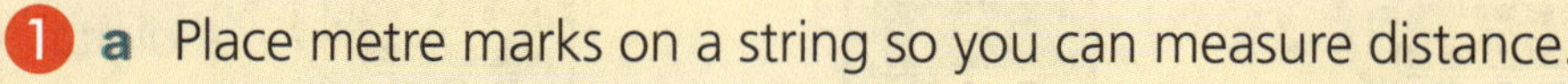

ACTIVITY

1 **a** Place metre marks on a string so you can measure distance.
b Estimate and measure each length to the nearest metre.

	Length	Estimate	Measurement
A	length of 10 steps	m	m
B	width of a gate	m	m
C	width of the classroom	m	m
D	distance to the canteen	m	m

c Write **A**, **B**, **C** and **D** to order the lengths from shortest to longest.

2 Match each length with the best answer.

width of a door	1 metre	height of yourself
length of a whiteboard	2 metres	length of a car
height of a door	5 metres	width of your desk
width of a window		length of ten steps

3 Measure the following. Show whether each length is less than, about or more than 1 metre.

	Less than 1 m	About 1 m	More than 1 m
shoulder to toe			
standing jump			
height of your teacher			

We use metres in athletics and swimming carnival events.

Clocks

In a digital clock, the number before the dots tell the hour.

1 Write the time shown.

a 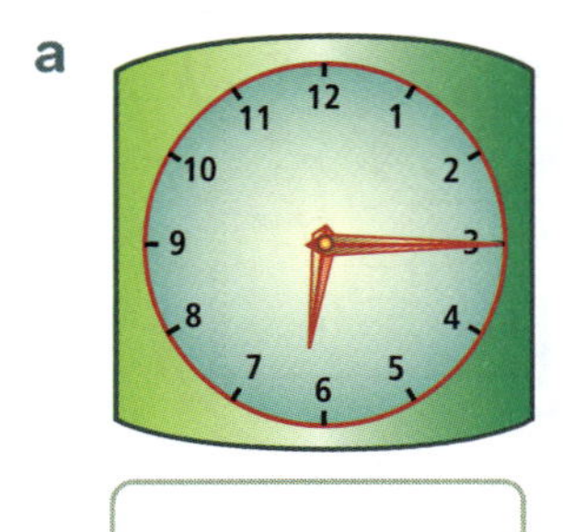

b 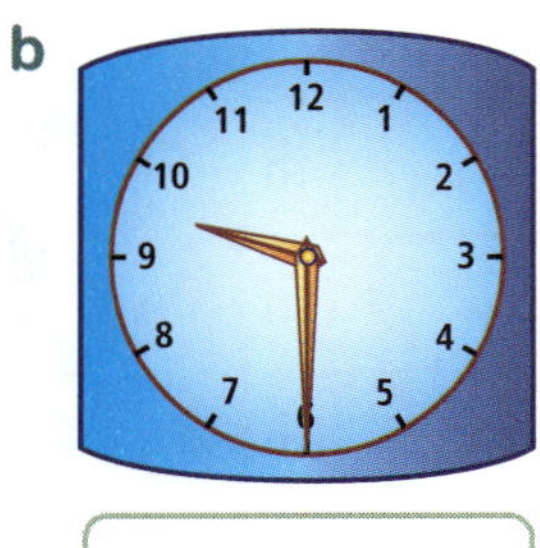

c 

d 

e 

f 

g 

h 

2 Show the time given.

a 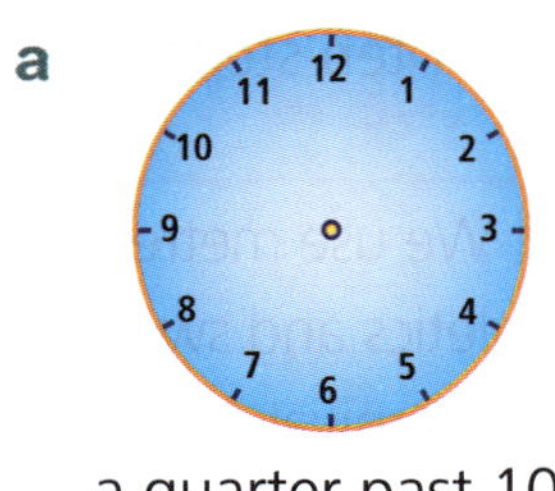

a quarter past 10

b 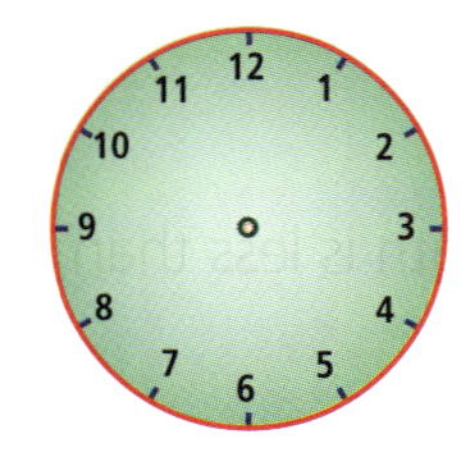

a quarter to 8

c 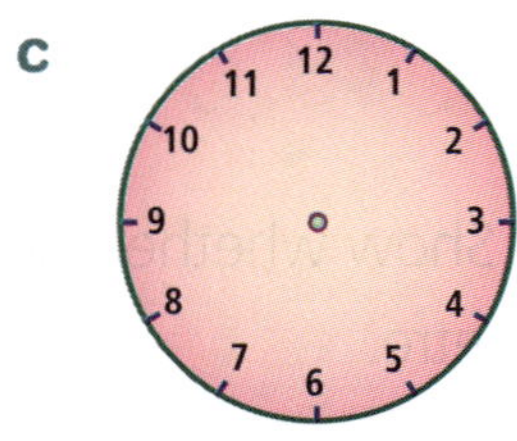

4 o'clock

d 

half past 7

e

a quarter past 8

f 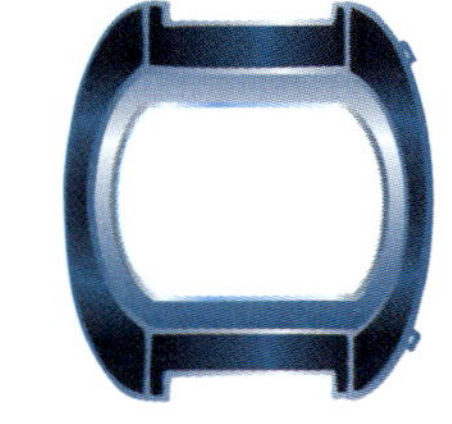

half past 2

g

a quarter to 1

h 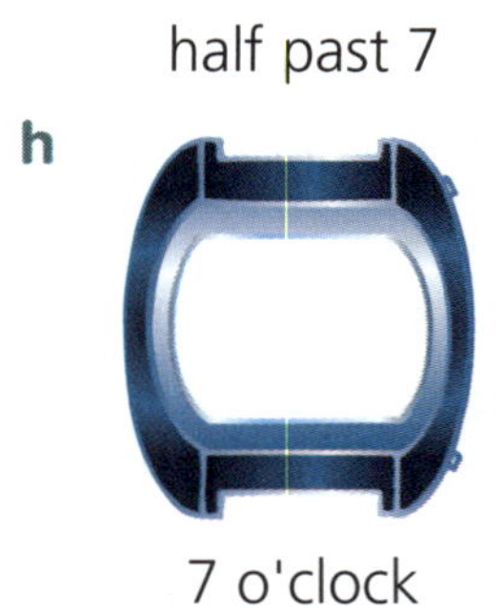

7 o'clock

 • *AUSTRALIAN SIGNPOST MATHS 3* • ISBN 9780655708773

Analog time

Ten past 5
10 minutes past 5
5:10

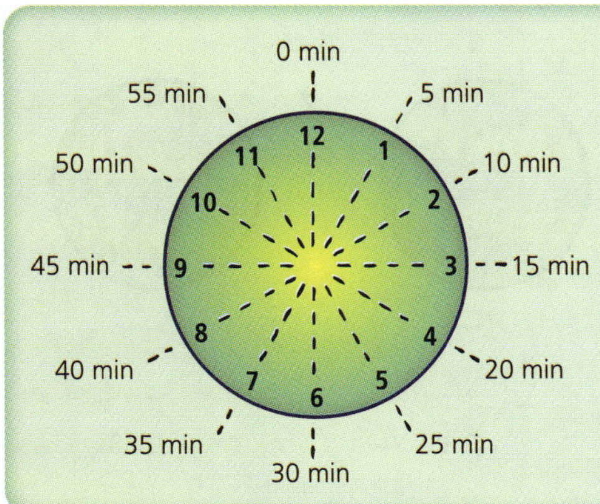

It takes 5 minutes for the minute hand to move from one numeral to the next.

20 past 7

- The hour hand has passed 7.
- The minute hand has moved 5, 10, 15, 20 minutes from 12.
- The time is **20 past 7**.

1. Write the time shown.

a

☐ minutes past ☐

b

☐ minutes past ☐

c

☐ minutes past ☐

d

☐ minutes past ☐

e

☐ past ☐

f

☐ past ☐

g

☐ past ☐

h

☐ past ☐

50 minutes past 2

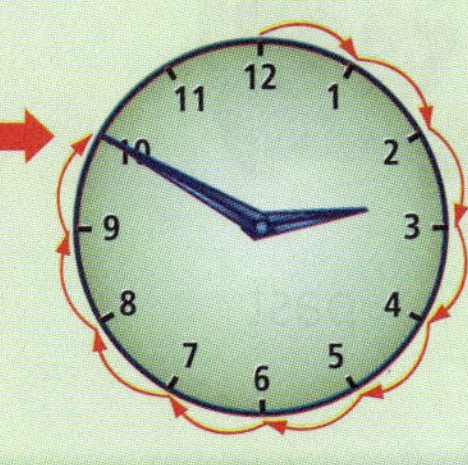

- The hour hand has passed 2.
- The minute hand has moved 5, 10, 15, … 50 minutes from 12.
- The time is **50 minutes past 2**.

2. Write the time shown.

a

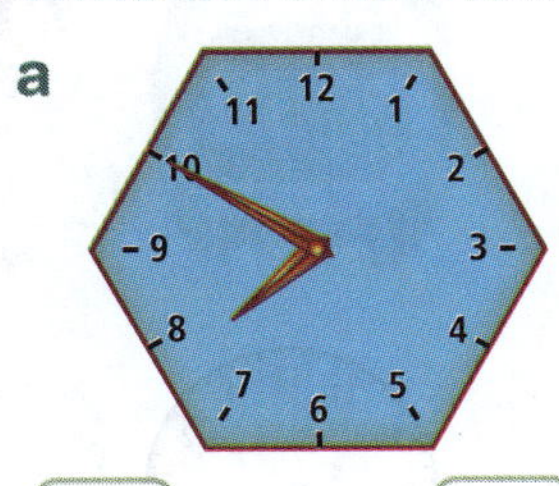

☐ past ☐

☐ minutes to ☐

b

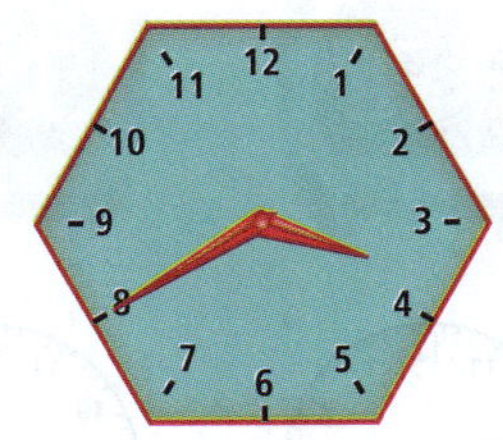

☐ past ☐

☐ minutes to ☐

c

☐ past ☐

☐ to ☐

d

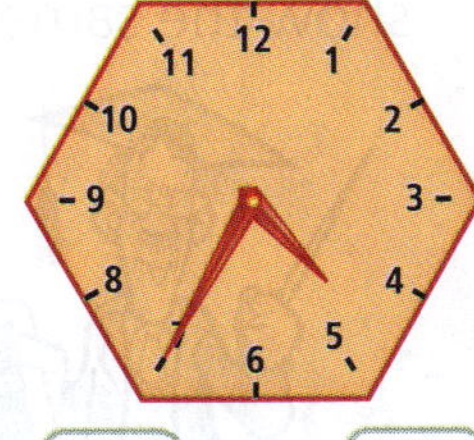

☐ past ☐

☐ to ☐

 • *AUSTRALIAN SIGNPOST MATHS 3* • ISBN 9780655708773

Analog and digital time

1:20
20 past 1

1 Look carefully at each clock face and complete the labels.

a 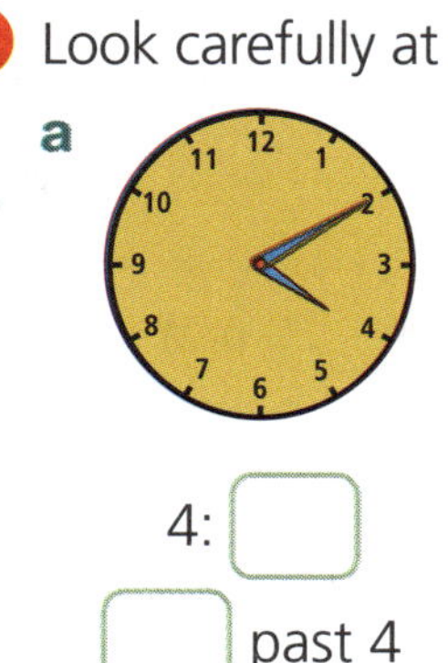
4: ☐
☐ past 4
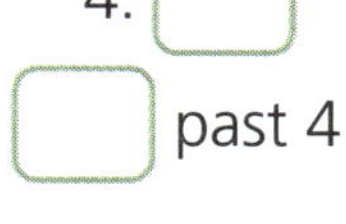

b 
7: ☐
☐ past 7
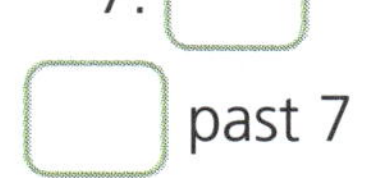

c 
12: ☐
☐ past 12

d 
4: ☐
☐ past 4

e 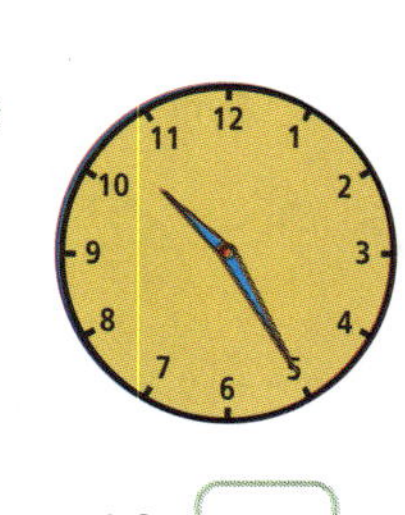
10: ☐
☐ past 10

f 
2: ☐
☐ past 2
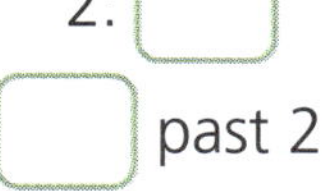

g 
11: ☐
☐ past 11
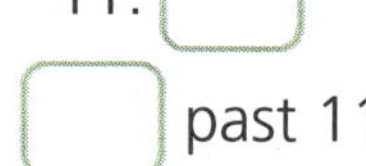

h 
8: ☐
☐ past 8
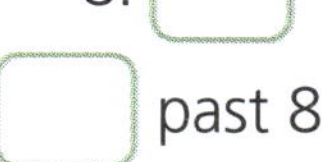

i 
3: ☐
☐ past 3

j 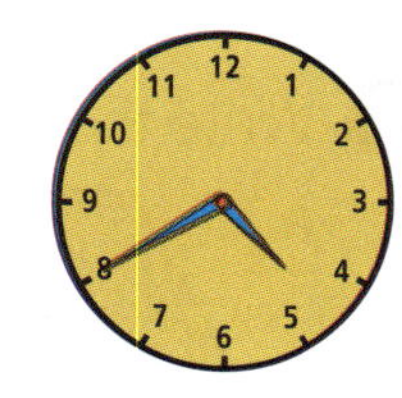
4: ☐
☐ past 4

k 

☐ past ☐

l 

☐ past ☐

m 

☐ past ☐

n 

☐ past ☐

o 

☐ past ☐

p 

☐ past ☐

q 

☐ past ☐

r 

☐ past ☐

s 

☐ past ☐

t 

☐ past ☐

Join the clocks that show the same time.

 • *AUSTRALIAN SIGNPOST MATHS 3* • ISBN 9780655708773

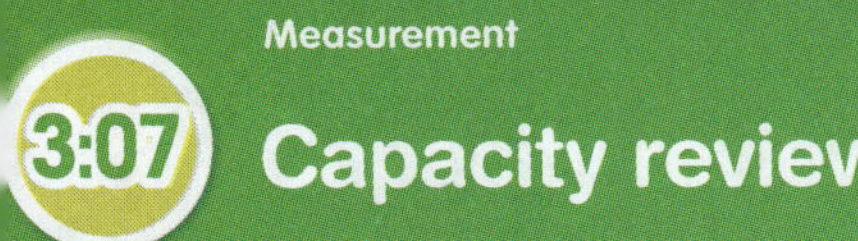

3:07 Capacity review

We can use full cups as an informal unit.

Capacity is how much a container can hold.
This full jug has been poured into these two cups.

If **more than** one and a half cups are used, round to two cups. If **less than** one and a half cups are used, round to 1 cup.

1 Submerging objects in water:

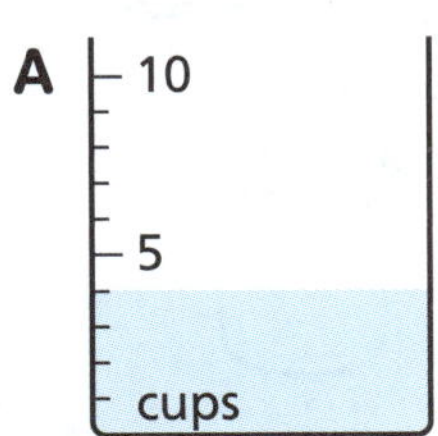

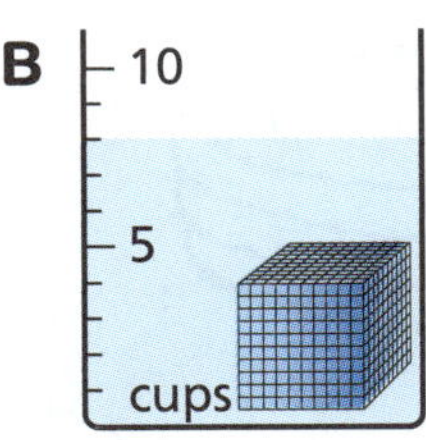

What's your capacity?

a What is the volume of water in container **A**? ☐ cups

b What is the volume of the 1000 block in **B**? ☐ cups

c What would the volume of two 1000s blocks be? ☐ cups

d What is the volume of the can of food in **C**? ☐ cups

e What would the volume of three cans of food be? ☐ cups

f How many cans would be the same volume as one 1000s block? ☐ cans

g How many cans would be the same volume as two 1000s block? ☐ cans

You could investigate and compare the volume of other objects using this method.

ACTIVITY

2 Choose containers and measure the capacity of each.
Use a full cup each time. Record your results in the table below.

Measure to the nearest whole container.

a

	Container	Estimate	Measure
A		cups	cups
B			
C			
D			

b Order the capacities **A**, **B**, **C** and **D** from smallest to largest.

☐

 • *AUSTRALIAN SIGNPOST MATHS 3* • ISBN 9780655708773

3:08 Estimating the litre

A standard unit is a unit that everybody uses.

- The litre is a standard unit for measuring capacity.
- **L** is short for **litre**.
  We write 1 litre as 1 L.

1 Colour in blue the containers that hold more than 1 litre.
Colour in red the containers that hold less than 1 litre.

2 Look at the pictures below. What is the total capacity of each pair of containers?

a drink bottle and esky ______

b storage box and bin ______

c esky and storage box ______

d bin and watering can ______

e Order the capacities **A**, **B**, **C**, **D** and **E** from largest to smallest. ______

A drink bottle: 1 L

B storage box: 50 L

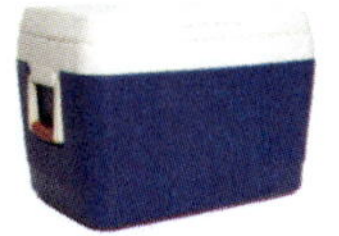
C esky: 10 L

D watering can: 9 L

E bin: 25 L

ACTIVITY

3 Use these two different containers to fill a 1 litre carton.
Write the number of containers needed to completely fill the carton.

Container	Estimated number to fill 1 L	Measured number to fill 1 L
one standard measuring cup		
500 mL small takeaway container		

3:09 The litre

How many cups would we need to fill a litre?

1 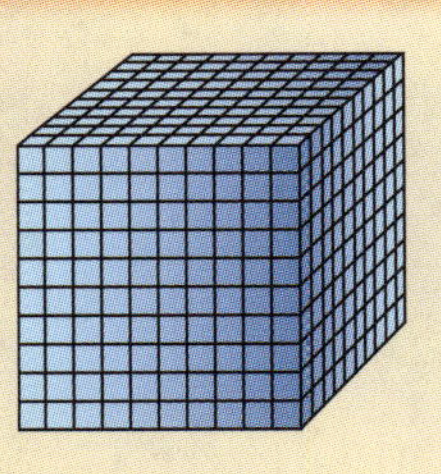 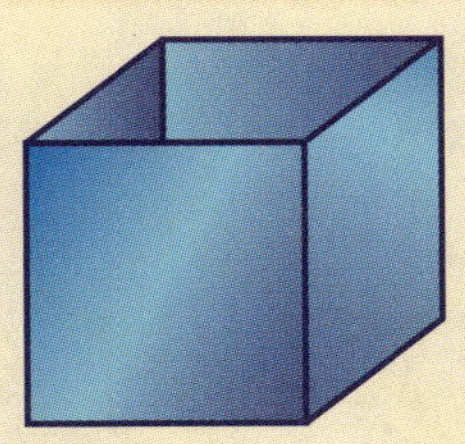

1000 block — 1 litre measure

Compare a 1 litre measure with a 1000 block. Do they have about the same volume? ______

- 1 litre of water has the same volume as a 1000 block.

2 Compare a 1 L, 2 L and 3 L milk container.
Discuss the shape and size of each container.

1 L — 2 L — 3 L

3 **Capacity of a bucket**

Use a 1 L, 2 L and 3 L milk container to find the capacity of a bucket.

Unit	Estimate	Measure
1 L milk container	containers	containers
2 L milk container	containers	containers
3 L milk container	containers	containers

4 **Make a 3 L measuring container**

- Estimate where the 1 L, 2 L and 3 L marks would be on a 3 L milk container.
- Use a funnel to pour 1 L of water into your 3 L milk container.
- Label the 1 L mark on your 3 L container. Repeat and label the 2 L and 3 L marks.
- Discuss: Does 1 L of water always have the same shape?
  Why was there room left at the top or why did it overflow?

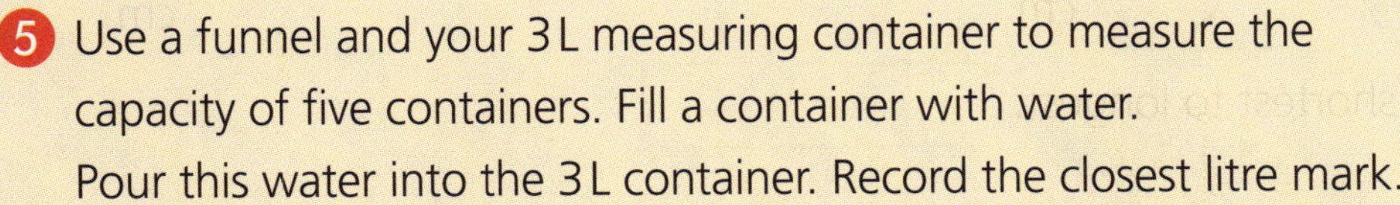

5 Use a funnel and your 3 L measuring container to measure the capacity of five containers. Fill a container with water.
Pour this water into the 3 L container. Record the closest litre mark.

	Closer to 1 L	Closer to 2 L	Closer to 3 L
Containers			

 • *AUSTRALIAN SIGNPOST MATHS 3* • ISBN 9780655708773

3:10 Centimetres

CONCEPT

- **cm** is short for **centimetre**.
- 100 centimetres is the same as 1 metre.

100 cm = 1 m

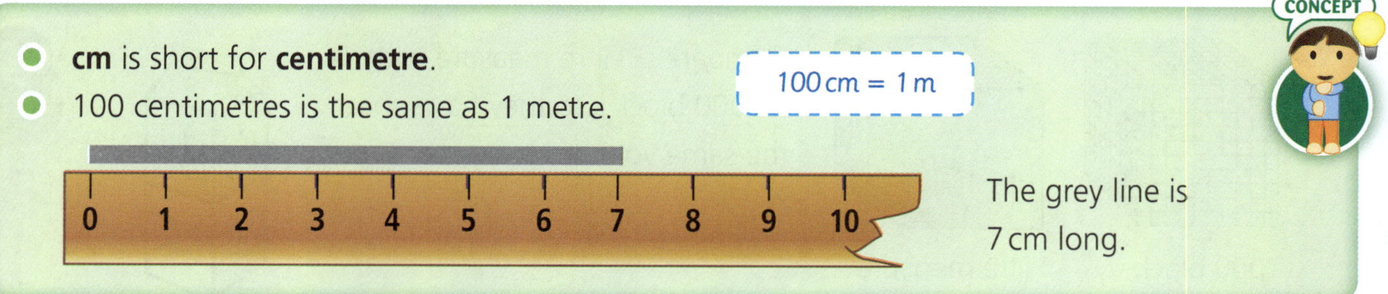

The grey line is 7 cm long.

1 How long is each line?

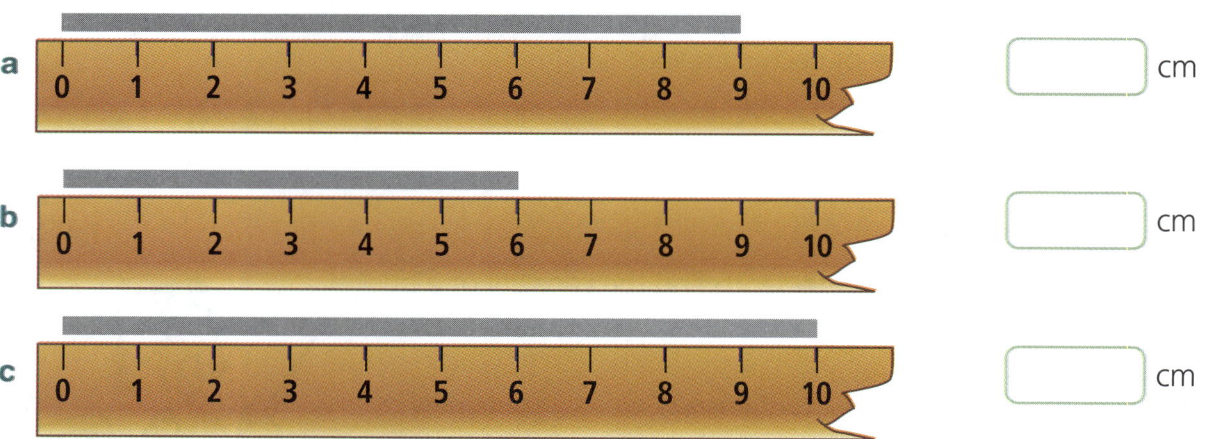

a ___ cm

b ___ cm

c ___ cm

2 Estimate and then measure the length of each item. Write your measurement.

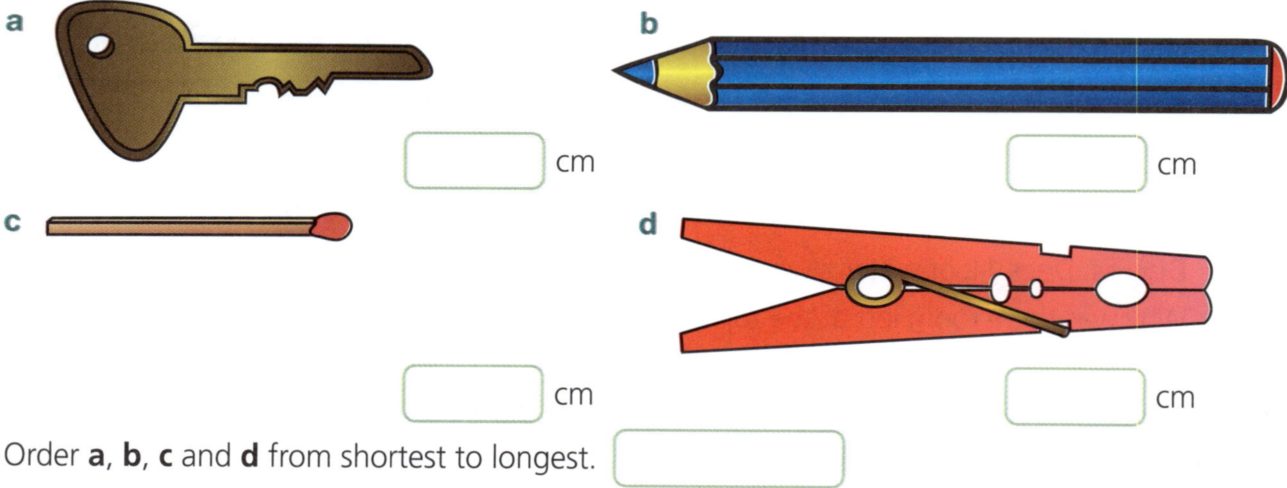

a ___ cm

b ___ cm

c ___ cm

d ___ cm

Order **a**, **b**, **c** and **d** from shortest to longest. ___

3 Estimate and then measure the length of each bar. Write your measurement.

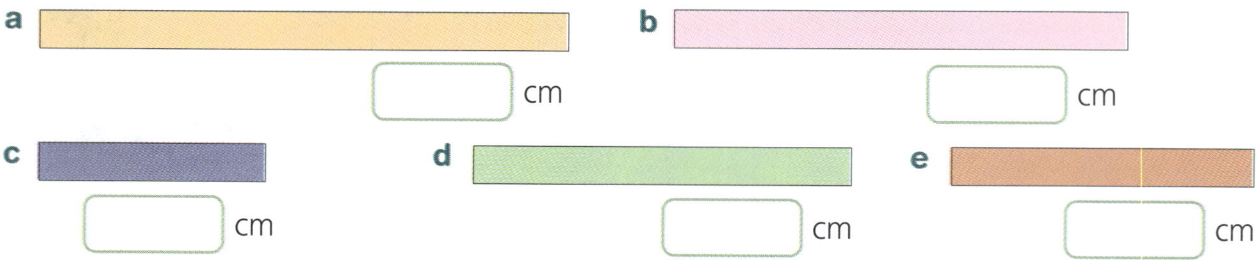

a ___ cm

b ___ cm

c ___ cm

d ___ cm

e ___ cm

3:11 Measuring with centimetres

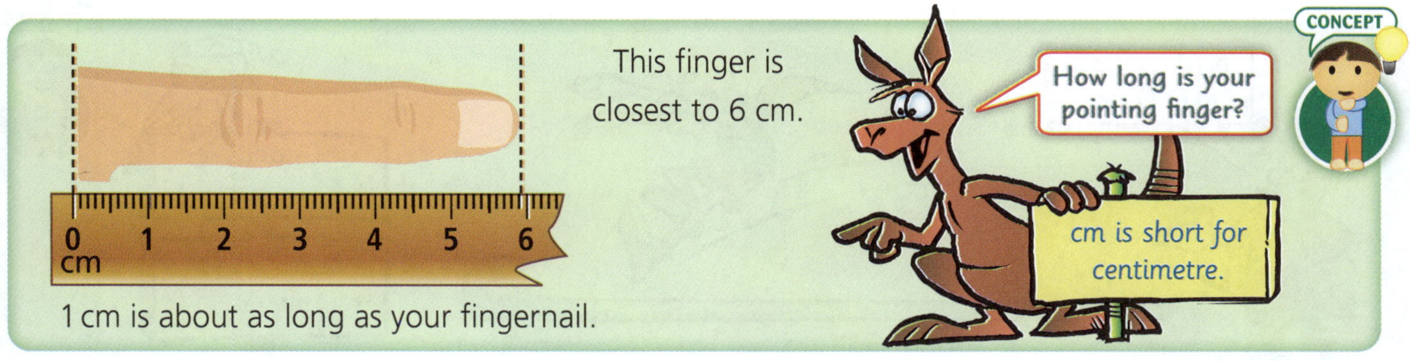

1 Estimate and then measure the length of each bar. Write the measurements.

2 Estimate and then measure the sides of each shape. Write your measurements.

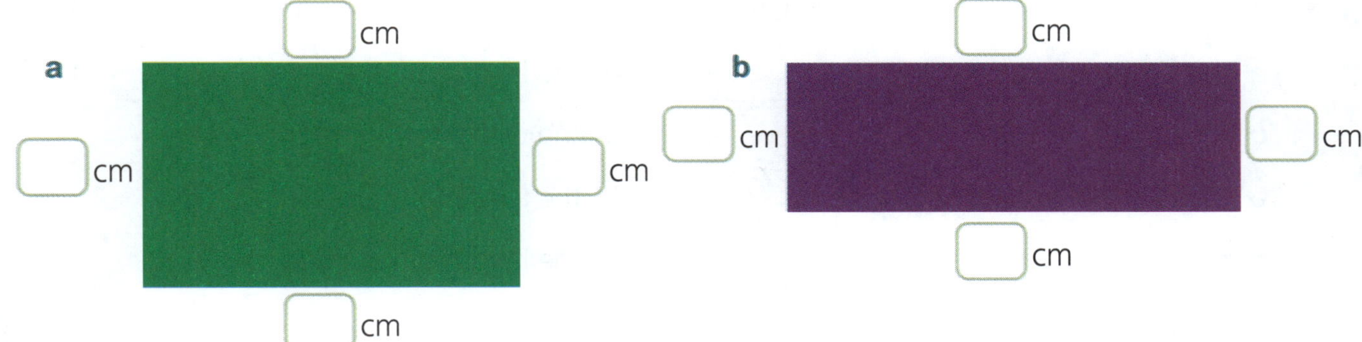

Make your own measuring tape.

You will need: centimetre grid paper, scissors and a pencil.

A paper ruler can measure curved objects.

1 Cut a long strip of 1 cm grid paper.
2 Write numbers to show centimetre marks.
3 Mark the halfway point for each centimetre.

0 1 2 3 4 5 6 7

Use your paper ruler to measure an item in your classroom, then around these body parts. Use your halfway points to help you round to the nearest centimetre. Compare your results.

Draw and label one item	Measurement
	Length: cm
	Width: cm
	Height: cm

Measure around these	Measurement
your wrist	
your ankle	
your pointing finger	

 • *AUSTRALIAN SIGNPOST MATHS 3* • ISBN 9780655708773

3:12 Recording length

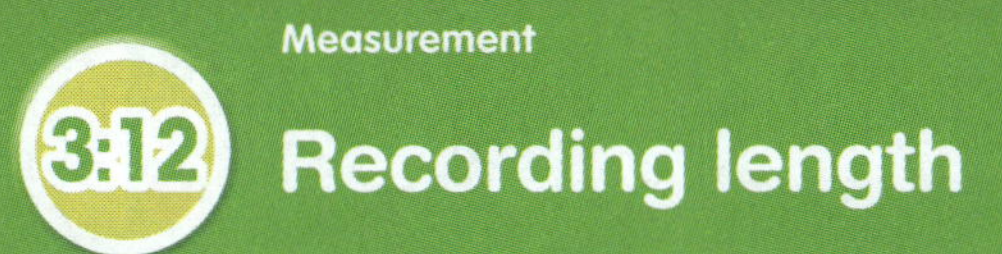

CONCEPT

1. Write the lengths in short form.

a 1 metre 70 centimetres ☐ m ☐ cm **b** 3 metres 36 centimetres ☐ m ☐ cm

c 4 metres 26 centimetres ☐ m ☐ cm **d** 7 metres 13 centimetres ☐ m ☐ cm

e 6 metres 83 centimetres ☐ m ☐ cm **f** 5 metres 42 centimetres ☐ m ☐ cm

2. Would you use metres (m) or centimetres (cm) to measure the following things?

a the height of your house ☐ **b** the length of an eraser ☐

c the length of your hair ☐ **d** the width of your room ☐

e the width of your thumb ☐ **f** the length of a pencil ☐

g the length of a path ☐ **h** the height of your desk ☐

INVESTIGATION

- Find some items that you think would match the lengths in this table.
  Use a tape measure to measure the items and complete the table.
- Use a trundle wheel to find these lengths:
  - the length of a fence
  - the width of the school playground
  - the distance from your classroom to the office.
- Measure the length of your steps.
  - How many of your steps make 1 metre? ☐
    Now roll a ball along the ground.
  - It rolled ☐ steps.
  - That is about ☐ metres.

Length	Item	Measured length
50 cm		
1 m		
13 cm		
2 m		
4 m		

trundle wheel

3:13 Perimeter

cm is short for centimetres.
1 metre = 100 centimetres
1 m = 100 cm

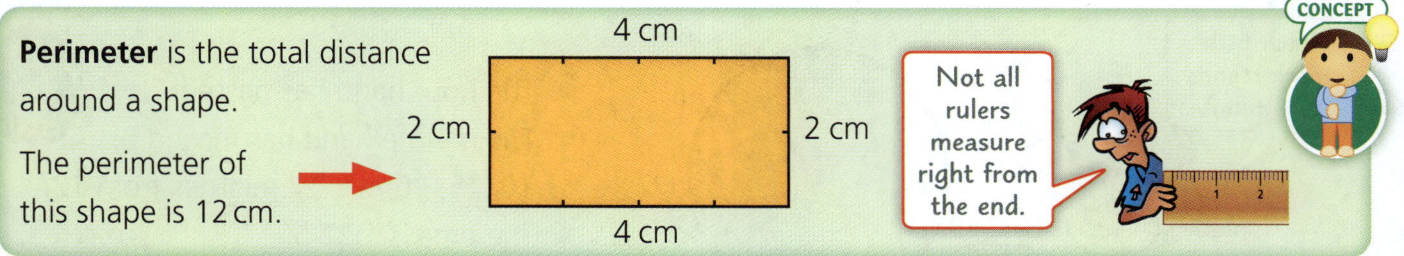

1. Estimate and then measure the perimeter of each shape.

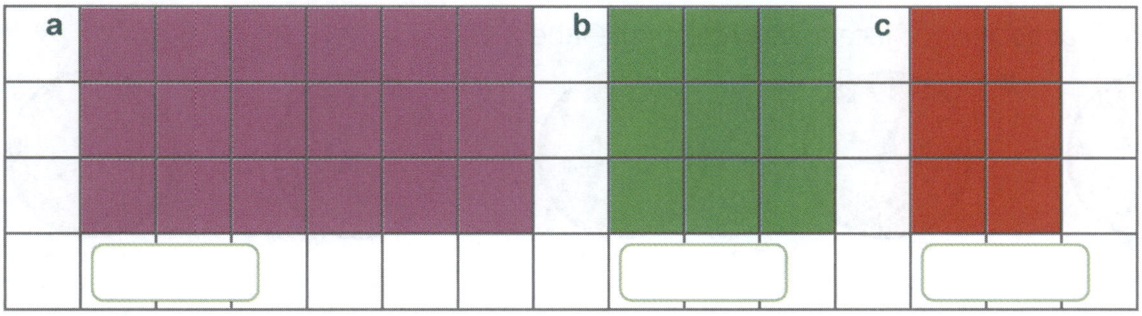

a

b

c

d

e

f

g ☐ cm ☐ cm ☐ cm ☐ cm

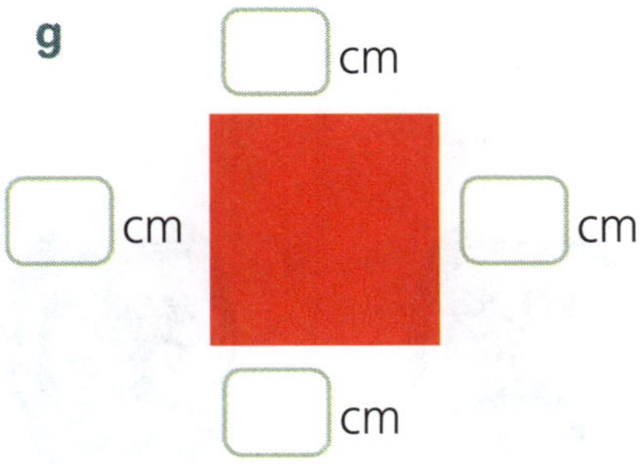

perimeter = ☐ cm

h ☐ cm ☐ cm ☐ cm

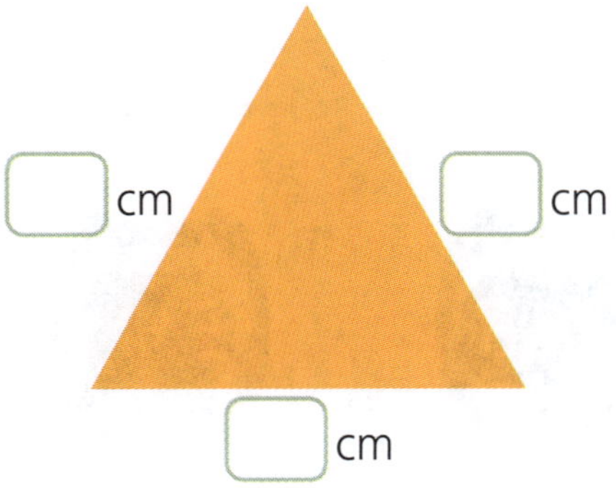

perimeter = ☐ cm

i ☐ cm ☐ cm ☐ cm

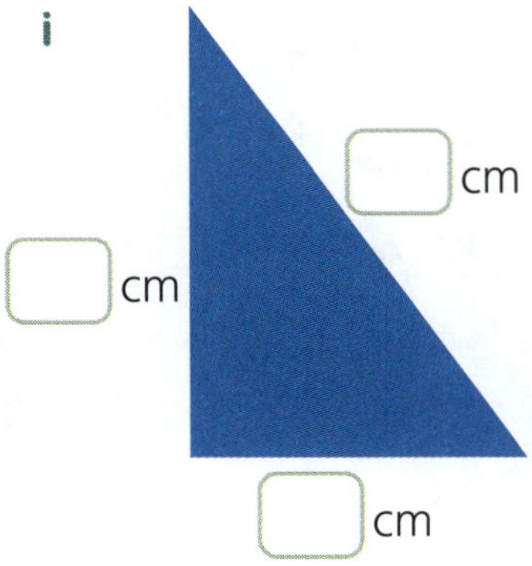

perimeter = ☐ cm

j Order parts **a** – **c** above from shortest to longest perimeter. ☐

2. Write the lengths in centimetres.

a 1 m 26 cm ☐ **b** 1 m 73 cm ☐

My fingernail is 1 cm wide.

3. Write the lengths as metres and centimetres.

a 238 cm ☐ **b** 213 cm ☐

c 347 cm ☐ **d** 724 cm ☐

3:14 Analog and digital time

60 minutes makes 1 hour.

CONCEPT

- The hour hand has passed 1.
- The minute hand has moved 5, 10, 15, 20, 21, 22 minutes from 12.
- The time is **1:22** or **22 minutes past 1**.

1 Look carefully at each clock face and complete the labels.

a 10: ☐	b 11: ☐	c 3: ☐	d 2: ☐	e 4: ☐
☐ past 10	☐ past 11	☐ past 3	☐ past 2	☐ past 4
f 5: ☐	g 2: ☐	h 4: ☐	i 7: ☐	j 2: ☐
☐ past 5	☐ past 2	☐ past 4	☐ past 7	☐ past 2
k 9:34	l 2:28	m 5:41	n 8:47	o 6:59
☐ past ☐	☐ past ☐	☐ past ☐	☐ past ☐	☐ past ☐

2 Draw lines to join the same times together.

a

11:36	12 minutes past 6
6:12	57 minutes past 9
9:57	eleven thirty-six

b

1:43	26 minutes past 8
8:26	five-oh-seven
5:07	43 minutes past 1

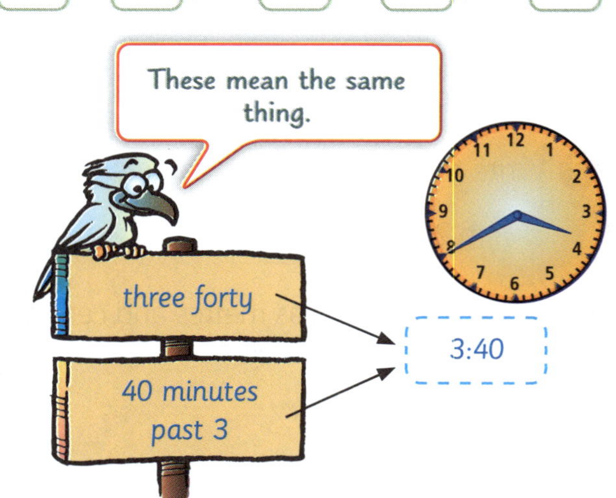

 • *AUSTRALIAN SIGNPOST MATHS 3* • ISBN 9780655708773

Analog time

Analog clocks have 60 1-minute marks around the clock.

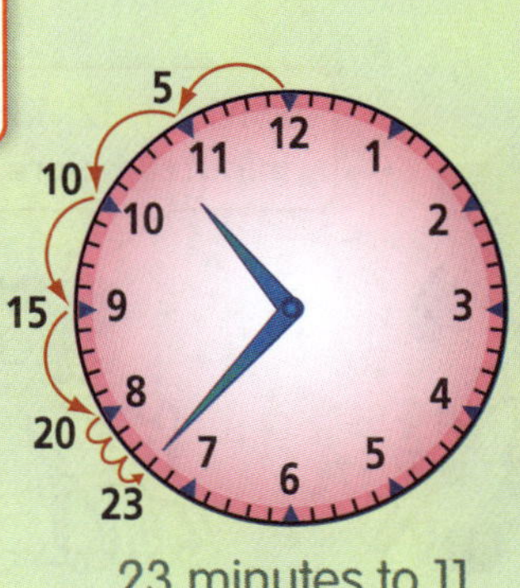

23 minutes to 11

- The hour hand is approaching 11.
- The minute hand has 23 minutes to go before it reaches the 12.
- The time is **23 to 11**.

1. Write the time shown.

a  ☐ to ☐

b  ☐ to ☐

c  ☐ to ☐

d  ☐ to ☐

e  ☐ to ☐

f  ☐ to ☐

g  ☐ to ☐

h  ☐ to ☐

2. Show the time given.

a 

17 to 3

b 

14 to 8

c 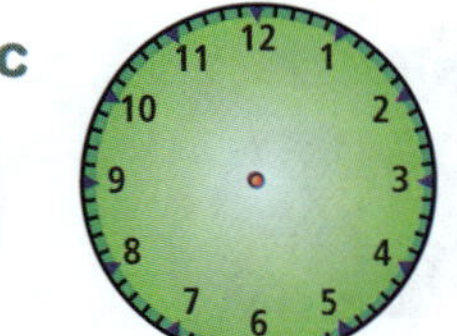

28 to 1

d 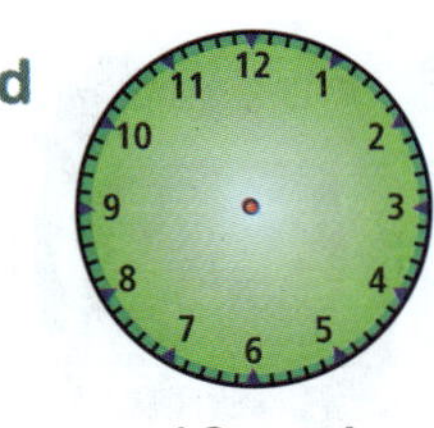

12 to 4

3. Write the time that is four minutes after.

a 20 to 6 ☐ **b** 15 to 9 ☐ **c** 25 to 3 ☐
d 20 to 10 ☐ **e** 25 to 11 ☐ **f** 10 to 7 ☐

4. Write the time that is three minutes before.

a 5 to 6 ☐ **b** 15 to 11 ☐ **c** 20 to 9 ☐
d 10 to 12 ☐ **e** 20 to 8 ☐ **f** 12 o'clock ☐

3:16 Analog and digital time

Count by 5s around the clock then count on the ones.

CONCEPT

22 past 5
5:22

14 to 6
5:46

1 Write the time shown.

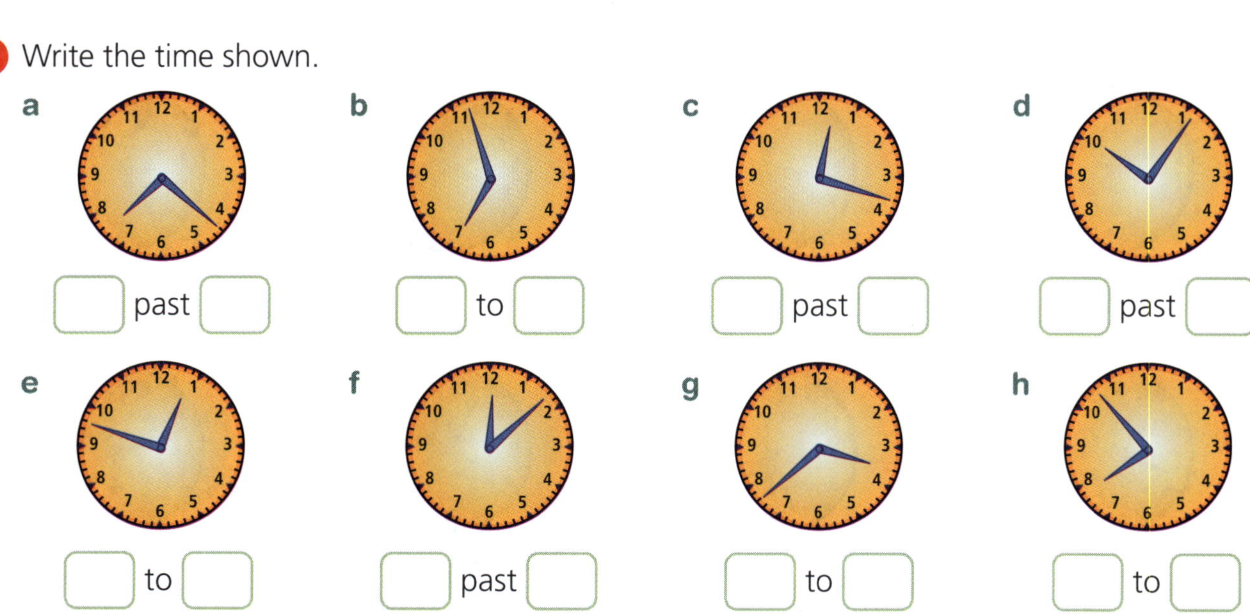

a ☐ past ☐
b ☐ to ☐
c ☐ past ☐
d ☐ past ☐
e ☐ to ☐
f ☐ past ☐
g ☐ to ☐
h ☐ to ☐

2 Write the time shown.

a ☐ past ☐
b ☐ past ☐
c ☐ past ☐
d ☐ past ☐
e ☐ past ☐

f ☐ to ☐
g ☐ to ☐
h ☐ to ☐
i ☐ to ☐
j ☐ to ☐

 • *AUSTRALIAN SIGNPOST MATHS 3* • ISBN 9780655708773

The kilogram

We can measure mass in kilograms.

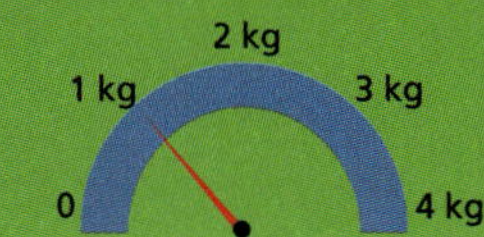

CONCEPT

1 litre of water has a mass of 1 kilogram.

ACTIVITY

1 **a** On one side of a balance scale, put a 1 kilogram mass. On the other side of the scale, put a bag of sand that you estimate to have the same mass.

b Does it balance? [ ] Was the bag of sand lighter or heavier than 1 kg? [ ]

c Repeat this activity with nails or stones instead of sand.

2 Estimate whether the items listed below are heavier or lighter than 1 kilogram. Use balance scales to check.

Item	Estimate (less than 1 kg?)	Measurement (less than 1 kg?)
3 pencils	yes	yes
10 books		
5 shoes		

Item	Estimate (less than 1 kg?)	Measurement (less than 1 kg?)
drink bottle	yes	yes
pencil case		
lunch box		

Find some other items to weigh.

INVESTIGATION

3 **The mass of water**

On balance scales, place a milk container with 1 L of water on one side and a 1 kg mass with an identical milk container on the other side. Do they balance? [ ]
Discuss why or why not.

How much does 1L of water weigh?

3:18 Comparing masses

CONCEPT

ACTIVITY

1 Complete this table. Estimate first, then use a balance scale and a 1 kg mass to check.

Item	Less than 1 kg	About 1 kg	More than 1 kg
book			
large milk container			
full drink bottle			
vase			

2 Repeat this activity with other items in the classroom.
Draw each item on this chart to show where it belongs.

Less than 1 kg							
About 1 kg	Milk 1L						
More than 1 kg							

3 Collect labels from packages that show kilograms. Display the labels on a chart.

4 Circle the items that would have a mass greater than 2 kilograms (a 2 L container of milk).

a television **b** ant **c** pair of socks **d** car battery
e football **f** dog collar **g** horse **h** ruler
i slice of bread **j** spoon **k** table **l** refrigerator

5 Circle the items that would be measured in kilograms.

a packet of jelly beans **b** bag of potatoes **c** suitcase of clothes
d jar of jam **e** bag of onions **f** a person
g packet of sultanas **h** packet of chips **i** sack of flour

3:19 Using the kilogram

Do you think 7 cockatoos would weigh more than 3 kg?

1 Use the short form to write these measurements.

a 3 kilograms ☐ **b** 10 kilograms ☐ **c** 8 kilograms ☐

d 5 kilograms ☐ **e** 7 kilograms ☐ **f** 11 kilograms ☐

2 Circle the items that would have a mass greater than 1 kilogram.

a bicycle **b** chair **c** nail **d** your teacher

e desk **f** marble **g** computer **h** brick

i matchbox **j** car tyre **k** large dog **l** golf ball

Flour 25 kg

ONIONS 20 kg

Grapes 3 kg

Meat 7 kg

Laundry Powder 4 kg

CHEESE 1 kg

3 Look at the pictures. What is the total mass of the items together?

a grapes and cheese ☐ **b** meat and grapes ☐

c flour and laundry powder ☐ **d** onions and meat ☐

e onions and grapes ☐ **f** cheese and meat ☐

g flour and onions ☐ **h** cheese and onions ☐

4 Circle the labels that are written correctly.

a 9 kg **b** 9 KG **c** 7 kg **d** 6 k.g. **e** 11 Kg

f 14 kg **g** 3 kg **h** 17 kg. **i** 21 kgs **j** 32 kg

Choose and check

- Choose 10 classroom items that you think are heavier than 1 kg. Use balance scales and a 1 kg mass to check.
- Choose 10 items that you think are lighter than 1 kg. Use balance scales to check.
- Without measuring, arrange six different items in order from lightest to heaviest. Use balance scales to check if you were right.

 • *AUSTRALIAN SIGNPOST MATHS 3* • ISBN 9780655708773

Area

For larger areas, we need a larger unit.

1 Write the area of each shape.

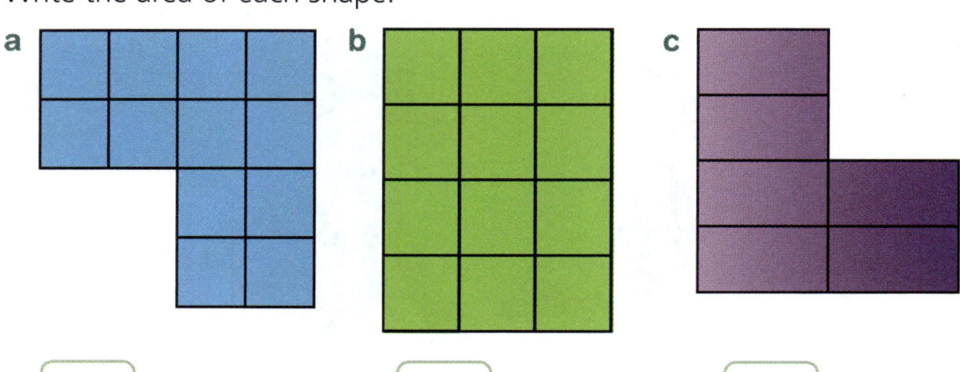

a ☐ squares   b ☐ squares   c ☐ rectangles   d ☐ rectangles

2 Shape **A** has 2 rows of 4 (or 4 columns of 2). Describe the area of shape:

a **B** ☐

b **C** ☐

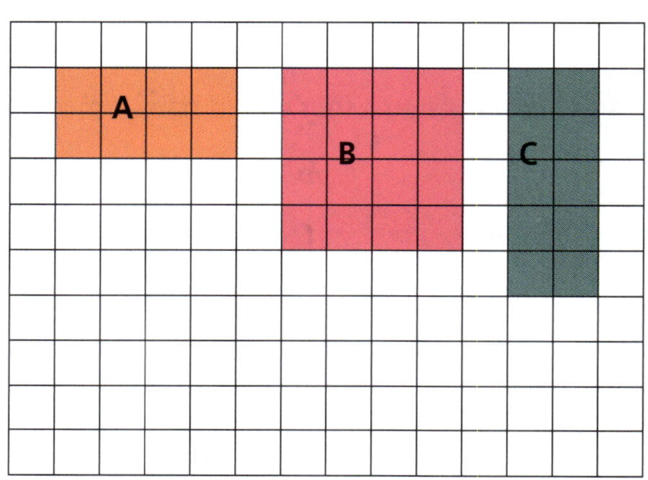

Draw a shape with:

c 3 rows of 4. Label it with a **D**.

d 2 columns of 2. Label it with an **E**.

Which shape has:

e the largest area? ☐

f the smallest area? ☐

3 Books were used to cover this desk.

a Did the books cover the desk exactly? ☐

b Estimate the amount of overhang. ☐

c If we could cut the books, how many books would cover the table? ☐

d Do you think a book would be a good unit of area? ☐

Why or why not? ☐

Visualise to estimate, then use sheets of A4 paper to measure the area of a desktop.
Measure and compare other larger areas using this method.

Remember:
no gaps, no overlaps.

3:21 Area

3 rows of 5

The area of this array is 3 × 5 squares.

1 **a** How many squares make up the area of each shape?

L

M

N

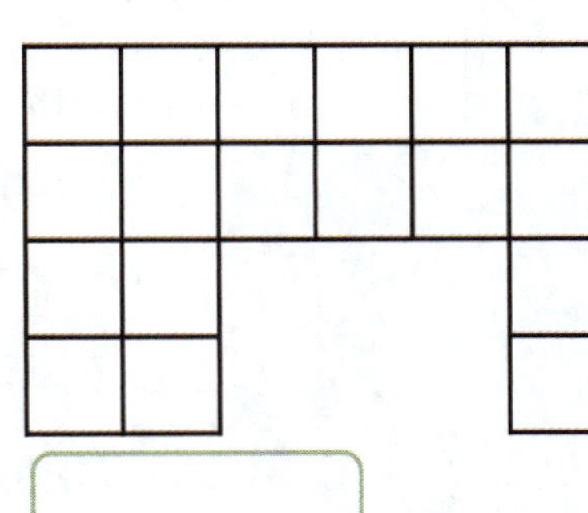

b Write **L**, **M** and **N** in order from least area to most area.

2 Estimate which area is the largest. Count the number of squares and discuss what you find.

X

Y

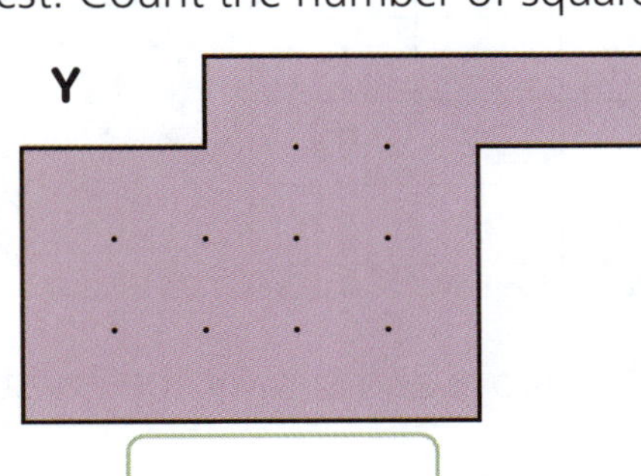

Z

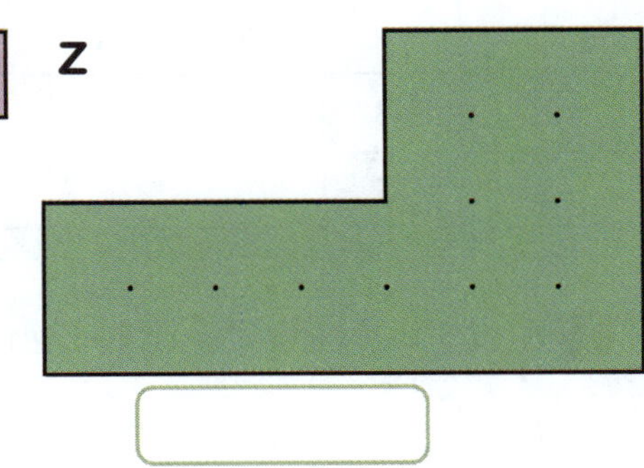

3 **a** Describe each area as an array. How many times does the square cover these areas?

A

× squares

squares

B

× squares

squares

C

× squares

squares

b Order these areas, **A**, **B** and **C**, from smallest to largest.

FUN SPOT

Trace your hand on 1 cm grid paper. Count any square where more than half of the square is within your hand outline. Do not count any square where less than half is within your outline.

Area of your hand = squares

Compare the area of your hand with others in the class.

 • *AUSTRALIAN SIGNPOST MATHS 3* • ISBN 9780655708773

3:22 The calendar

There are 7 days in a week and 365 days in a year.

There are 12 months in each year. How many days in each month?

30 days has September, April, June and November. All the rest have 31 except for February alone, which has 28 days clear but 29 in each leap year.

November 2024						
Sun	Mon	Tues	Wed	Thurs	Fri	Sat
					1	2
3	4	5	6	7	8	9
10	11	12	13	14	15	16
17	18	19	20	21	22	23
24	25	26	27	28	29	30

How to know the number of days in each month.

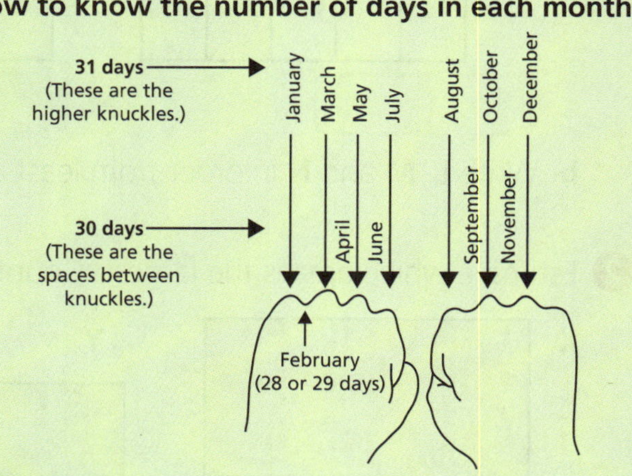

1. Study the calendar of November above and answer the questions.
   - **a** What day of the week is 1 November?
   - **b** What day of the week is 17 November?
   - **c** What is the date of the first Friday?
   - **d** What is the date of the first Monday?
   - **e** What is the date of the last Saturday?
   - **f** Write the dates of all the Mondays in November.
   - **g** How many Thursdays are in November?
   - **h** How many weekend days are there in November?

2. How many days are in the following?
   - **a** one week
   - **b** one fortnight
   - **c** January
   - **d** June
   - **e** March
   - **f** May
   - **g** April
   - **h** July
   - **i** October
   - **j** September
   - **k** November
   - **l** August

3. Write these dates in short form.
   - **a** first Sunday in November
   - **b** last Friday in November
   - **c** last Wednesday in November

13/11/24

When we write dates in short form we use numbers.

The calendar

A calendar shows how a year is divided into months, weeks and days.

Study the calendar for November 2024 to January 2025.

November 2024						
Sun	Mon	Tues	Wed	Thurs	Fri	Sat
					1	2
3	4	5	6	7	8	9
10	11	12	13	14	15	16
17	18	19	20	21	22	23
24	25	26	27	28	29	30

December 2024						
Sun	Mon	Tues	Wed	Thurs	Fri	Sat
1	2	3	4	5	6	7
8	9	10	11	12	13	14
15	16	17	18	19	20	21
22	23	24	25	26	27	28
29	30	31				

January 2025						
Sun	Mon	Tues	Wed	Thurs	Fri	Sat
			1	2	3	4
5	6	7	8	9	10	11
12	13	14	15	16	17	18
19	20	21	22	23	24	25
26	27	28	29	30	31	

1. If the date is November 11, how many weeks and days will it be until my birthday on January 17?

2. If today is 2/11/24, how many weeks and days is it until Christmas Day?

3. Akash played cricket every Saturday from November 9 until December 21 for 5 hours. How many hours of cricket did he play?

4. I earn $3 pocket money every Friday. I need to save $12 so I can buy a new book. What is the earliest date that I could save the money if today's date is November 5?

5. Priya did gymnastics for 2 hours every Monday and Thursday during November. How many hours of gymnastics did she do during that time?

6. On November 18, Mia has 7 weeks and 5 days to wait until it is her birthday. What is the date of Mia's birthday?

7. Circle these dates on the calendar: 14/11/24, 18/12/24, 29/1/25, 30/11/24, 1/1/25

Make up your own question about this calendar. See if your classmates can solve it.

 • *AUSTRALIAN SIGNPOST MATHS 3* • ISBN 9780655708773

3:24 The gram

500 grams is half of a kilogram.
250 grams is quarter of a kilogram.

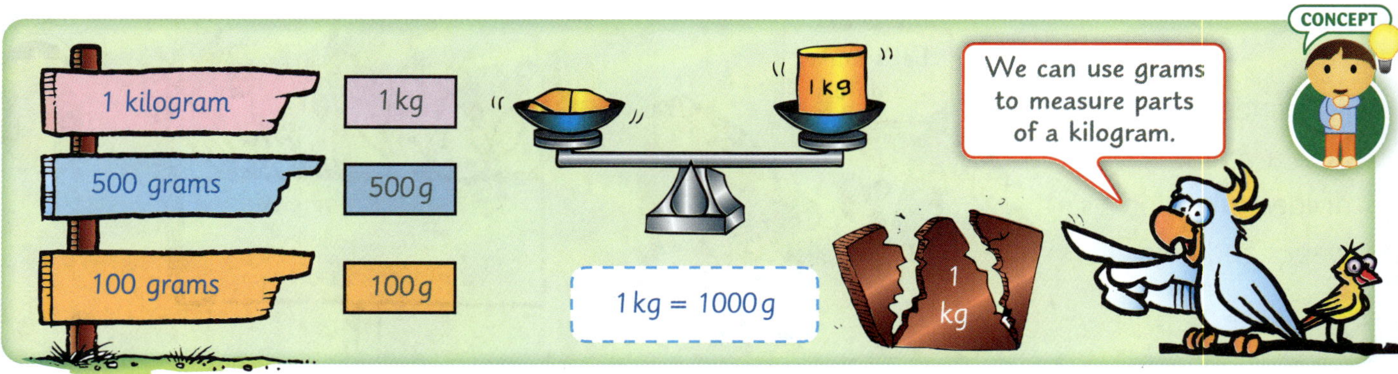

ACTIVITY

1. Using balance scales, slowly fill a plastic bag with sand until it balances a 500 g mass. Seal the bag and label it 500 g. Prepare 3 more bags like this.
   - Use balance scales to find:
     - How many 500 g bags balance a 1 kg mass? ☐
     - How many 500 g bags balance a 2 kg mass? ☐
   - Use balance scales and your bags of sand to complete the table.

Mass	Items in the classroom
less than 500 g	
between 500 g and 1 kg	
more than 1 kg	

2. Write the mass in short form.
   - **a** forty grams ☐
   - **b** one hundred grams ☐
   - **c** six hundred grams ☐
   - **d** three hundred grams ☐

3. Look at the pictures. What is the total mass of the items together?
   - **a** lollies and orange ☐
   - **b** cheese and jam ☐
   - **c** chocolate and jam ☐
   - **d** orange and chocolate ☐

4. Kitchen scales can be used to measure mass. Use the marks on the scales to write the mass to the closest mark shown.

a

☐

b

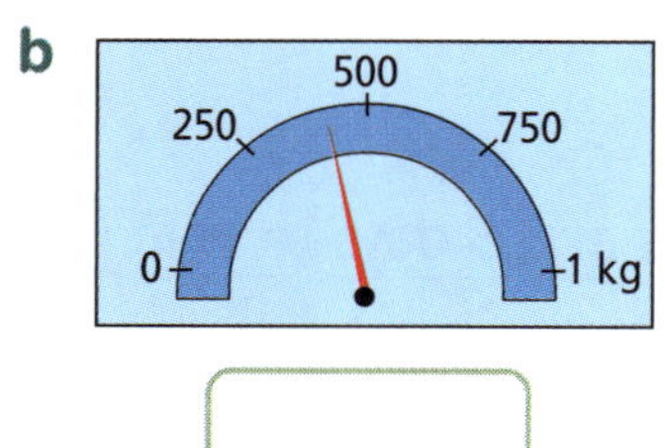

☐

c

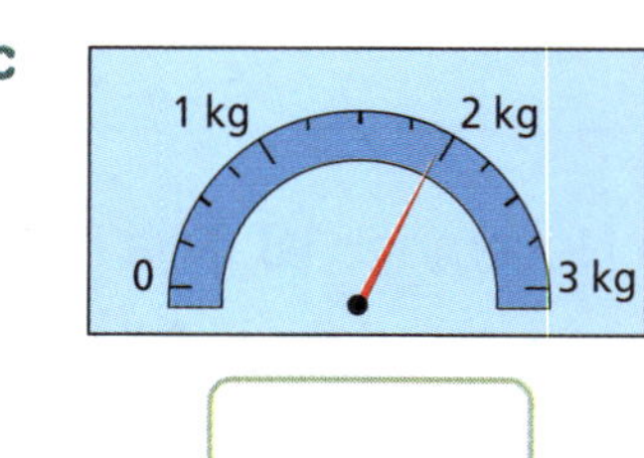

☐

 • *AUSTRALIAN SIGNPOST MATHS 3* • ISBN 9780655708773

Using grams

One millilitre of water has a mass of about 1 gram.

CONCEPT

Analog and digital scales can be used to measure mass.

Investigate what the marks mean on different scales.

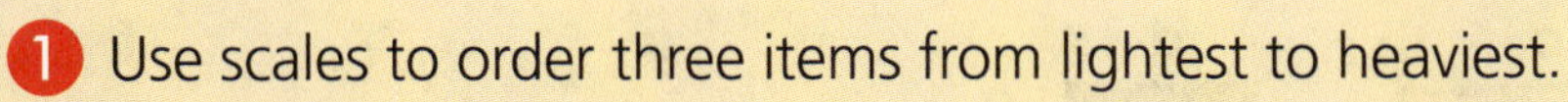

ACTIVITY

1 Use scales to order three items from lightest to heaviest.

2 Use scales to find items that have a mass of about 500 g.

3 Place a pile of tens blocks on the top of your scales.

- How many did you use? ☐ tens blocks
- What was the total mass of your tens blocks? ☐
- What is the mass of a tens block? ☐

4 Write the mass in short form.

a sixty grams ☐
b one hundred grams ☐
c forty kilograms ☐
d thirty grams ☐
e nine kilograms ☐
f seventy grams ☐

5 Which unit of measurement (**g** or **kg**) has been left off each package?

a

b

c

d

e

6 Use the marks on the scales to write the mass closest to the mark shown.

a
0 g, 200, 400, 600, 800, 1 kg

b
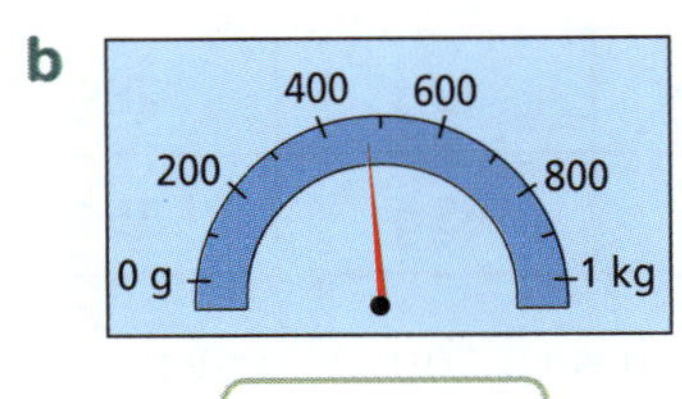

c
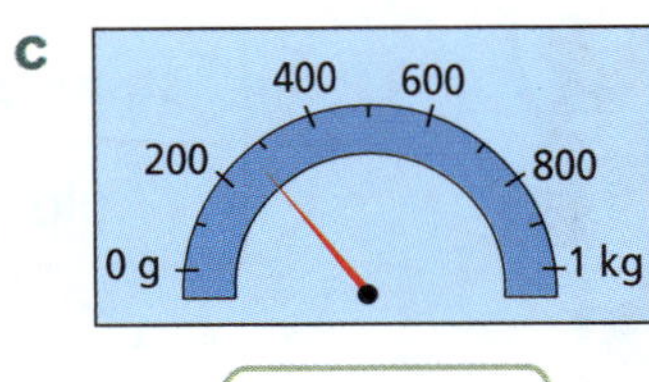

 • *AUSTRALIAN SIGNPOST MATHS 3* • ISBN 9780655708773

Mass problem solving

Always show the units in your answer.

1 Zara's boat can only carry a mass of 30 kg or less.

Use the table to find which two creatures she can take with her.

	Mass
Zara	23 kg
dog	6 kg
duck	3 kg
pelican	2 kg

2 Write **g** for grams or **kg** for kilograms to show what unit would be used to measure these items.

a 

b 

c 

d 

e 

f 

3 What would the contents of my trolley weigh if it held:

a the jam and the chips?

b the dog food and the flour?

c the cake and the tuna?

d the cake, the jam and the tuna?

4 What is the difference in mass between these items?

a the fridge and the dishwasher

b the stove and the washing machine

c the fridge and the stove

d What is the total mass of all these items?

Item	Mass
fridge	23 kg
washing machine	78 kg
dishwasher	18 kg
stove	69 kg

INVESTIGATION

- Find the difference between the largest recorded mass and my fruit's mass.

Fruit	My fruit's mass	Largest recorded mass	Difference between the largest and my fruit
watermelon	9 kg	119 kg	119 kg – 9 kg = kg
pineapple	18 kg	28 kg	
strawberry	12 g	289 g	
plum	65 g	354 g	

- Find photos of the largest recorded fruits.

 • *AUSTRALIAN SIGNPOST MATHS 3* • ISBN 9780655708773

The millilitre

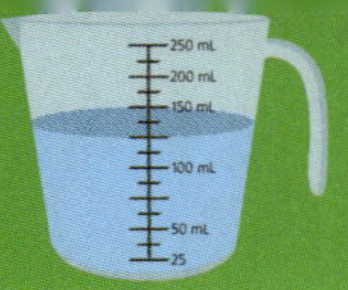

How much water do I have?

- Millilitres are used to measure capacities smaller than 1 litre.
- **mL** stands for millilitres.
- One litre is **1000 mL**.
  Half a litre is **500 mL**.
  A quarter of a litre is **250 mL**.

Capacity is the space within a container.

Volume is the space taken up by an object.

1 Which measure (**L** or **mL**) has been left off each label?

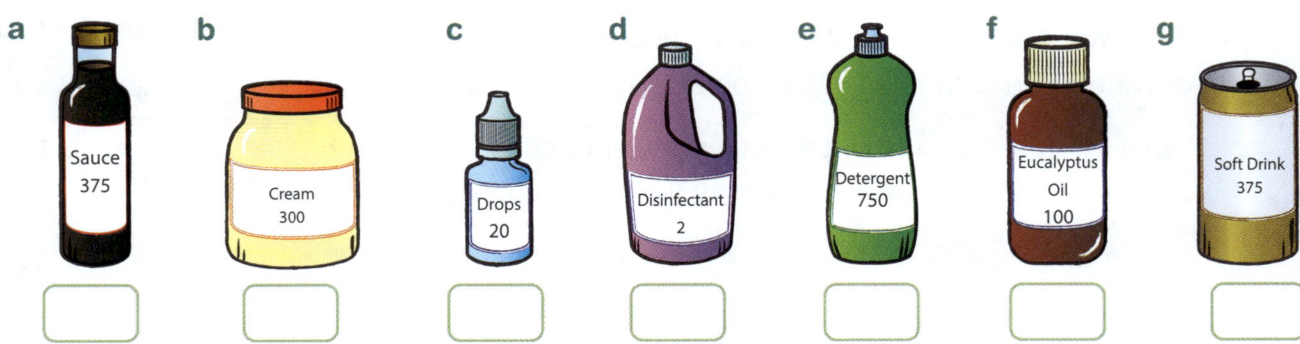

2 Research the capacity of four familiar containers you would find in a shop. Complete the table.

Container	Capacity	Order (smallest to largest)
A		
B		
C		
D		

Make a collage of familiar containers with each capacity label displayed.

Which of the containers on this page is closest to a 600 mL bottle of water?

3 **a** Write the closest measuring line for each volume of water.

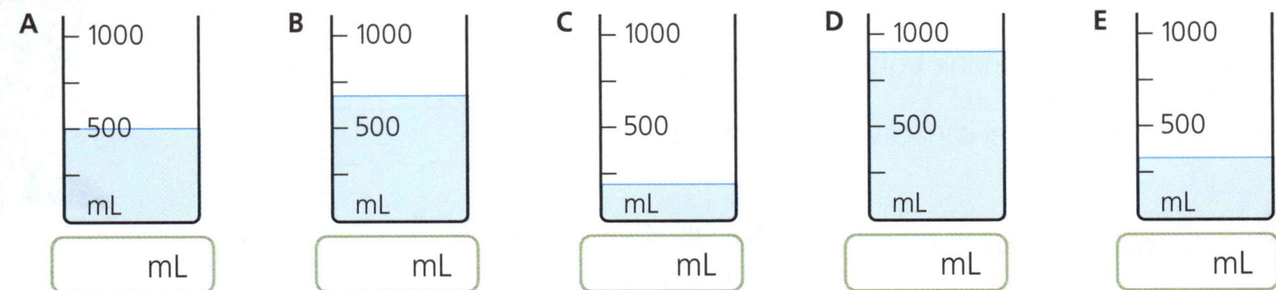

mL mL mL mL mL

b Order these volumes of water from smallest to largest (**A**, **B**, **C**, **D** and **E**).

c On container **C** above, draw a water level of 750 mL.

ACTIVITY

Use the marks on a measuring container to pour certain measures into a cup.

1. It takes 6 cups to fill my water bottle to the top.

   a How many half cups would it take to fill my water bottle to the top? ☐ half cups

   b How many cups would it take to fill 5 water bottles? ☐ cups

2. I completed this chart after measuring the capacity of containers **A** to **D**.

	Container	Estimate	Measure
A	bottle	3 cups	4 cups
B	jug	5 cups	6 cups
C	vase	3 cups	3 cups
D	tub	34 cups	40 cups

   a How many vases of water would I need to fill a jug? ☐

   b How many cups of water did I estimate it would take to fill a vase and a bottle? ☐ cups

   c What was my estimate of the total number of cups of water needed to fill all of the containers? ☐ cups

   What was the measure of the total number of cups of water needed to fill all of the containers? ☐ cups

   How many more cups of water were needed than I estimated? ☐ cups

   d How many bottles of water would I need to fill the tub? ☐ bottles

3.

drink bottle: 500 mL | storage box: 50 L | esky: 10 L | watering can: 9 L | bin: 25 L

   a How many full bins would I need to fill the storage box? ☐ bins

   b How many full eskys would I need to fill the storage box? ☐ eskys

   c How many full watering cans would I need to fill the bin? ☐ watering cans

   d How many full drink bottles would I need to fill the esky? ☐ drink bottles

   e What is the total capacity of the last four containers? ☐

4.

Container	Capacity
bucket	10 L
bin	
esky	50 L
storage box	30 L

   a The total capacity of these containers is 150 L. What is the capacity of the bin? ☐

   b Which of these containers would I need for a total capacity of 110 L? ☐

3:29 The millimetre

Millimetres can be used to measure small lengths more accurately.
1 cm = 10 mm

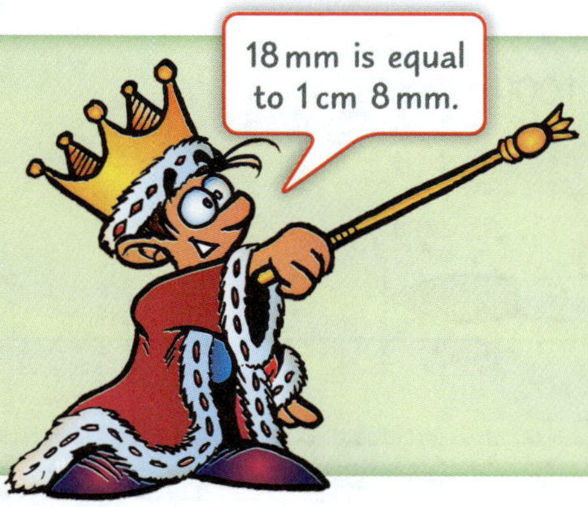

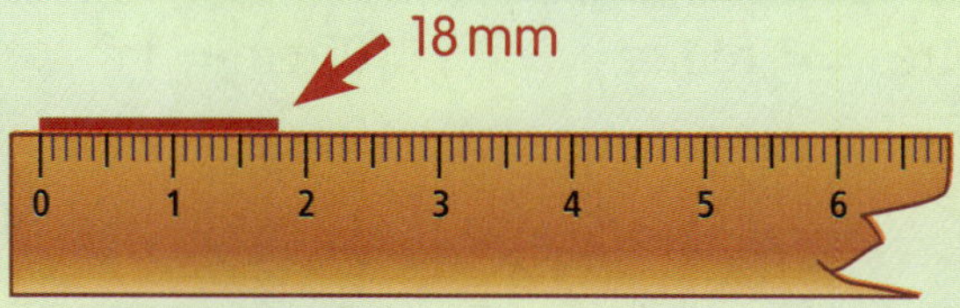

CONCEPT

18 mm is equal to 1 cm 8 mm.

18 mm

1 centimetre is divided into 10 millimetres.

mm is short for millimetres.

1 cm = 10 mm

1 Write the length of each red line.

a ☐ mm

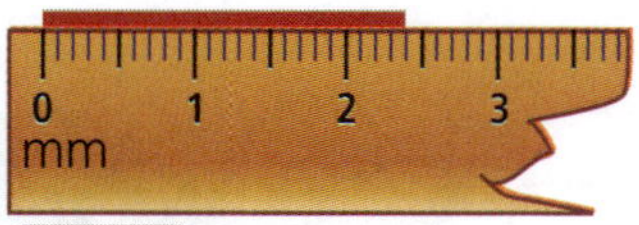

b ☐ mm

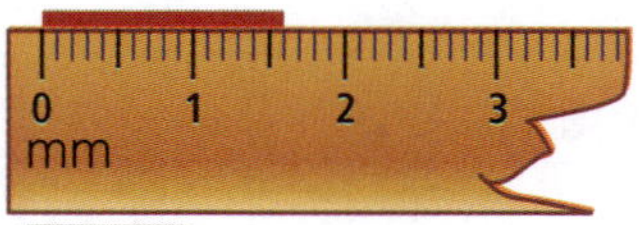

c ☐ mm

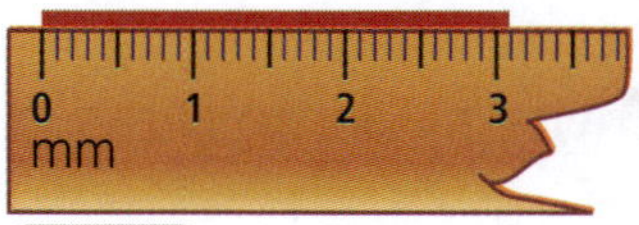

d ☐ mm

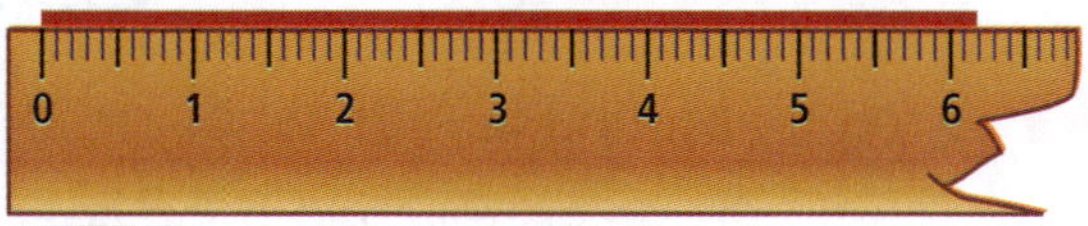

e ☐ mm

2 Estimate and then measure the length of each line. Write the measurement.

a ☐ mm

b ☐ mm

c ☐ mm

d ☐ mm

e ☐ mm

f ☐ mm

FUN SPOT

- Play this game with a partner.
  - Take turns to choose an object.
  - Each player estimates the length and width of the object to the nearest millimetre.
  - Measure the object. The closest estimate gets 1 point.
  - The first player to 10 points wins.

Remember this.

1 cm = 10 mm

- Choose a suitable unit to measure each item. Record the measurements.
  - width of this book ☐
  - length of a pen ☐
  - length of a ruler ☐
  - length of a fingernail ☐
  - width of your hand ☐
  - width of a ruler ☐

Compare your measurements with others. Discuss the results.

 • *AUSTRALIAN SIGNPOST MATHS 3* • ISBN 9780655708773

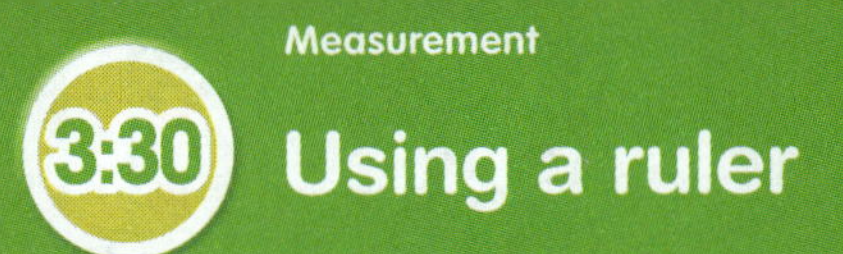

3:30 Using a ruler

Some rulers have a different scale on each edge: cm and mm.

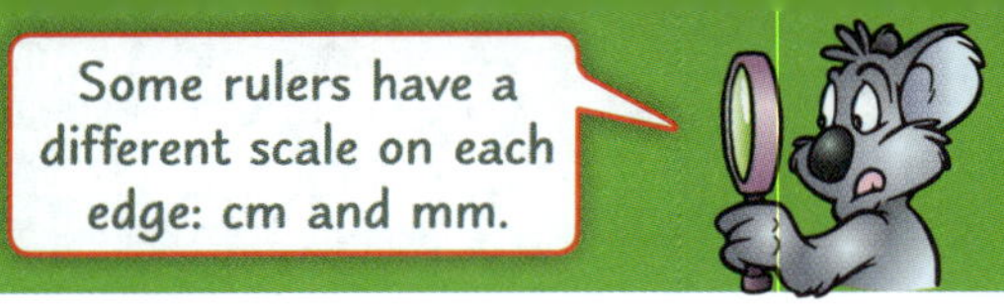

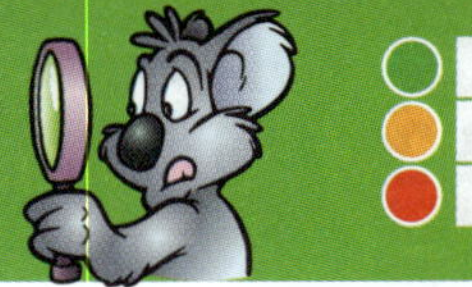

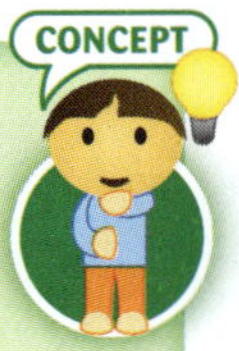

CONCEPT

100 centimetres = 1 metre   100 cm = 1 m   1000 mm = 1 m
10 millimetres = 1 centimetre   10 mm = 1 cm

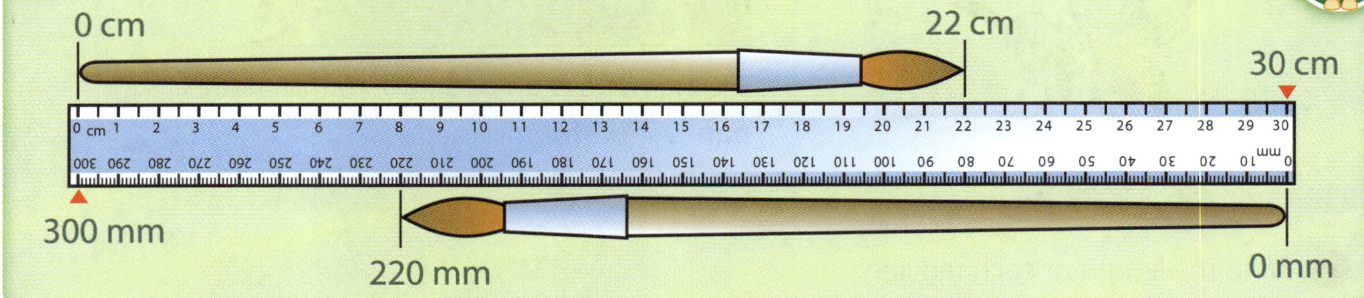

0 cm
22 cm
30 cm
300 mm
220 mm
0 mm

1. Use a ruler to measure these lengths.

   a Place-value ones block

   Length in centimetres = ☐ cm

   Length in millimetres = ☐ mm

   b Place-value long block

   Length in centimetres = ☐ cm

   Length in millimetres = ☐ mm

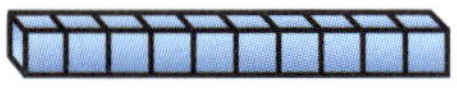

Measure correct to the closest unit used.

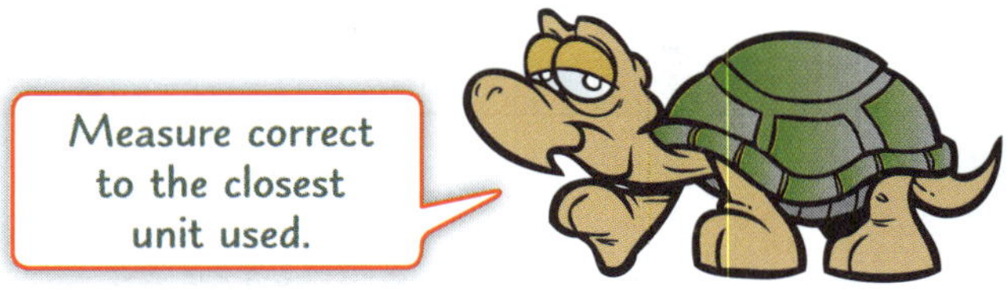

2. When measuring length, why would centimetres be better than hand spans?

3. When would it be better to use millimetres rather than centimetres?

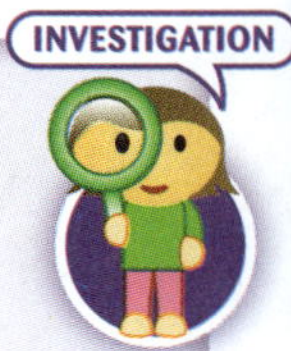

INVESTIGATION

- Use a ruler to measure the lengths of 4 items in millimetres or to the closest centimetre.

Name of item				
Length				

- Measure the height of a ball in millimetres. How did you do this?

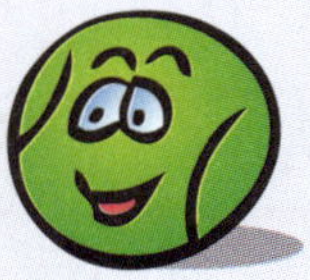

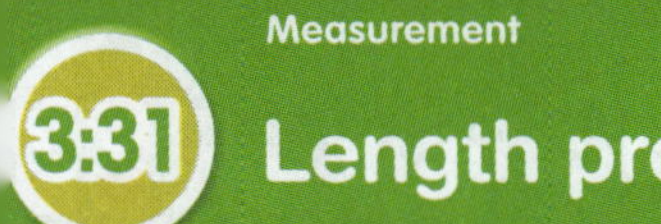

3:31 Length problem solving

1 m = 100 cm
10 mm = 1 cm

1 **a** Use a ruler to measure the length of each animal.

b Order the animals from shortest to longest.

2 On Riley's 9th birthday he was 133 cm tall. The previous year he grew 5 cm. How tall was he on his 8th birthday?

3 Zara's height is 123 cm and the height of her fishing rod is 155 cm. How much taller is her fishing rod?

4 Kasey has 50 cm of elastic. She needs 24 cm to make a bracelet. How many bracelets could she make?

5 33 cm

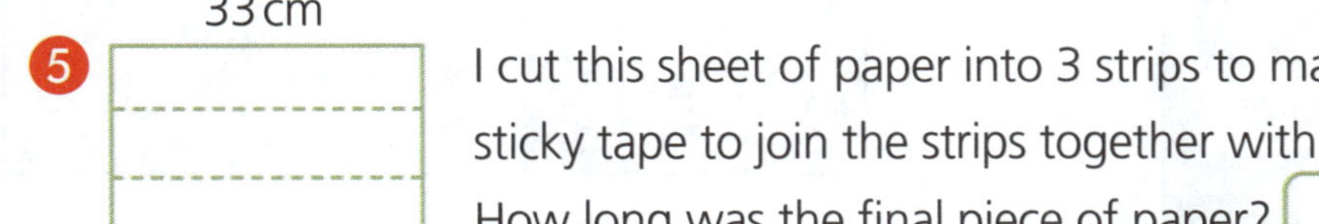

I cut this sheet of paper into 3 strips to make one long strip. I used sticky tape to join the strips together with no gaps or overlaps. How long was the final piece of paper?

6 On Monday I walked 300 metres to school and 300 metres back again in the afternoon. On Tuesday I walked an extra 400 metres to visit the shops on my way home. How far did I walk to and from school altogether on Monday and Tuesday?

7 I ran around an 800 m track two and a half times. How far did I run altogether?

8 25 m, 50 m

My paddock is 50 metres long and 25 metres wide.
How long would the fence around the paddock be?
Start at the top left corner of the paddock and draw a light post (use a dot).
If I put a light post every 25 metres around the fence line, how many lights would I need?

3:32 Area problems

2 rows of 4 squares.
The area is 8 squares.

No gaps.
No overlaps.

CONCEPT

Isaac used 3 rows of 5 tiles to cover his laundry floor.
How many tiles did he use? ☐

You could count by 5s to find your answer.

1 Draw squares to find the area of each shape. Describe the array for each area.
Tick the larger area of each pair.

a

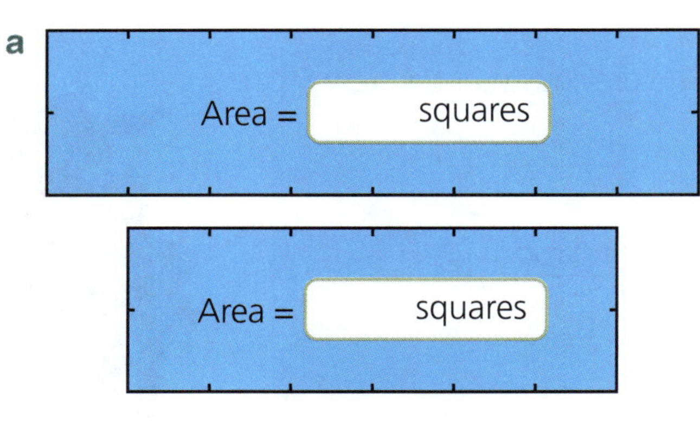

b

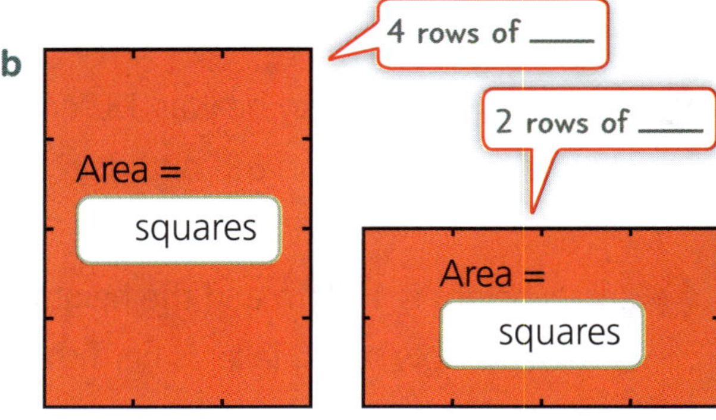

c

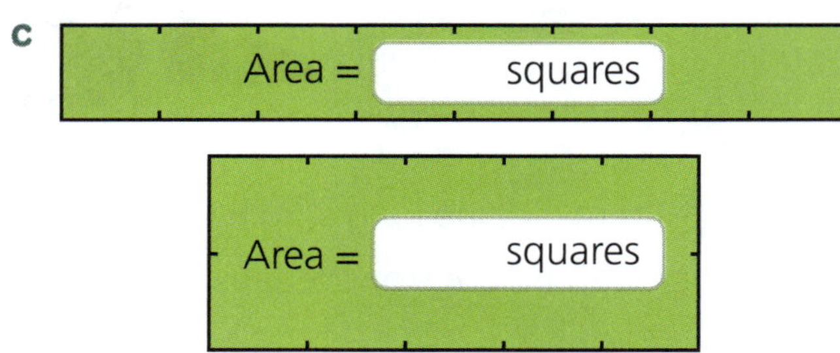

d

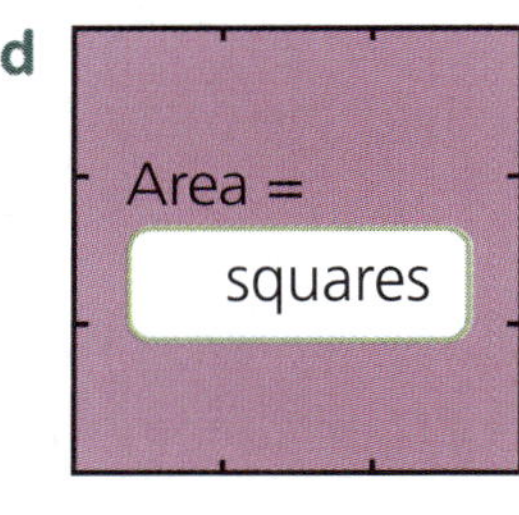

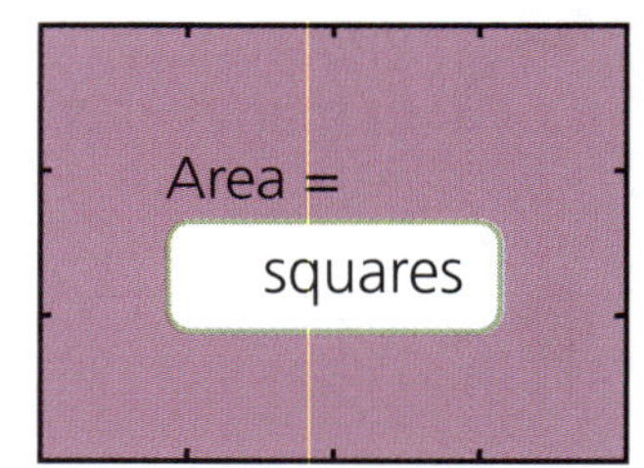

2 Write a number sentence to describe each array, then find the area.

a Jake measured the area of the whiteboard. He needed 8 sheets of paper along the top and 4 sheets of paper down the side. How many sheets of paper did he need to cover the whiteboard? ☐ rows of ☐ = ☐ sheets of paper

b My chocolate bar has 4 pieces down the side and 5 pieces across the top. How many pieces of chocolate are in my bar altogether? ☐ rows of ☐ = ☐ pieces

ACTIVITY

Estimate, then use sheets of paper, the same size, to find the area of three surfaces.

Item	Estimated area	Measured area	Order
			☐
			☐
			☐

Order these areas from smallest to largest.

Area using square centimetres

1 cm squares are a useful unit. They are square centimetres.

CONCEPT

The bottom of a ones block is a square centimetre (cm²).

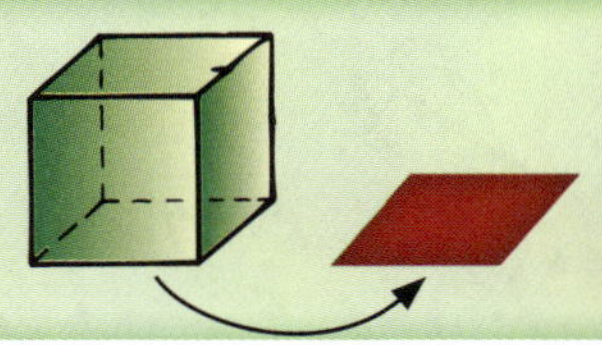

1 Each square on 1 cm grid paper is 1 square centimetre.
How many square centimetres make up the area of each shape?

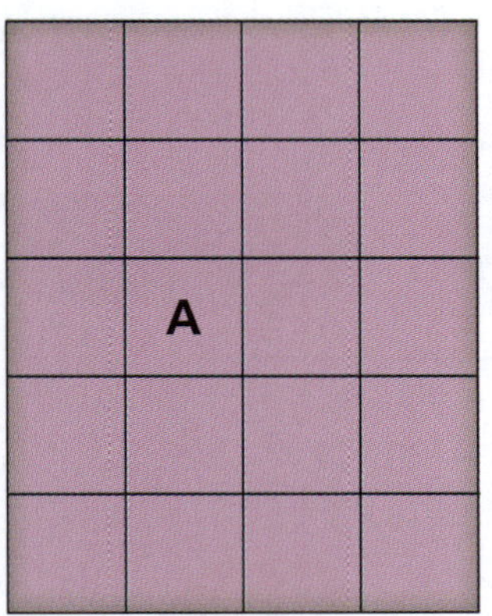

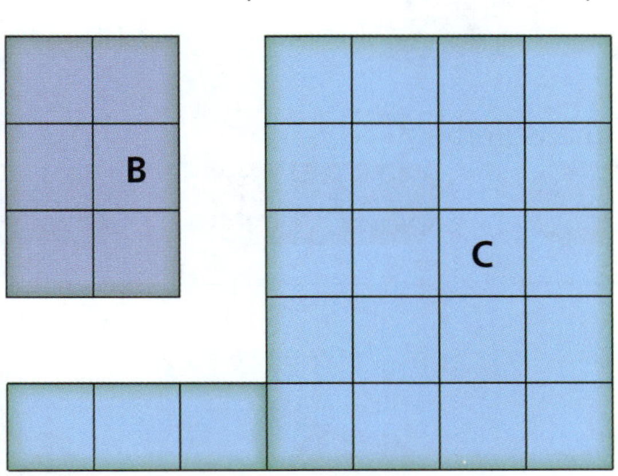

Area	Square centimetres (cm²)
A	
B	
C	
D	
E	
F	

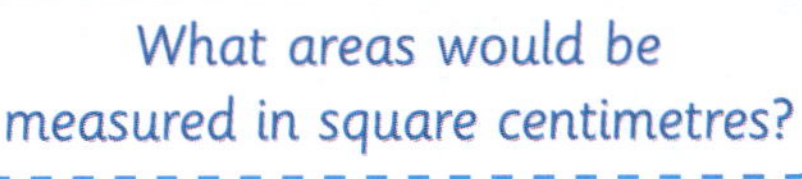

D

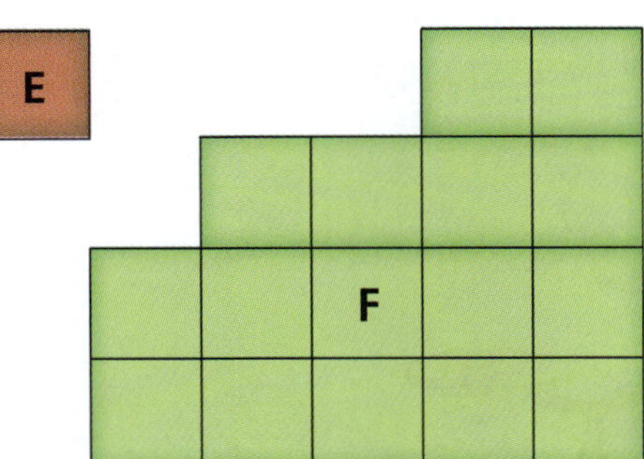

2 Which shape in Question 1 has:

a the greatest area? ☐ **b** the least area? ☐

c an area less than **B**? ☐ **d** an area more than **F**? ☐

e an area less than **A** but greater than **F**? ☐

ACTIVITY

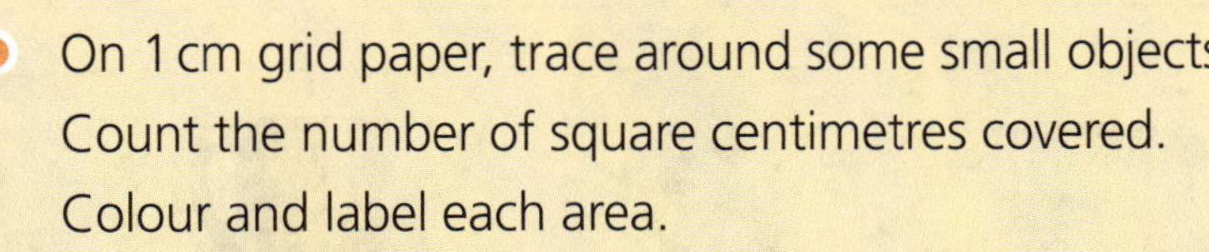

- On 1 cm grid paper, trace around some small objects. Count the number of square centimetres covered. Colour and label each area.
- Place small flat objects on top of 1 cm grid paper. Count the number of square centimetres covered. Label each area measured.

sharpener: 9 squares

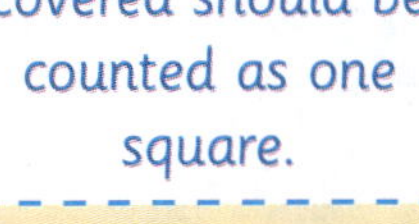

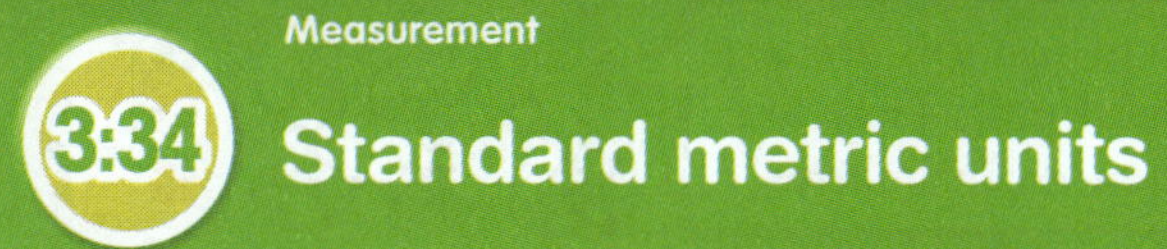

3:34 Standard metric units

Using metric units is easier.

CONCEPT

We use **standard metric units** so everybody can use the same units.

mass	capacity	length
kilograms grams	litre millilitre	metre centimetre millimetre

1 Match the unit to the type of measurement.

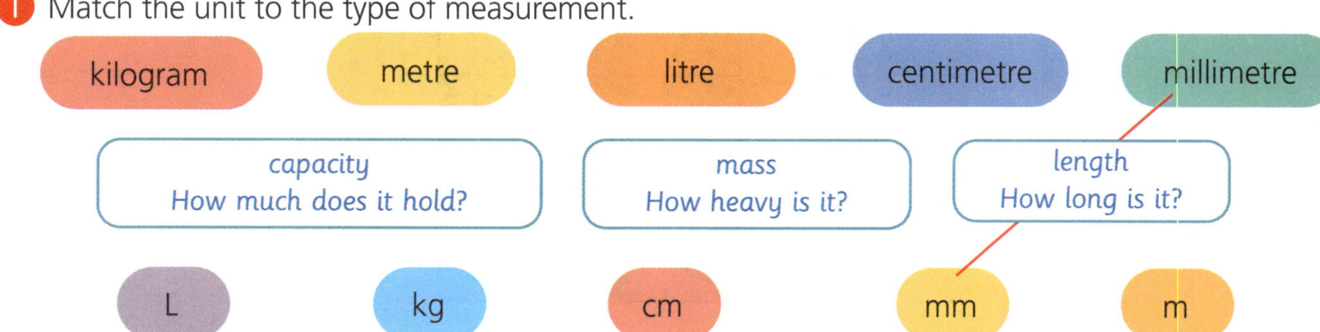

2 Which quantity does each tool measure: capacity, mass or length?

a 1 litre container

b balance scales

c rulers

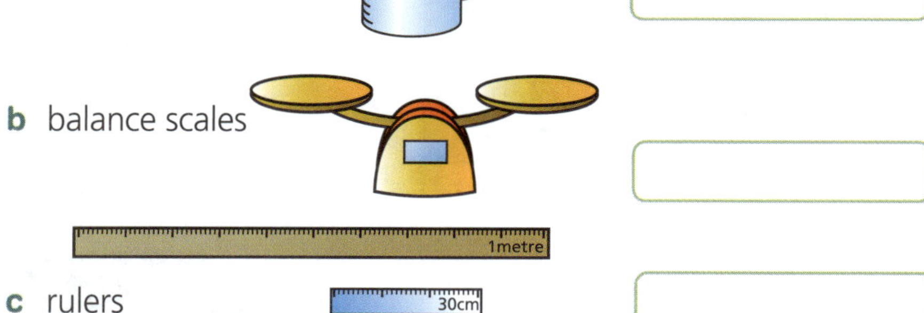

3 What is one advantage of using standard units to describe and compare objects?

FUN SPOT

4 Choose a container.

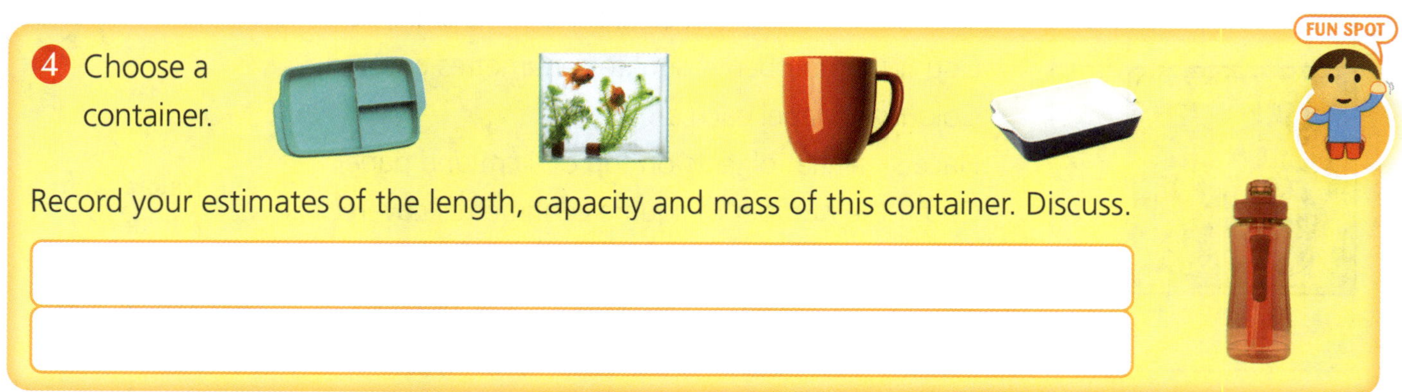

Record your estimates of the length, capacity and mass of this container. Discuss.

3:35 Personal benchmarks

I can estimate more accurately if I use personal benchmarks.

1 a Draw a 1-metre line on the ground. Practise taking two steps that would cover one metre.
   - From a starting point, use the steps you have practised to estimate a length of 5 metres. Use a tape measure to see how good your estimate was. Was your estimate close? ☐
   - Use this method to estimate other distances.

  b Use your practised steps to estimate the length of a building. ☐

  c Place a 1-metre ruler vertically beside you. Remember how high it reaches on your body. Record this personal measurement for one metre. The metre ruler reached my ☐.

2 1 L of water has a mass of 1 kg. Pour one litre of water into a plastic jug.

  a Use hefting to find objects that have a mass of about 1 kg.

  ☐

  b Use hefting to estimate the mass of a box of toys.

  c Try to remember the mass and volume of a litre of water. These will be your personal benchmarks for one kilogram and one litre.

TOYS

3 a Use a 1 L container to measure the capacity of a bucket. ☐ litres
  Use this as your benchmark for larger volumes.
   - Half fill a bucket with water. Use your benchmark for a full bucket to estimate how much water is now in the bucket. ☐ litres
     Use a 1-litre container to check your estimate. Was your estimate close? ☐
   - If two buckets of water are needed to fill a fish tank, estimate its capacity. ☐

4 Write your personal benchmarks for length, mass and capacity.

☐

☐

☐

Measurement

3:36 The stopwatch

minutes
seconds

We round the time to the nearest second.

Stopwatches measure the time an activity takes.

This **analog stopwatch** shows 3 minutes and 50 seconds to the nearest second.

This **digital stopwatch** shows 12 minutes and 21 seconds to the nearest second.

1 **a** Estimate how long it would take for the class to do each activity.
Select students to use stopwatches to measure the time taken for each activity. Record below.

	Estimated time	Actual time	Shortest (1) to longest (4)
Pack up classroom			
Line up at the door			
Walk to the ____________ and back			
Walk into classroom and sit at a desk			

b Choose another activity to measure (e.g. time taken to tie your shoelaces). Estimate, then use a countdown timer to check if the activity can be completed in the estimated time.

Activity	Estimate time	Actual time

2 Circle the faster time in each pair.

a $00{:}29_{15}$ / $00{:}31_{14}$

b $04{:}59_{06}$ / $04{:}39_{19}$

c $19{:}02_{06}$ / $16{:}15_{38}$

d $00{:}41_{92}$ / $00{:}28_{35}$

e $02{:}43_{08}$ / $02{:}43_{00}$

3 Write the longer times from Question 2 parts **a** and **b** in full to the nearest second (e.g. for $03{:}23_{46}$ write 3 minutes and 24 seconds).

a ______________________ **b** ______________________

Set a stopwatch timer at the beginning of the school day. Use lap times to record the time taken to complete events that occur throughout the day, using hours, minutes and seconds.

4:01 Properties of 3D objects

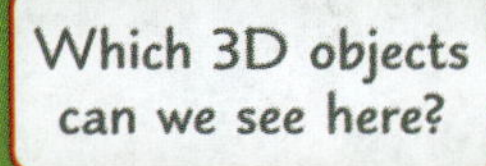

A 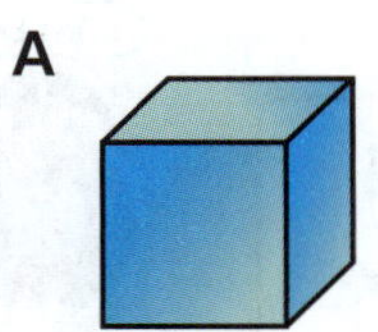 B  C 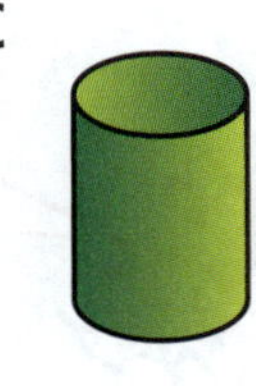 D 

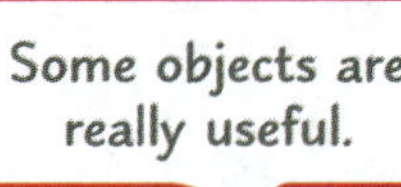

E 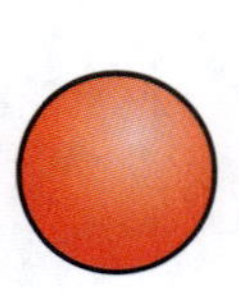 F 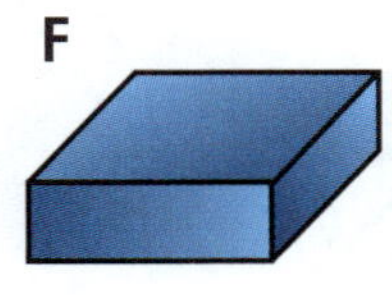 G  H 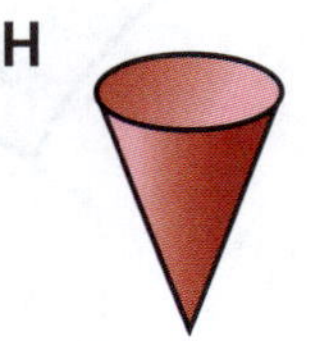

1 This picture shows holes cut in a block of wood.
Which of the objects **A** to **H** would fit through the holes?

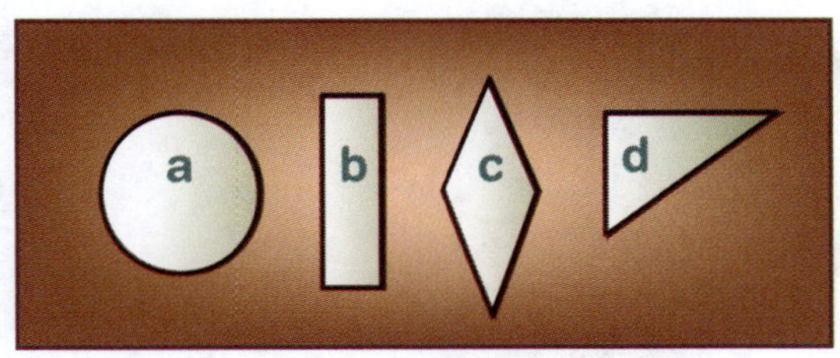

a circle hole ______

b rectangle hole ______

c rhombus hole ______

d triangle hole ______

2 Which of the objects **A** to **H** can't be easily stacked? ______

3 Which of the objects **A** to **H** are the same shape as these?

a 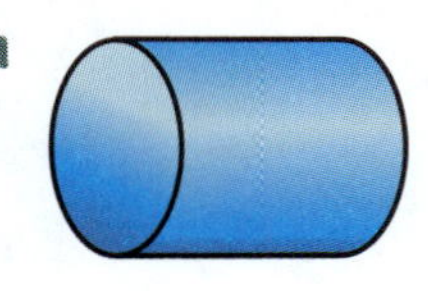  ______

b  ______

c  ______

d  ______

4 Which of the objects **A** to **H** could fit together like this?

a 

______ and ______

b 

______ and ______

c 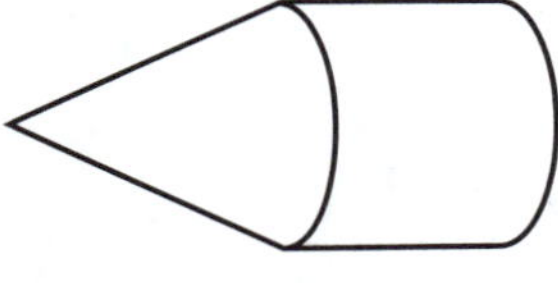

______ and ______

d Draw the hidden lines to make the diagram in part **c** look 3D.

5 Draw the missing object in each pattern.

a 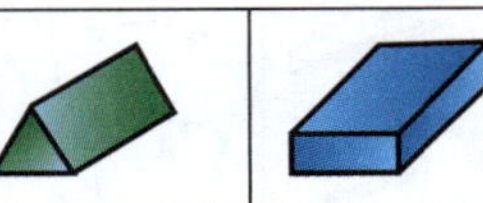  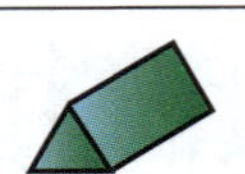 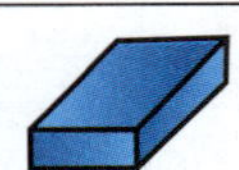   ______ 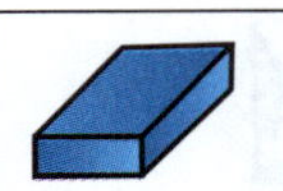

b  ______  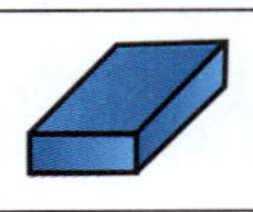 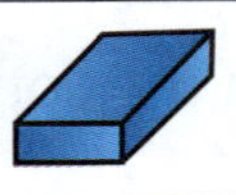 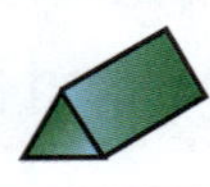 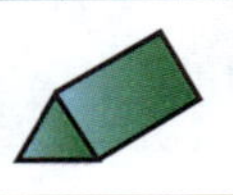  

 • *AUSTRALIAN SIGNPOST MATHS 3* • ISBN 9780655708773

Draw the lines of symmetry.

1 Use a ruler to draw a line of symmetry on each picture.

2 Draw lines of symmetry on these letters.

A C D E M V

Draw the other half of each picture below.

3 Use a ruler and pencil to draw all of the lines of symmetry on each shape.

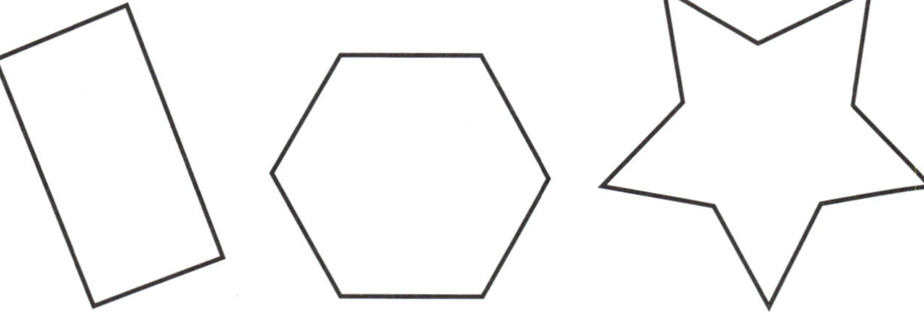

Making a symmetrical picture

1 Fold a piece of paper.
2 Draw half of a picture on one side of the fold.
3 Fold the paper under, with the drawing on top.
4 Use a marker (that shows through) at the corners.
5 Unfold the paper and join the dots.

ACTIVITY

4:03 Properties of 3D objects

We usually cut cross-sections parallel to the end.

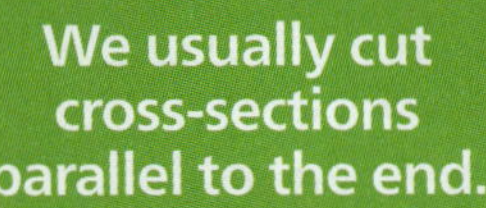

- How would you describe the shape of this tent?

1 How many flat surfaces does each object have? Name each object.

Cross-sections?

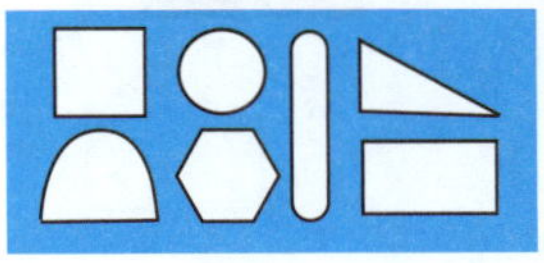

a

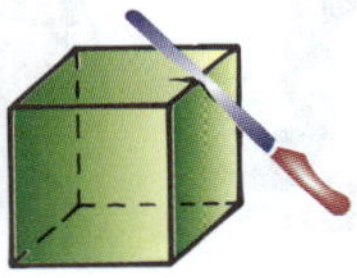

b

c

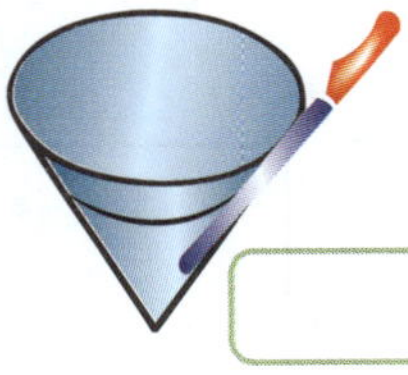

d

e

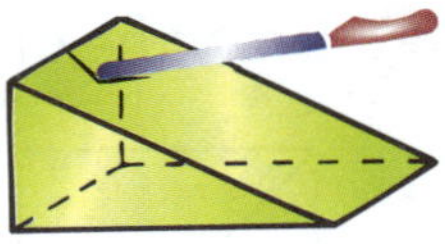

2 What is the shape of each object's cross-section?

a

b

c

d

e

3 a Which of the objects in Question 1 has six corners?

b Which has 8 corners?

c Which has 12 edges?

d Which has 1 corner?

e Which has 5 faces?

f Which has 9 edges?

g Which has only curved surfaces?

h Which has only 2 flat surfaces?

i Which have a circular cross-section?

4 Which block would fit into which hole? Write the number.

a Hole A

b Hole B

c Hole C

d Hole D

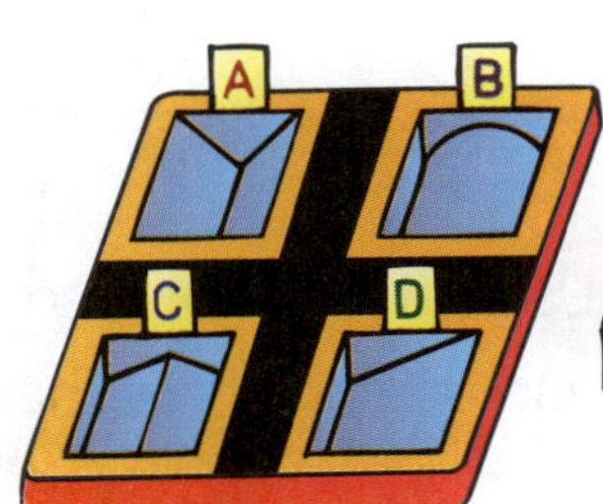

1 2 3 4

4:04 Symmetry around us

Each side is a reflection of the other.

It is hard to find perfect symmetry, but there are many examples of symmetry that are close to perfect.

We use the term symmetrical in these cases.

Discuss the symmetry.

1. Order the heads from 'most symmetrical' (1) to 'least symmetrical' (6).

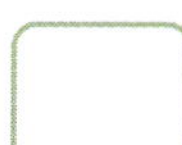

2. Draw the other half to make each picture symmetrical.

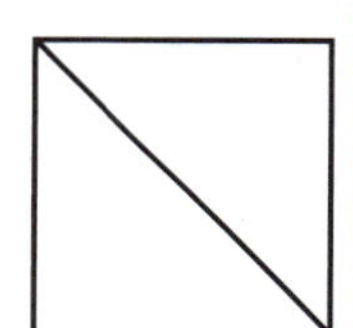
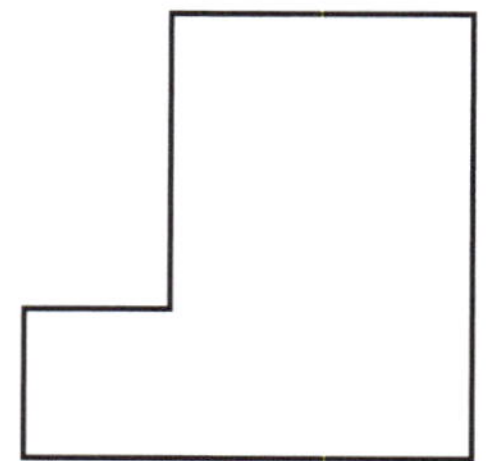
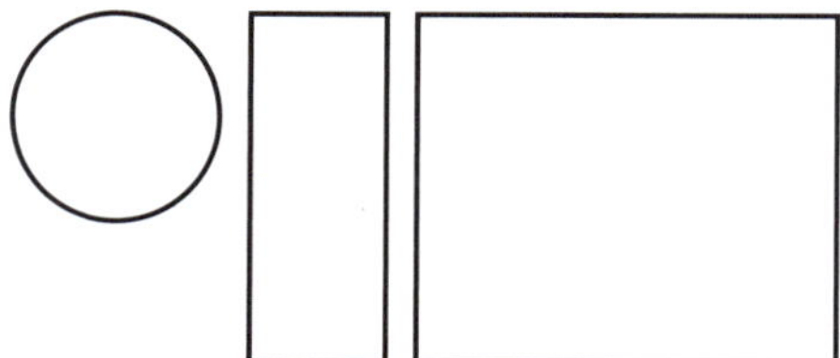

Slide back the edge of this page so that it matches the pictures on page 114 underneath. What do you see?

- Colour 8 of these shapes to make a symmetrical design.

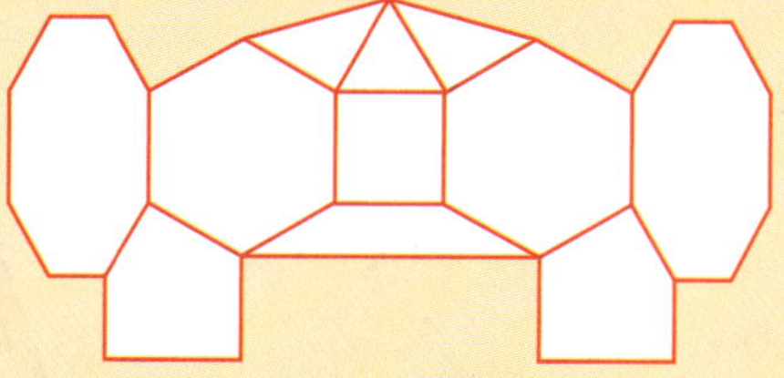

- Use pattern blocks to make your own symmetrical design and describe how the pattern was made.

4:05 Parallel and perpendicular lines

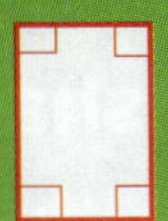

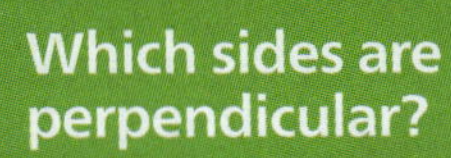

Parallel lines are always the same distance apart.

- They are straight lines.
- They are in the same direction.
- They never touch.

Perpendicular lines meet at right angles.

- They are straight lines.
- They cross over at right angles.

1 At how many points does each group of lines cross?

a 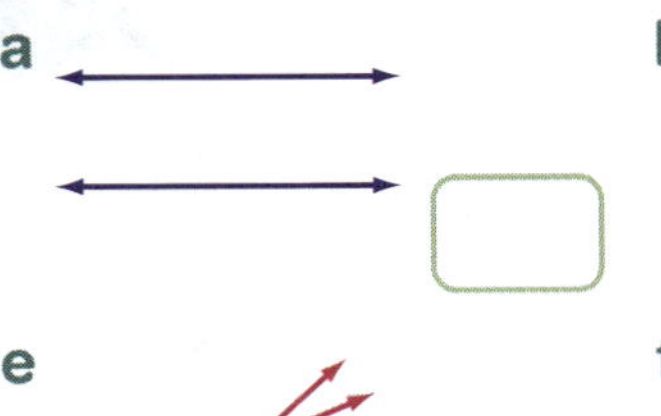

b 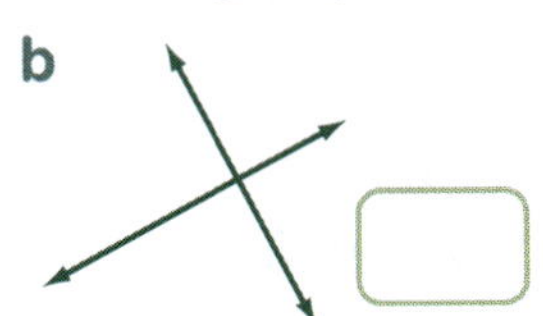

c 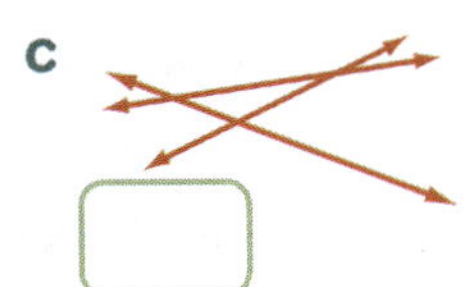

d 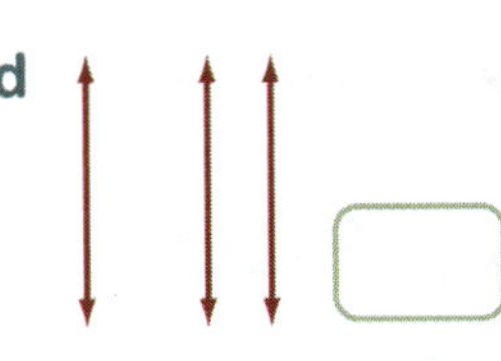

e 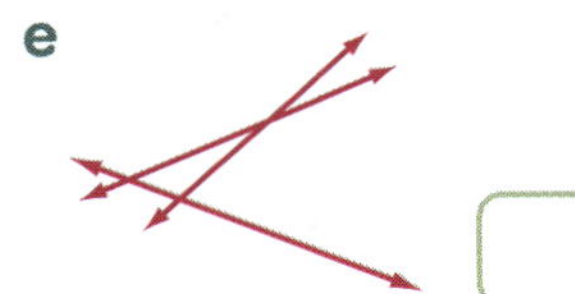

f 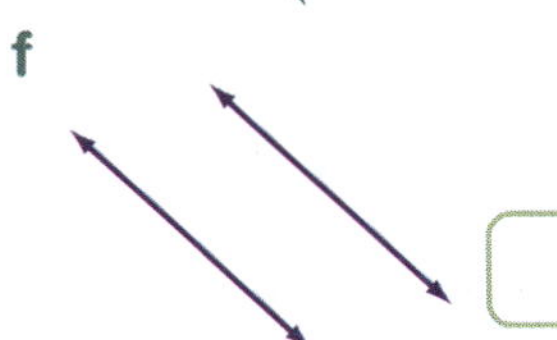

g 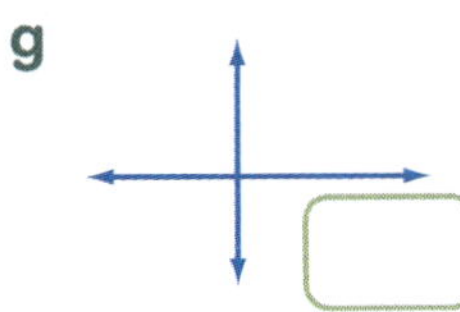

h 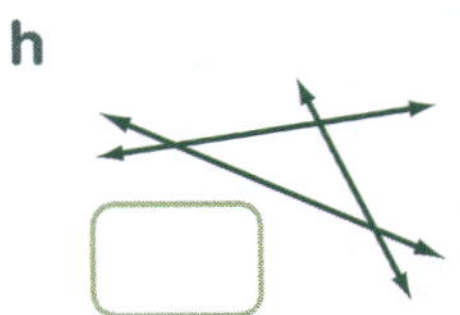

2 Which sets of lines in Question 1 are parallel?

Why are they parallel?

3 Why are the lines in 1**b** perpendicular?

4 Name two shapes that have perpendicular sides.

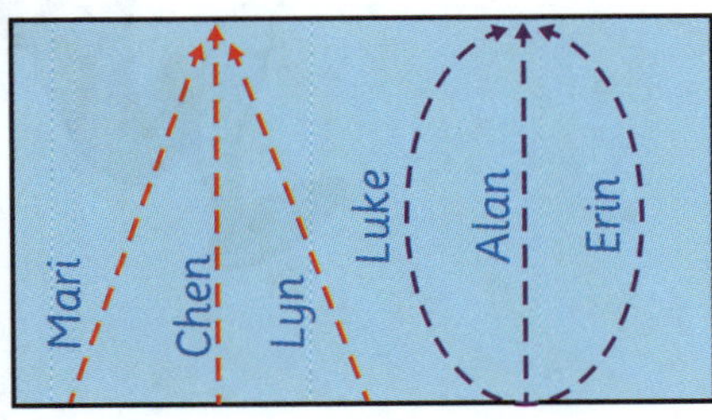

5 Six people swam across a swimming pool.

a Who swam the shortest path?

b Who swam perpendicular to the sides?

c Who swam parallel paths?

6 

a List things in this picture that are parallel.

b When parallel lines continue further away from us, do they look like they are coming together?

Are they really coming together?  Discuss.

 • *AUSTRALIAN SIGNPOST MATHS 3* • ISBN 9780655708773

4:06 Regular and irregular shapes

Irregular shapes do not have all sides and angles equal.

1. Join the dots to complete these regular shapes. Under each shape, write its name.

a b c d

For regular shapes:
- Are all sides equal?
- Are all angles equal?

2. Which shapes in Question 1 have opposite sides parallel?

3. Join the dots to complete these irregular shapes. Under each shape, write its name.

a b c d

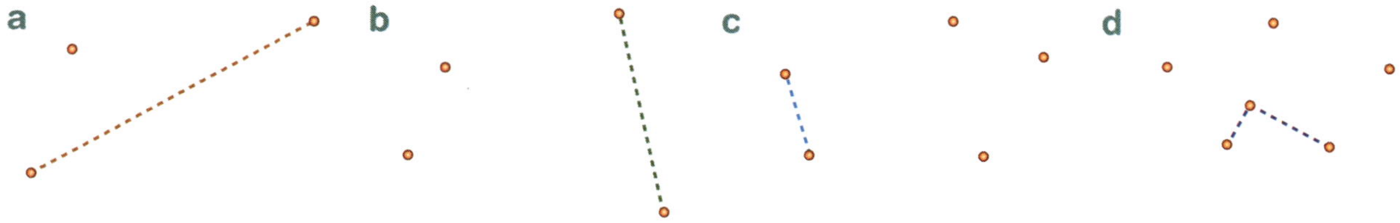

For irregular shapes:
- Are all sides equal?
- Are all angles equal?

4. Trapeze artists swing on trapeziums. A trapezium has at least one pair of parallel lines. Join the dots to complete each trapezium.

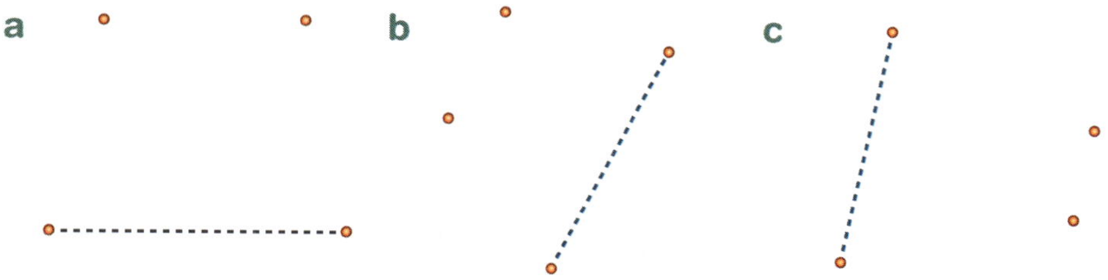

a b c

Are trapeziums regular or irregular shapes?

ACTIVITY

- Use diagonal parallel lines to join these dots in both directions.
- In this lattice pattern, what shape is repeated?

Use grid paper to draw your own lattice pattern.
Are rhombuses regular or irregular?

Position and giving directions

CONCEPT

A map gives us a view from above.

- Circle the camping area.
- Draw a straight line from the roundabout to the traffic light.

1 Write directions to get from place to place.

a **A** to **C** ____

b **A** to **D** ____

c **A** to **E** ____

d **A** to **F** ____

2 Follow these directions. Where do they lead? Draw each path on the map.

a Start at **A**. Turn right, then the first right, then the second left.

____

b Start at **A**. Turn right, then the first right, then the first right, then the first left, then the first right.

____

D B C A E F H G

Key: School, Library, Hospital, Post office

- Circle the school and the library.

3 **a** Jenna is sitting in seat **J**. She moves two seats to the right, then one seat forwards. Where is she now? ____

b Patrick is sitting in seat **P**. He moves three seats to the left, then two seats forwards. Where is he now? ____

c Dmitri is sitting in seat **D**. He moves three seats backwards, then two seats to the left. Where is he now? ____

d Erin is sitting in seat **E**. She moves one seat to the right, then two seats backwards, then one seat left, then two seats forwards. Where is she now? ____

Classroom

Forwards ↑

T			
A	B	C	D
E	F	G	H
I	J	K	L
M	N	O	P

4:08 Giving directions

1 Follow the spider's path and write the letter for the point where it stops.

a 4 spaces up, 2 right, 3 up

b 3 spaces up, 1 left, 4 up

c 2 up, 4 right, 3 up, 5 left, 2 up

d 6 up, 2 right, 4 down, 1 left, 5 up

e 1 right, 7 up

f 2 up, 1 left, 2 up, 5 right, 3 up

g Write directions to take the spider to **E**.

2 Use directions like those above to describe these paths.

a **A** to **Y**

b **B** to **X**

c **C** to **Z**

d **X** to **B**

e **Y** to **A**

3 You are in a car at **A**. To get to **E** you would follow these directions: 1 forwards, turn right, 6 forwards, turn left, 4 forwards.
Write directions for these paths.

a **A** to **B**

b **A** to **C**

c **A** to **D**

d **F** to **D**

e **F** to **E**

 • *AUSTRALIAN SIGNPOST MATHS 3* • ISBN 9780655708773

4:09 Shapes revision

Which three shapes below have all angles equal?

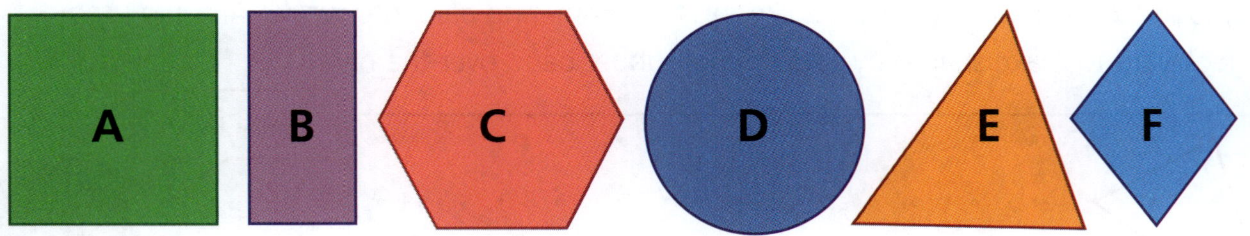

1 Write **A**, **B**, **C**, **D**, **E** or **F** to match the shape name.

a circle ☐ **b** square ☐ **c** triangle ☐

d hexagon ☐ **e** rhombus ☐ **f** rectangle ☐

Why is **B** a rectangle?

2 Write **A**, **B**, **C**, **D**, **E** or **F** to match the description.

a three sides ☐ **b** four sides ☐, ☐ and ☐

c six sides ☐ **d** no straight sides ☐

3 **a** Which of the shapes above have all sides equal? ☐

b Which of the shapes above have opposite sides equal? ☐

4 Write the names of the two shapes used in each picture.

a

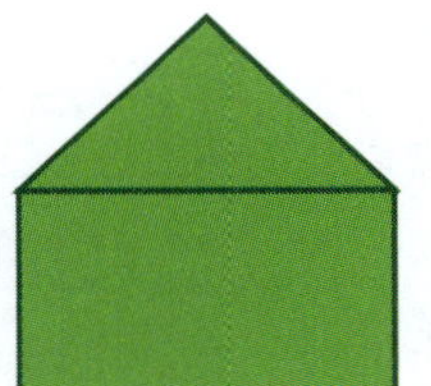

b

c

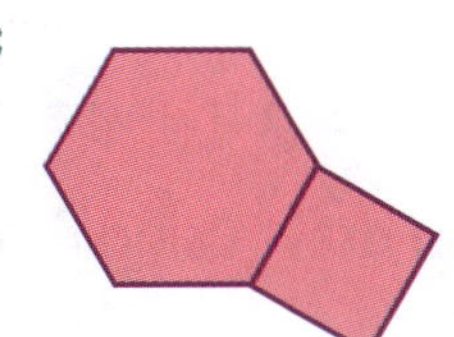

d

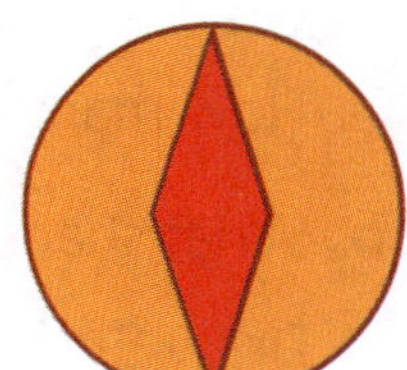

5 How many shapes are in the picture?

a squares ☐

b triangles ☐

c rectangles ☐

d circles ☐

- Draw your own picture using shapes.

ACTIVITY

This is not as easy as it looks.

© PEARSON AUSTRALIA 2024 • *AUSTRALIAN SIGNPOST MATHS 3* • ISBN 9780655708773

4:10 Properties of 2D shapes

This is like using square grid paper.

Antonio's teacher made a **geoboard** like this by hammering nails into wood. Antonio used the geoboard to make shapes by stretching a rubber band over the nails.

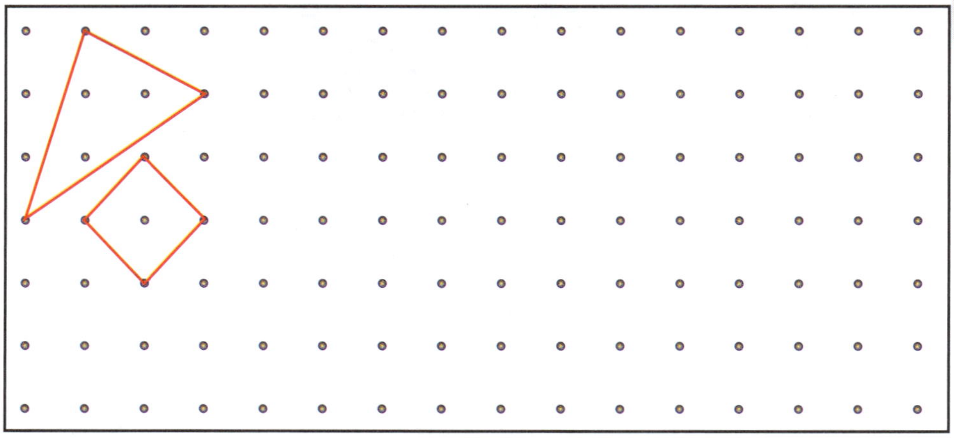

I made those.

- You can use an online geoboard.

1. a How many nails were used to make the triangle? ☐ Number of corners = ☐
   b How many nails were used to make the square? ☐ Number of corners = ☐
   c How many sides on a triangle? ☐ d How many sides on a square? ☐

2. Every corner of each shape on the geoboard must be at a nail.
   a On the geoboard above, draw 3 triangles of different shapes and sizes. How many sides does each triangle have? ☐
   b What shapes can you draw using 4 nails as corners? ☐ Draw 3 of them on the geoboard above. ☐
   c A pentagon has 5 sides. How many corners would you need to draw a pentagon? ☐ Draw a pentagon on the geoboard.
   d Draw a shape on the geoboard that has 6 corners. What is this shape called? ☐

ACTIVITY

Olena cut a square of paper into 5 pieces. She asked her friend to put the square back together again. Then she asked her friend to make a picture using the pieces.

- Cut your own square of paper into 5 pieces. Colour one side.
- Discuss the shapes you cut out.
- Mix up your 5 pieces and ask a partner to put the square back together again.
- Use your pieces of paper to make pictures.

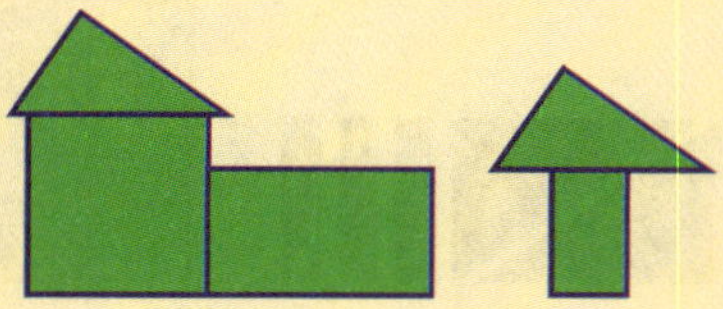

 • *AUSTRALIAN SIGNPOST MATHS 3* • ISBN 9780655708773

Investigating angles

CONCEPT

- Take 2 straight strips of cardboard and join them at one end with a paper fastener.
- By turning the arms, you can make the movable angle small or large.

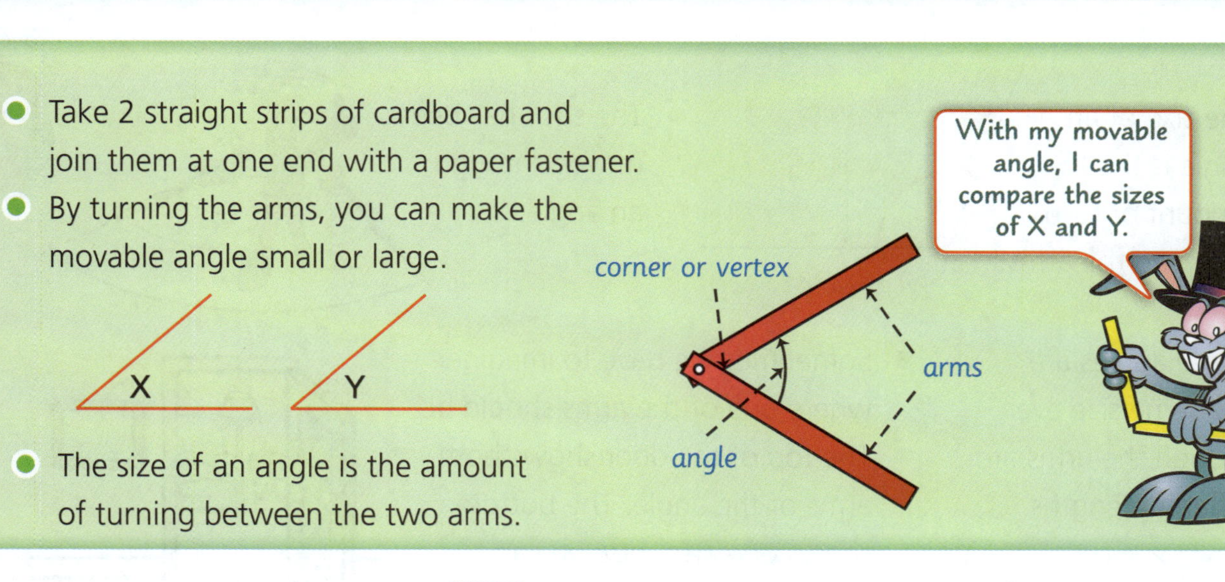

- The size of an angle is the amount of turning between the two arms.

1. Which angle is the largest? ☐
2. Which angle is the smallest? ☐

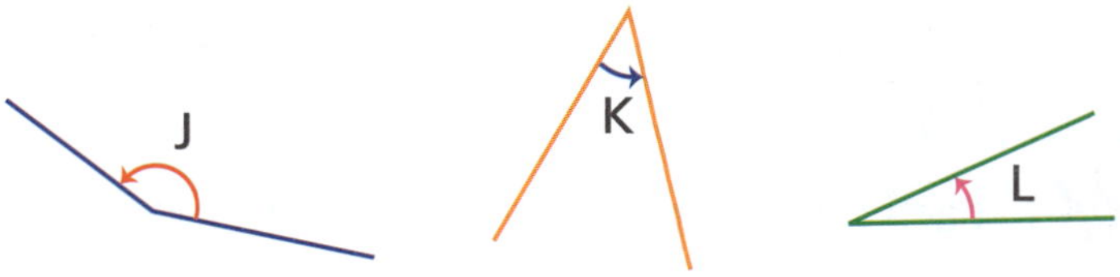

J K L

3. Use a movable angle to answer these questions about the angles below.
   - **a** Which of these angles are the same size as angle **A**? ☐
   - **b** Which angles are the same size as angle **B**? ☐
   - **c** Which angle is smaller (less turn) than angle **B**? ☐
   - **d** Which angle is bigger (more turn) than angle **A**? ☐
   - **e** Is **F** the same size angle as the corner of a square? ☐

My arms are like a movable angle.

A B C D

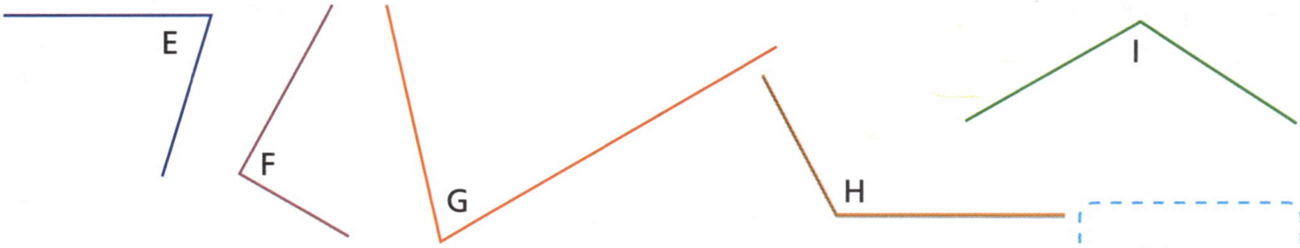

E F G H I

A square corner is called a right angle.

INVESTIGATION

- Compare the angles you can see in your classroom.

 ISBN 9780655708773

4:12 Angles

How many angles in each?

CONCEPT

- The size of an angle is the amount of turn between the arms.

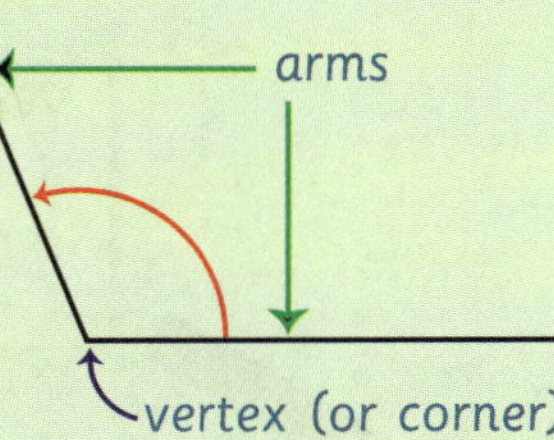

- The stick has been moved through an angle.

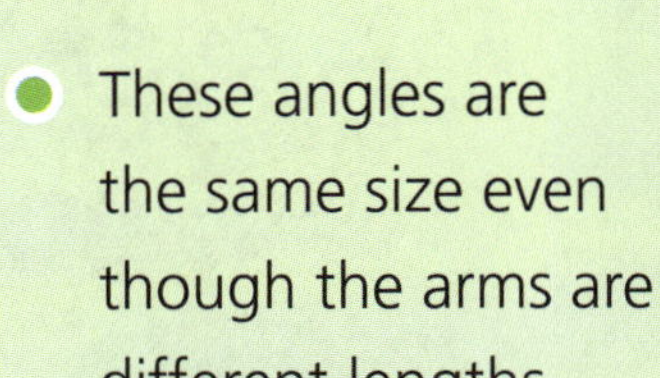

- These angles are the same size even though the arms are different lengths.

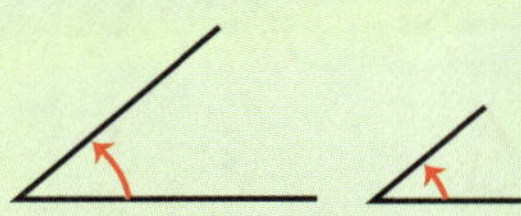

- Sometimes we have to imagine where one of the arms should be.
- The top of the door shows both arms of the angle. The bottom shows one arm, but we can imagine the other.

1 In each part, number the angles from the smallest turn (1) to the largest turn (4).

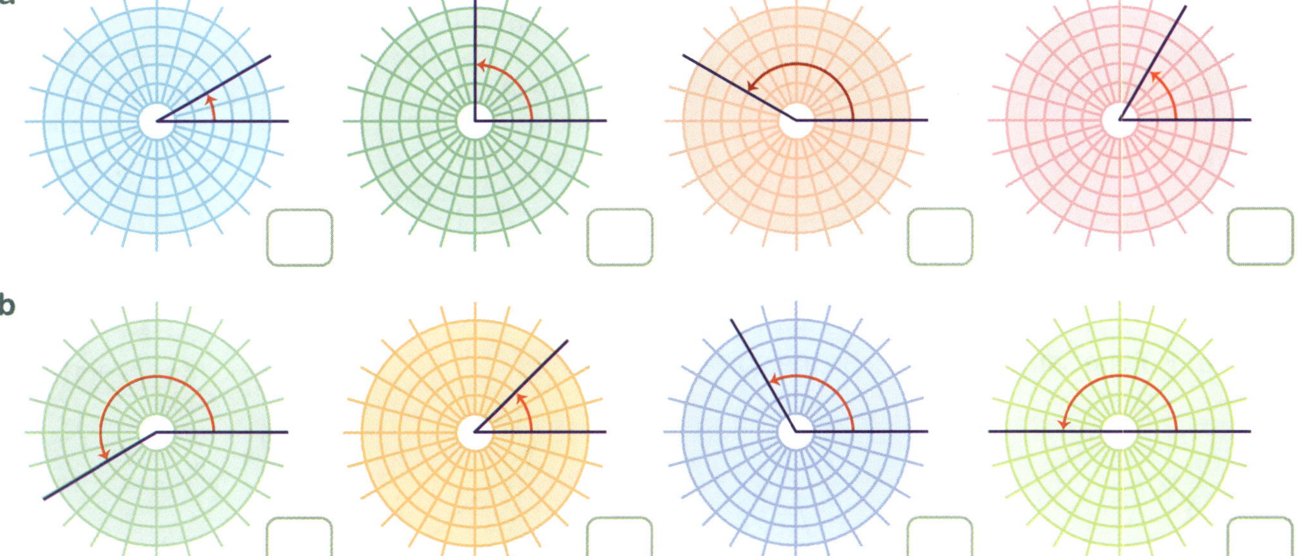

2 Use a ruler to draw angles on the dot grids.

a Draw an angle the same size as **A**.

A

b Draw an angle the same size as **B**.

B

c Why is **B** a right angle?

 • *AUSTRALIAN SIGNPOST MATHS 3* • ISBN 9780655708773

Trapezium and parallelogram

A rectangle?
A trapezium?
A parallelogram?

CONCEPT

- Arrows are used to show parallel sides.

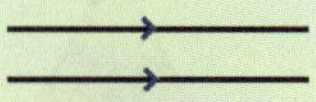

This is a trapezium.

This is a parallelogram.

- A **trapezium** has one pair of parallel sides.
- A **parallelogram** has two pairs of parallel sides.
- Both shapes have 4 straight sides.
- A parallelogram is a special trapezium.
- Trapeziums and parallelograms are both quadrilaterals.

1

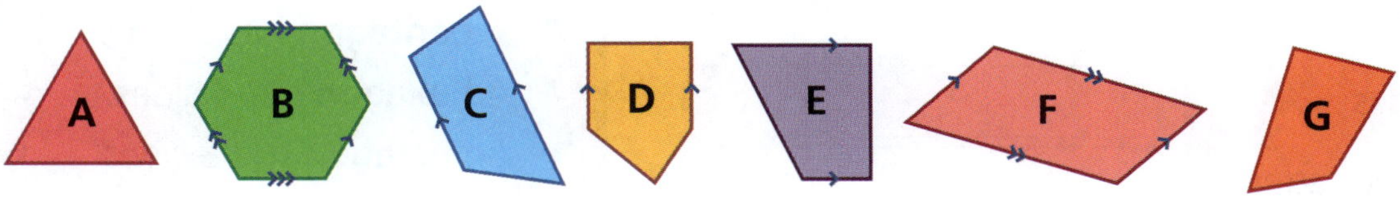

A B C D E F G

a Which of these shapes are trapeziums?

b Which shape is a parallelogram?

2 Match each shape name with one shape picture.

oval
square
triangle
rhombus (diamond)
octagon

rectangle
parallelogram
pentagon
trapezium
hexagon

3 a On this dot grid, draw three trapeziums.

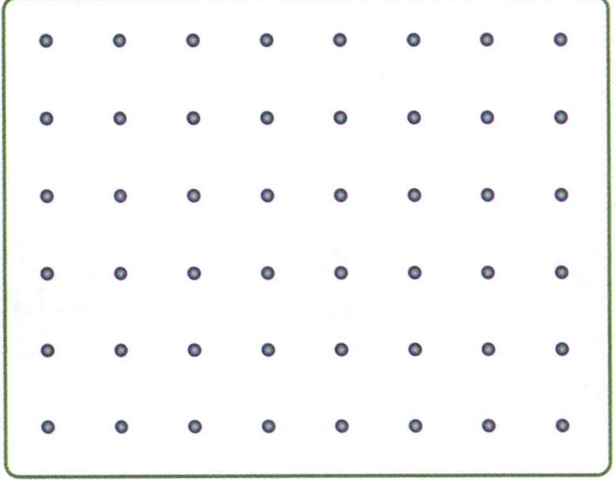

b On this dot grid, draw three parallelograms.

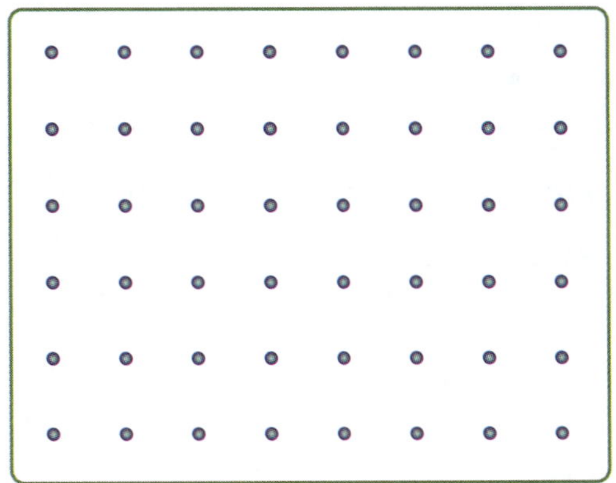

 • *AUSTRALIAN SIGNPOST MATHS 3* • ISBN 9780655708773

4:14 Features of 2D shapes

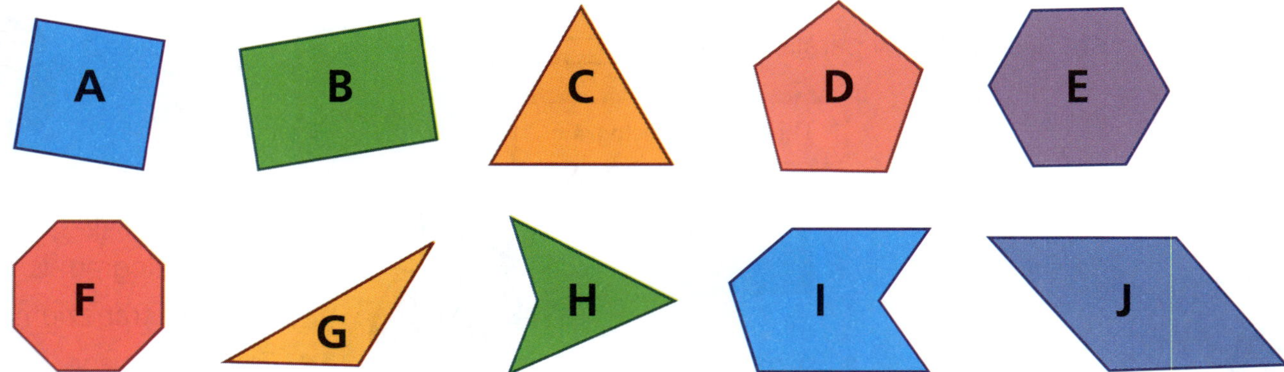

1. Write which of the shapes above have:
   - **a** 3 sides
   - **b** 4 sides
   - **c** 6 sides
   - **d** all sides equal
   - **e** sides that jut in

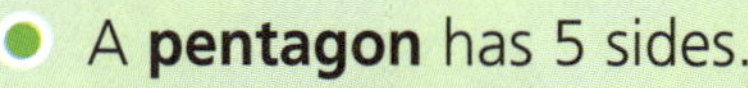

- A **quadrilateral** has 4 sides.
- A **pentagon** has 5 sides.
- A **hexagon** has 6 sides.
- An **octagon** has 8 sides.
- A **rhombus** is a diamond.
- A **kite** has symmetry.

2. **a** Which of the quadrilaterals above have all sides equal?

   b Which of the shapes above is an octagon?

3. What shape is a closed shape with the least possible number of straight sides and no curved sides?

4. 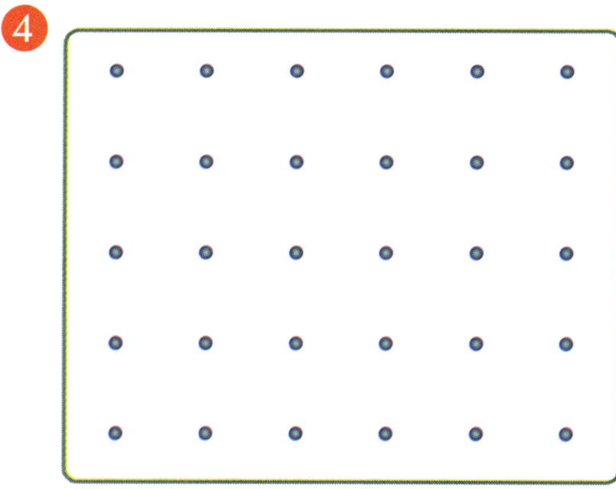

   a On this dot grid, draw 5 different quadrilaterals.

   b How many different sizes of squares could be drawn on this dot grid?

   c How many dots would be inside the largest square you could draw?

   d How many dots would be inside the largest hexagon you could draw on this dot grid?

5. How are these shapes different from the shapes at the top of the page?

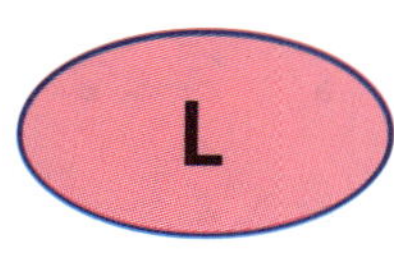

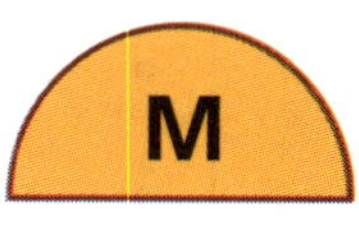

 • *AUSTRALIAN SIGNPOST MATHS 3* • ISBN 9780655708773

Right angles

The angles at the corners of a square are called right angles.

CONCEPT

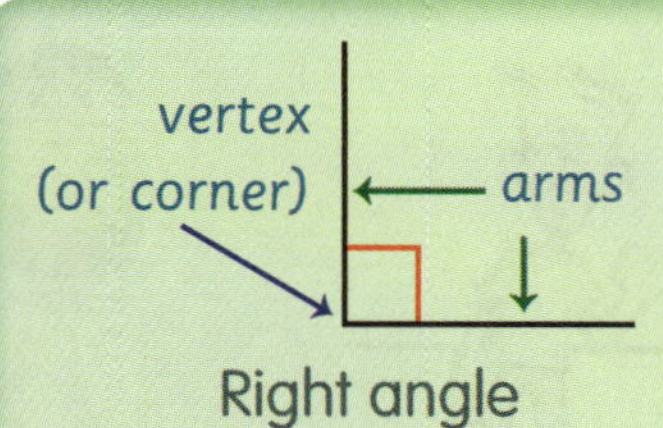

The angle at the corner of a square is called a **right angle**.
Two right angles make a half turn.

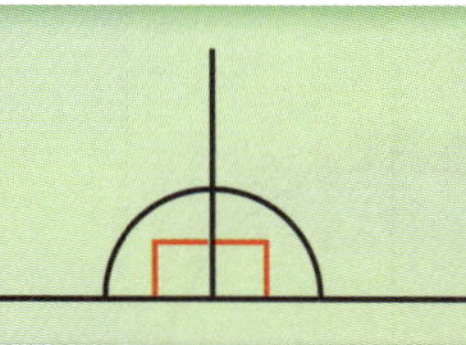

A small square drawn in the corner shows that it is a right angle.

To make a square corner, follow these steps:

1 Fold a piece of paper once to form a half turn.

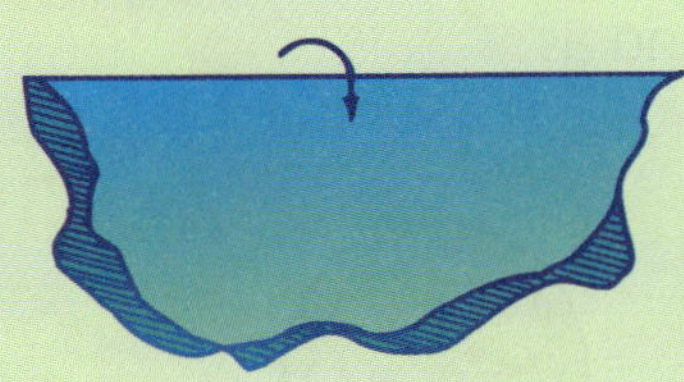

2 Fold the paper again so that the second fold lies exactly on top of the first.

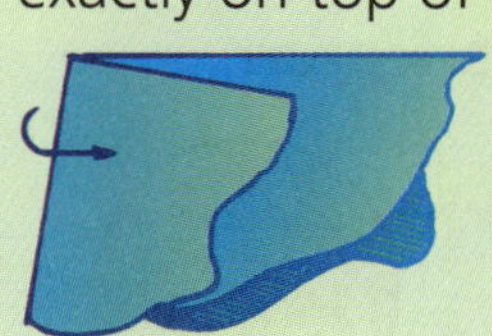

Just like magic!

3 Press all the folds down firmly. Where the folds meet, you have a square corner.

Square corner

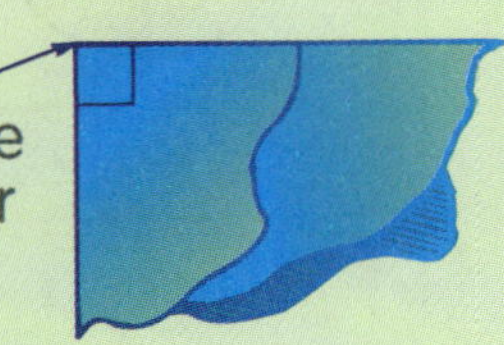

Practise making your own square corners.

1 Use a square corner to test these angles. Which are right angles?

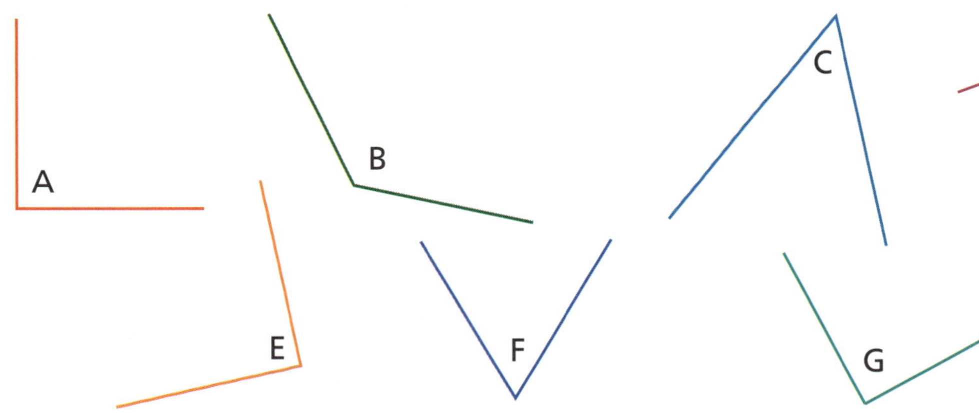

2 Which angle is larger than a right angle?

3 Use a square corner to test the corners of this page. Are they right angles?

INVESTIGATION

Make a list of all the right angles that you can see right now.

 • *AUSTRALIAN SIGNPOST MATHS 3* • ISBN 9780655708773

Angles

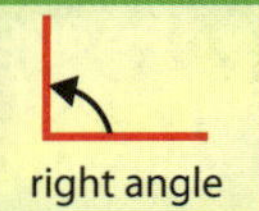

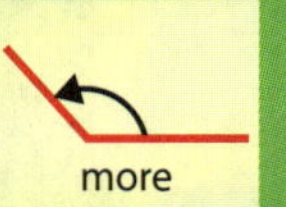

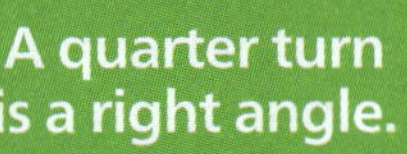

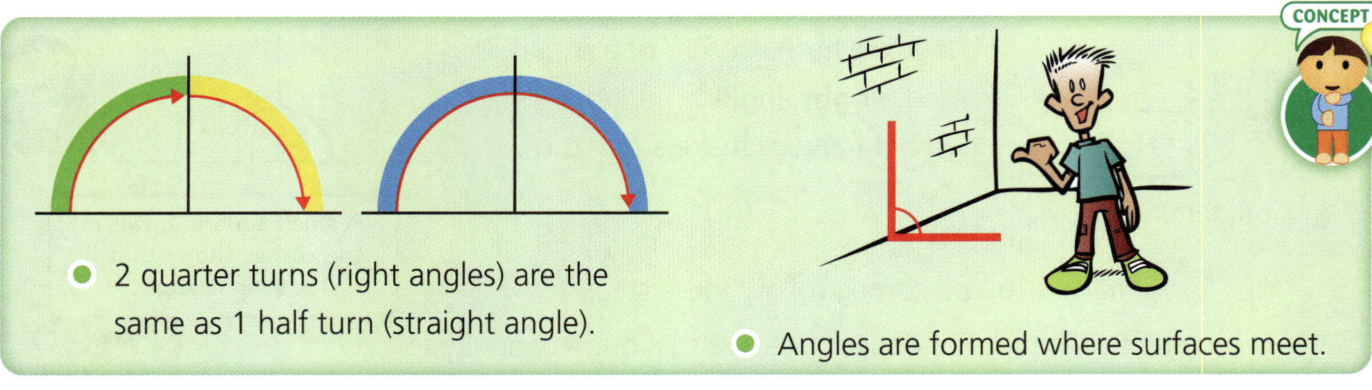

- 2 quarter turns (right angles) are the same as 1 half turn (straight angle).
- Angles are formed where surfaces meet.

1. Describe each turn as **clockwise** or **anticlockwise**, and as a **quarter**, **half** or **three-quarter turn**.

a 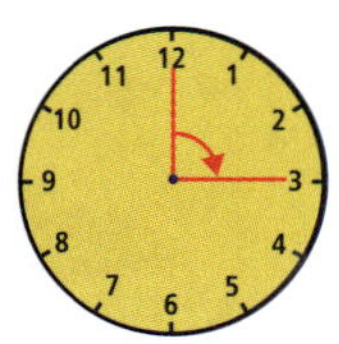

b 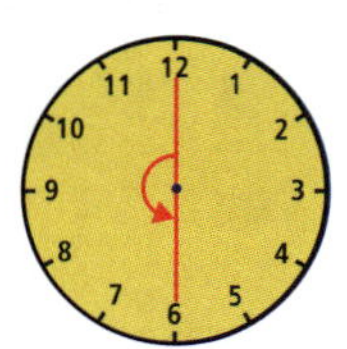

c 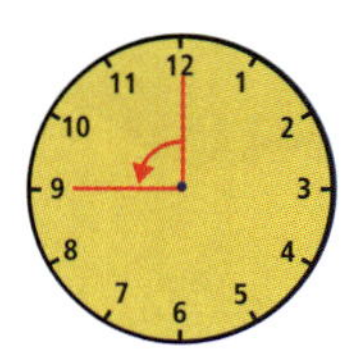

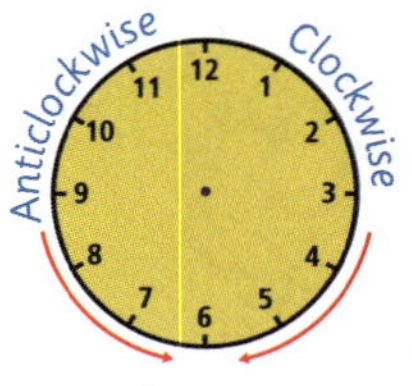

d

e 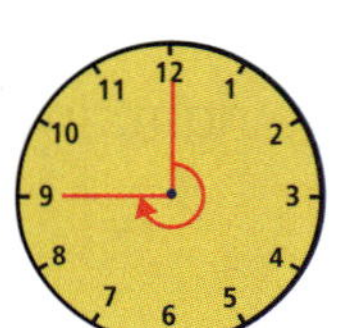

f 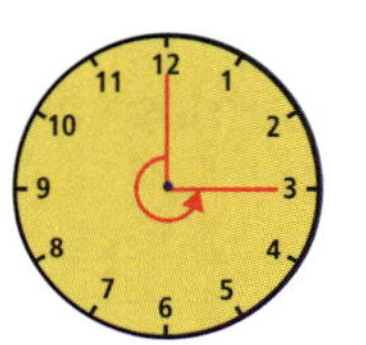

The minute hand turns a half turn in half an hour.

2. a Draw a quarter turn anticlockwise.

   b Draw a three-quarter turn clockwise.

   c Is a quarter turn clockwise the same as a three-quarter turn anticlockwise?

INVESTIGATION

List examples of angles made where surfaces meet.

4:17 Describing position

A B C D E F

4th from the left ☐ 3rd from the right ☐

1. Which items are in these positions?

a middle of the top shelf ☐

b right side of the top shelf ☐

c left side of the middle shelf ☐

d right side of the bottom shelf ☐

In which positions are these items?

e duck ☐ f book ☐ g bottle ☐

2. Which items are kept in these cupboards?

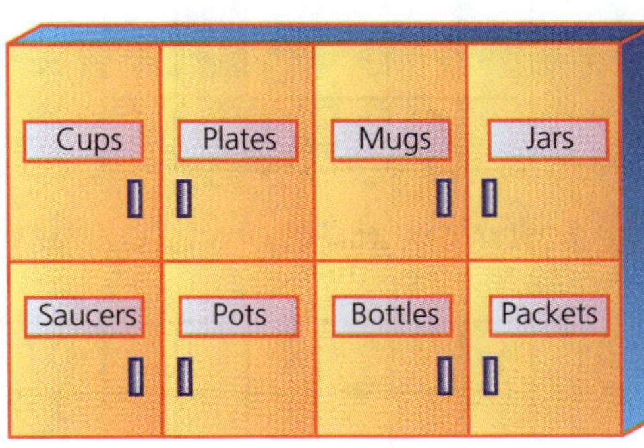

a left cupboard on the bottom row ☐

b second from the left on the top row ☐

c third from the left on the top row ☐

d second from the left on the bottom row ☐

In which cupboards are these items?

e cups ☐

f bottles ☐

g packets ☐

h jars ☐

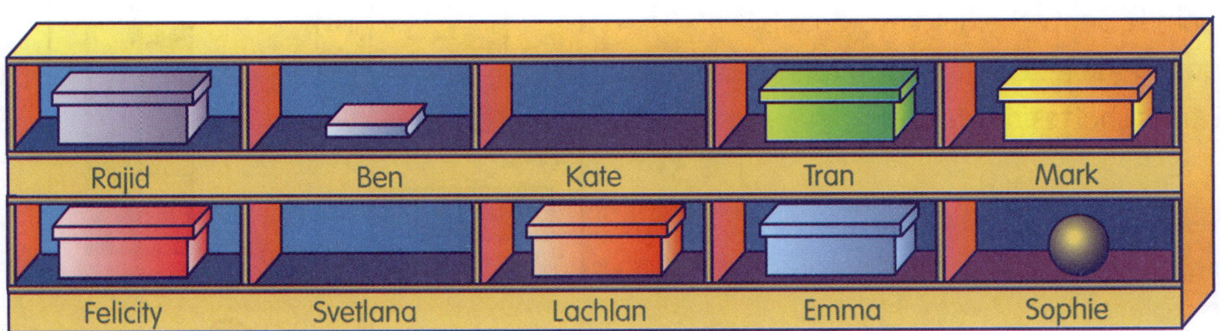

3. Each student has their own shelf. Whose shelves are in these positions?

a fourth from the left on the top ☐

b at the far right on the bottom ☐

c fifth from the left on the top ☐

d first on the left on the bottom ☐

e What is the position of Ben's shelf? ☐

f What is the position of Emma's shelf? ☐

 • *AUSTRALIAN SIGNPOST MATHS 3* • ISBN 9780655708773

4:18 Pathways between places

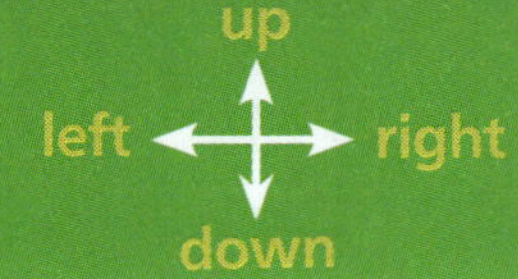

1 Move the counter along the path. Write each move in the table.

a

Moves
3 right
4 up
1
2

b

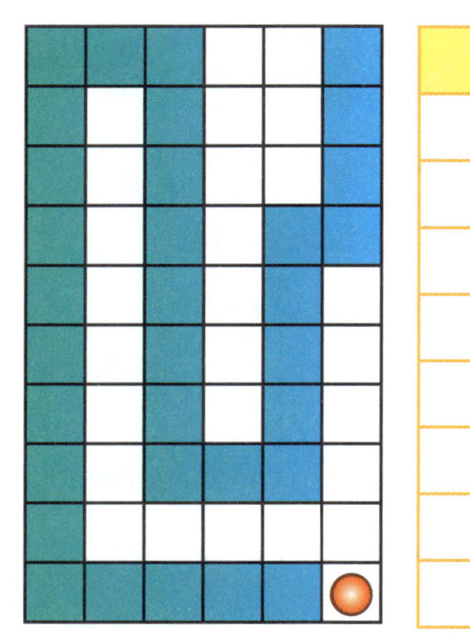

2 Follow the directions to colour the path of the counter.

a

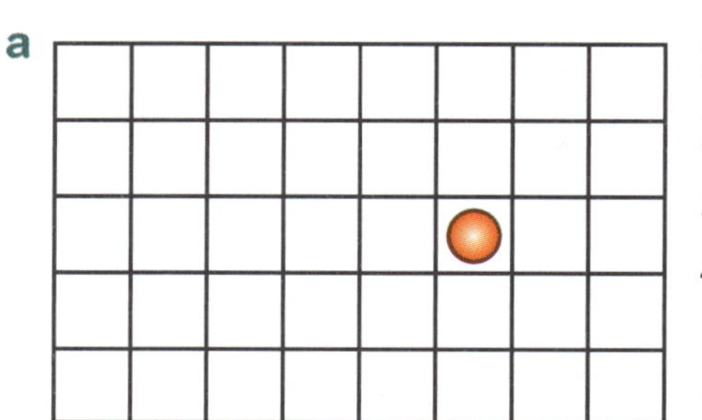

2 right,
2 down,
3 left,
4 up,
1 left,
1 down.

b

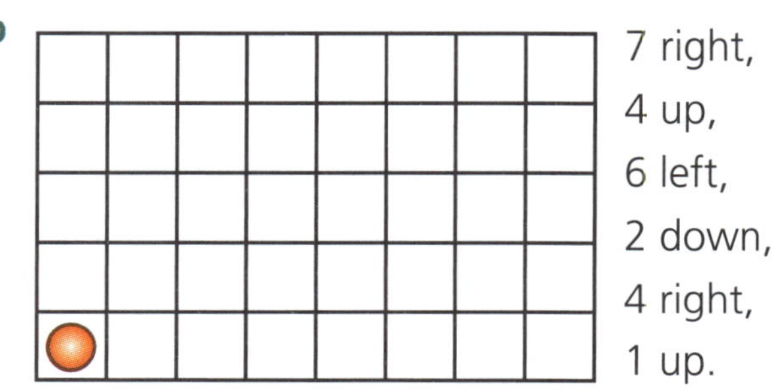

7 right,
4 up,
6 left,
2 down,
4 right,
1 up.

3 Carla has to go to every classroom and then to the office. Starting with room **H**, show the quickest route by writing the letters of the rooms in order.

Carla's shortest route is:

H C ______________________ **G O**

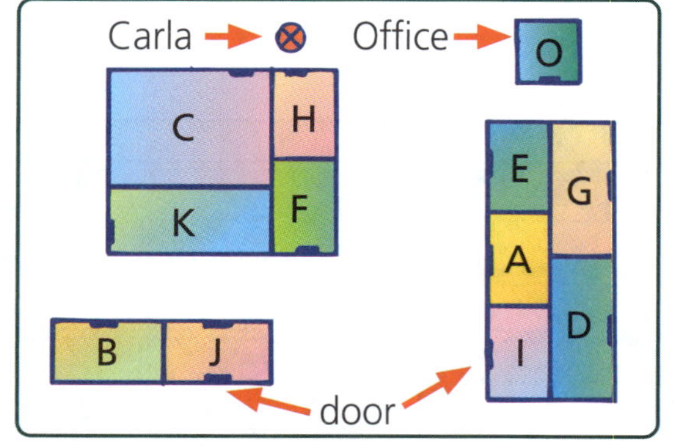

- In your school playground, mark a starting point.
- Students work in pairs to follow directions from the starting point to a secret destination. Everyone should measure distances using metre rulers or paces.
- Example directions: Move 3 m forwards, then 5 m to the right, then 7 m forwards, then 10 m to the left.

 • *AUSTRALIAN SIGNPOST MATHS 3* • ISBN 9780655708773

Prisms and cylinders

A face is a flat surface with straight sides.

CONCEPT

Prisms and **cylinders** are 3D objects.

- Their two ends are the same shape and size.
- Their **cross-section** is the same shape and size as their ends.
- The prism's other **faces** are rectangles.
- The cylinder's other **surface** is curved.

Prism

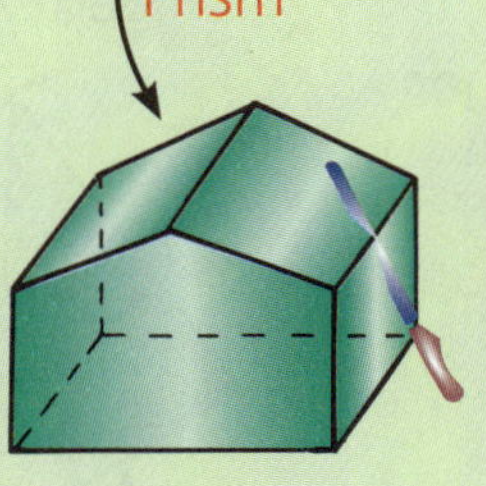
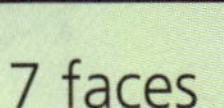

7 faces

Cylinder

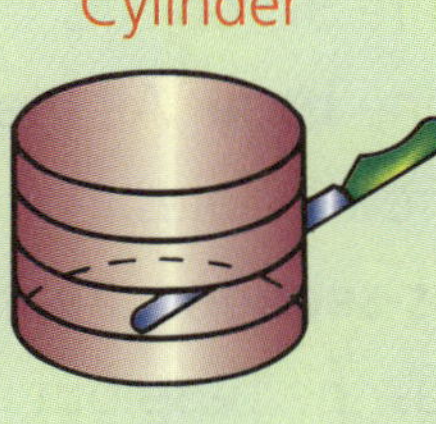

0 faces
2 flat surfaces
1 curved surface

1 Write **prism**, **cylinder** or **neither** under each picture.

a 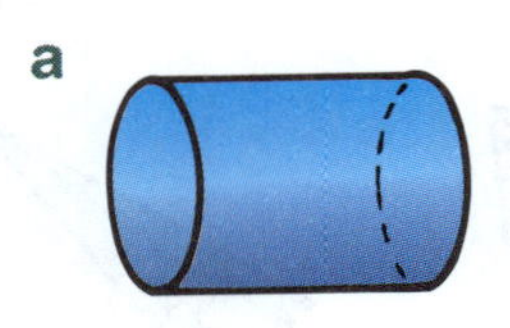

b 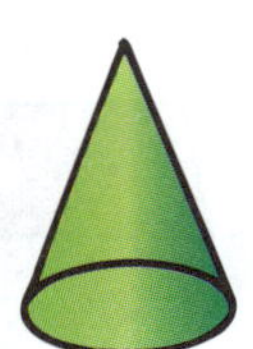

c 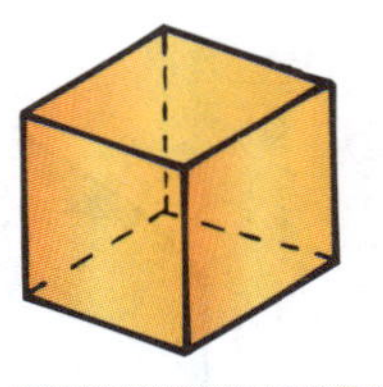

d 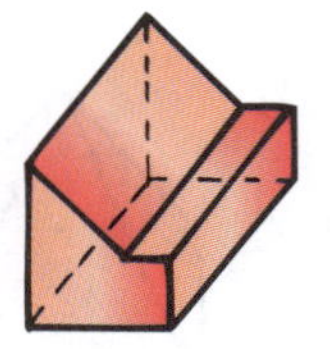

e 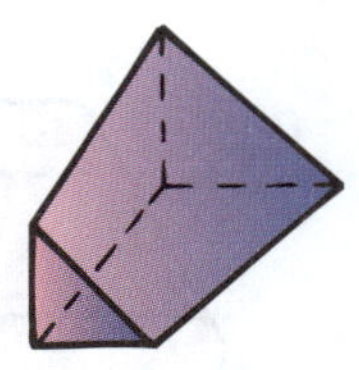

f 

g 

h 

i 

2 Match the object label **X**, **Y** or **Z** with the description.

a I have a curved surface.

b All my faces are rectangles.

c My cross-section is a hexagon.

d My base is a circle.

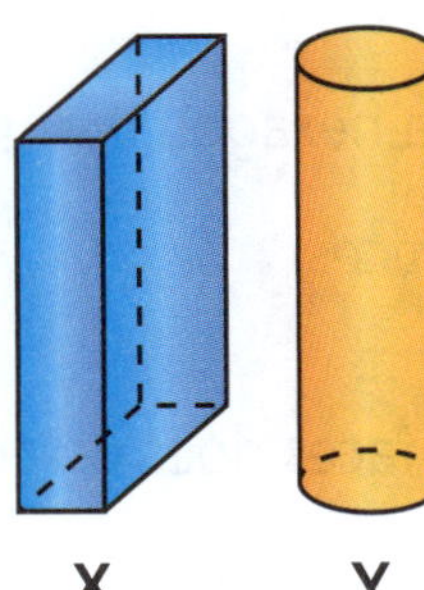
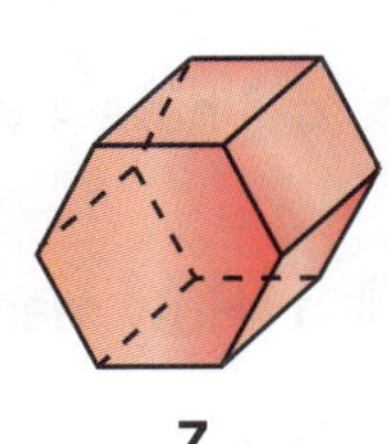

3 a How many faces does object **Z** have?

b How many edges does object **Z** have?

c How many vertices does object **Z** have?

Corners are also called vertices.

4 Draw each face.

The faces are:

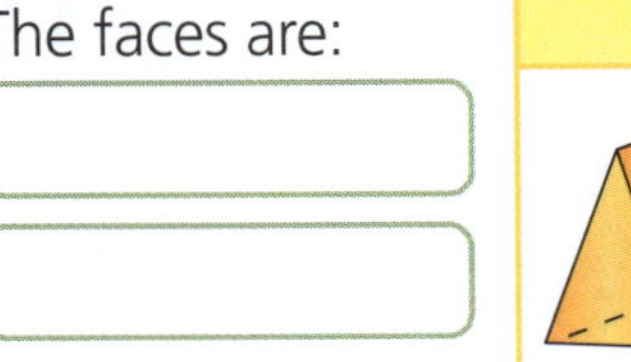

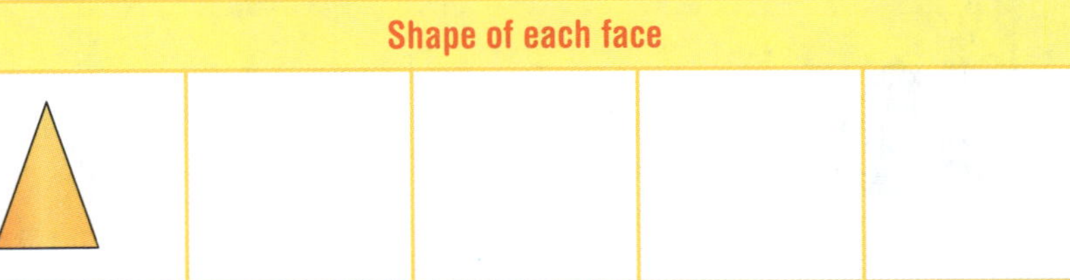

Prism	Shape of each face				

 ISBN 9780655708773

4:20 Pyramids

Cross-sections are usually made parallel to the base.

Pyramids are 3D objects.

- It has one **base**. All the other faces are triangles.
- Its **cross-sections** are the same shape as the base but not the same size.
- One end tapers to a point.

1. Which of these pictures are pyramids?

a  b 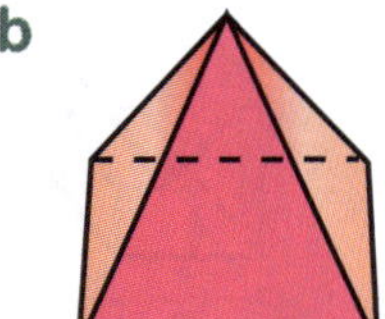 c 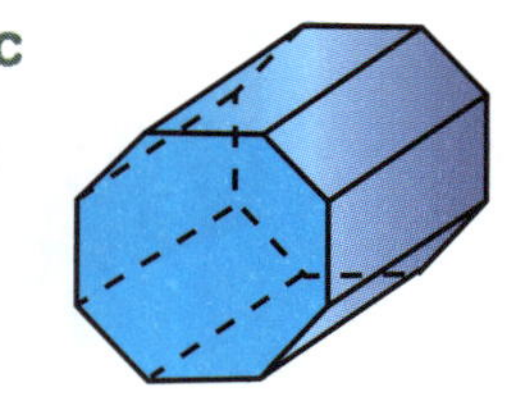 d 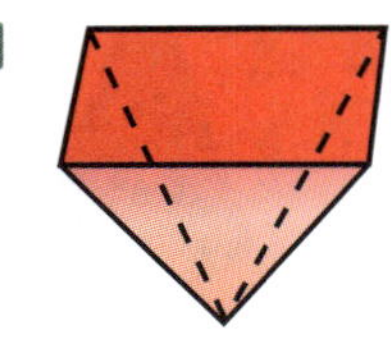 e 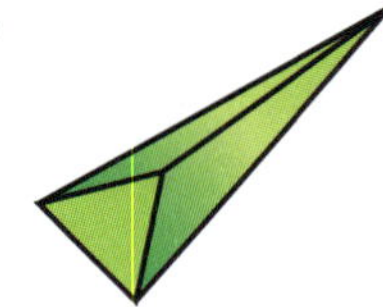

f  g 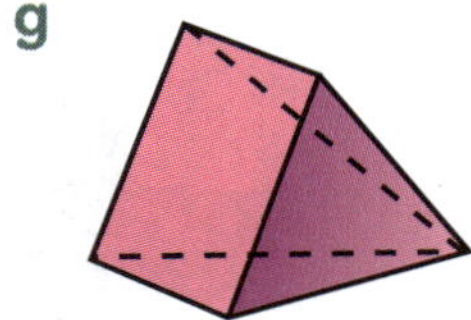 h 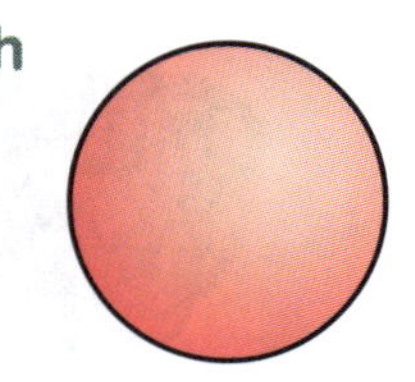 i 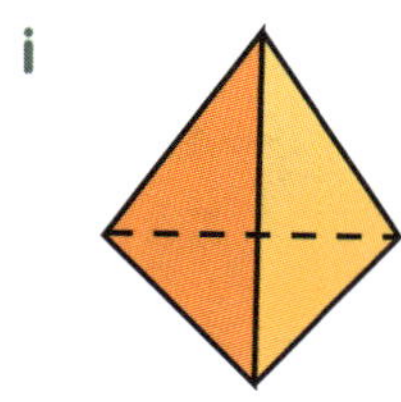 j 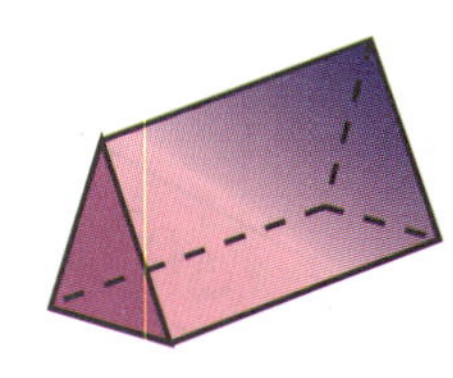

2. Match the object label **A**, **B** or **C** with the description.
   - a All my faces are triangles.
   - b My base is a hexagon.
   - c I have 4 vertices.

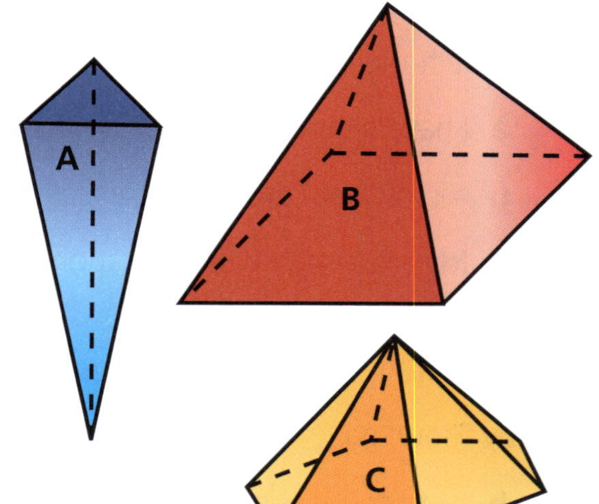

3.
   - a How many faces does object **B** have?
   - b How many edges does object **B** have?
   - c How many vertices does object **B** have?
   - d How many faces does object **A** have?

4. Draw each face of the pyramid. A square pyramid has a square base.

Pyramid	Shape of each face				

The faces are:

4:21 Creating maps

When I look down, it's like looking at a map.

CONCEPT

- **Maps** show where things are, as if you were looking down on them from above.
- This is a map of a classroom.
- Beside the map is a **key**. It describes the symbols on the map.

Key: B = board　　C = cupboard
D = desk　　E = entry
N = noticeboard　　S = sinks
W = window

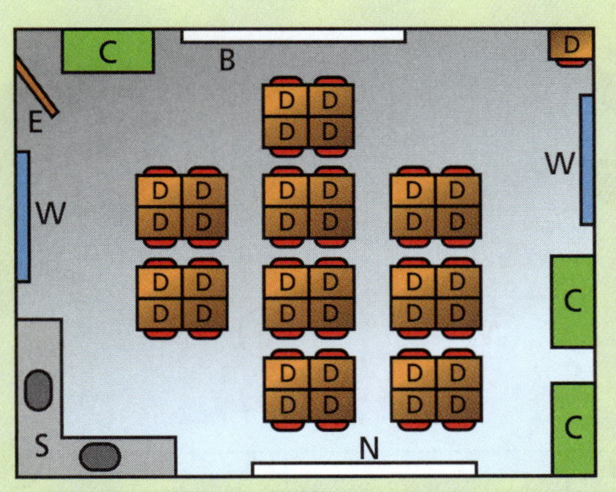

1 Use the classroom map above to answer the questions.

a How many desks are in the classroom?

b How many cupboards are there?

c What is to the left of the board?

d Where is the noticeboard?

2 Draw a map of your own classroom or a room at home.

Key:

Place a red cross at the place where you spend the most time.

INVESTIGATION

Copy a map of your local area. Make a key and use it to show places of interest on the map.

 • *AUSTRALIAN SIGNPOST MATHS 3* • ISBN 9780655708773

4:22 Mazes

Which animal reaches the food? Colour their path.

1

2

3

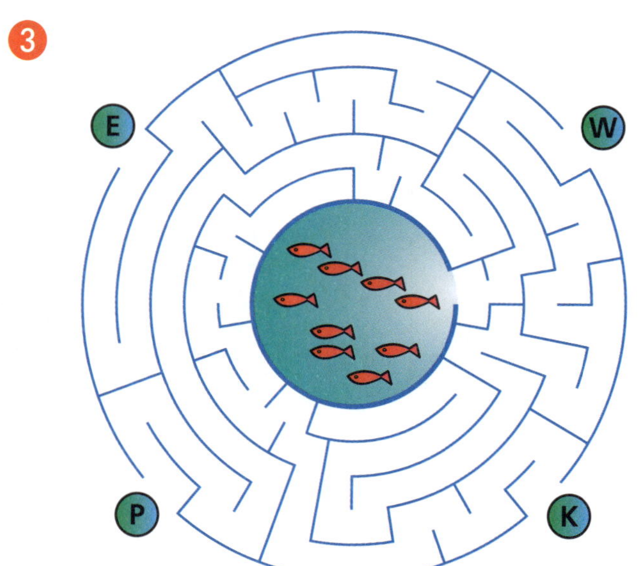

4

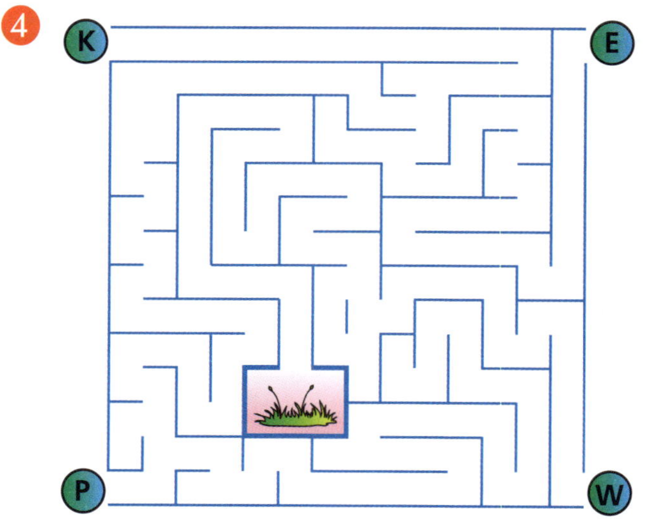

- Use grid paper to make your own maze.

Spheres

CONCEPT

A **sphere** is a 3D object.

- It is like a ball.
- It has one **curved surface**.
- All of the points on the surface are the same distance from the centre.
- Its **cross-section** is always a circle. The circles can be different sizes.

Which countries can you see?

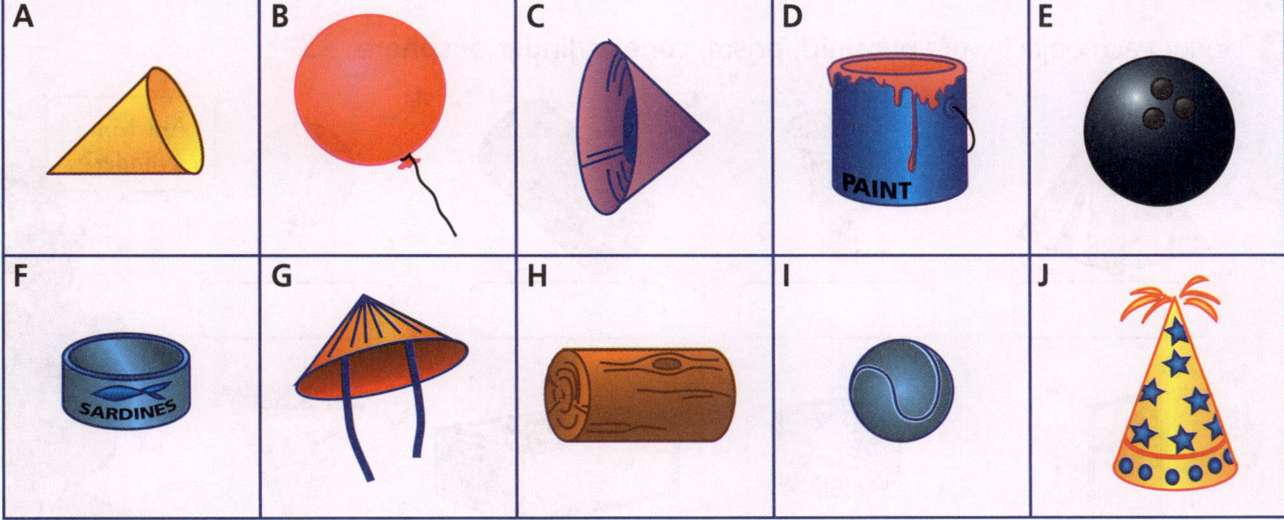

1 a Which pictures show a sphere?

b Which have 2 flat surfaces?

c Which have no vertices (corner points)?

2 Write **true** or **false**. A sphere:

a can stack

b can roll

c can slide

d has a flat surface

e looks like a marble

f looks like a can

ACTIVITY

Draw objects that have the shape of a sphere or part of a sphere.

  ISBN 9780655708773

3D objects

To draw a prism:
- draw two identical shapes
- Join the matching vertices.

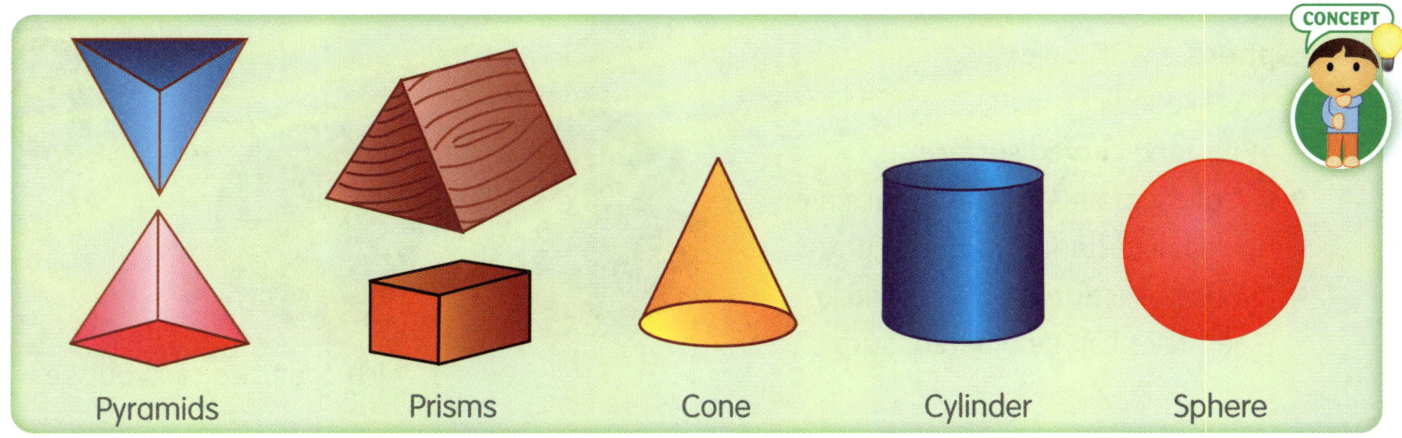

1. Under each object write **pyramid**, **prism**, **cone**, **cylinder** or **sphere**.

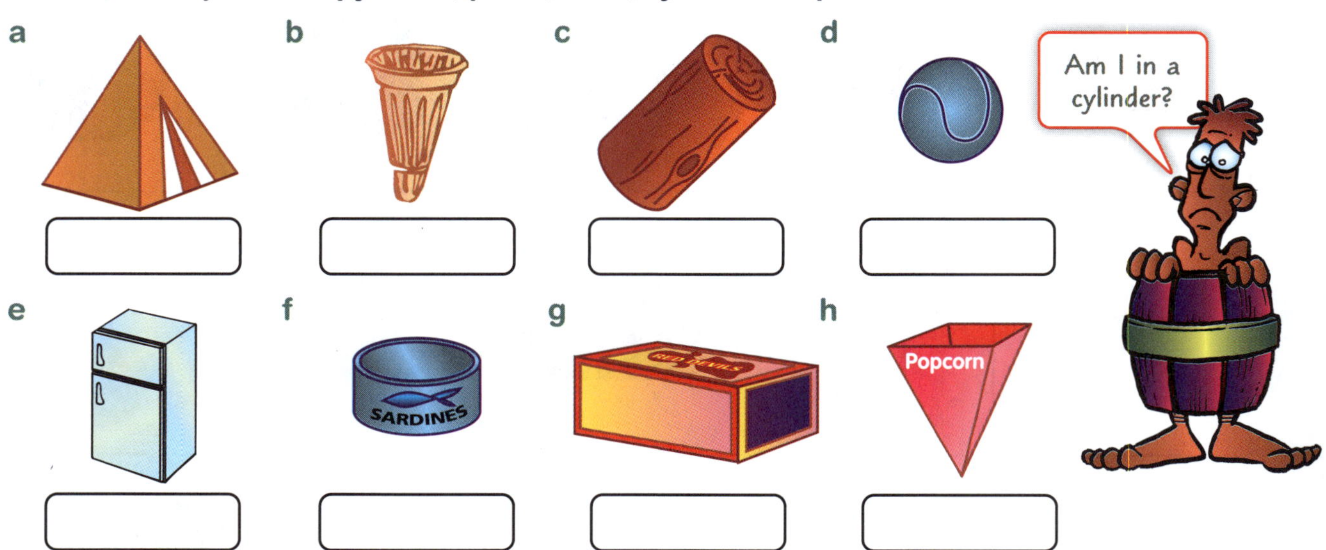

2. Complete the drawings.

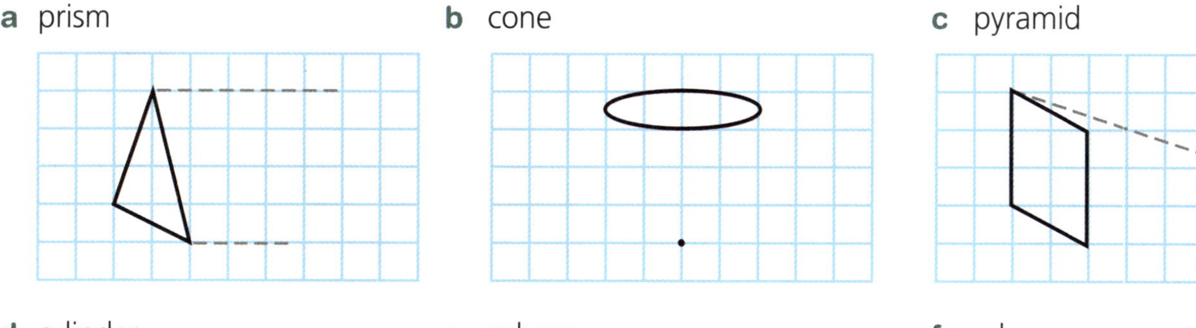

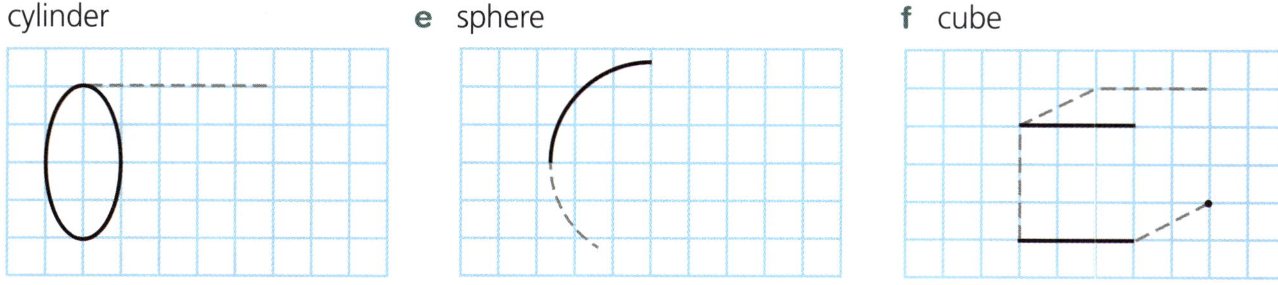

The net of a cube

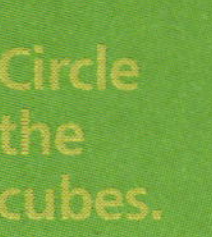

Circle the cubes.

A square box is a cube.

This is the net of a cube.

1. Which of these nets would **not** fold to make a cube? ☐

A

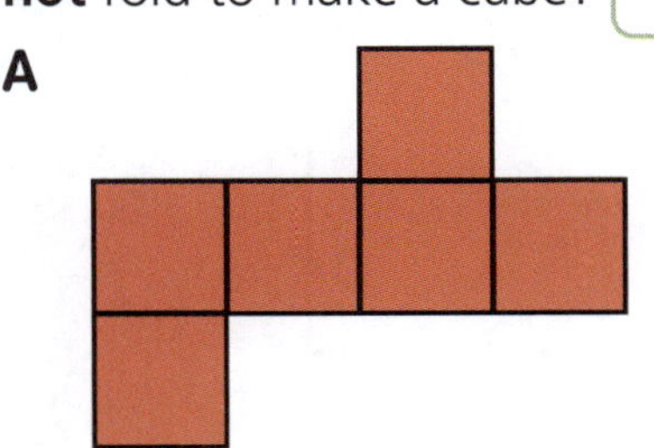

B

C

ACTIVITY

- Trace this net.
- Cut out the net.
- Fold the net to make your own cube.

2. A cube has:

☐ faces

☐ vertices

☐ edges

- Investigate other nets that could make a cube.

 • *AUSTRALIAN SIGNPOST MATHS 3* • ISBN 9780655708773

3D models

This is a skeletal model.
How many vertices (joining points)?
How many edges (toothpicks)?

1 These models have the same height and depth but different lengths.

a Write the number of blocks used for each model.

A 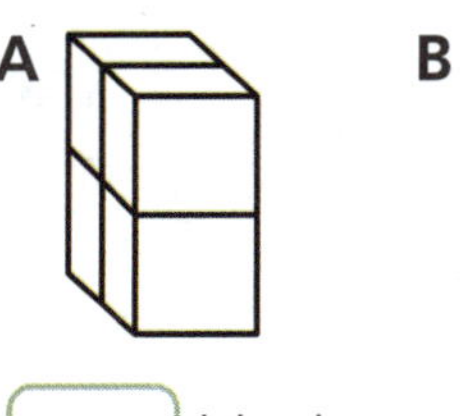
B 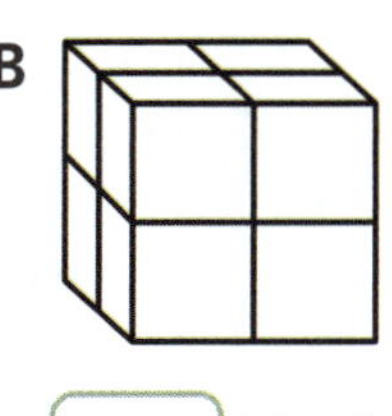
C 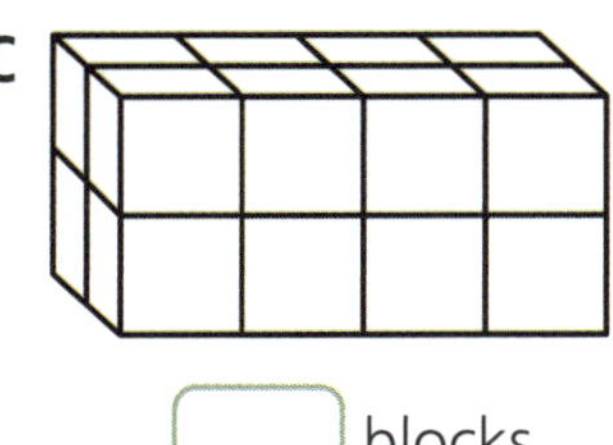
D 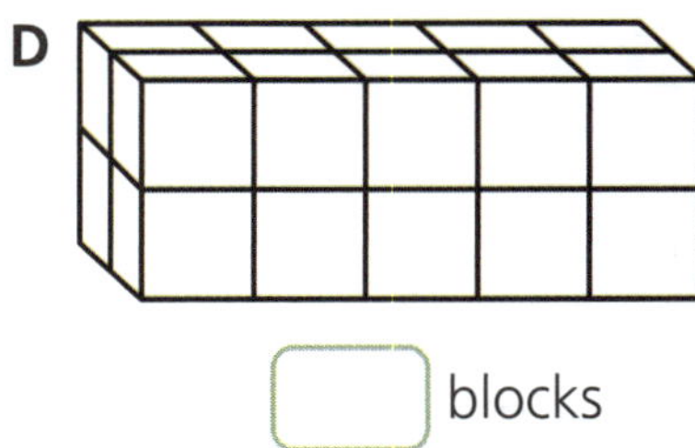

☐ blocks ☐ blocks ☐ blocks ☐ blocks

b What is the connection between the length of the base and the number of blocks?

2 Use straws or toothpicks and plasticine, Blu Tack or modelling clay to make models of:

a a rectangular prism **b** a triangular prism **c** a square pyramid

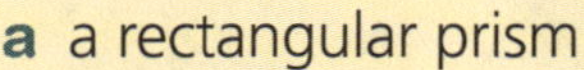
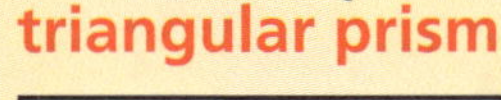

Draw the models you made here.

rectangular prism

triangular prism

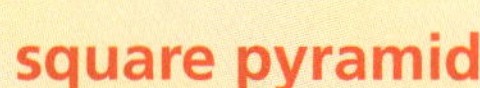

square pyramid

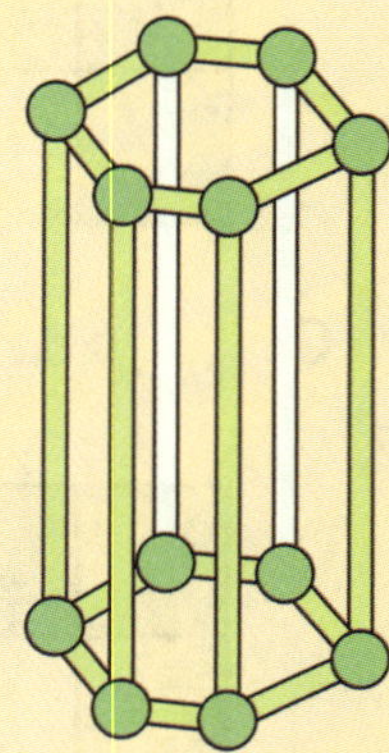

 • *AUSTRALIAN SIGNPOST MATHS 3* • ISBN 9780655708773

Chance words

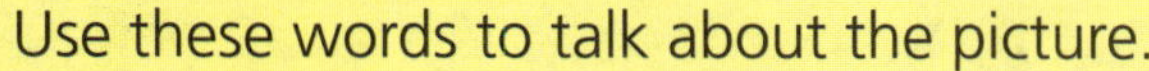

FUN SPOT

Use these words to talk about the picture.

will happen (certain)

won't happen (impossible)

maybe
(rarely happens)

probably
(usually happens)

might happen
(happens sometimes)

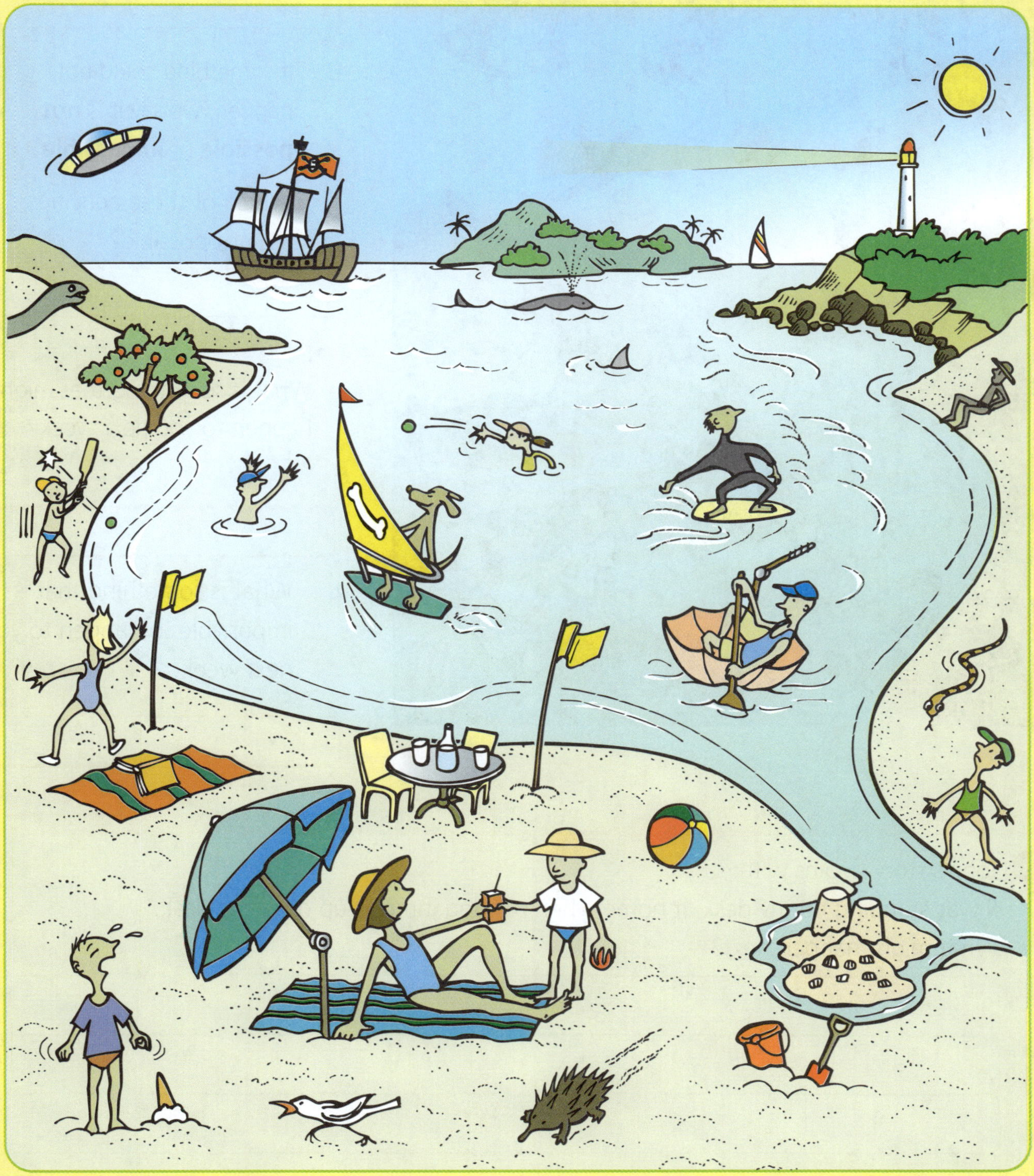

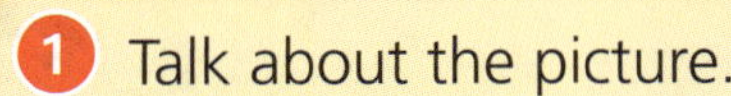

5:02 Chance

Will it rain tomorrow?

Will I pick my name out of this hat?

1 Talk about the picture.

a If something could happen, we say it is **possible**.

Which of these activities are possible?

b If something could not happen, we say it is **not possible** or **impossible**.

Which of these activities are not possible?

2 a What is something that might happen to you next week?

b What is something that is impossible to happen to you next week.

3 John's story begins with:

'I was standing on my desk at home when my dog jumped up onto the desk.'

What might happen next?

What's the chance of this happening?

1 Link each event to the better label.

a

more likely

less likely

b

more likely

less likely

c

more likely

less likely

2 Write what you think is most likely to happen to this tower.

Write something that is impossible to happen to this tower.

3 Sam will take one counter from the container.

What colours can he choose?

Match each box with the label that suits it.

Certain means that it will happen.

red	yellow	blue	red or blue

or

impossible **likely** **certain** **unlikely**

Tables

Tables are used to show the data collected.

1 Each student in the class chose a colour. The results are in the **Colours chosen** table.

Colours chosen			
Blue	Green	Orange	Red
12	8	4	6

a The most popular colour was ______.

b The least popular colour was ______.

c How many students chose green? ______

d How many students are in the class? ______

2 Use the **Collections** table to answer these questions.

Collections		
Person	Number of cards	Number of stickers
Darcy	825	173
Nasha	72	201
Rachel	300	88
Rajiv	166	193
Rhonda	46	405

How many cards were collected by each person?

a Darcy ______ b Rhonda ______

c Rajiv ______ d Nasha ______

How many stickers were collected by each person?

e Rachel ______ f Nasha ______

g Rhonda ______ h Rajiv ______

i How many cards and stickers altogether were collected by Rachel? ______

3 How old is each person?

Name	Age	Name	Age
Alana	27	Alan	57
Diane	38	Luke	20
Deklyn	0	Rachel	23
Greg	10	Tom	87
Heather	17	Naomi	22

a Tom ______

b Alana ______

c Rachel ______

d Deklyn ______

e Make up your own question that could be answered using this table.

______

______

INVESTIGATION

- Do you think there are more left-handed or right-handed students in your class?
- Investigate the question by completing this tally.
- By how many is one group bigger than the other? ______

Right-handed		
Left-handed		

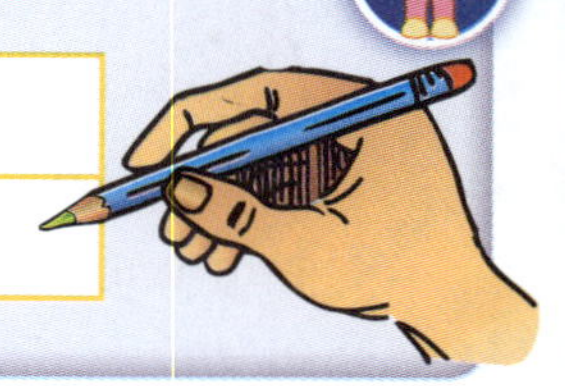

5:05 Tables and graphs

How is data displayed on this page?

Pets kept in the classroom

Birds	🐦 🐦 🐦
Fish	🐟 🐟 🐟 🐟 🐟 🐟
Mice	🐭 🐭 🐭 🐭 🐭 🐭
Turtles	🐢

1. **a** How many turtles are kept? ☐
   b How many birds are kept? ☐
   c Which rows are longest? ☐
   d Three of which pet are kept? ☐
   e How many pets altogether? ☐

2. Use the graph to complete these tables.

A

Pets kept in the classroom			
Birds	Fish	Mice	Turtles

B

Pets kept in the classroom	
Birds	
Fish	
Mice	
Turtles	

Pets kept in the classroom

Birds								
Fish								
Mice								
Turtles								
	0 1	2	3	4	5	6	7	8

   a How many classroom pets can fly? ☐
   b How many classroom pets are there altogether? ☐
   c Which table do you think looks better, **A** or **B**? ☐
   d Complete the graph.

When the parts of a graph are aligned, it is quicker to compare the categories.

3. **a** Use this table to complete the graph.

Youth group attendance				
Carmen	Erika	Holly	Paul	Yong
4	5	3	7	6

Youth group attendance

Carmen	● ● ● ●
Erika	● ● ● ● ●
Holly	
Paul	
Yong	

   b Who has attended the least? ☐
   c Did Yong attend more often than Erika? ☐
   d Erika has been away three times. How many times has the group met? ☐

4. **Collecting and displaying data**

INVESTIGATION

Step 1: Decide on a class topic of interest. ☐
Step 2: Collect your data. (Discuss the best way to do this.)
Step 3: Record your data in a table or spreadsheet.
Step 4: Create a graph to display your data.
Step 5: Reflect on and share what you discovered.

 • *AUSTRALIAN SIGNPOST MATHS 3* • ISBN 9780655708773

5:06 Picture graphs

In Question 1, each picture stands for 2 trains.

1 a How many trains were sold on Monday?

b On which day were the most trains sold?

c How many trains were sold altogether?

d If there were 30 trains for sale, how many trains were not sold?

Discuss what else this graph tells us.

Toy trains sold

Day	
Monday	
Tuesday	
Wednesday	
Thursday	
Friday	

Key: stands for 2 toy trains

2 Students cut out shapes to show some of the languages spoken at home. They made this graph using one shape for each student.

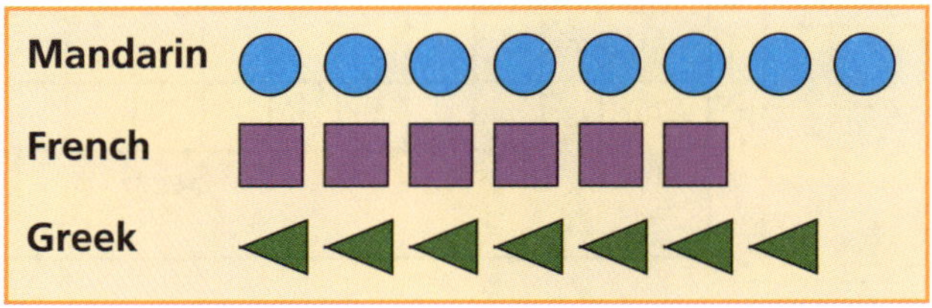

a How many students speak Greek?

b How many students speak French?

c How many students speak Mandarin?

d Which row is the longest?

3 Liz made this graph using stones, blocks and counters. She used a stone for each car she saw, a block for each truck and a counter for each van.

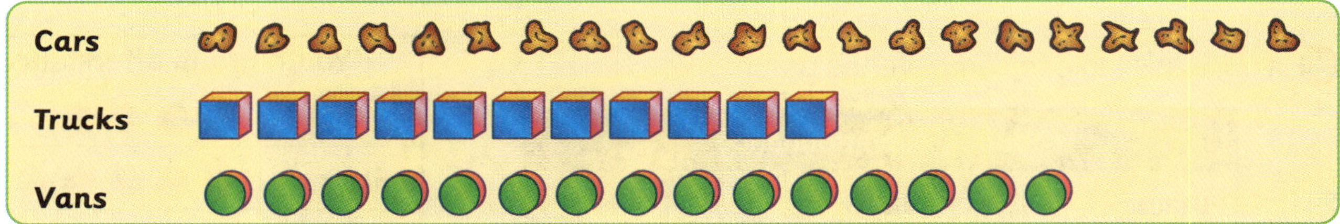

a How many cars did Liz see?

b How many vans did she see?

c How many more cars than trucks did she see?

d How many vehicles were seen altogether?

Car colour tallies

- Work in groups. Each group records the colours of cars that drive by in 10 minutes.
- Use tally marks to record the colours of cars.
- Groups discuss and compare their results.
- Create a graph showing the popular colours.

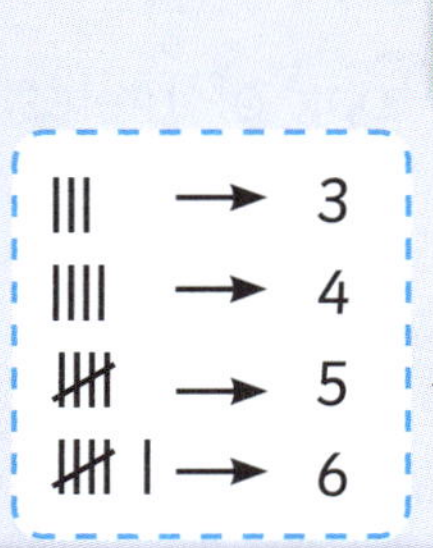

 • *AUSTRALIAN SIGNPOST MATHS 3* • ISBN 9780655708773

Making graphs

卌 A tally is used to record the data collected.

1 Tina rolled these dice. Finish the graph to show how many of each number she rolled.

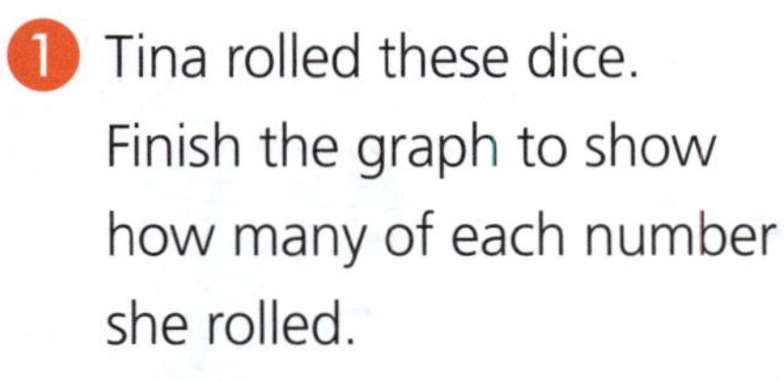

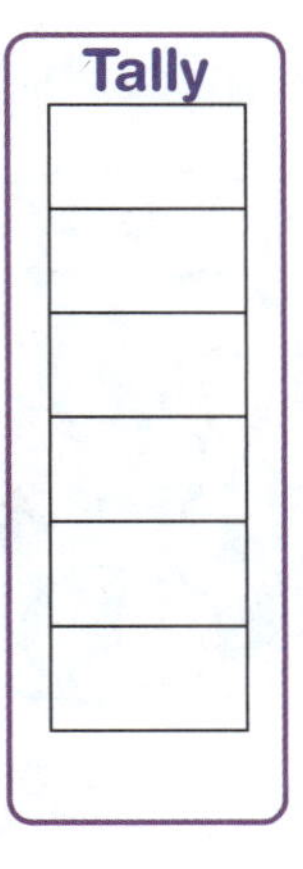

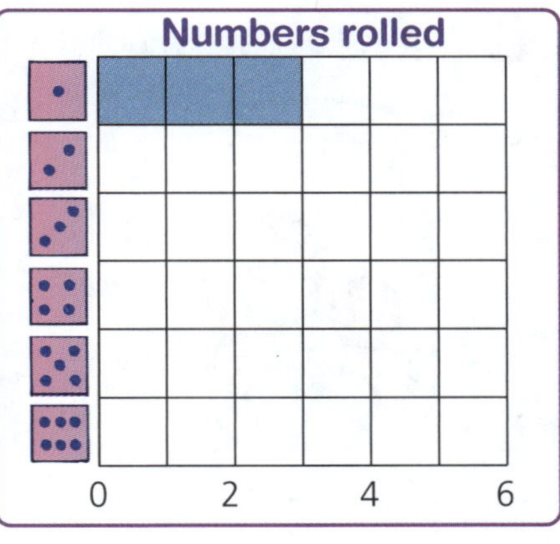

2 Gino made this table using tally marks. It shows the favourite game of each of his friends. Use this information to complete both graphs.

Game	Tally	Number
Handball	卌 III	8
Hopscotch	卌 II	7
Marbles	卌 卌	10
Skipping	IIII	4

Columns in a graph can go up or across.

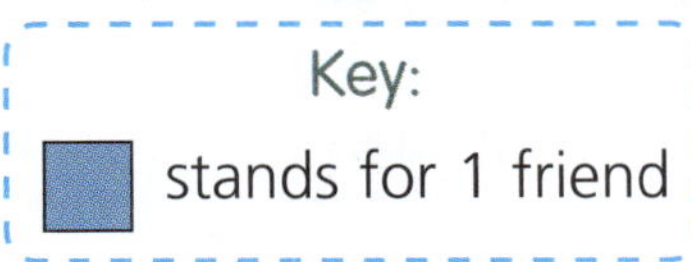

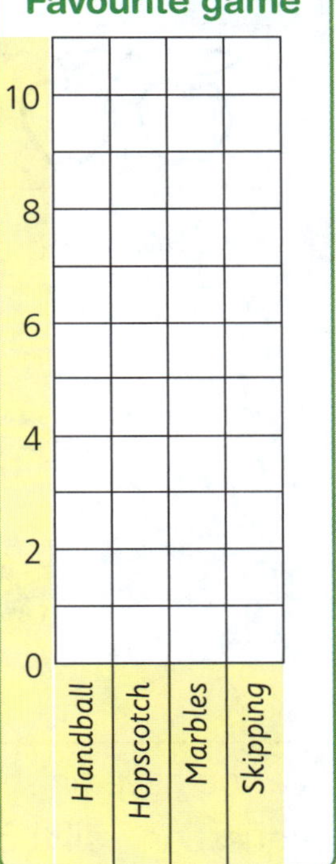

Favourite game

Handball										
Hopscotch										
Marbles										
Skipping										

0 2 4 6 8 10

3
- After talking to your friends, choose four popular games they like.
- Write them in the table and graph below.
- Ask people in your class to choose the game they like best out of the four games. Keep a tally of the answers in the table.
- Draw a graph to display the data.

Game	Tally	Total

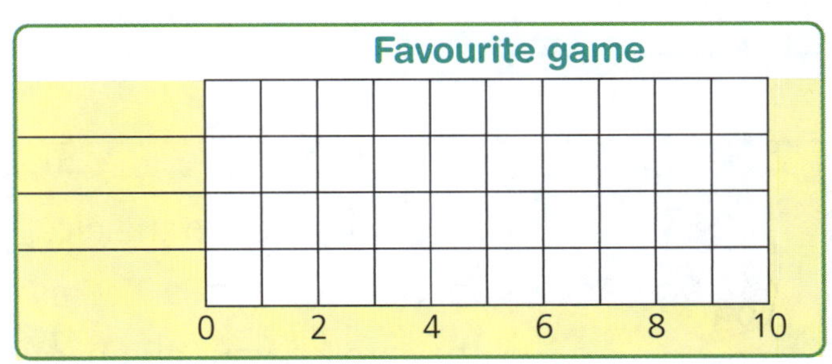

 • *AUSTRALIAN SIGNPOST MATHS 3* • ISBN 9780655708773

5:08 Chance

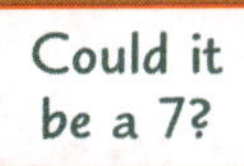

1 Is it certain, likely, unlikely or impossible that a red ball would be chosen?

a

6 red, 4 blue

b

3 red, 7 blue

c

all red

d

all blue

2 Colour these apples red or green so that green is more likely to be chosen if you are not looking.

3 A dice is rolled once. What are the possible outcomes?

Each outcome is equally likely to happen.

4 Roll a dice six times. Write each number rolled.

a Which number (or numbers) was rolled most?

b Which numbers were not rolled?

c Is it possible to throw six ones in a row?

Why is this almost impossible?

Once you have finished this question, roll the dice again and compare the results.

- Choose a number on the dice.
- Count how many rolls it takes until you have rolled your number twice. ____ rolls

Prediction: ____ rolls

Tally	Total

5:09 Possible outcomes

Will my plant die?
What should I do?

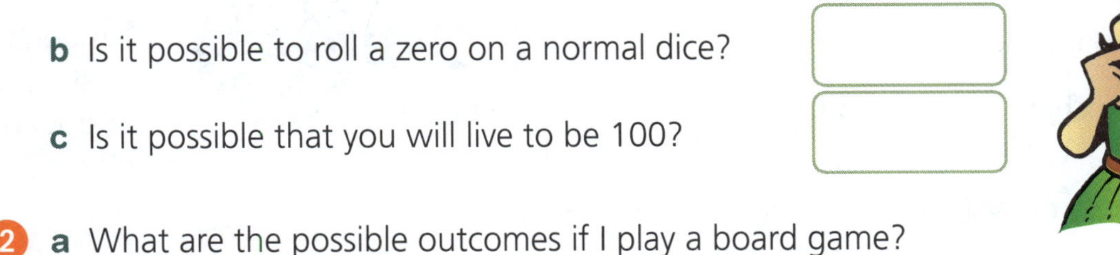

1 a Is it possible that it will rain tomorrow?

b Is it possible to roll a zero on a normal dice?

c Is it possible that you will live to be 100?

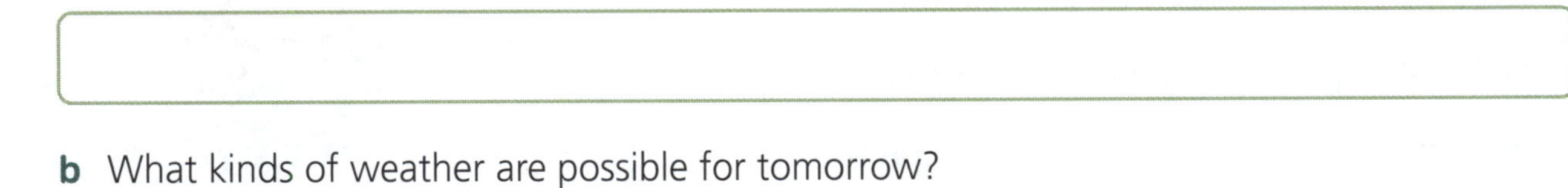

2 a What are the possible outcomes if I play a board game?

b What kinds of weather are possible for tomorrow?

3

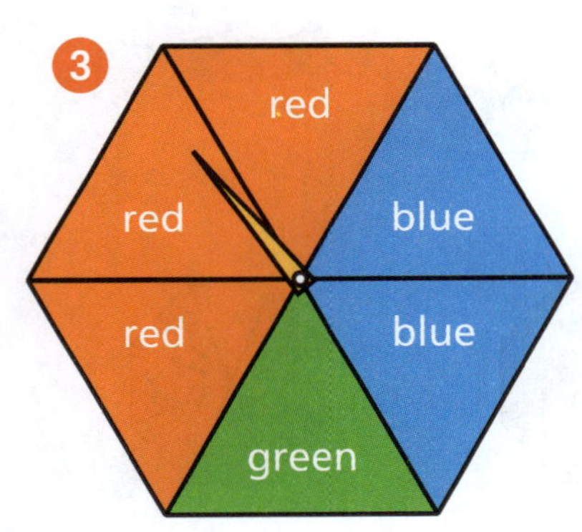

a List all possible outcomes for this spinner.

b Which colour is most likely to be spun?

c Which colour is least likely to be spun?

d Is it possible to spin yellow?

e Is there an even chance of spinning red?

4 How likely is it that a three will be rolled on a dice and the three of diamonds will also be selected from the boy's hand?

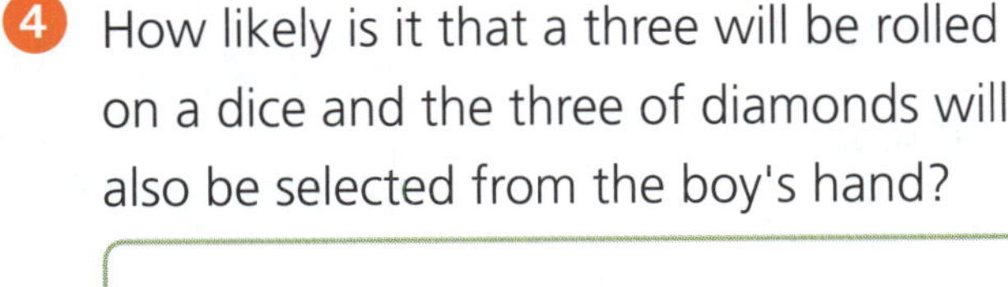

Possible answers: Impossible, highly unlikely, even chance, highly likely, certain

INVESTIGATION

- Toss a coin until you have tossed 3 heads.
  Have a friend count the number of tosses needed.
- Guess how many times it will take you to toss three heads next time.
  Repeat the experiment. It took ☐ tosses.

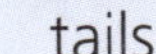

head tails

 • *AUSTRALIAN SIGNPOST MATHS 3* • ISBN 9780655708773

Chance

Tallies

1			4		
2			5		
3			6		

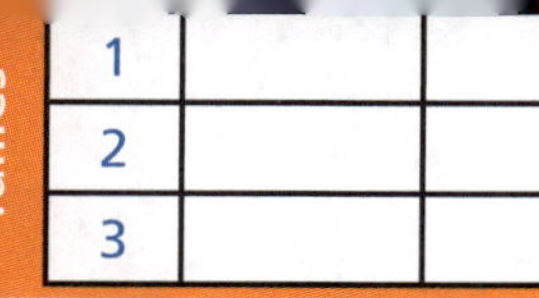

Toss a dice 50 times.

An even chance means it should happen half the time.

1. If you toss a coin, it can come up heads or tails.
   - a Is heads more likely than tails?
   - b Is there an even chance of tossing tails?

2. If you spin the arrow on a spinner, it can land on any colour.
   - a Is there 1 chance in 3 of spinning red?
   - b Do all colours have an equal chance of being spun?
   - c Is there an even chance it will land on blue?

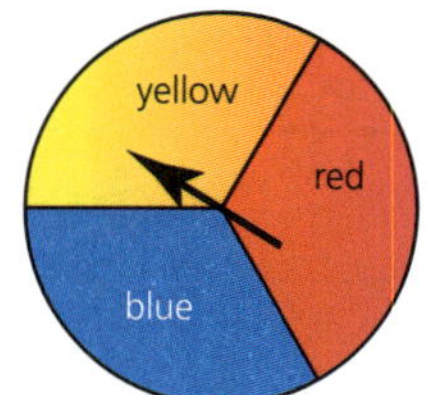

3. Without looking, Jai took a coloured ball from the bowl.
   - a Which colour is more likely to be taken?
   - b Is it possible to take a yellow ball?
   - c Is there an even chance of taking green?

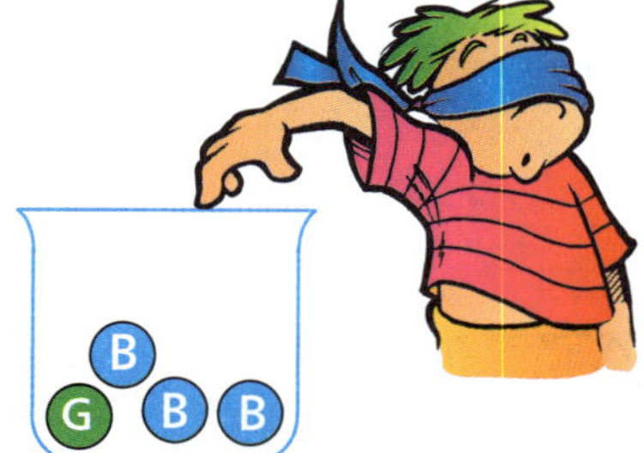

4. These spinners can stop on red or yellow.

A B C D E

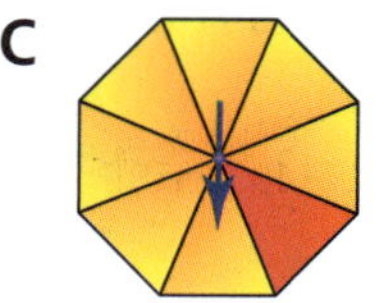
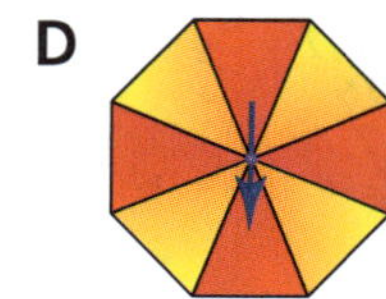
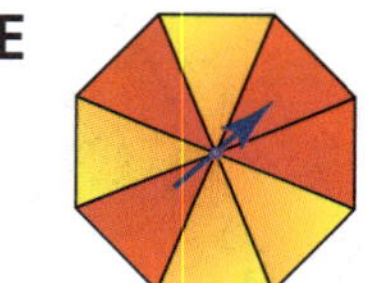

   - a Which spinner is most likely to stop on yellow?
   - b Which spinner is most likely to stop on red?
   - c Which spinners are equally likely to stop on red or yellow?
   - d Is there an even chance that spinner **D** will stop on red?
   - e Is there an even chance that spinner **B** will stop on yellow?
   - f On spinner **B**, is it fair if Ben wins on red and Michelle wins on yellow?
   - g On spinner **D**, is it fair if Ben wins on red and Michelle wins on yellow?

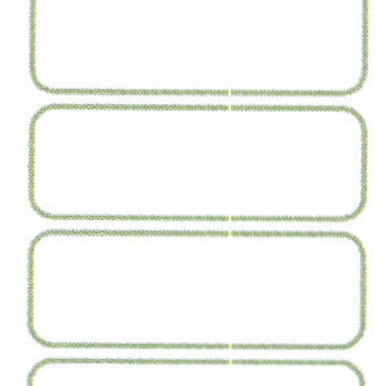

INVESTIGATION

- Make a spinner like this.
- Spin the arrow 50 times. Keep a tally of the colours that you spin.
- Is your spinner fair? How can you tell? Discuss.

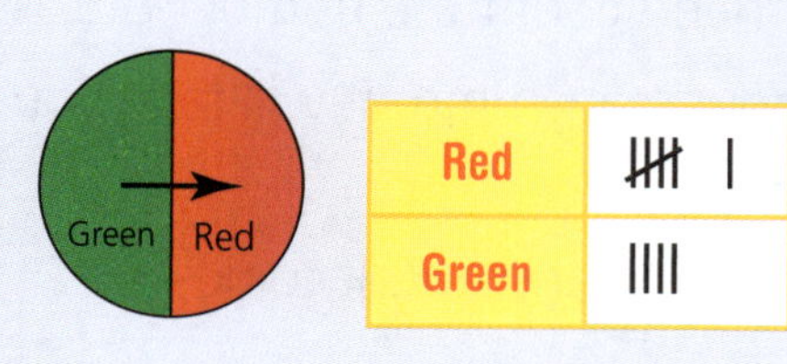

Red	𝍸 I
Green	IIII

 • *AUSTRALIAN SIGNPOST MATHS 3* • ISBN 9780655708773

Reading tables and graphs

Tables can be read across or down.

Use the tables and graphs to answer the questions.

1 How many of these people were at the play?

a female teachers ☐

b male students ☐

c female parents ☐

d teachers ☐

e males ☐

f altogether ☐

This is called a **two-way** table.

People at the school play

	Parents	Students	Teachers
Female	70	120	6
Male	80	100	4

2 a Who has the most merit stamps? ☐

b Who has the least stamps? ☐

c How many stamps does Adiva have? ☐

d How many stamps does Juan have? ☐

e How many stamps do Benjamin and Amanda have altogether? ☐

f What is the total number of stamps that Adiva and Brittany have? ☐

Merit stamps

Adiva
Amanda
Benjamin
Brittany
Juan

0 2 4 6 8 10 12 14 16 18

3 a How many students practised on:

Monday? ☐ Friday? ☐

b On which two days did the same number of students practise? ☐

c What was the total number of students who practised on Wednesday and Friday? ☐

d How many more students practised on Thursday than on Wednesday? ☐

e Can we tell how many different students practised during the week? ☐

Students at sports practice

Mon
Tues
Wed
Thurs
Fri

stands for 2 students

Graph display

- Collect or create different types of graphs.
- Compare and discuss the graphs.
- Use them to make a display in your classroom.

 • *AUSTRALIAN SIGNPOST MATHS 3* • ISBN 9780655708773

5:12 Reading picture graphs

Each picture can stand for many items.

1 a How many pears did Peter grow in 2009?

b How many more pears were grown in 2009 than in 2008?

c In which year was the least number of pears grown?

d How many pears were grown in these four years?

e If one [pear] stands for 100 pears, what would half of a [pear] stand for?

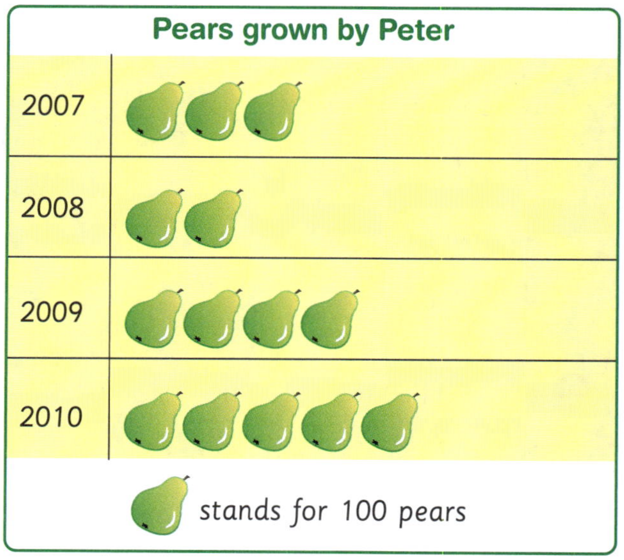

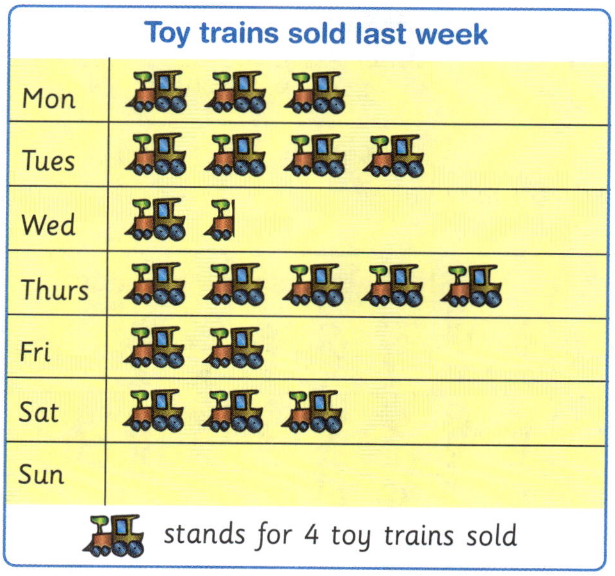

Pears grown by Peter

Year	Pears
2007	🍐🍐🍐
2008	🍐🍐
2009	🍐🍐🍐🍐
2010	🍐🍐🍐🍐🍐

[pear] stands for 100 pears

Toy trains sold last week

Day	Trains
Mon	3 trains
Tues	4 trains
Wed	1 and a half trains
Thurs	5 trains
Fri	2 trains
Sat	3 trains
Sun	

[train] stands for 4 toy trains sold

2 a How many toy trains were sold on Tuesday?

b How many toy trains were sold on Saturday?

c On which day were the most trains sold?

d On what two days were the same number of trains sold?

e How many more trains were sold on Thursday than on Friday?

f What was the total number of trains sold?

g Why do you think no sales were made on Sunday?

3 a How many cars crossed the bridge from 1 pm to 2 pm?

b During which hour did the least number of cars cross the bridge?

c During which hour did 30 cars cross?

d How many cars crossed altogether?

e Why do you think so many cars crossed between 4 pm and 6 pm?

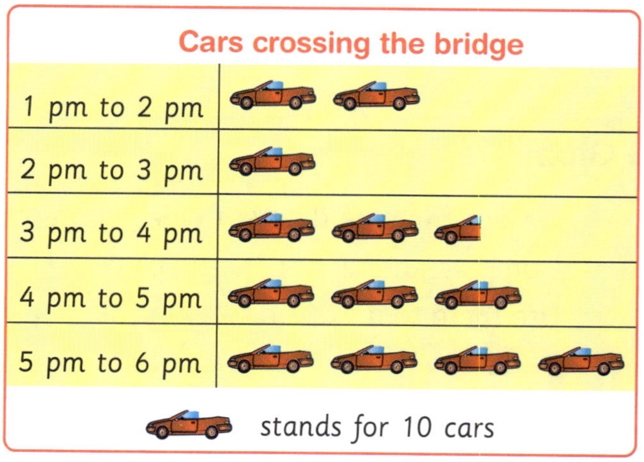

Cars crossing the bridge

Time	Cars
1 pm to 2 pm	2 cars
2 pm to 3 pm	1 car
3 pm to 4 pm	2 and a half cars
4 pm to 5 pm	3 cars
5 pm to 6 pm	4 cars

[car] stands for 10 cars

Dicey graphs

If I tossed a dice 10 times would I throw every number?

Class investigation

There is an equal chance of throwing each number on a dice but the results do not always show this.

Question: If we throw a dice many times would the number of 1s, 2s, 3s, 4s, 5s and 6s be very close? How close do you think?

Step 1: Form small groups in your class.

Step 2: In your group, toss a dice 100 times.

Step 3: Record the numbers thrown in the table.

My results for 100 throws

Number on dice	Tally	Total
1		
2		
3		
4		
5		
6		

1. How close are the totals?

Step 4: Use the table below to combine your results with the results of other groups.

2. How close are these totals?

Combined results

Number on dice	Results for our group	Results for group 1	Results for group 2	Results for group 3	Total
1					
2					
3					
4					
5					
6					

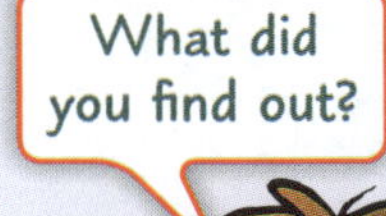

Step 5: Graph the combined total and discuss the results.

The results for ____ throws

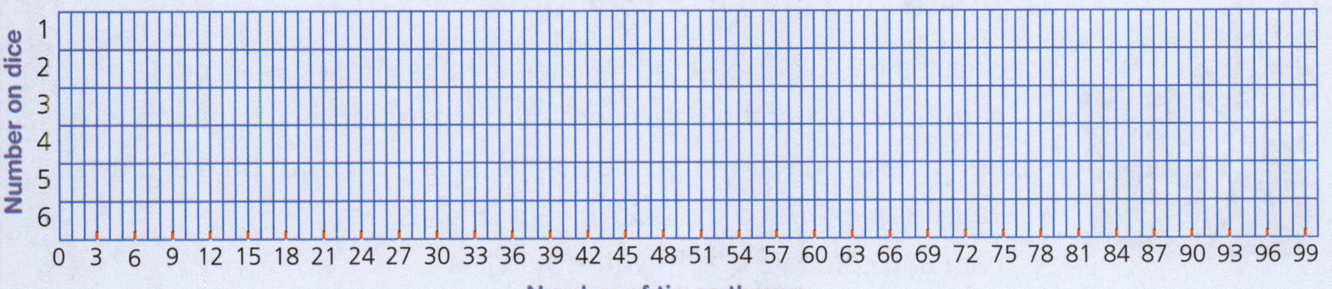

 • *AUSTRALIAN SIGNPOST MATHS 3* • ISBN 9780655708773

5:14 Class investigation

We need to decide on a question of interest first.

INVESTIGATION

Question of interest: Who has the longest and the shortest shoe, a boy or a girl?

Step 1: Ask for volunteers to take part (about 8 boys and 8 girls).

Each student taking part measures one of their shoes.

Step 2: Decide how you will measure the shoe lengths.

Stand on a ruler? Trace your shoe?

Step 3: Predict who will have the longest shoe length, a boy or a girl?

Predict who will have the shortest shoe length, a boy or a girl?

Step 4: Measure and record the shoe length of boys and girls (to the nearest cm).

Shoe lengths of boys and girls

Measurement (cm)	Boys' tally	Total	Girls' tally	Total
1				
2				
3				
4				
5				
6				

This is an example of a spreadsheet.

Shoe lengths

cm	Boys	Girls
21		1
22	1	1
23	1	2
24	3	1
25	2	2
26		1
27	1	
Total	8	8

Step 5: Discuss your results.

The longest shoe length belonged to a ______.

The shortest shoe length belonged to a ______.

The steps are like a flowchart.

Organise your data in a spreadsheet

ICT

- Enter the data you collected for shoe lengths into a spreadsheet.
- Learn how to **sort** the data in order from smallest shoe length to longest.
- Use the **sum function** to calculate the total number of boys and girls.
- Create a graph using the data in your spreadsheet.
- Share and compare graphs with your class.

 • *AUSTRALIAN SIGNPOST MATHS 3* • ISBN 9780655708773

Predicting outcomes

I predict that all of my guests will like gum leaves.

1 Without looking, Meg took a coloured ball from the beaker and did not replace it.

a Which colour is least likely to be taken?

b Which colour is most likely to be taken?

c Is there an even chance of taking a yellow ball?

d Could Meg take the red ball first?

e If Meg took the red ball first, what colours could she take next?

f If Meg took a blue ball first, what colours could she take next?

2 Put 1 yellow, 3 blue and 5 red counters into a bag.
Pick one counter at random.

a Which colour is most likely to be picked?

b Which colour is least likely to be picked?

3 This spinner is spun 10 times.

a Would you be surprised if blue was spun every time?

Why or why not?

b If 3 blues are spun in a row, would this affect the chance of spinning a blue on the next spin?

Why or why not?

4 a Are all three colours equally likely to be spun?

b How many red spins would you expect out of 6 spins?

- There would be 1 chance out of 243 of spinning 5 reds in a row. This is not impossible but it is highly unlikely.

INVESTIGATION

- Put 1 yellow, 3 blue and 5 red counters into a bag.
- Randomly pick one counter from the bag.
- Record a tally mark for that colour.
- Put the counter back in the bag.
- Repeat this experiment 50 times.
- What do the tallies show? Discuss your results.

Taking counters from a bag		
Blue		
Red		
Yellow		

Ordering events

I'm more likely to see the next bird than he is.

1 Choose a label to match each statement.

impossible | unlikely | even chance | very likely | certain

a I bought a ticket in a raffle and I will win.

b Our next teacher will be six years old.

c The next school captain will be a student.

d If I drop an egg on the road, it will break.

e We will do maths on our next day at school.

f It will be warmer in December than in May.

g I will see a lion on the way home from school.

h This year, half the students in my class will grow tails.

i The next student I see will have been born after 1900.

j If I toss a coin, it will come up heads.

2 Write the letter of each part of Question 1 in the table below to show each statement's chance.

Will always happen	It can happen (but not always)	Will never happen

3 Put the following events in order from least likely to most likely.

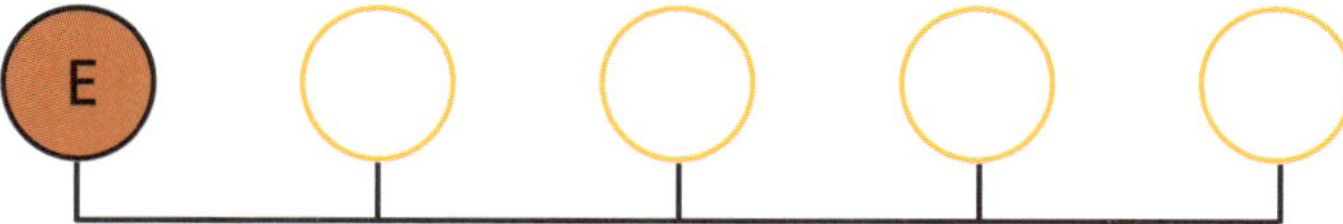

Least Likely — Most Likely

A We will have an earthquake today.

B I will go to school in November.

C I will stay up late tonight.

D We will be given homework on our next school day.

E A dinosaur will walk into our classroom tomorrow.

FUN SPOT

- Use this picture to make up four events that could happen. For example, the man could drop the spinning plate.
- Write your four events in order from least likely to most likely.

 • *AUSTRALIAN SIGNPOST MATHS 3* • ISBN 9780655708773

5:17 Drawing graphs

What is your favourite way to display data?

1 Kai-Lin kept a tally of the hair colour of students in her class. Use the table to finish the graph.

Hair colour	Tally	Number
Black	卌 卌 ||	12
Blonde	卌 卌	10
Brown	||||	4
Red	||	2

a Which colour was the most common?

b How many students had grey hair?

c How many more students had blonde hair than brown hair?

d How many students were there altogether?

e What is the key on the graph used for?

f Why do you think people use picture graphs?

Hair colour in Kai-Lin's class

Black	● ● ● ● ● ●
Blonde	
Brown	
Red	

Key: ● stands for 2 students

2 What are the advantages of showing information as a:

a tally?

b column graph?

c sector graph?

Cars washed		
Monday	Tuesday	Friday
6	8	4

Cars washed	
Monday	卌 |
Tuesday	卌 |||
Friday	||||

Cars washed

Monday	■■■
Tuesday	■■■■
Friday	■■
	0 2 4 6 8 10

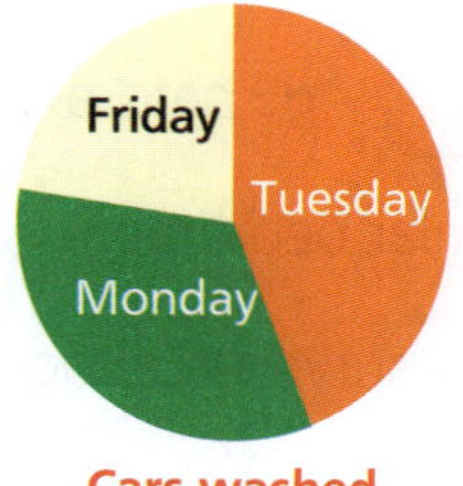

Cars washed

Cars washed

Monday	🚗 🚗 🚗
Tuesday	🚗 🚗 🚗 🚗
Friday	🚗 🚗

🚗 stands for 2 cars

Using computers

- Using a computer spreadsheet program, create a table to organise collected data for a question of interest.
- Use the spreadsheet program to make a variety of graphs from your data.
- Share and compare the graphs you made with your class.

ICT

Do you like cats?
Yes ☐ No ☐

CONCEPT

- **Surveys** are used to discover information, to give us a general view of a situation or to check predictions.
- If everyone is surveyed from the group we wish to study, we have carried out a **census**.
- Surveys can be written or digital.

1 Jared chose as his survey topic: *The time my classmates go to bed.* He asked everyone in his class.

Jared's survey *When my classmates go to bed.*

Tick the box next to the time you went to bed last night.

- ☐ before 8 pm
- ☐ between 8 pm and 9 pm
- ☐ between 9 pm and 10 pm
- ☐ between 10 pm and 11 pm
- ☐ after 11 pm

Jared's results *When my classmates go to bed.*

before 8 pm	𝍸 𝍸 ||| (13)
between 8 pm and 9 pm	𝍸 𝍸 (10)
between 9 pm and 10 pm	||||
between 10 pm and 11 pm	||
after 11 pm	|

How many students went to bed:

a before 8 pm? ☐ **b** between 9 pm and 10 pm? ☐

c after 11 pm? ☐ **d** before 9 pm? ☐ **e** before 11 pm? ☐

f What was the most popular bed time? ☐

g How many students were surveyed altogether? ☐ Was this a census? ☐

h Make up a question of your own that could be answered using these results.

☐

2 Write down a topic that you would like to use in a survey of your class.

☐

Write two questions you would like to ask about this topic.

a ☐

b ☐

Carry out your own survey

Do you like dogs?
Yes ☐ No ☐

INVESTIGATION

Step 1: Choose a topic you are interested in for your survey.

Topic:

Step 2: Write a question to ask people about your topic.

Question:

Step 3: Decide how you will collect and record the answers (data).

Step 4: Predict what the data will show.

I think

Step 5: Represent your results using tables and graphs. (You could use technology to do this.)

Step 6: Reflect and write what you have learnt from your data.

I found

Step 7: Share your results.

Reflection: Was using a survey useful? What did you do well and what could you do better next time? What other topics could you research using a survey?

ICT

- Research written and online surveys.
- Learn about the Australian census and research some data that has been collected.
- Use a digital tool such as Google Forms, Microsoft Forms, Kahoot or Survey Monkey.

Researching data

Each graph needs a title. There are many data displays online.

1

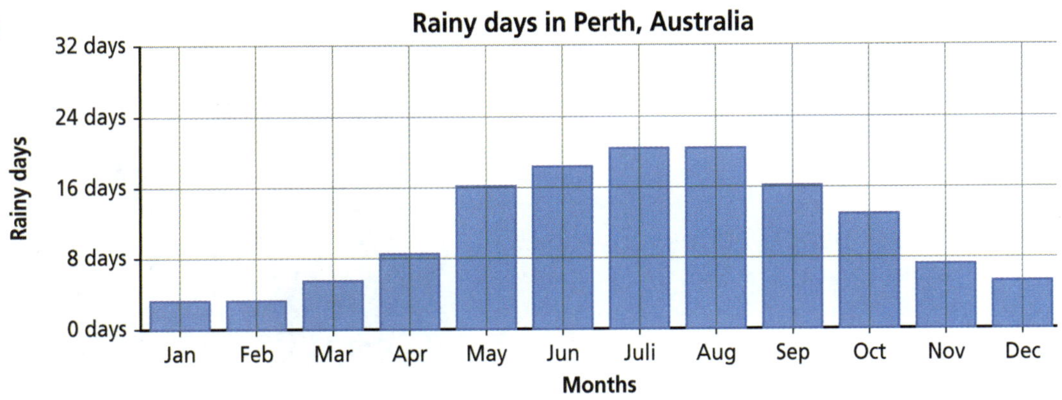

a Which months had the least rainy days in Perth?

b How many days did it rain in May?

c Which season had the most rainy days?

d Which two months had closest to 8 days of rain?

e Is it possible that June had more rain than August?

2

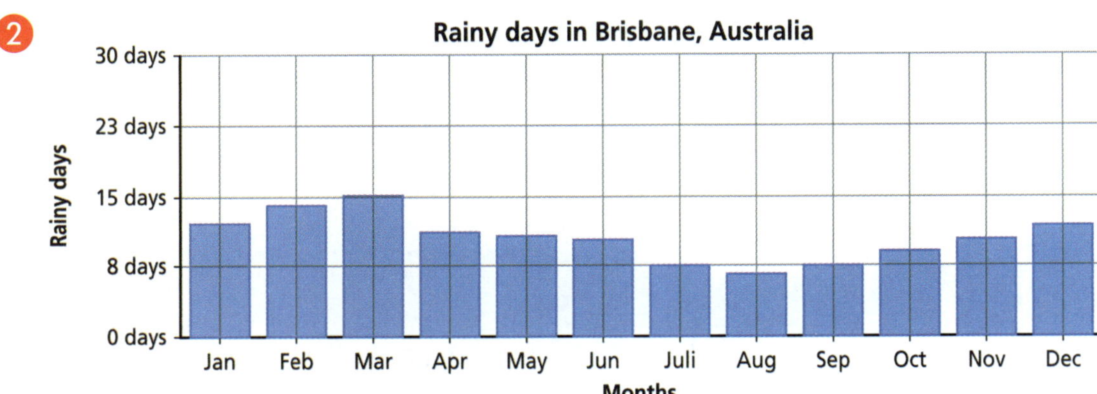

a Which month had:

i) the most rainy days? **ii)** the least rainy days?

b Which season had the most rainy days in Brisbane?

c How is the rainfall for Brisbane different from the rainfall for Perth, shown in Question 1.

Let's research data!

Step 1: Select a topic of interest.

Step 2: Search online for data displays of your topic.

Step 3: Discuss and share what you found.

You could research weather records, data collected in the census or Google trends.

 • *AUSTRALIAN SIGNPOST MATHS 3* • ISBN 9780655708773

5:21 Dot plots

A dot plot is like a tally.
We use dots instead of lines.

Drawing a dot plot

CONCEPT

- The members of our class were asked how many pets they had at home.
- The student with the most pets had 5. We wrote the numbers 0 to 6 under the line.
- As each student told us the number of pets, we put a dot above that number.

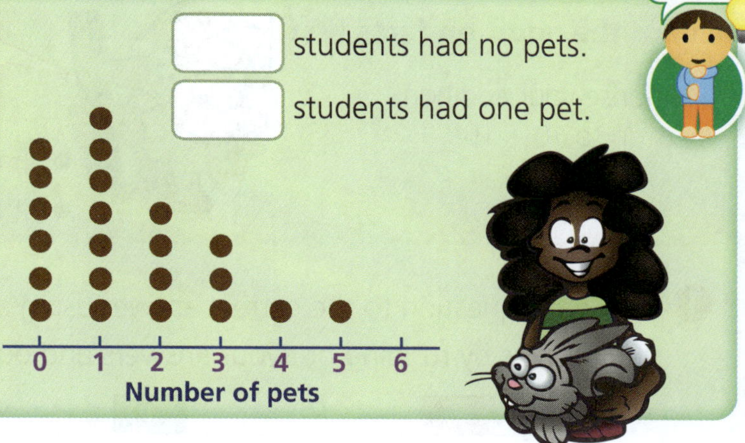

☐ students had no pets.

☐ students had one pet.

1 I stayed in hospital for 7 days and kept a dot plot of my visitors.
How many people visited me:

a on Sunday? ☐ **b** on Wednesday? ☐

c On which day did I have no visitors? ☐

d How many visitors did I have during this time? ☐

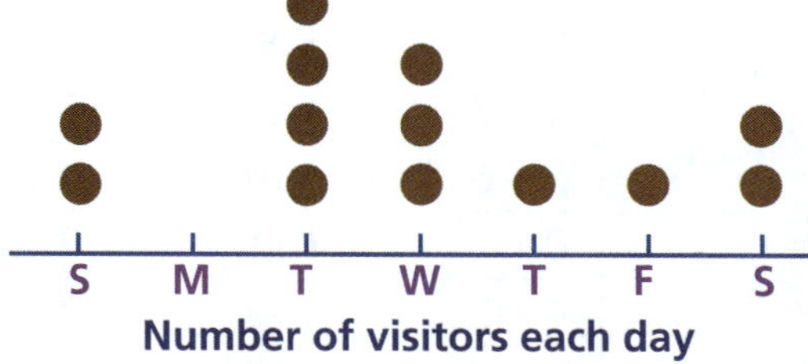

2

Fruit chosen	
apple	●●●●●●●
orange	●●●●●●
banana	●●●●●●●
pear	●●●●

At camp, each of us took one piece of fruit.
We could have an apple, orange, banana or pear.
We made a dot plot of the fruit chosen.

a How many of us chose a banana? ☐

b How many pieces of fruit were taken? ☐

c How many more apples than pears were chosen? ☐

3

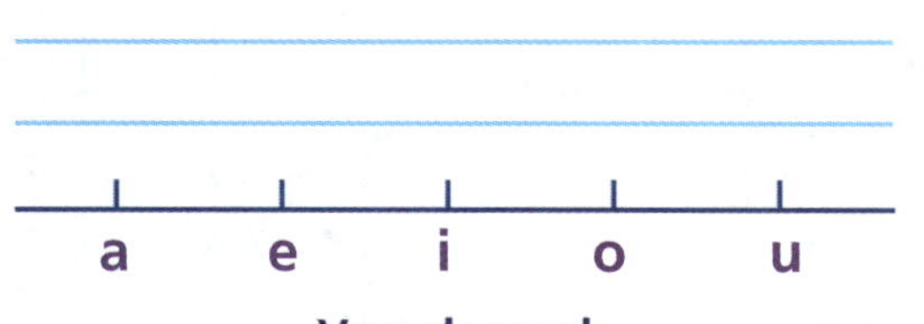

The letters **a**, **e**, **i**, **o** and **u** are called vowels. Make a dot plot of the vowels used in the graph of Question 2.

a Which vowel was used the most? ☐

b Which two vowels were used the same number of times? ☐

c How many vowels were used altogether? ☐

d What is the difference in number of the most used and least used vowel? ☐

4 The letter most used in the English language is a vowel. Discover which one it is.

Method: Make a dot plot like the one in Question 2 using 10 lines of text.

If you have no text to use, use 10 lines of text from Questions 3 and 4.

Results: The vowel that occurred the most is ☐. Compare class results.

Extra Support 1

Addition and subtraction facts

Learn the addition facts first.

Memorise your addition facts up to 10 + 10.

Once you learn your addition tables, use them for subtraction.

- If 6 + 7 = 13, then 13 − 6 = 7 and 13 − 7 = 6.
- If 8 + 9 = 17, then 17 − 8 = 9 and 17 − 9 = 8.

1 Join each question to the correct answer using a pencil. You could practise your tables facts by rubbing out your answers and doing them again.

a +

Question	Answer
2 + 6	1
4 + 6	7
0 + 1	8
5 + 7	9
5 + 6	10
0 + 7	11
4 + 5	12
7 + 10	15
8 + 7	17
10 + 10	18
9 + 9	20

Scores:

b +

Question	Answer
2 + 3	4
4 + 3	5
2 + 2	7
5 + 4	9
8 + 5	8
8 + 0	10
7 + 5	11
1 + 9	12
10 + 5	13
6 + 5	15
10 + 9	19

Scores:

c +

Question	Answer
3 + 6	6
2 + 8	7
4 + 2	8
5 + 2	9
4 + 7	10
3 + 5	11
9 + 6	12
6 + 6	13
8 + 8	14
7 + 6	15
10 + 4	16

Scores:

d +

Question	Answer
3 + 4	5
6 + 2	6
4 + 5	7
3 + 2	8
2 + 4	9
8 + 4	10
4 + 9	11
5 + 5	12
4 + 7	13
7 + 8	14
5 + 9	15

Scores:

e −

Question	Answer
8 − 6	1
10 − 4	0
1 − 0	2
12 − 5	4
11 − 6	6
7 − 7	5
9 − 5	7
17 − 7	8
15 − 7	10
11 − 8	9
18 − 9	3

Scores:

f −

Question	Answer
5 − 2	2
7 − 3	3
4 − 2	4
9 − 4	5
13 − 5	0
8 − 8	1
12 − 5	6
10 − 9	7
15 − 5	8
11 − 5	10
19 − 10	9

Scores:

g −

Question	Answer
6 − 4	0
5 − 2	1
10 − 9	2
7 − 7	3
9 − 3	4
7 − 3	5
10 − 3	6
14 − 5	7
9 − 4	8
18 − 8	9
10 − 2	10

Scores:

h −

Question	Answer
6 − 5	0
9 − 9	1
6 − 3	2
8 − 6	3
8 − 4	4
16 − 9	5
9 − 4	6
16 − 7	7
17 − 7	8
10 − 4	9
17 − 9	10

Scores:

See 2:03 (Addition and subtraction).

 • *AUSTRALIAN SIGNPOST MATHS 3* • ISBN 9780655708773

Addition facts to 20

Learn your addition facts.

1

A	1 + 1	2 + 4	5 + 1	2 + 3	4 + 5
B	3 + 4	0 + 4	3 + 1	1 + 6	2 + 5
C	0 + 7	7 + 1	1 + 3	2 + 6	3 + 6
D	7 + 0	9 + 3	2 + 7	3 + 5	6 + 5
E	4 + 1	8 + 3	0 + 5	9 + 0	9 + 4
F	2 + 2	3 + 7	6 + 3	6 + 0	5 + 2
G	5 + 3	3 + 2	2 + 8	4 + 2	1 + 7
H	5 + 5	8 + 2	6 + 4	4 + 4	7 + 2
I	4 + 3	5 + 4	7 + 3	6 + 2	6 + 6
J	1 + 8	2 + 1	6 + 1	3 + 3	4 + 6
K	7 + 7	9 + 1	5 + 6	1 + 4	9 + 9
L	8 + 1	1 + 2	4 + 8	6 + 7	9 + 8
M	1 + 5	0 + 9	8 + 8	8 + 0	1 + 9
N	9 + 2	8 + 4	4 + 7	7 + 9	9 + 6
O	7 + 6	2 + 9	7 + 4	3 + 8	5 + 7
P	3 + 9	4 + 0	9 + 7	6 + 8	5 + 9
Q	8 + 6	4 + 9	8 + 7	5 + 8	7 + 5
R	7 + 8	8 + 9	8 + 5	6 + 9	9 + 5

See 2:03 (Addition and subtraction).

 • *AUSTRALIAN SIGNPOST MATHS 3* • ISBN 9780655708773

Subtraction facts to 20

Use your addition facts to do subtraction.

You could also use the number line.

0 1 2 3 4 5 6 7 8 9 10 11 12 13 14 15 16 17 18 19 20

1

A	14 – 7 ☐	12 – 3 ☐	11 – 6 ☐	18 – 9 ☐
B	12 – 8 ☐	13 – 7 ☐	17 – 8 ☐	16 – 8 ☐
C	10 – 9 ☐	10 – 3 ☐	12 – 3 ☐	11 – 5 ☐
D	11 – 3 ☐	13 – 4 ☐	10 – 5 ☐	10 – 8 ☐
E	11 – 2 ☐	12 – 4 ☐	11 – 7 ☐	16 – 9 ☐
F	13 – 6 ☐	11 – 9 ☐	11 – 4 ☐	11 – 8 ☐
G	14 – 6 ☐	13 – 9 ☐	15 – 7 ☐	13 – 8 ☐
H	10 – 7 ☐	16 – 7 ☐	14 – 8 ☐	15 – 9 ☐
I	15 – 6 ☐	10 – 4 ☐	12 – 7 ☐	14 – 9 ☐
J	12 – 9 ☐	14 – 5 ☐	12 – 5 ☐	12 – 6 ☐
K	13 – 5 ☐	10 – 6 ☐	15 – 8 ☐	17 – 9 ☐

See 2:03 (Addition and subtraction).

Know your addition facts

6 + 8 = 14
so
14 − 8 = 6 and 14 − 6 = 8

+	1	2	3	4	5	6	7	8	9	10
1	2	3	4	5	6	7	8	9	10	11
2	3	4	5	6	7	8	9	10	11	12
3	4	5	6	7	8	9	10	11	12	13
4	5	6	7	8	9	10	11	12	13	14
5	6	7	8	9	10	11	12	13	14	15
6	7	8	9	10	11	12	13	14	15	16
7	8	9	10	11	12	13	14	15	16	17
8	9	10	11	12	13	14	15	16	17	18
9	10	11	12	13	14	15	16	17	18	19
10	11	12	13	14	15	16	17	18	19	20

- Learn the addition tables with answers up to 10. (**2 + 5 = 5 + 2 = 7**)
- Learn the addition tables with answers up to 20. (**7 + 6 = 6 + 7 = 13**)
- Learn your doubles and halves.

7 | 6
6 | 7

Numbers	1	2	3	4	5	6	7	8	9	10
Doubles	**2**	**4**	**6**	**8**	**10**	**12**	**14**	**16**	**18**	**20**

4 + 4 = 8 **double 4 = 8** **2 x 4 = 8**

Numbers	2	4	6	8	10	12	14	16	18	20
Halves	**1**	**2**	**3**	**4**	**5**	**6**	**7**	**8**	**9**	**10**

half of 10 = 5 **10 ÷ 2 = 5**

See 2:03 (Addition and subtraction).

Addition problems to 99

Round off to the nearest 10 when checking answers.

Problem solving

How many pencils does Maddy have if she has 24 in her bag and 47 in her desk?

Find: How many pencils?

Number sentence: 24 + 47 = ☐

Answer: Maddy has 71 pencils.

Working

	tens	ones
	1	
	2	4
+	4	7
	7	1

Use these blanks for working. Work in pencil so they can be reused.

1 Answer these questions, setting them out as shown above.

a Luke's test had 27 mistakes. Naomi's had 22 mistakes. How many mistakes do they have together? ☐ mistakes

b Brianna had 56 pet ants. Jordan caught 8 more and gave them to her. How many did she have then? ☐ ants

c Wen, an ancient Chinese king, began the first zoo 3000 years ago. He received 56 animals from the north and 27 from the south. How many animals did he receive altogether? ☐ animals

d At night, an owl can see about 100 times better than a human. In one week an owl caught 53 mice. In the next week it caught 38. How many mice did it catch altogether? ☐ mice

e At a waterhole, Michelle photographed 31 magpie geese, 12 Burdekin ducks and 8 pied herons. How many birds did she photograph altogether? ☐ birds

f A family of 18 bandicoots lived near 13 possums and 6 native rats. How many animals were there altogether? ☐ animals

2 **a** Alan saw three varieties of finch in one paddock. There were 35 zebra finches, 15 double-bar finches and 27 spice finches. How many were there altogether? ☐ finches

b On Phillip Island, 37 penguins came ashore before 6 pm. In the next hour 18 more arrived. How many had arrived by 7 pm? ☐ penguins

c Consecutive numbers follow one after the other. Find the sum of the consecutive numbers 28, 29 and 30. ☐ is the sum

d In a Test cricket series, Eric batted three times. His scores were 44, 28 and 19. What was his total score? ☐ runs

tens	ones

tens	ones

tens	ones

See 2:33 (Addition to 99 with trading) and 2:34 (Addition with trading).

Addition to 999

H stands for hundreds.
T stands for tens.
U stands for units (or ones)

CONCEPT

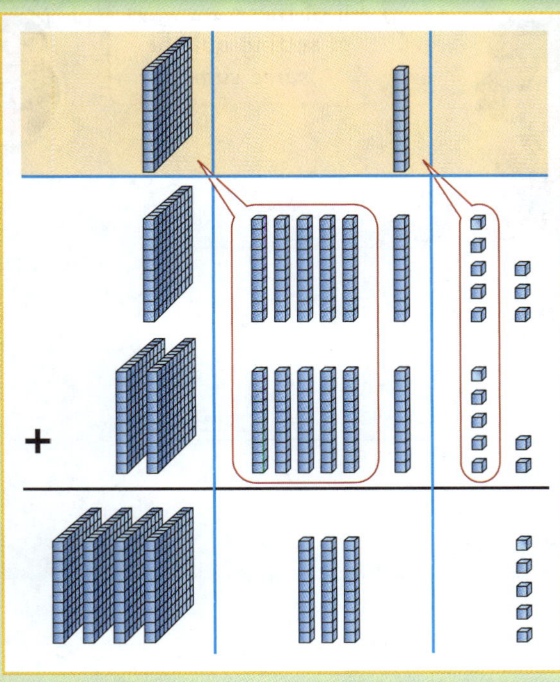

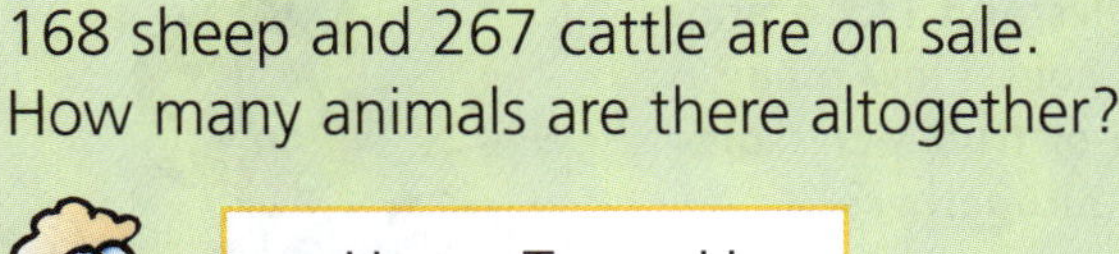

168 sheep and 267 cattle are on sale.
How many animals are there altogether?

H	T	U
1	1	
1	6	8
+ 2	6	7
4	3	5

There are 435 animals altogether.
We can check the answer by rounding to the nearest 100 (or 10).
200 + 300 = 500
435 is reasonably close to 500.

1

a

H	T	U
	6	1
+	9	3

b

H	T	U
	7	2
+	4	5

c

H	T	U
	3	0
+	7	8

d

H	T	U
2	5	8
+	2	5

e

H	T	U
	7	6
+ 7	1	4

f

H	T	U
3	6	9
+	1	9

g

H	T	U
4	3	6
+	8	0

h

H	T	U
4	2	5
+	8	5

i

H	T	U
	8	7
+ 3	4	1

j

H	T	U
1	8	8
+ 1	4	3

k

H	T	U
3	6	5
+ 1	4	9

l

H	T	U
4	5	9
+ 2	7	4

2 Check your answers by rounding each number to the nearest 100 (or 10) then adding.

See 2:36–2:38 (Addition to 999 with trading).

 • *AUSTRALIAN SIGNPOST MATHS 3* • ISBN 9780655708773

Writing the addition algorithm

Be careful to keep your columns aligned.

CONCEPT

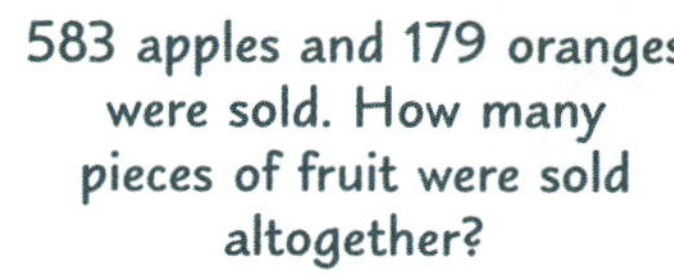

Hund	Tens	Ones
1	1	
5	8	3
+ 1	7	9
7	6	2

H	T	U
1	1	
5	8	3
+ 1	7	9
7	6	2

1	1	
5	8	3
+ 1	7	9
7	6	2

762 pieces of fruit were sold altogether.

1

	a	b	c	d	e
	250	534	154	92	245
+	84	128	207	340	370

	f	g	h	i	j
	365	209	345	507	365
+	166	583	312	220	397

	k	l	m	n	o
	188	365	509	381	777
+	133	366	296	259	185

2 Estimate each answer and use the estimate to check your answers.

a Luke watched 287 minutes of television on Saturday and 145 minutes on Sunday. How much did he watch altogether? Give your answer in minutes. ☐ minutes

b The attendances at two concerts on Sunday were 156 and 218. How many people attended altogether? ☐ people

c This year farmer McDonald sold 180 bags of corn. Last year he sold 17 bags more than this. How many bags were sold in the two years? ☐ bags

d Rex and Lyn bought the house next door and added 346 square metres to their original block of 575 square metres. How large is the block now? ☐ square metres

3 Use estimation to check your answers to Question 1.

See 2:36–2:38 (Addition to 999 with trading).

Addition of money

A decimal point (or full stop) separates the dollars and cents.
10 lots of 10 cents make 1 dollar.

1

a $0.41 + $0.37	**b** $0.64 + $0.88	**c** $1.26 + $3.47	**d** $2.24 + $3.07	**e** $3.75 + $2.94
f $4.69 + $3.56	**g** $2.63 + $2.07	**h** $5.83 + $2.68	**i** $4.96 + $1.47	**j** $2.79 + $4.32
k $2.41 + $3.67	**l** $4.06 + $2.91	**m** $3.77 + $1.63	**n** $1.92 + $4.37	**o** $5.16 + $1.98

2 Write each as an algorithm or use a mental strategy to find your answer.

a $1.56 + $2.23 ☐ **b** $4.01 + $1.76 ☐
c $3.51 + $2.17 ☐ **d** $5.03 + $3.65 ☐
e $2.37 + $4.12 ☐ **f** $6.45 + $2.03 ☐

3 Find the total if I bought:

a a cake for $5.50 and a drink for $4.05. ☐
b a dessert for $4.95 and a drink for $3.25. ☐
c a sandwich for $7.30 and a drink for $1.55. ☐
d a biscuit for $3.75 and a drink for $4.95. ☐

4

a $2.21 + $0.85 + $1.82	**b** $1.61 + $3.17 + $4.05	**c** $4.68 + $1.83 + $2.86	**d** $5.91 + $1.45 + $1.65

See 2:36–2:38 (Addition to 999 with trading).

Extra Support 9 — Addition to 9999

Th means thousands. H means hundreds.
T means tens. U means ones.

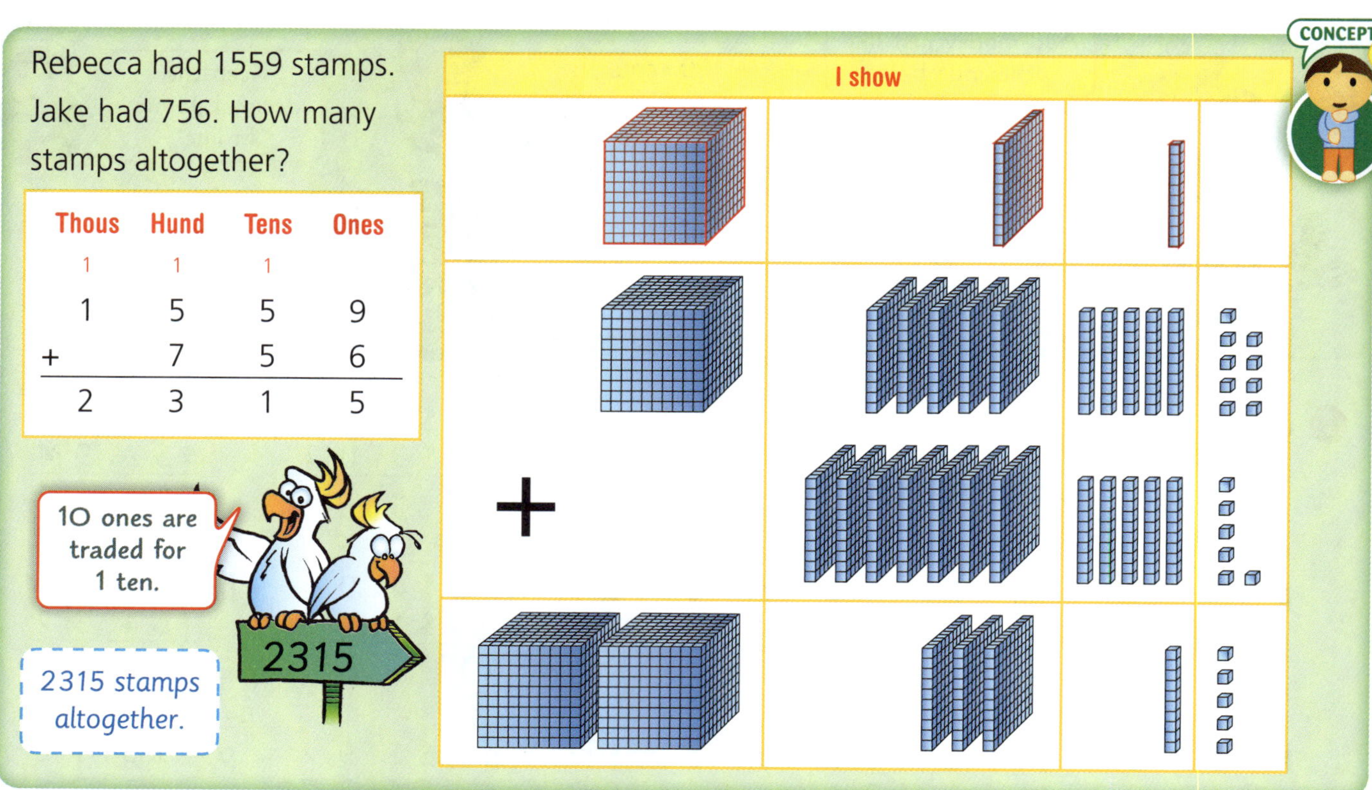

Rebecca had 1559 stamps. Jake had 756. How many stamps altogether?

	Thous	Hund	Tens	Ones
	1	1	1	
	1	5	5	9
+		7	5	6
	2	3	1	5

1

a) Th H T U
3416 + 2052

b) Th H T U
8104 + 871

c) Th H T U
6318 + 1270

d) Th H T U
392 + 3406

e) Th H T U
35 + 7932

f) 3418 + 2906

g) 7950 + 650

h) 6087 + 1164

i) 946 + 2627

j) 6492 + 1748

2

a) 5071 + 2124

b) 3831 + 1054

c) 2516 + 1827

d) 3195 + 5730

e) 7041 + 978

f) 4692 + 2813

g) 7472 + 1809

h) 479 + 3860

i) 1793 + 5824

j) 6097 + 1835

3

a) \$7542 + \$1607

b) \$6549 + \$1742

c) \$3581 + \$4328

d) \$2591 + \$3706

e) \$7059 + \$2371

See 2:35–2:37 (Addition to 999 with trading).

 • *AUSTRALIAN SIGNPOST MATHS 3* • ISBN 9780655708773

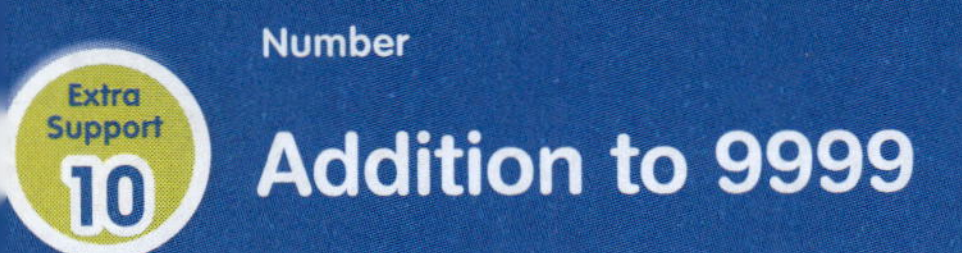

Addition to 9999

13 hundreds
= 1 thousand + 3 hundreds

CONCEPT

I have three stamp albums. In the first is 3087 stamps, in the second 1872 stamps and in the third 4378. How many stamps do I have altogether?

How many stamps?

3087 + 1872 + 4378 = ☐

Answer

I have 9337 stamps.

	Thous	Hund	Tens	Ones
	1	2	1	
	3	0	8	7
	1	8	7	2
+	4	3	7	8
	9	3	3	7

1

a

	Th	H	T	U
	1	8	3	5
		4	0	8
+	5	3	1	8

b

	Th	H	T	U
		9	9	9
	4	2	5	6
+	1	6	8	0

c

	Th	H	T	U
	8	4	1	8
		6	4	7
+		7	5	3

d

	Th	H	T	U
	3	8	4	2
		7	0	6
+	2	9	3	4

2

a

```
   386
  2514
   977
+   27
```

b

```
   183
   964
  1863
+ 2098
```

c

```
  5142
   863
   744
+ 1088
```

d

```
  2099
  1847
  1935
+ 1207
```

3

a

```
  $61.29
  $13.91
+ $10.94
```

b

```
  $28.18
  $14.63
+ $ 9.72
```

c

```
  $ 8.47
  $60.08
+ $21.55
```

d

```
  $28.47
  $29.66
+ $28.67
```

4 Estimate then calculate. (E = estimate, A = answer)

a Residents were phoned at 3187 homes in Bendigo, 1394 in Ballarat and 914 in Geelong. How many residents were phoned? E = ☐ A = ☐

b A bookshop kept 3096 books in room A, 2515 in room B and 2845 in room C. How many books were in the three rooms? E = ☐ A = ☐

c Sandy spent $3245 renovating her laundry, $2188 on landscaping and $2840 on furniture. How much did she spend? E = ☐ A = ☐

See 2:36–2:38 (Addition two trades).

 ISBN 9780655708773

Subtraction, no trading to 999

'hund' means hundreds.

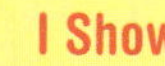

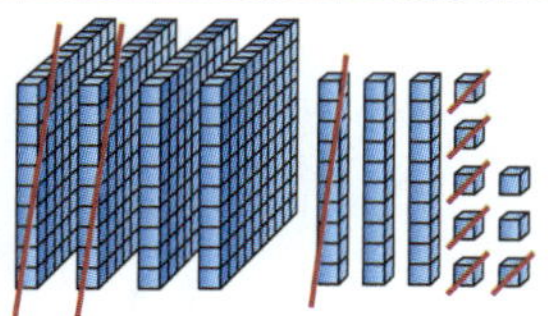

Take away 6 ones.
Take away 1 ten.
Take away 2 hundreds.

I Write

	hund	tens	ones
	4	3	8
−	2	1	6
	2	2	2

1 **a** 4 hundreds 7 tens 6 ones
− 2 hundreds 3 tens 1 one

b 8 hundreds 9 tens 7 ones
− 2 hundreds 5 tens 2 ones

2

a

	hund	tens	ones
	8	5	2
−	7	2	1

b

	hund	tens	ones
	9	6	7
−	2	3	4

c

	hund	tens	ones
	9	9	8
−	4	6	5

d

	hund	tens	ones
	3	4	2
−		1	1

e

	hund	tens	ones
	6	9	8
−		2	4

f

	hund	tens	ones
	9	4	5
−		4	3

g

	hund	tens	ones
	6	8	6
−			4

h

	hund	tens	ones
	7	4	7
−		3	4

i

	hund	tens	ones
	3	6	9
−			7

j

	hund	tens	ones
	5	5	9
−	4	3	0

k

	hund	tens	ones
	1	7	3
−		5	0

l

	hund	tens	ones
	6	4	6
−	2	0	3

m

	hund	tens	ones
	7	7	8
−	6	0	0

n

	hund	tens	ones
	5	2	9
−	1	2	9

o

	hund	tens	ones
	5	8	7
−	3	8	2

Estimate to check each answer.

- Make up a problem to match each of parts **e** to **h**, in Question 2 above.

See 2:32 (Subtraction no trading).

Subtraction, one trade to 999

8 tens is the same as 7 tens and 10 ones.

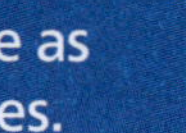

CONCEPT

28 of my 384 stamps are Chinese. How many are not Chinese?

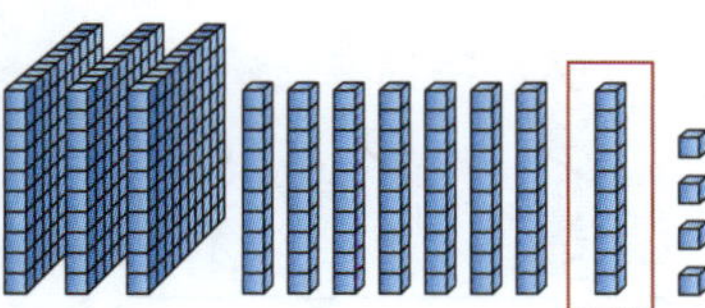

We can't take 8 ones from 4 ones, so trade 1 ten for 10 ones.

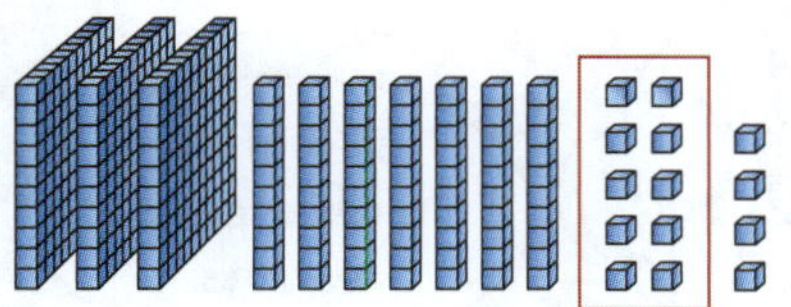

356 stamps are not Chinese.

From this we take 2 tens and 8 ones.

	Hund	Tens	Ones
		7	14
	3	~~8~~	~~4~~
–		2	8
	3	5	6

1

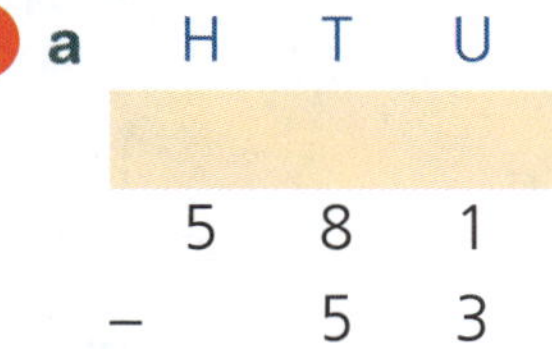

	a H	T	U	b H	T	U	c H	T	U	d H	T	U
	5	8	1	3	4	3	2	9	6	4	6	0
–		5	3		2	8		6	7		3	9

	e H	T	U	f H	T	U	g H	T	U	h H	T	U
	2	7	3	1	6	6	8	4	4	9	7	3
–			9		5	8			8		6	5

	i H	T	U	j H	T	U	k H	T	U	l H	T	U
	7	5	0	3	4	1	2	8	0	6	4	7
–		3	9		2	6		3	2		1	9

	m			n			o			p		
	8	3	5	8	9	1	5	2	0	6	8	4
–	1	0	8	8	3	6	4	1	5		7	6

	q			r			s			t		
	2	1	4	7	8	4	3	9	1	6	6	4
–	2	0	8		5	0	3	7	5	5	5	7

2 Check your answers to Question 1 by rounding the numbers to the nearest 100 (or 10).

See 2:39–2:41 (Subtraction with trading).

 • AUSTRALIAN SIGNPOST MATHS 3 • ISBN 9780655708773

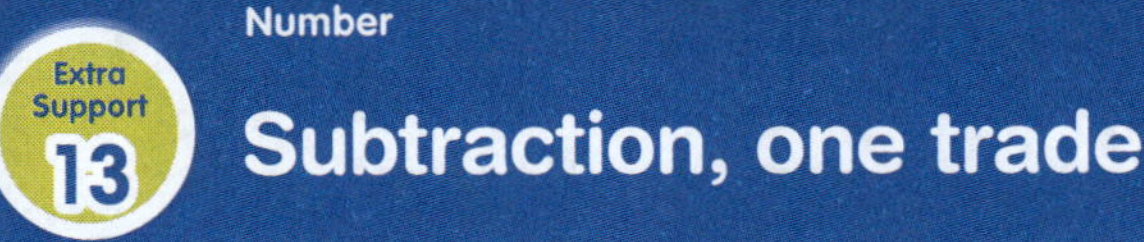

Subtraction, one trade to 999

Trade 1 hundred for 10 tens.

1

	H	T	U
a			
	6	1	7
−	1	5	3

	H	T	U
b			
	8	2	6
−	5	7	1

	H	T	U
c			
	4	3	4
−	2	4	0

	H	T	U
d			
	7	2	9
−		3	8

	H	T	U
e			
	5	2	8
−	1	5	2

	H	T	U
f			
	6	0	7
−	3	5	2

	H	T	U
g			
	6	8	5
−		9	1

	H	T	U
h			
	2	1	5
−	1	7	5

	H	T	U
i			
	4	3	9
−	1	5	0

	H	T	U
j			
	6	1	7
−	3	2	6

	H	T	U
k			
	5	0	4
−	1	9	2

	H	T	U
l			
	9	0	9
−	3	4	7

m

	7	0	8
−	1	3	3

n

	9	1	6
−	8	3	6

o

	6	0	8
−	4	1	5

p

	7	2	9
−	2	7	6

q

	4	0	7
−	2	1	7

r

	9	2	4
−	5	6	0

s

	8	6	6
−	3	7	5

Use rounding to check your answers.

See 2:39–2:41 (Subtraction with trading).

 • *AUSTRALIAN SIGNPOST MATHS 3* • ISBN 9780655708773

Subtraction, two trades to 999

Trade 1 ten for 10 ones.
Trade 1 hundred for 10 tens.

CONCEPT

I had \$524 and spent \$245. How much do I have left?

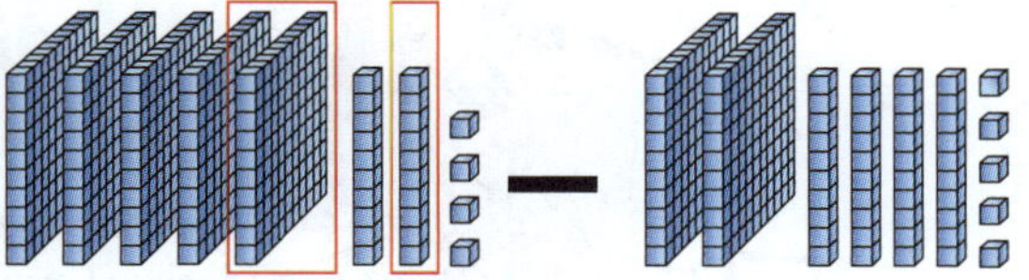

I trade 1 ten for 10 ones, and 1 hundred for 10 tens.

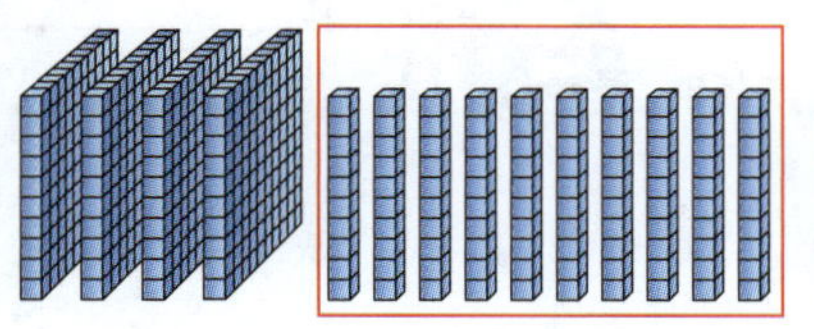

From this we take 2 hundreds, 4 tens and 5 ones.

	Hund	Tens	Ones
		11	
	4	~~1~~	14
	~~5~~	~~2~~	~~4~~
−	2	4	5
	2	7	9

I had \$279 left.

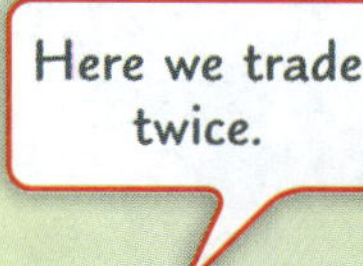

Here we trade twice.

Use rounding to check your answers.

1

	a			b			c			d		
	H	T	U	H	T	U	H	T	U	H	T	U
	3	1	4	2	4	6	1	3	2	7	3	5
−		5	6		6	7		9	8		8	9

	e			f			g			h		
	H	T	U	H	T	U	H	T	U	H	T	U
	4	3	0	3	4	1	6	2	4	9	2	2
−	1	5	6	2	7	8	1	3	5	3	3	3

	i			j			k			l		
	H	T	U	H	T	U	H	T	U	H	T	U
	7	1	5	4	7	0	8	4	2	9	1	1
−	5	7	7	2	9	3	1	8	3	3	4	4

	m			n			o			p		
	6	1	4	5	2	8	7	5	5	4	1	5
−	5	8	5	4	2	9	6	6	8	3	8	7

	q			r			s		
	7	0	6	6	0	1	5	0	6
−	2	4	9	1	8	4	2	7	8

In Questions 1q–1s, start by trading 1 hundred for 10 tens.

See 2:39–2:41 (Subtraction with trading).

 ISBN 9780655708773

Subtraction of money

Trade $1 for 10 ten-cent coins.
Trade a ten-cent coin for 10 cents.

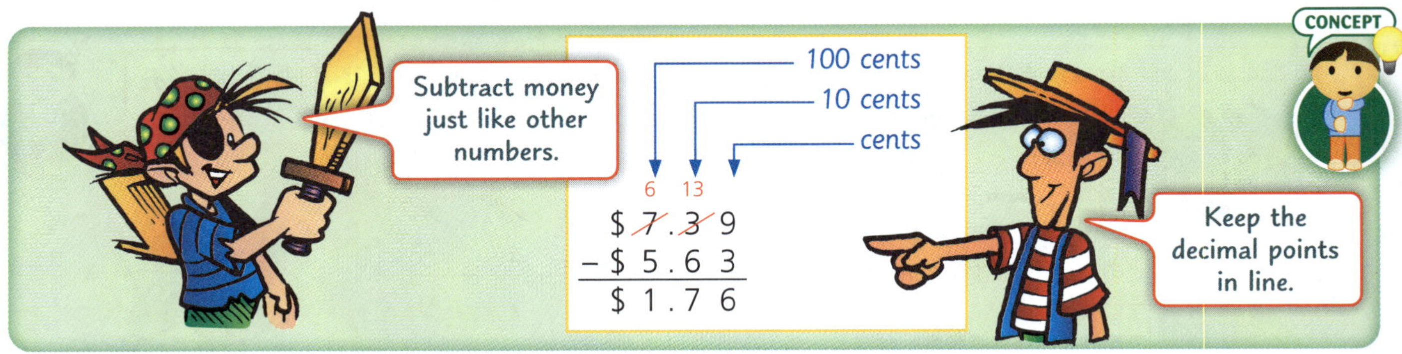

1

a \$6.52 − \$1.30	**b** \$8.79 − \$3.62	**c** \$9.85 − \$3.51	**d** \$7.82 − \$5.43	**e** \$6.24 − \$2.07
f \$4.47 − \$2.63	**g** \$5.38 − \$2.61	**h** \$7.50 − \$1.42	**i** \$3.54 − \$0.20	**j** \$7.55 − \$3.47
k \$8.57 − \$6.87	**l** \$9.57 − \$6.99	**m** \$6.50 − \$2.61	**n** \$7.90 − \$2.45	**o** \$3.52 − \$1.48

2 Write each as an algorithm or use a mental strategy to find your answer.

a $3.35 – $1.24 ☐ **b** $8.98 – $4.00 ☐

c $8.56 – $3.21 ☐ **d** $4.54 – $4.49 ☐

e $7.00 – $1.50 ☐ **f** $3.50 – $1.99 ☐

3 I started with $8.50. What do I have left if I buy:

a a book for $7.45?  **b** an icy pole for $2.30? ☐

c a drink for $3.05? ☐ **d** a keyring for $7.30? ☐

e a pen for $4.95 ☐ **f** marbles for $3.55? ☐

First to $5

FUN SPOT

- Each player begins the game with $10 and takes turns to roll a dice.
- The number shown on each dice is multiplied by 10 and that number of cents is subtracted from the player's total.
- The game continues until one player reaches $5.

See 2:39–2:41 (Subtraction with trading).

Answers

1:01

1 a–d

1	2	3	4	5	6	7	8	9	10
11	12	13	14	15	16	17	18	19	20
21	22	23	24	25	26	27	28	29	30
31	32	33	34	35	36	37	38	39	40
41	42	43	44	45	46	47	48	49	50
51	52	53	54	55	56	57	58	59	60
61	62	63	64	65	66	67	68	69	70
71	72	73	74	75	76	77	78	79	80
81	82	83	84	85	86	87	88	89	90
91	92	93	94	95	96	97	98	99	100

c (Answers will vary): Every second even number is the pattern for counting by 4s.

d 8, 16, 24, 32, 40, 48, 56, 64, 72, 80

2 2, 4, 6, 8 or 0

3 5 or 0

4 0

5 a 253, 263, 273, 283, 293 b 800, 795, 790, 785, 780
c 120, 118, 116, 114, 112 d 700, 600, 500, 400, 300

6 a The rule is start at 223 and add 10 each time.

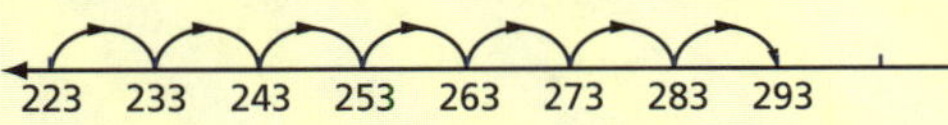

b The rule is start at 815 and subtract 5 each time.

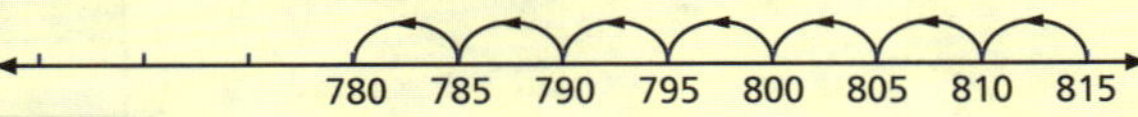

1:02

1 a 76, 78, 80, 82, 84, 86, 88, 90, 92, 94
b 1000, 900, 800, 700, 600, 500, 400, 300, 200, 100, 0
c 645, 650, 655, 660, 665, 670, 675, 680, 685, 690
d 500, 490, 480, 470, 460, 450, 440, 430, 420, 410, 400

2 a 855, 835, 825, 805, 795
b 615, 610, 600, 595, 590
c 408, 406, 402, 400, 398

3 2, (4), 6, (8), 10, (12), 14, (16), 18, (20), 22, (24), 26, (28), 30, (32), 34, (36), 38, (40)
The pattern is counting by 4, or add 4.

4 5, (10), 15, (20), 25, (30), 35, (40), 45, (50), 55, (60), 65, (70), 75, (80), 85, (90), 95, (100)
The pattern is counting by 10, or add 10.

5 Group the coins into stacks of ten. Group stacks into ten lots of ten to make one hundred. Make sure that you have three groups of ten stacks of ten.

6 a The rule is start at 76 and add 2 each time.

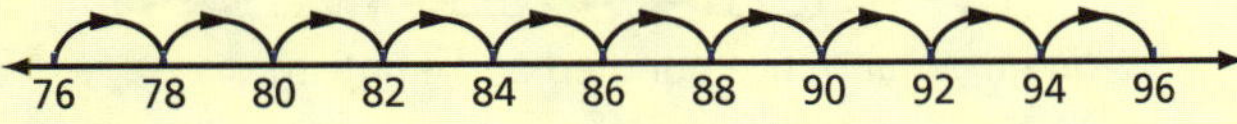

b The rule is start at 1000 and subtract 100 each time.

c The rule is start at 645 and add 5 each time.

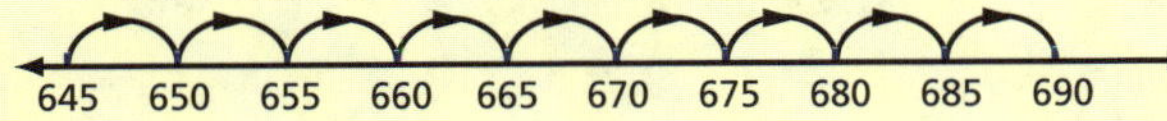

1:03

Header: 2 hundreds 3 tens 8 ones

1 a 316 b 512 c 145 d 224
e 232 f 129 g 221 h 324
i 268 j 519 k 674 l 953

2 a 346 b 723 c 962 d 634
e 572 f 914

3 a 137, 446, 653 b 237, 491, 974
c 106, 567, 819 d 250, 683, 749

1:04

Header:

380,	38,	308,	803,	83
4	1	3	5	2

1 a 413 4 hundreds 1 tens 3 ones
four hundred and thirteen

b 324 3 hundreds 2 tens 4 ones
three hundred and twenty-four

2 a 2 b 3 c 3 d 2 e 3
f 2 g 1 h 3 i 4 j 3

3 a 260 b 152 c 940 d 718
e 679 f 534 g 868 h 306

4 a 998, 1000 b 862, 864 c 658, 660
d 305, 307 e 498, 500 f 708, 710

Activity: Numbers will be modelled using place-value blocks.

1:05

1 a

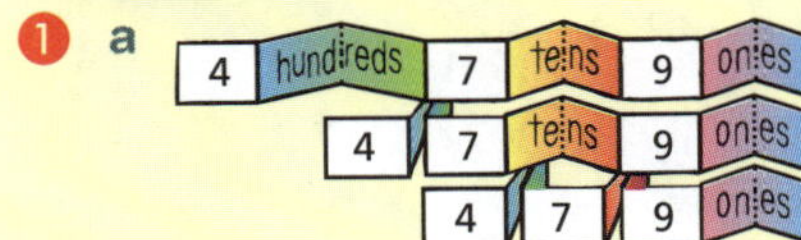

b

c

d

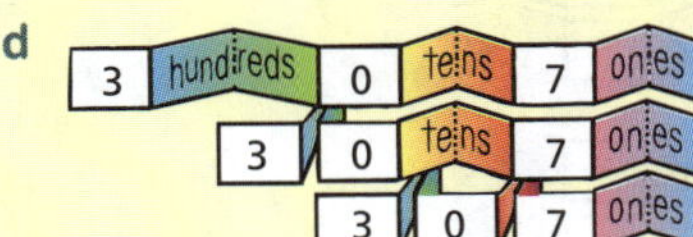

2 a 632 b 817 c 429 d 763
e 238 f 562 g 940 h 351

3 a one hundred and six b six hundred and seven
c three hundred and ten
d eight hundred and forty-one

Activity: The numbers in Question 3 will be modelled.

1:06

1. a 10 b 80 c 20
   d 90 e 30 f 110
2. a 20 b 40 c 60 d 50
   e 90 f 70 g 60 h 80
   i 100 j 120 k 120 l 130
3. a 57, 58, 64, 61, 62, 56 will be circled.
   b 187, 186, 194, 193, 185, 189, 188, 191 will be circled.
4. a 60 + 20 b 40 − 20 c 130 − 30
   d 70 + 70 e 120 − 30 f 240 − 60
   g 50 + 80 h 670 − 50 i 450 − 120

1:07

1. a 200 b 400 c 500 d 600
   e 400 f 300 g 800 h 300
2. a 100 b 400 c 500 d 500
   e 200 f 800 g 900 h 600
   i 200 j 500 k 400 l 900
   m 400 n 200 o 700 p 600
3. a 163, 220, 186, 217, 237, 205 will be circled.
   b 467, 456, 483, 532, 521 will be circled.
4. a false b false c true d true
   e true f false g true h true

Activity: Answers will vary.

1:08

Header:

421	3
42 tens	2
4 hundreds	1

1. a 746 b 183 c 575 d 397
2. a 513

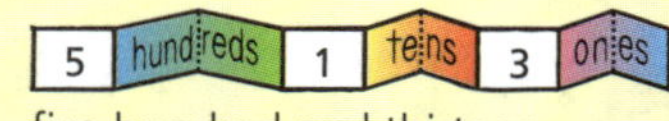

five hundred and thirteen

b 342

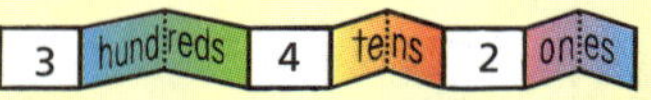

three hundred and forty-two

3. a

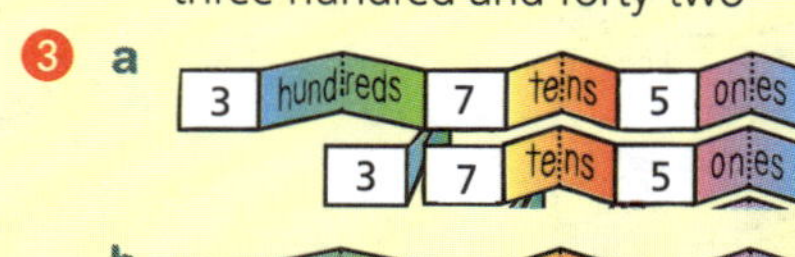

b

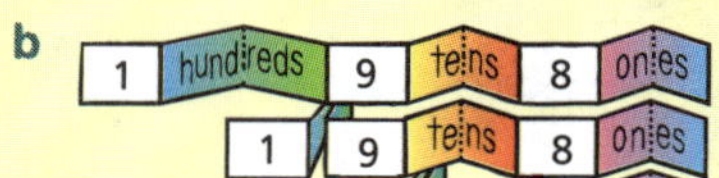

4. a 400 b 800 c 300
   d 400 e 700 f 300
   g 900 h 500 i 800

Fun spot: Answers will vary.

1:09

1.

Group	Number coloured	Total in group	Fraction coloured
	4	5	$\frac{4}{5}$
	3	4	$\frac{3}{4}$
	5	8	$\frac{5}{8}$
	2	4	$\frac{2}{4}$

2. a $\frac{5}{8}, \frac{3}{8}$ b $\frac{3}{4}, \frac{1}{4}$ c $\frac{5}{6}, \frac{1}{6}$
   d $\frac{3}{6}, \frac{3}{6}$ e $\frac{5}{8}, \frac{3}{8}$ f $\frac{8}{10}, \frac{2}{10}$
3. a 4 fish are coloured. b 7 beetles are coloured.
   c 8 fruits are coloured. d 3 bats are coloured.
   e 2 mushrooms are coloured. f 5 pencils are coloured.

Activity: Answers will vary.

1:10

1. a <u>4</u> of <u>5</u>, $\frac{4}{5}$ b <u>3</u> of <u>4</u>, $\frac{3}{4}$ c <u>5</u> of <u>6</u>, $\frac{5}{6}$
2. a $\frac{1}{2}$ b $\frac{7}{10}$ c $\frac{5}{6}$
   d $\frac{3}{8}$ e $\frac{2}{3}$ f $\frac{2}{4}$
3. a

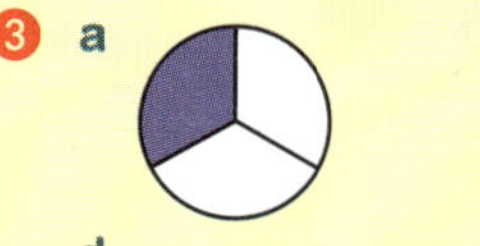

b

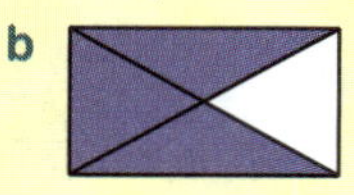

c

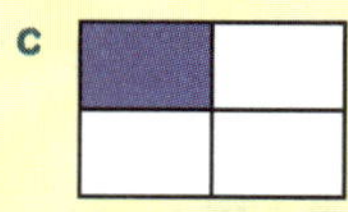

d

e

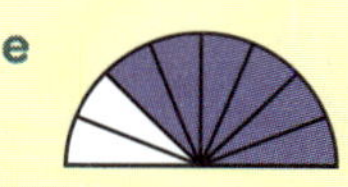

f

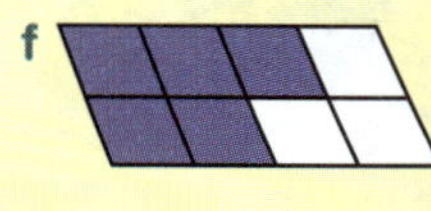

g

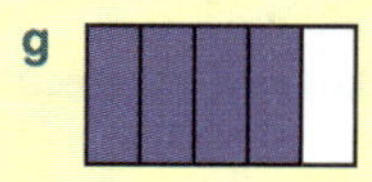

h

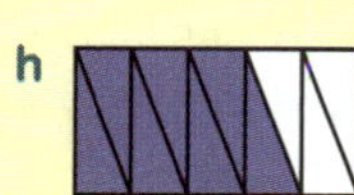

i

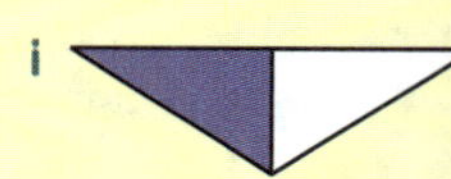

Challenge: $\frac{1}{6}$ is greater than $\frac{1}{8}$.

1:11

Header:

100	1
10 000	3
1000	2

1. a 1518

one thousand, five hundred and eighteen

b 1332

one thousand, three hundred and thirty-two

2. a 2 b 4 c 1 d 2
   e 4 f 2 g 4 h 4

Activity: Answers will vary.

1:12

Header: The letter 'O' can be mistaken for zero.

1. **a** 1519 **b** 1354 **c** 1395 **d** 8405 **e** 4092
2. **a** 5837 **b** 6902 **c** 4189
3. In each case the larger number will be circled.
   a 2547 **b** 4263 **c** 5409
   d 2157 **e** 4312 **f** 10 000

Investigation: 100 is ten tens
1000 is ten hundreds

1:13

Header: 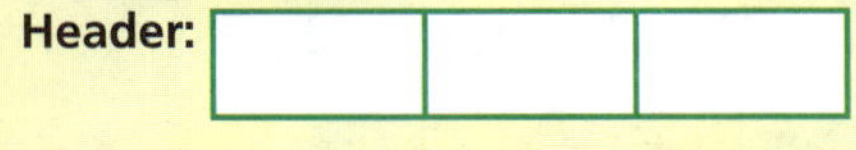

1. **a** $\frac{1}{4}$ **b** $\frac{2}{2}$ or 1 **c** $\frac{3}{8}$ **d** $\frac{4}{4}$ or 1
   e $\frac{5}{8}$ **f** $\frac{8}{8}$ or 1 **g** $\frac{3}{4}$ **h** $\frac{7}{8}$
2. **a** **b** **c** **d** **e** **f** **g** **h**

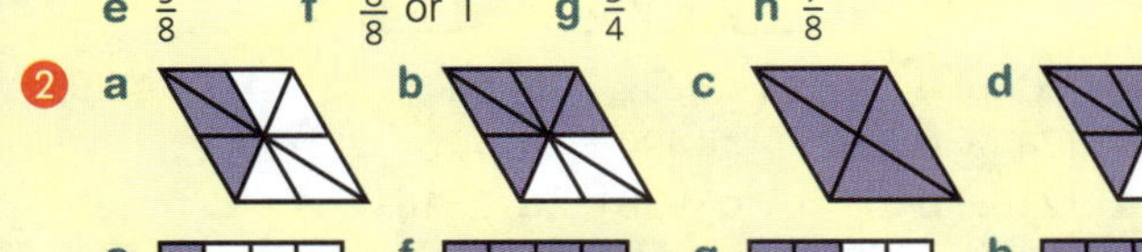

Investigation

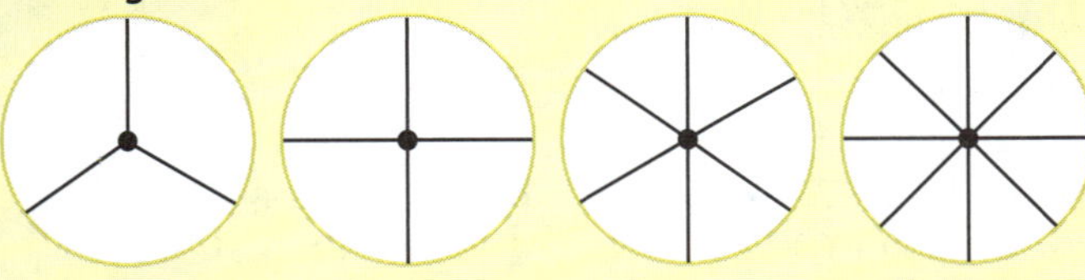

3 guests 4 guests 6 guests 8 guests

The more guests there are, the smaller the pieces will be.

1:14

Header: 3 squares will be coloured green and 7 will be coloured yellow.
$\frac{3}{10}$ and $\frac{7}{10}$ makes 10 tenths or one whole.

1. **a** **b** **c** **d** **e** **f** **g** **h** **i** **j** **k** **l**

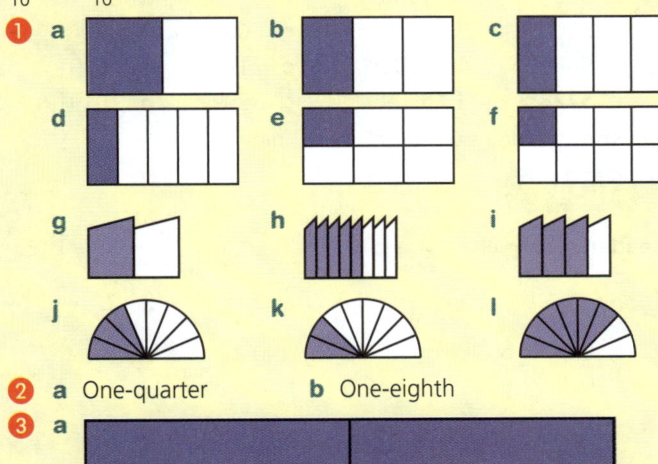

2. **a** One-quarter **b** One-eighth
3. **a**
   b

Investigation: These shapes will be circled.

a  **b** 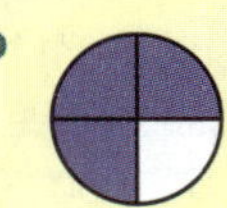

1:15

1. **a** 7 **b** 16 **c** 40
   d 8 **e** 30 **f** 11
   g 22 **h** 60 **i** 62
2. **a** Add 2 **b** Add 3 **c** Add 10
   d Subtract 4 **e** Subtract 1 **f** Subtract 11
   g Add 4 **h** Subtract 5 **i** Add 8
3. **a** 27, 33, 39 **b** 40, 39, 38 **c** 72, 70, 68
   d 42, 50, 58 **e** 43, 63, 83 **f** 36, 32, 28
   g 6, 12, 24 **h** 20, 35, 50 **i** 53, 43, 33 **j** 2, 4, 8
4. **a** 6, 9, 12, Add 3. **b** 15, 20, 25, Add 5.

1:16

Concept: The rule is multiply by 2 and the next number would be 400.

1. **a** 8, 16 **b** 24, 48 **c** 200, 400,
   d 40, 80 **e** 4, 8, 16 **f** 10, 20, 40
   g 12, 24, 48 **h** 40, 80, 160 **i** 8, 16, 32 **j** 14, 28, 56
2. **a** 27, 81 **b** 54, 162 **c** 9, 27, 81
   d 30, 90, 270 **e** 12, 36, 108 **f** 60, 180, 540
3. **a** 1000, 10 000 **b** 2000, 20 000
   c 30, 300, 3000 **d** 100, 1000, 10 000

Fun Spot: Answers will vary.

1:17

Header: 3210

1. **a** 1594 **b** 1625 **c** 1465 **e** 1613 **f** 1079
2. **a** 1514

one thousand, five hundred and fourteen

3. **a** 3 **b** 2 **c** 4 **d** 3
   e 2 **f** 4 **g** 4 **h** 1
4. **a** 4370, 4400, 4420, 4430
   b 7905, 8005, 8405, 8505
   c 4763, 5763, 9763, 10 763
5. **a** 347 **b** 680 **c** 1000 **d** 1317
   e 4877 **f** 3208 **g** 2650 **h** 3641
   i 2200 **j** 5011 **k** 10 000 **l** 1002

1:18

1. **a** **b** **c** **d**

2 a 5763 b 8956 c 6275 d 4649 e 9582
3 a six thousand, eight hundred and twenty-four
b two thousand, three hundred and nineteen
4 a 5000 b 3000 c 10 000

1:19

Header: $\frac{3}{4}$

1 a $\frac{3}{6}$ or $\frac{1}{2}$ b $\frac{4}{6}$ or $\frac{2}{3}$ c $\frac{5}{6}$
d $\frac{3}{8}$ e $\frac{5}{8}$ f $\frac{7}{8}$

2 These fractions will be circled:
a $\frac{4}{8}$ b $\frac{3}{4}$ c $\frac{7}{8}$
d $\frac{3}{4}$ e $\frac{6}{8}$ f $\frac{5}{8}$

3 These fractions will be circled:
a $\frac{4}{10}$ b $\frac{9}{10}$ c $\frac{1}{2}$ d $\frac{8}{10}$
e $\frac{7}{10}$ f $\frac{1}{2}$ g $\frac{3}{4}$ h $\frac{3}{10}$

1:20

1 a b c d
2 a b c d

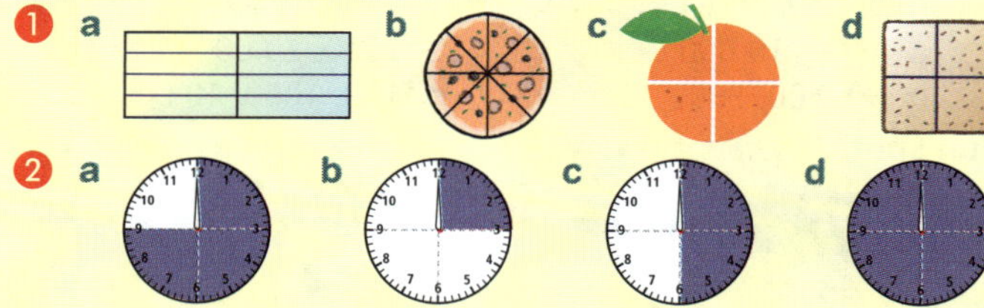

3 a 4 b 8 c 12 d 16 e 6 f 10

Activity: There are 6 halves in 3 oranges.

Activity: Answers will vary, e.g. cooking, telling the time and test results.

1:21

Header: 3019

1 a 1352 b 1234 c 1392 d 9646 e 1255
f 9708 g 2055 h 4249 i 9030
2 a 723 b 965 c 631
d 1264 e 2753 f 4194
3 a 600 or 6 hundreds b 6000 or 6 thousands
c 60 or 6 tens

Activity: Students will play 'Wipe out a digit'.

1:22

1 a

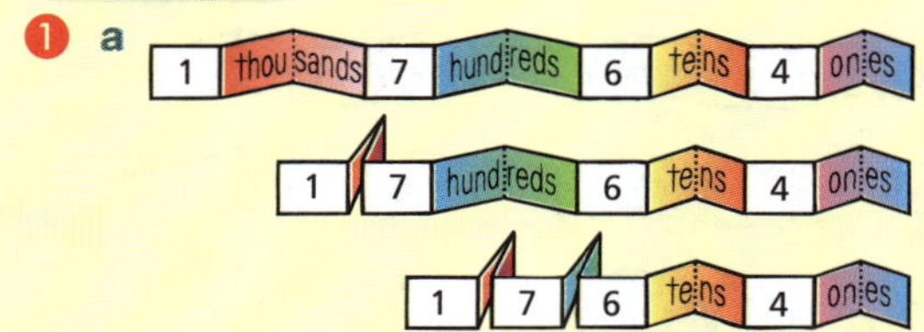

b c d

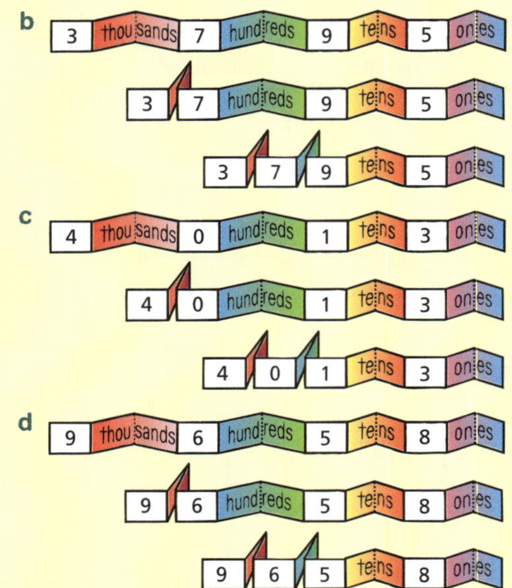

2 a 15 b 12 c 23 d 61 e 74 f 93
3 a 174 b 162 c 490 d 726
4 a 1210 b 5641 c 6301 d 2516
5 a 300 tens = 30 hundreds
b 70 tens = 7 hundreds

1:23

1 a 3769 b 4637 c 2581
d 5476 e 3958 f 6843
2 a 4000 + 200 + 40 + 7 b 3000 + 100 + 60 + 9
c 2000 + 600 + 70 + 5 d 5000 + 100 + 90 + 2
3

	Thousands	Hundreds	Tens	Units
a	4	3	7	8
b	6	2	4	9
c	3	8	2	1
d	5	8	7	3

4 a 900 b 4000 c 9 d 80
e 3000 f 5 g 600 h 30
5 a 966 b 1235 c 2190 d 4629
e 5728 f 6309 g 3399 h 7019

Fun spot: Students will play Dicey numbers.

1:24

Header: $\frac{2}{10}$ are yellow. $\frac{1}{5}$ is blue.

1 a $\frac{3}{10}$ b $\frac{5}{10}$ c $\frac{9}{10}$ d $\frac{7}{10}$
2 a 0·2 b 0·5 c 0·1 d 0·8 e 0·3
f 0.7 g 0·4 h 0·6 i 0·9
3 a $\frac{5}{5}$ b $\frac{1}{5}$ c $\frac{2}{5}$
d $\frac{4}{5}$ e $\frac{3}{5}$ f $\frac{5}{5}$

1:25

Header: $\frac{1}{10}$ is yellow. $\frac{3}{10}$ are red.

1. a 2·9 b 1·5
2. a 0·1 b 0·3 c 0·5
   d 0·4 e 0·2 f 0·8
   g 0·9 h 0·7 i 0·6
3. a 1·1 b 1·6 c 1·2
   d 2·3 e 2·4 f 2·9
   g 3·5 h 3·8 i 3·7
4. a $\frac{5}{10}$ or $\frac{1}{2}$ b $\frac{7}{10}$ c $\frac{2}{10}$ or $\frac{1}{5}$
   d $1\frac{4}{10}$ or $1\frac{2}{5}$ e $3\frac{1}{10}$ f $2\frac{8}{10}$ or $2\frac{4}{5}$
   g $6\frac{9}{10}$ h $5\frac{3}{10}$ i $7\frac{6}{10}$ or $7\frac{3}{5}$
5. a 4·1 b 8·3 c 5·2 d 3·4

1:26

1. a 0·5 b 0·3 c 0·6 d 0·1
   e 0·8 f 0·9 g 0·2 h 0·4
   i 1·1 j 1·3 k 1·9 l 1·8
2. a

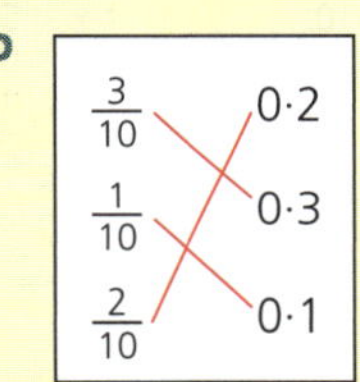

b

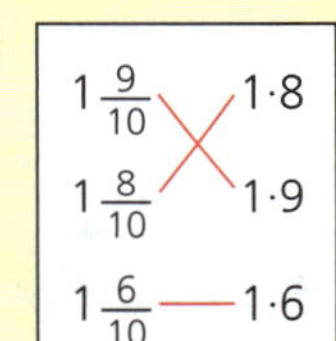

c $1\frac{9}{10}$ — 1·9, $1\frac{8}{10}$ — 1·8, $1\frac{6}{10}$ — 1·6

3. a 0·5 b 0·3 c 0·9 d 0·7
   e 0·4 f 0·8 g 0·6 h 1 or 1·0
   i 0·1 j 0·8 k 0·5 l 1·9 m 1·3 n 1·0
4. a $\frac{2}{10}, \frac{4}{10}, \frac{5}{10}, \frac{7}{10}, \frac{8}{10}, \frac{9}{10}$
   0·2, 0·3, 0·4, 0·7, 0·8, 0·9
   b $\frac{4}{10}, \frac{5}{10}, \frac{6}{10}, \frac{7}{10}, \frac{8}{10}, \frac{9}{10}, 1$
   0·4, 0·5, 0·6, 0·7, 0·8, 0·9, 1

1:27

1. a 49 734 b 68 392 c 56 438
2.

	T Thous	Thousands	Hundreds	Tens	Units
a	2	6	3	2	4
b	3	5	1	6	2
c	8	2	9	7	0
d	5	2	8	1	4
e	7	4	2	6	0

3. a 34 528 b 67 934 c 58 462
   d 92 748 e 82 359 f 48 673
4.

	Thousands	Hundreds, Tens, Ones
a	47	500
b	263	280
c	984	000

1:28

1. a 58 437 b 50 437 c 81 526 d 14 201
   e 35 832 f 72 600 g 462 937
2. These numbers will be circled.
   a 87 352 b 90 651 c 97 702
   d 75 098 e 112 403 f 105 206
3. a 9752, 50 712, 50 752, 51 270
   b 69 999, 70 789, 75 098, 508 970
4. a 5 b 4 c 5 d 6
5.

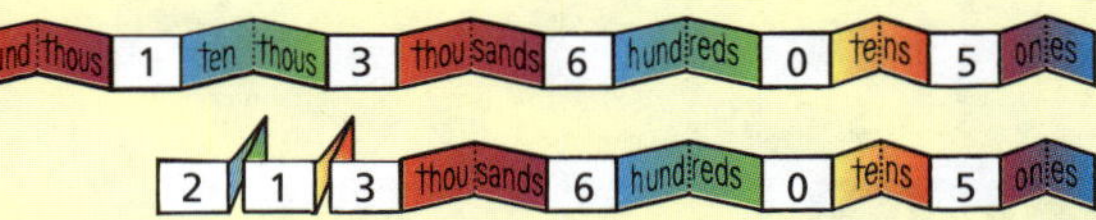

2 1 3 thou sands 6 hund reds 0 tens 5 ones

6. a 10 b 10 c 10 d 10

1:29

1. a 8 412 693 b 3 729 549
   c 5 030 024 d 9 000 701
2.

	Millions	Thousands	Hundreds, tens, ones
a	1	347	791
b	2	527	013
c	1	729	742
d		984	321

3. South Australia, Northern Territory, Queensland, Western Australia
4.

4 millions 3 6 8 thou sands 0 hund reds 2 tens 4 ones

5. $462 000

2:01

Header: 50c = 20c + 20c + <u>10c</u>
= 20c + <u>10c</u> + <u>10c</u> + <u>10c</u>

1. 5 cents, 2 dollars, 10 cents, 1 dollar, 20 cents, 50 cents
2.

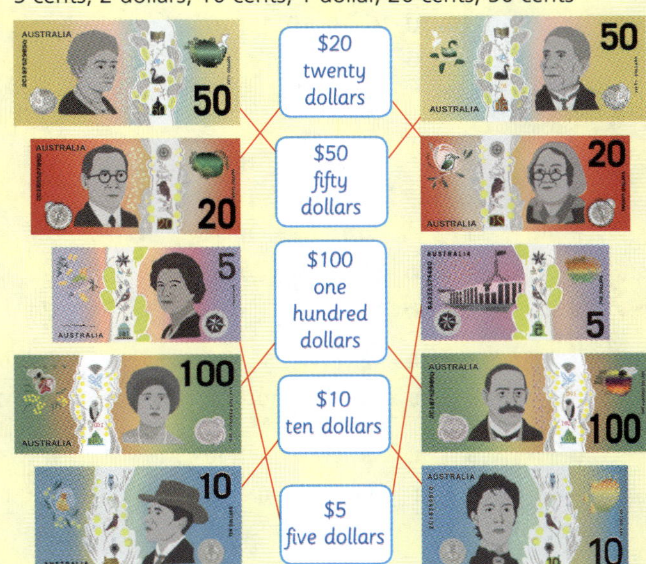

 • • ISBN 9780655708773

3 two $50 notes, or five $20 notes
ten $10 notes, or twenty $5 notes

4 $5, $10, $20, $50, $100

2:02

1 **a** $25 **b** $60 **c** $20 **d** $50

2 **a** The amount on the left will be circled.
b The amount on the right will be circled.
c The amount on the right will be circled.

3 **a** $55, $60, $75
b $50, $80, $85
c $35, $40, $90

2:03

1 **a** 5, 5, 1, 4 **b** 6, 6, 2, 4 **c** 10, 10, 9, 1
d 10, 10, 8, 2 **e** 15, 15, 9, 6

2

+	0	1	2	3	4	5	6	7	8	9	10
0	0										
1		2									
2			4			7					
3				6							
4					8				12		
5			7			10	11	12		14	
6						11	12	13			
7						12	13	14	15	16	
8					12			15	16	17	
9						14		16	17	18	
10											20

Matching pairs of numbers will be coloured.

3 **a** 10, 10, 10, 10, 10, 10, 10, 10, 10
b 1, 2, 3, 4, 5, 6, 7, 8, 9

2:04

1 **a** 2 **b** 4 **c** 6 **d** 8 **e** 10
f 12 **g** 14 **h** 16 **i** 18 **j** 20
k 4 **l** 8 **m** 12 **n** 16 **o** 20

2 **a** 16, 6, 22 **b** 14, 10, 24 **c** 8, 18, 26 **d** 20, 12, 8

3 **a** 14 **b** 16 **c** 22 **d** 24

4 **a**

	3	10	2	1	5	4	7	9	8	6
× 2	6	20	4	2	10	8	14	18	16	12

b

	6	4	8	2	5	10	1	7	9	3
× 2	12	8	16	4	10	20	2	14	18	6

c

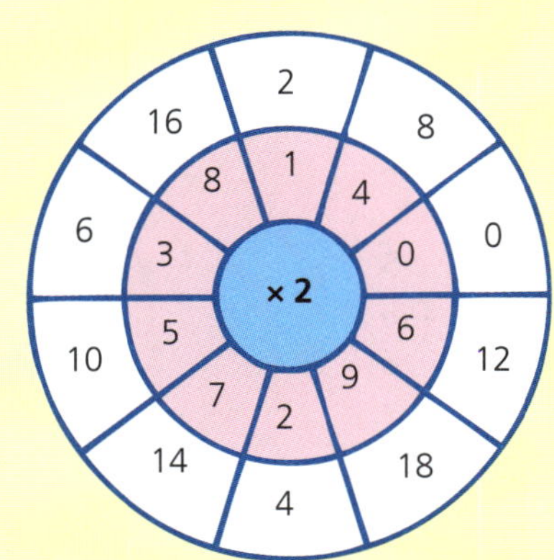

2:05

1 **a** 5 **b** 10 **c** 15 **d** 20 **e** 25
f 30 **g** 35 **h** 40 **i** 45 **j** 50
k 10 **l** 20 **m** 30 **n** 40 **o** 50

2 **a** 60 **b** 70 **c** 80 **d** 90 **e** 100

3 **a**

	3	10	2	1	5	4	7	9	8	6
× 10	30	100	20	10	50	40	70	90	80	60

b

	3	10	2	1	5	4	7	9	8	6
× 5	15	50	10	5	25	20	35	45	40	30

c yes **d** yes **e** yes **f** yes **g** yes

2:06

1 **a** 12 **b** 35 **c** 14 **d** 80 **e** 70 **f** 16
g 25 **h** 50 **i** 18 **j** 30 **k** 60 **l** 90
m 40 **n** 22 **o** 45 **p** 55

2 **a** 2, 2 **b** 10, 10 **c** 20, 20
d 5, 5 **e** 0, 0 **f** 50, 50

3 **a** 0, 7, 30, 50, 6, 25, 40, 12, 40, 70
b 0, 6, 45, 100, 4, 20, 50, 18, 35, 80
c 0, 9, 40, 20, 10, 15, 20, 14, 45, 60
d 0, 8, 35, 10, 8, 10, 30, 16, 30, 90

2:07

1 **a**

	=
2 × 2	0
4 × 2	2
0 × 2	4
1 × 2	6
3 × 2	8
7 × 2	10
5 × 2	12
10 × 2	14
9 × 2	16
6 × 2	18
8 × 2	20

b

	=
3 × 2	0
0 × 2	2
5 × 2	4
1 × 2	6
7 × 2	8
2 × 2	10
8 × 2	12
4 × 2	14
6 × 2	16
10 × 2	18
9 × 2	20

c

	=
1 × 10	0
3 × 10	10
0 × 10	20
5 × 10	30
2 × 10	40
10 × 7	50
4 × 10	60
6 × 10	70
10 × 10	80
9 × 10	90
8 × 10	100

 ISBN 9780655708773

d

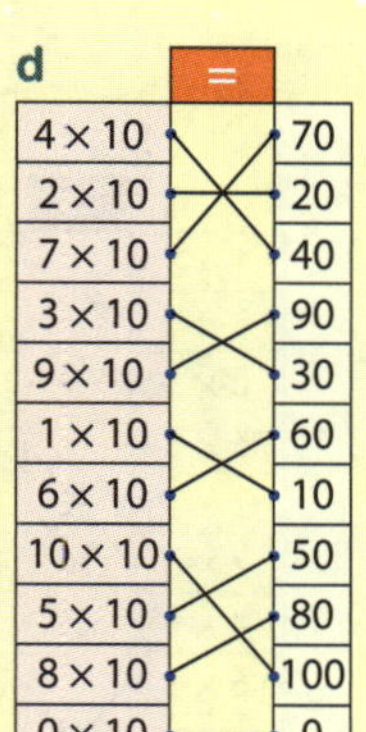

e

=	
1 × 5	50
6 × 5	25
10 × 5	5
5 × 5	30
8 × 5	0
0 × 5	40
2 × 5	15
9 × 5	35
3 × 5	20
7 × 5	10
4 × 5	45

f

=	
0 × 5	0
6 × 5	15
3 × 5	30
8 × 5	20
4 × 5	25
10 × 5	40
5 × 5	10
2 × 5	50
1 × 5	35
7 × 5	45
9 × 5	5

20 is 1 × 20, 2 × 10, 4 × 5, 5 × 4, 10 × 2 or 20 × 1.

2:08

1 The tens digit: increases by one
The ones digit: decreases by one
So, to add 9 we can add 10 and then subtract 1.

2 The tens digit: decreases by one
The ones digit: increases by one
So, to subtract 9 we can subtract 10 and then add 1.

3 **a** 16 **b** 25 **c** 37 **d** 51 **e** 8 **f** 25 **g** 72, 63, 54, 45

4 **a** 14 **b** 27 **c** 61 **d** 83 **e** 15 **f** 59 **g** 56, 64, 72, 80

5 **a** 9 **b** 15 **c** 9

6 **a** 27, 37, 47 **b** 26, 36, 46 **c** 29, 39, 49

2:09

Concept: 33 – 15 =18; 15 + 18 = 33

1 **a** 8, 8, 8 **b** 7, 7, 7 **c** 9, 9, 9 **d** 6, 6, 6 **e** 19, 19 **f** 28, 28

Activity: Answers will vary.

2:10

1 How many bones were left?
100 – 40 = 60
There were 60 bones left.

2 How many pies?
3 × 10 = 30
There were 30 pies.

3 How many friends?
24 ÷ 2 = 12
There were 12 friends.

4 How many books?
24 + 55 = 79
There were 79 books.

5 How many people got off?
15 + 10 + 8 = 33
33 people got off altogether.

6 How many bottles?
(3 × 5) + 2 = 17
There were 17 bottles.

7 How many rows of bottles?
45 ÷ 5 = 9
You could make 9 rows.

8 **a** 899 **b** 890 **c** 590 **d** 490 **e** 698 **f** 198 **g** yes

2:11

1 Coloured coins:
a 50c, 20c, 20c **b** $1, 50c, 20, 10c, 5c
c $2, 50c, 20c **d** $2, $1, 20c, 10c, 10c, 10c, 10c
e $2, 50c, 20c, 20c, 5c **f** $2, $1, 20c
g $5, $2, 50c, 20c **h** $5, 20c, 10c

2 Answers will vary. Examples:
a $2, $1, 50c, 20c, 10c **b** $2, 50c, 20c, 20c, 5c
c $2, $2, 20c, 10c, 5c **d** $5, $2, $2, 10c
e $10, $2, 50c, 20c **f** $10, $5, 50c

2:12

Header: two $1 coins, ten 20c coins, four 50c coins, twenty 10c coins

A:65c, **B**:$2.35, **C**:$1.15, **D**:65c, **E**:$1.30, **F**:$2.35, **G**:35c, **H**:$2.60

1 **a** D **b** B **c** G **d** H

2 **a** $1.30 **b** $3.65 **c** $1.50

3 **a** O **b** Q **c** M **d** S

M:$15, **N**:$50, **O**:$20, **P**:$20, **Q**:$60, **R**:$30, **S**:$200, **T**:$60

2:13

1 **a** 5 + 12 = 17 **b** 13 + 32 = 45

2 **a** 27 **b** 43 **c** 37 **d** 53 **e** 48 **f** 39 **g** 48 **h** 29

3 **a** 4 tens and 7 ones **b** 4 tens and 9 ones **c** 3 tens and 9 ones

4 **a** 98 **b** 88 **c** 68

2:14

Header: 25

1 **a** 35 **b** 33 **c** 51 **d** 93 **e** 64 **f** 72

2 **a** 14 **b** 8 **c** 14 **d** 19 **e** 37 **f** 31 **g** 7 **h** 17 **i** 29

2:15

Header: 95

1 **a** 91 **b** 82 **c** 63 **d** 72 **e** 78 **f** 92 **g** 101 **h** 103

2 **a** 73 **b** 38 **c** 19 **d** 37 **e** 31 **f** 7 **g** 17 **h** 59

3 **a** 83 **b** 36 **c** 124

2:16

1 **a** 700 **b** 900 **c** 700 **d** 600

2 **a** 27 **b** 34 **c** 78 **d** 34

3 **a** 46 **b** 33 **c** 43 **d** 61

4 **a** 56 **b** 92 **c** 67 **d** 64

5 **a** 73 **b** 89 **c** 39 **d** 48 **e** 57 **f** 80

6 **a** 89

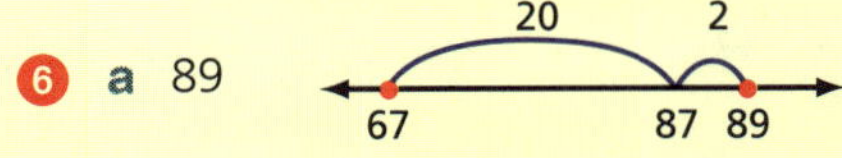

b 78

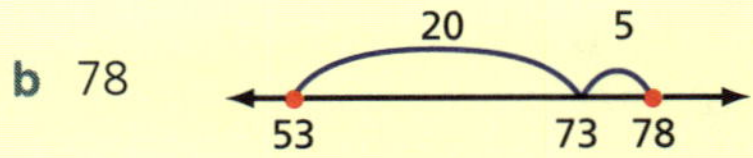

c 61

30 4
27 57 61

d 62

10 6 2
44 54 60 62

7 **Investigation:** Strategies used may vary.

a 88, E **b** 43, B **c** 53, C or D
d 45, C or D **e** 800, A **f** 66, D or F

2:17

Example: 37 + (37 + 5) = 79

1 How many cards?
43 + 25 = 68
68 cards

2 How many books each?
45 ÷ 5 = 9
9 books each

3 How many sheep left?
96 − 28 = 68
68 sheep left

4 How many cans?
54 + 37 = 91
91 cans

5 How many seeds?
(6 × 5) + 4 = 34
34 seeds

6 **Investigation:** **a** 10 **b** 5 **c** 3

2:18

1 **a** 3 **b** 6 **c** 9 **d** 12 **e** 15
f 18 **g** 21 **h** 24 **i** 27 **j** 30

2 **a** 0 **b** 0 **c** 30 **d** 30
e 6 **f** 6 **g** 3 **h** 3
i 15 **j** 15 **k** 24 **l** 12
m 27 **n** 18 **o** 9 **p** 21

3 **a** 5 **b** 5 **c** 10 **d** 10
e 0 **f** 0 **g** 50 **h** 50
i 20 **j** 20 **k** 25 **l** 100

4 **a**
3
× 8
= 24

b
3
× 9
= 27

5 **a**

	4	7	9	5	8	6
× 3	12	21	27	15	24	18

b

	4	7	9	5	8	6
× 5	20	35	45	25	40	30

c

	4	7	9	5	8	6
× 2	8	14	18	10	16	12

d

	4	7	9	5	8	6
× 10	40	70	90	50	80	60

2:19

1 **a**

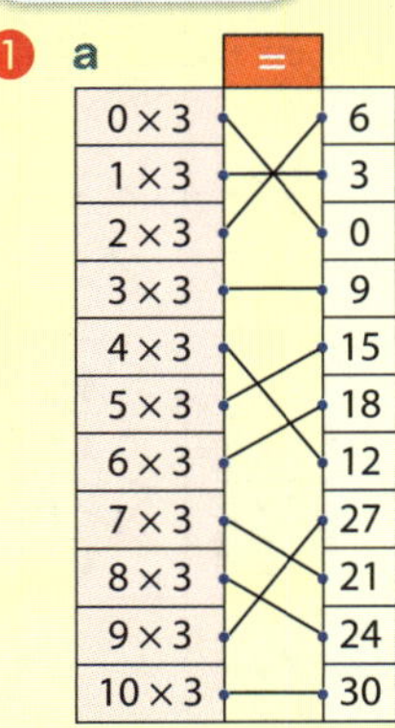

b

	=
3 × 3	0
0 × 3	3
5 × 3	6
1 × 3	9
7 × 3	12
2 × 3	15
8 × 3	18
4 × 3	21
6 × 3	24
10 × 3	27
9 × 3	30

c

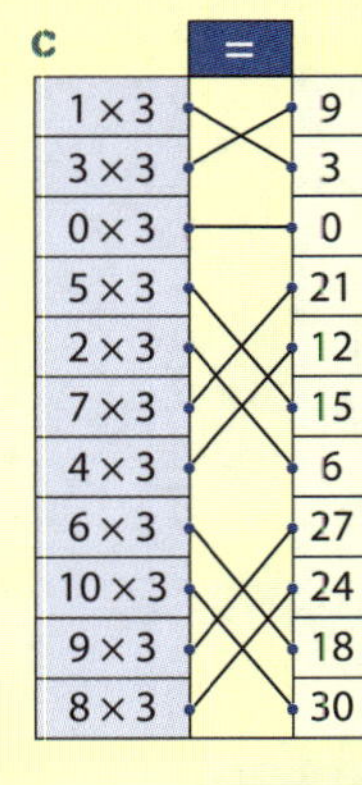

d

	=
4 × 2	35
2 × 3	6
7 × 5	8
3 × 10	9
9 × 1	30
4 × 0	40
8 × 5	0
10 × 2	50
5 × 10	20
8 × 0	21
7 × 3	0

e

	=
1 × 5	18
6 × 3	50
10 × 5	5
5 × 5	24
8 × 3	0
0 × 5	25
2 × 5	27
9 × 3	10
3 × 5	21
7 × 3	12
4 × 3	15

f

	=
7 × 1	18
6 × 3	7
3 × 5	24
8 × 3	15
4 × 3	10
8 × 5	40
5 × 2	12
6 × 5	21
1 × 0	30
7 × 3	27
9 × 3	0

30 is <u>3</u> × 10, <u>10</u> × 3, <u>6</u> × 5.

2:20

1 **a** 6, 6 **b** 15, 15 **c** 30, 30
d 3, 3 **e** 0, 0 **f** 18, 18

2 **a** 0, 7, 18, 50, 9, 25, 40, 12, 24, 70
b 0, 6, 9, 100, 6, 20, 50, 27, 21, 80
c 0, 9, 24, 18, 15, 15, 20, 21, 27, 60
d 0, 3, 21, 10, 12, 10, 30, 24, 18, 90

3 **a** 6 **b** 21 **c** 3 **d** 12 **e** 15 **f** 24
g 25 **h** 30 **i** 27 **j** 30 **k** 9 **l** 18
m 40 **n** 15 **o** 45 **p** 33

4 12, 15, 18, 21, 24, 27, 30

2:21

1 **a** 4 **b** 8 **c** 12 **d** 16 **e** 20 **f** 24
g 28 **h** 32 **i** 36 **j** 40

2 **a** 20 **b** 4 **c** 24 **d** 8 **e** 28 **f** 4
g 32 **h** 12 **i** 36 **j** 4 **k** 40 **l** 16

3 **a**

x 2
6 3 9 7 5 8 2 4
12 6 18 14 10 16 4 8

b

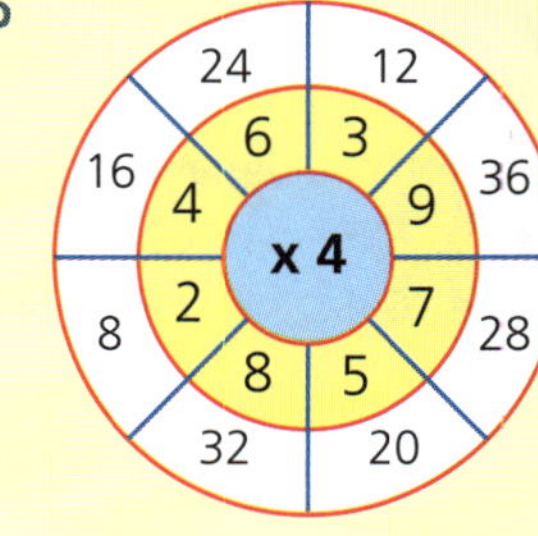

c

× 5		
Inner	6, 3, 9, 7, 5, 8, 2, 4	
Outer	30, 15, 45, 35, 25, 40, 10, 20	

d

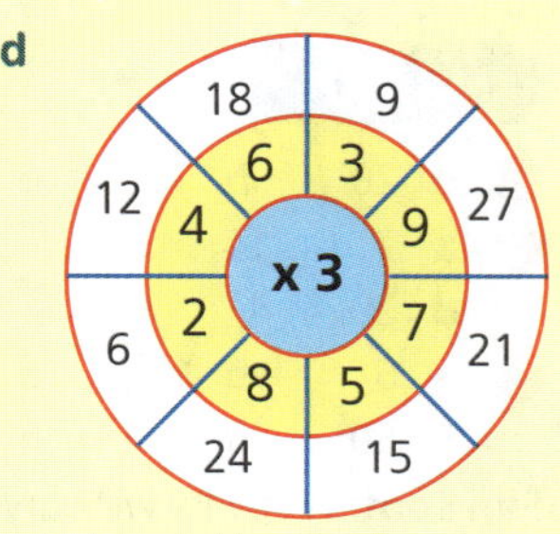

× 3		
Inner	6, 3, 9, 7, 5, 8, 2, 4	
Outer	18, 9, 27, 21, 15, 24, 6, 12	

4 **a** 20, 4, 24 **b** 24, 4, 28

5 **a**

	2	1	5	10	3	4	8
× 4	8	4	20	40	12	16	32

b

	4	6	8	5	9	7	3
× 4	16	24	32	20	36	28	12

2:22

1 **a**

	=
3 × 3	0
2 × 3	3
4 × 3	6
0 × 3	9
1 × 3	12
7 × 3	15
5 × 3	18
6 × 3	21
10 × 3	24
8 × 3	27
9 × 3	30

b

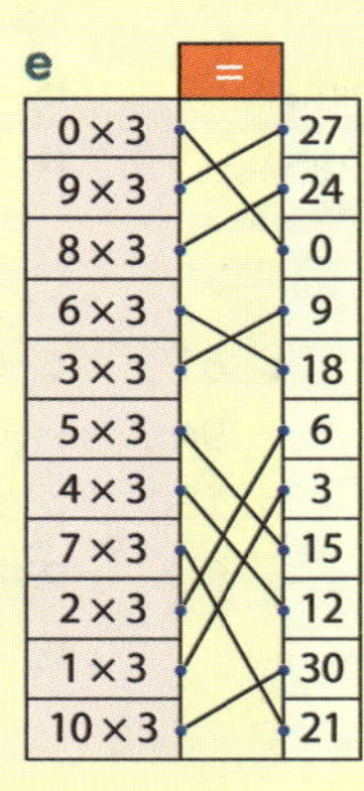

	=
3 × 4	0
2 × 4	4
0 × 4	8
6 × 4	12
1 × 4	16
4 × 4	20
5 × 4	24
9 × 4	28
10 × 4	32
7 × 4	36
8 × 4	40

c

	=
2 × 10	10
4 × 10	0
1 × 10	60
0 × 10	20
6 × 10	40
3 × 10	50
5 × 10	30
8 × 10	90
7 × 10	100
9 × 10	80
10 × 10	70

d

	=
2 × 2	0
4 × 2	2
1 × 2	4
0 × 2	6
6 × 2	8
3 × 2	10
5 × 2	12
8 × 2	14
7 × 2	16
9 × 2	18
10 × 2	20

e

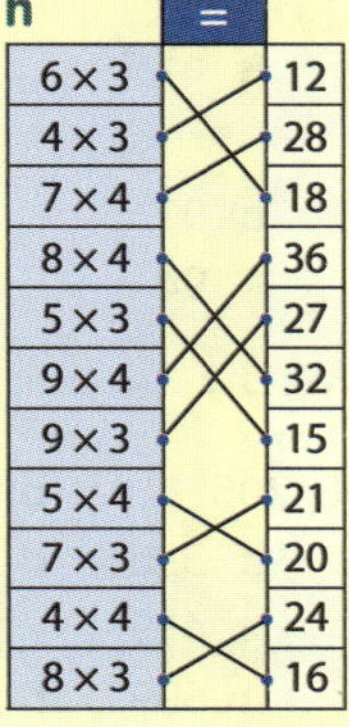

	=
0 × 3	27
9 × 3	24
8 × 3	0
6 × 3	9
3 × 3	18
5 × 3	6
4 × 3	3
7 × 3	15
2 × 3	12
1 × 3	30
10 × 3	21

f

	=
0 × 4	4
6 × 4	12
1 × 4	0
3 × 4	20
10 × 4	24
4 × 4	40
8 × 4	16
5 × 4	36
9 × 4	32
2 × 4	28
7 × 4	8

g

	=
1 × 5	0
3 × 5	25
0 × 5	5
5 × 5	15
2 × 5	30
6 × 5	10
4 × 5	45
9 × 5	35
7 × 5	20
10 × 5	40
8 × 5	50

h

	=
6 × 3	12
4 × 3	28
7 × 4	18
8 × 4	36
5 × 3	27
9 × 4	32
9 × 3	15
5 × 4	21
7 × 3	20
4 × 4	24
8 × 3	16

2 **a**

	5	3	4	8	6	9	7
× 3	15	9	12	24	18	27	21

b

	5	3	4	8	6	9	7
× 4	20	12	16	32	24	36	28

2:23

1 **a** 7 × 5 = 35 **b** 4 × 10 = 40 **c** 5 × 5 = 25

d $\begin{array}{r} 5 \\ \times\ 8 \\ \hline 40 \end{array}$ **e** $\begin{array}{r} 5 \\ \times\ 6 \\ \hline 30 \end{array}$

2 **a** 18 **b** 20 **c** 80 **d** 14 **e** 4 **f** 12
g 30 **h** 10 **i** 15 **j** 3 **k** 70 **l** 0

3 The numbers 2, 4, 6, 8, 10, 12, 14, 16, 18, 20, 22, 24, 26, 28, 30, 32, 34, 36, 38, 40, 42, 44, 46, 48, 50 will be coloured yellow. The numbers 3, 6, 9, 12, 15, 18, 21, 24, 27, 30, 33, 36, 39, 42, 45, 48 will be coloured green. The numbers 4, 8, 12, 16, 20, 24, 28, 32, 36, 40, 44, 48 will be circled.

4

×	0	1	2	3	4	5	6	7	8	9	10
0			0	0	0	0					
1			2	3	4	5					
2	0	2	4	6	8	10	12	14	16	18	20
3	0	3	6	9	12	15	18	21	24	27	30
4	0	4	8	12	16	20	24	28	32	36	40
5	0	5	10	15	20	25	30	35	40	45	50
6			12	18	24	30					
7			14	21	28	35					
8			16	24	32	40					
9			18	27	36	45					
10			20	30	40	50					

2:24

Header: 6

1 **a** 4 **b** 3 **c** 2 **d** 3 **e** 4
f 7 **g** 7 **h** 4 **i** 5

2 **a** 3 **b** 2 **c** 6 **d** 2 **e** 5 **f** 6

3 **a** 6 pieces each **b** 4 pieces each **c** 3 pieces each

4 **a** 3 mugs each with 1 left over
b 2 mugs each with 2 left over **c** 2 mugs each

2:25

Concept: 15 ÷ 3 = 5

1 **a** 7, 7, 7 **b** 3, 3, 3 **c** 3, 3, 3 **d** 3, 3, 3

2 **a** 5, 5, 4, 4 **b** 4, 4, 2, 2 **c** 7, 7, 70 **d** 6, 6, 5

3 **a** 3 **b** 4 **c** 7 pens

2:26

Concept: 15, 5

1. a 10, 5, 10, 5 b 18, 6, 18, 6 c 25, 5, 5
   d 40, 4, 4 e 35, 7, 7, 7 f 16, 8, 8
2. a 9 b 6 c 4 d 7 e 5 f 8 g 10
3. a 6 b 7 c 9 d 7 e 7 f 10 g 8
4. a 10 b 3

2:27

1. a 20, 20 b 4, 4 c 5, 5
2. a 20, 20 b 5, 5 c 4, 4
3. a 24, 24 b 3, 3 c 8, 8
4. a 18, 18 b 9, 9 c 2, 2
5. a 5, 2 b 10, 3 c 7, 2 d 9, 3
6. a 4, 4 b 7, 7 c 5, 5 d 8, 8

2:28

Header: 7

1. a 4, 4 b 10, 10 c 5, 5 d 4, 4
   e 9, 9 f 6, 6 g 7, 7 h 8, 8
2. a 2, 10 b 6, 2 c 5, 3 d 8, 5
3. a 1 b 10 c 6 d 5
   e 1 f 10 g 2 h 8
4. a 5 b 4 c 7 d 6 e 5 f 6
   g 8 h 9 i 2 j 8 k 9 l 7
5. a 5, 5 b no c no

Activity: Answers will vary.

2:29

1. a

	=
2 × 3	0
4 × 3	3
0 × 3	12
1 × 3	6
3 × 3	21
7 × 3	15
5 × 3	9
10 × 3	27
9 × 3	30
6 × 3	24
8 × 3	18

b

	=
3 × 4	4
0 × 4	20
5 × 4	0
1 × 4	8
7 × 4	32
2 × 4	16
8 × 4	12
4 × 4	28
6 × 4	36
10 × 4	24
9 × 4	40

c

	=
6 × 10	25
9 × 2	3
5 × 5	40
3 × 1	18
8 × 5	60
9 × 10	14
7 × 2	35
7 × 5	20
8 × 1	90
4 × 5	40
8 × 5	8

d

	=
4 ÷ 2	8
60 ÷ 10	3
16 ÷ 2	9
30 ÷ 10	2
18 ÷ 2	6
70 ÷ 10	1
6 ÷ 6	7
50 ÷ 10	4
20 ÷ 2	0
8 ÷ 2	5
0 ÷ 10	10

e

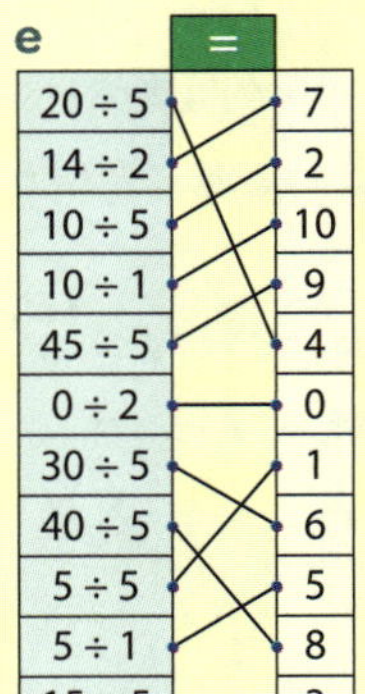

f

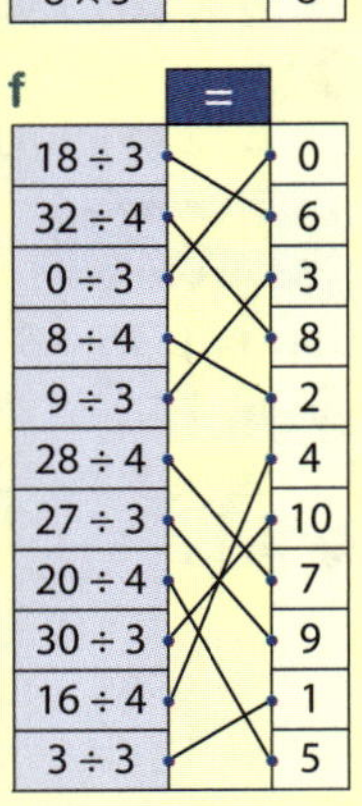

Answers will vary. 20 is 1 × 20, 2 × 10, 4 × 5, 5 × 4, 10 × 2 or 20 × 1.

2:30

1. a 20 b 10 c 3 d 30 e 8 f 60
2. a 7, 14, 14 b 3, 15, 15 c 40, 4, 4
   d 20, 4, 4 e 10, 5, 5 f 10, 20, 20
3. a 6 b 10 c 30 d 4 e 8
   f 50 g 9 h 7 i 45 j 6

Fun spot: Answers will vary.

2:31

1. a 58 b 78 c 77 d 89 e 96 f 77
   g 89 h 98 i $89 j $97 k $79 l $89
2. a 8 tens and 8 ones b 8 tens and 7 ones
   c 7 tens and 9 ones d 8 tens and 9 ones
   e 8 tens and 9 ones f 7 tens and 8 ones
3. a $96 b 29 c 57 d $77

2:32

1. a 36 – 4 = 32 b 55 – 23 = 32 c 47 – 5 = 42
   d 68 – 34 = 34 e 76 – 42 = 34 f 59 – 46 = 13
2. a 36 b 31 c 23 d 27 e 35 f 34
   g 42 h 34 i $63 j $40 k $4 l $52
3. Students will check their answers.

2:33

1. a 31 b 33 c 41 d 65 e 71
   f 74 g 90 h 82 i 72 j 58
   k 94 l 76 m $94 n $83 o $60
   p $97
2. a 4 + 29 = 33 animals b 16 + 27 = 43 birds
   c 65 + 28 = 93 insects d 57 + 26 = 83 coins

2:34

1. a 40 b 72 c 61 d 61 e 93 f 70
   g 93 h 52 i 94 j 95 k 82 l 82
   m $54 n $96 o $90 p $80
2. a 53 students b 80 cans
   c 72 stamps d 93 cards

2:35

1. a 73 b 45 c 83 d 65 e 73
   f 80 g 71 h 93
2. odd
3. a 83 b 70 c 91
   d 60 e 80 f 94

2:36

1. a 62 + 144 = 206, 206 b 173 + 251 = 424, 424
2. a 105 b 507 c 336 d 227 e 719
   f 688 g 325 h 419 i 828 j 718
   k 547 l 937 m 509 n 537 o 928
   p 827

 • *AUSTRALIAN SIGNPOST MATHS 3* • ISBN 9780655708773

2:37

1 a 159 b 842 c 618 d 173 e 459
f 557 g 674 h 485 i 978 j 585
k 780 l 870 m 612 n 893 o 490
p 619

2 a $470 b $825 c $907 d $754

3 Students will test their answers to Questions 1 and 2.

2:38

1 a 128 b 820 c 504 d 200 e 532
f 810 g 602 h 920 i 821 j 650
k 620 l 744 m 806 n 751 o 900
p 932

2 a 224 birds b 312 sheets
c 197 meals d 374 cows

2:39

1 a

tens	ones
4	10
~~5~~	~~0~~

b

tens	ones
6	10
~~7~~	~~0~~

c

tens	ones
3	10
~~4~~	~~0~~

d

tens	ones
8	10
~~9~~	~~0~~

2 a 56 b 73 c 44 d 82 e $14
f $13 g $45 h $48

3 a 16 b 53 c 14 d 12

4 a $53 b $34 c $22

2:40

1 a

tens	ones
2	14
~~3~~	~~4~~

b

tens	ones
4	17
~~5~~	~~7~~

c

tens	ones
3	16
~~4~~	~~6~~

d

tens	ones
6	12
~~7~~	~~2~~

e

tens	ones
5	13
~~6~~	~~3~~

f

tens	ones
7	15
~~8~~	~~5~~

2 a 18 b 16 c 29 d 49
e 68 f 57 g 28 h 37

2:41

1 a

tens	ones
3	15
~~4~~	~~5~~

b

tens	ones
1	17
~~2~~	~~7~~

c

tens	ones
2	11
~~3~~	~~1~~

d

tens	ones
6	12
~~7~~	~~2~~

2 a 38 b 54 c 28 d 19 e 14
f 29 g 25 h 57 i 25 j 38

2:42

1 a 22 b $45 c 38 d 16

2 a 19 km b 34 km c 28 km

3 a 12 km b 74 km c 62 km
d 35 km e 39 km f 27 km

2:43

1 a 160 b 680 c 269 d 187 e 35
f 87 g 69 h 282 i 155 j 793

2 a 61 b 885 c 33 d 72 e 96
f 44 g 24 h 73 i 33 j 74
k 293 l 525 m 881 n 365 o 13
p 884 q 565

2:44

1 a 15 b 44 c 35 d 559 e 884

2 a 55 b 18 c 25 d 219 e 413

3 a 46 b 68 c 748 d 637 e 357
f 519 g 25 h 44 i 173 j 486
k 73 l 49 m 28 n 35 o 19
p 57 q 46 r 48

2:45

1 a 107 b 140 c 120 d 180 e 220
f 360 g 780 h 505 i 930 j 920
k 808 l 947

2 a 60 b 58 c 46 d 160 e 736
f 573 g 306 h 320 i 120 j 162
k 670 l 290

3 a 798 b 941

2:46

1 Coloured coins:
a 50c, $1, 20c, 5c = $1.75 b $1, 20c, 10c, 5c = $1.35
c 50c, 20c, 10c, 5c = 85c

2 b 5c, 10c = 15c c 5c, 20c, 20c = 45c
d 5c, 20c = 25c

3 a $1.30 b 60c c $1.55 d 95c

2:47

1 a $6 b $1 c $8 d $5

2 1, 2, 4, 5 and 6

3 5-point stars = 3, 6-point stars = 1

4 a 10, 8, 6 or 10, 10, 4 or 8, 8, 8
b No. Answers will vary. Three even numbers can't add to an odd number.

5 2 × 10, 10 × 2, 1 × 20, 20 × 1, 4 × 5, 5 × 4

6 1 × 30, 30 × 1, 2 × 15, 15 × 2, 3 × 10, 10 × 3, 5 × 6, 6 × 5

3:01

1 a C b C c A

2 a A, B, C b B, A, C c C, B, A

Activity: Answers will vary.

 • *AUSTRALIAN SIGNPOST MATHS 3* • ISBN 9780655708773

3:02

1. Answers will vary, e.g. width of a standard door.
2. Answers will vary.
3. Some answers may vary.

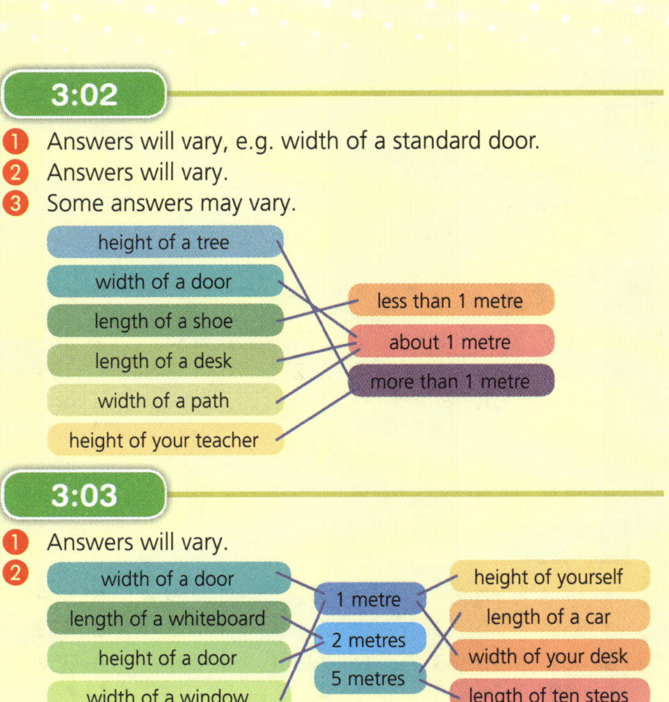

3:03

1. Answers will vary.
2. width of a door / length of a whiteboard / height of a door / width of a window — 1 metre / 2 metres / 5 metres — height of yourself / length of a car / width of your desk / length of ten steps
3. Answers will vary.

3:04

1. a a quarter past 6, 6 fifteen, 15 past 6 or 6:15
   b half past 9, 9 thirty, or 9:30
   c 1 o'clock or 1:00
   d a quarter to 2, 1 forty-five, 45 past 1 or 1:45
   e a quarter past 2, 2 fifteen, or 15 past 2
   f half past 5 or 5 thirty
   g 6 o'clock
   h a quarter to 9, 8 forty-five, or 45 past 8
2. a b c d

   e 8:15 f 2:30 g 12:45 h 7:00

3:05

1. a 5 minutes past 4 b 20 minutes past 1
   c 10 minutes past 11 d 25 minutes past 7
   e 20 past 5 f 5 past 9
   g 10 past 6 h 25 past 9
2. a 50 past 7, 10 minutes to 8 b 40 past 3, 20 minutes to 4
   c 55 past 1, 5 to 2 d 35 past 4, 25 to 5

3:06

1. a 4:10, 10 past 4 b 7:25, 25 past 7
   c 12:20, 20 past 12 d 4:05, 5 past 4
   e 10:25, 25 past 10 f 2:35, 35 past 2
   g 11:45, 45 past 11 h 8:50, 50 past 8
   i 3:55, 55 past 3 j 4:40, 40 past 4
   k 35 past 4 l 40 past 2
   m 25 past 8 n 45 past 3
   o 5 past 5 p 10 past 6
   q 35 past 12 r 50 past 11
   s 5 past 7 t 55 past 9

Activity:

3:07

Concept: rounds to 2 cups

1. a 4 cups b 4 cups c 8 cups d 2 cups
   e 6 cups f 2 cans g 4 cans
2. a Answers will vary. b Answers will vary.

3:08

1.

2. a 11 L b 75 L c 60 L d 34 L
   e **B, E, C, D, A**
3. Answers will vary.

3:09

1. Yes
2. Answers will vary.
3. Answers will vary.
4. A discussion will occur
5. Answers will vary.

3:10

1. a 9 cm b 6 cm c 10 cm
2. a 5 cm b 9 cm c 4 cm d 7 cm
   c, a, d, b
3. a 7 cm b 6 cm c 3 cm d 5 cm e 4 cm

3:11

1. a 7 cm b 4 cm c 8 cm
   d 3 cm e 2 cm f 9 cm
2. a 5 cm, 3 cm, 3 cm, 5 cm b 6 cm, 2 cm, 2 cm, 6 cm

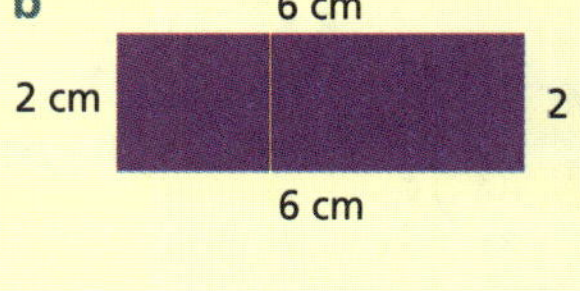

Activity: Answers will vary.

3:12

1. a 1 m 70 cm b 3 m 36 cm c 4 m 26 cm
   d 7 m 13 cm e 6 m 83 cm f 5 m 42 cm
2. a m b cm c cm d m e cm f cm g m h cm

Investigation: Answers will vary.

3:13

1. Estimates will vary.
   a 18 cm b 12 cm c 10 cm
   d 14 cm e 16 cm f 6 cm

g sides are 2 cm, perimeter = 8 cm
h sides are 4 cm, perimeter = 12 cm
i sides are 3 cm, 4 cm and 5 cm, and perimeter = 12 cm
j c, b, a

2 a 126 cm b 173 cm

3 a 2 m 38 cm b 2 m 13 cm
c 3 m 47 cm d 7 m 24 cm

3:14

1 a 10:26, 26 past 10 b 11:17, 17 past 11
c 3:39, 39 past 3 d 2:21, 21 past 2
e 4:07, 7 past 4 f 5:48, 48 past 5
g 2:37, 37 past 2 h 4:41, 41 past 4
i 7:54, 54 past 7 j 2:58, 58 past 2
k 34 past 9 l 28 past 2 m 41 past 5
n 47 past 8 o 59 past 6

2 a
11:36 — eleven thirty-six
6:12 — 12 minutes past 6
9:57 — 57 minutes past 9

b
1:43 — 43 minutes past 1
8:26 — 26 minutes past 8
5:07 — five-oh-seven

3:15

1 a 7 to 2 b 16 to 1 c 18 to 10 d 3 to 9
e 18 to 12 f 27 to 5 g 5 to 2 h 12 to 6

2 a  b  c 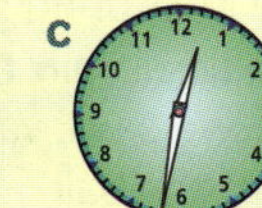 d 

3 a 16 to 6 b 11 to 9 c 21 to 3
d 16 to 10 e 21 to 11 f 6 to 7

4 a 8 to 6 b 18 to 11 c 23 to 9
d 13 to 12 e 23 to 8 f 3 to 12

3:16

1 a 22 past 7 b 3 to 7 c 18 past 12 d 6 past 10
e 12 to 1 f 8 past 12 g 22 to 4 h 7 to 8

2 a 27 past 6 b 18 past 7 c 10 past 8 d 4 past 12
e 26 past 4 f 27 to 6 g 19 to 2 h 6 to 5
i 18 to 12 j 1 to 7

3:17

1 Answers will vary.
2 Answers will vary.
3 1 L of water has the same mass as 1 kg. The container holding the water also has mass. Its mass is balanced by the empty container on the other side.

3:18

1 Answers will vary.
2 Answers will vary.
3 Answers will vary.
4 Answers with yes will be circled.
a yes b no c no d yes e no f no
g yes h no i no j no k yes l yes

5 Answers with yes will be circled.
a no b yes c yes d no e yes
f yes g no h no i yes

3:19

1 a 3 kg b 10 kg c 8 kg d 5 kg e 7 kg
f 11 kg

2 Answers with yes will be circled.
a yes b yes c no d yes e yes f no
g yes h yes i no j yes k yes l no

3 a 4 kg b 10 kg c 29 kg d 27 kg
e 23 kg f 8 kg g 45 kg h 21 kg

4 Answers with yes will be circled.
a yes b no c yes d no e no
f yes g yes h no i no j yes

Activity: Answers will vary.

3:20

1 a 12 b 12 c 6 d 6

2 a 4 rows of 4 or 4 columns of 4
b 5 rows of 2 or 2 columns of 5
c A rectangle with 3 rows of 4 will be drawn and labelled with a D.
d A rectangle with 2 columns of 2 will be drawn and labelled with an E.
e **B** f **E**

3 a no b 1 book c 8
d Books are a good unit because they fit together without leaving gaps or overlaps, however they would not be suitable to measure a small area.

Activity: Answers will vary.

3:21

1 a **L** 19 squares **M** 16 squares **N** 18 squares
b **M, N, L**

2 **X** 20 squares **Y** 20 squares **Z** 20 squares
Each one has a different shape, but the same area.

3 a **A** 6 × 4 squares, 24 squares
B 2 × 10 squares, 20 squares
C 6 × 10 squares, 60 squares
b **B, A, C**

Fun spot: Answers will vary.

3:22

1 a Friday b Sunday
c 1st November or November 1, 2024
d 4th November or November 4, 2024
e 30th November or November 30, 2024
f 4th November, 11th November, 18th November, 25th November, 2024
g 4 h 9

2 a 7 b 14 c 31 d 30
e 31 f 31 g 30 h 31
i 31 j 30 k 30 l 31

3 a 3/11/24
b 29/11/24 c 27/11/24

3:23

1. 9 weeks and 4 days
2. 7 weeks and 4 days
3. 35 hours (Note: Akash has 7 matches.)
4. 29th November
5. 16 hours
6. January 11th
7.

November 2024						
Sun	Mon	Tues	Wed	Thurs	Fri	Sat
					1	2
3	4	5	6	7	8	9
10	11	12	13	(14)	15	16
17	18	19	20	21	22	23
24	25	26	27	28	29	(30)

December 2024						
Sun	Mon	Tues	Wed	Thurs	Fri	Sat
1	2	3	4	5	6	7
8	9	10	11	12	13	14
15	16	17	(18)	19	20	21
22	23	24	25	26	27	28
29	30	31				

January 2025						
Sun	Mon	Tues	Wed	Thurs	Fri	Sat
			(1)	2	3	4
5	6	7	8	9	10	11
12	13	14	15	16	17	18
19	20	21	22	23	24	25
26	27	28	(29)	30	31	

3:24

1. 2 (Two 500 g bags balance a 1 kg mass.)
   4 (Four 500 g bags would balance a 2 kg mass.)
   Answers will vary.
2. **a** 40 g **b** 100 g **c** 600 g **d** 300 g
3. **a** 300 g **b** 800 g **c** 700 g **d** 600 g
4. **a** 750 g **b** 500 g **c** 2 kg

3:25

1. Answers will vary.
2. Answers will vary.
3. Answers will vary.
4. **a** 60 g **b** 100 g **c** 40 kg **d** 30 g **e** 9 kg **f** 70 g
5. **a** g **b** g **c** kg **d** kg **e** g
6. **a** 700 g **b** 500 g **c** 300 g

3:26

1. The duck and the pelican.
2. **a** g **b** g **c** kg **d** kg **e** g **f** g
3. **a** 450 g **b** 12 kg **c** 775 g **d** 1125 g
4. **a** 5 kg **b** 9 kg **c** 46 kg **d** 188 kg

Investigation:

Fruit	My fruit's mass	Largest recorded mass	Difference between the largest and my fruit
watermelon	9 kg	119 kg	119 kg – 9 kg = 110 kg
pineapple	18 kg	28 kg	28 kg – 18 kg = 10 kg
strawberry	12 g	289 g	289 g – 12 g = 277 g
plum	65 g	354 g	354 g – 65 g = 289 g

3:27

1. **a** mL **b** mL **c** mL **d** L **e** mL **f** mL **g** mL
2. Answers will vary.
3. **a** **A** 500 mL **B** 750 mL **C** 250 mL **D** 1000 mL **E** 250 mL
   b **C, E, A, B, D**

c
1000
500
mL

Activity: Answers will vary.

3:28

1. **a** 12 **b** 30
2. **a** 2 **b** 6 **c** 45, 53, 8 **d** 10
3. **a** 2 **b** 5 **c** 3 **d** 20 **e** 94 L
4. **a** 60 L **b** the bin and esky

3:29

1. **a** 24 mm **b** 16 mm **c** 31 mm **d** 62 mm **e** 47 mm
2. **a** 27 mm **b** 57 mm **c** 65 mm **d** 36 mm **e** 17 mm
   f 72 mm

Fun spot: Answers will vary.

3:30

1. **a** 1 cm, 10 mm **b** 10 cm, 100 mm
2. Answers will vary. Example: Centimetres are a better unit because they are always the same length, while handspans vary in length for each person.
3. We use millimetres when we need exact measurements (e.g. when building or making clothing).
   Also, if we are measuring small objects (less than 5 cm), millimetres would usually be preferred over centimetres.

Investigation: Answers will vary. You could place a ruler on the left and right side of the ball, mark the position of the rulers and measure the distance between them.

3:31

1. **a** Echidna: 37 mm, Lizard: 44 mm, Platypus: 41 mm, Koala: 38 mm
   b echidna, koala, platypus, lizard
2. 128 cm
3. 32 cm
4. 2
5. 99 cm
6. 1600 m (or 1 km 600 m)
7. 2000 m (or 2 km)
8. 150 m fence, 6 lights

3:32

Concept: 15 tiles

1. **a**
   2 rows of 8 Area = 16 squares ✔
   2 rows of 6 Area = 12 squares
   b
   4 rows of 3 Area = 12 squares ✔
   2 rows of 4 Area = 8 squares
   c
   1 row of 8 Area = 8 squares
   2 rows of 5 Area = 10 squares ✔
   d
   3 rows of 3 Area = 9 squares
   3 rows of 4 Area = 12 squares ✔

   16 squares, 12 squares, 10 squares and 12 squares will be ticked.

 • *AUSTRALIAN SIGNPOST MATHS 3* • ISBN 9780655708773

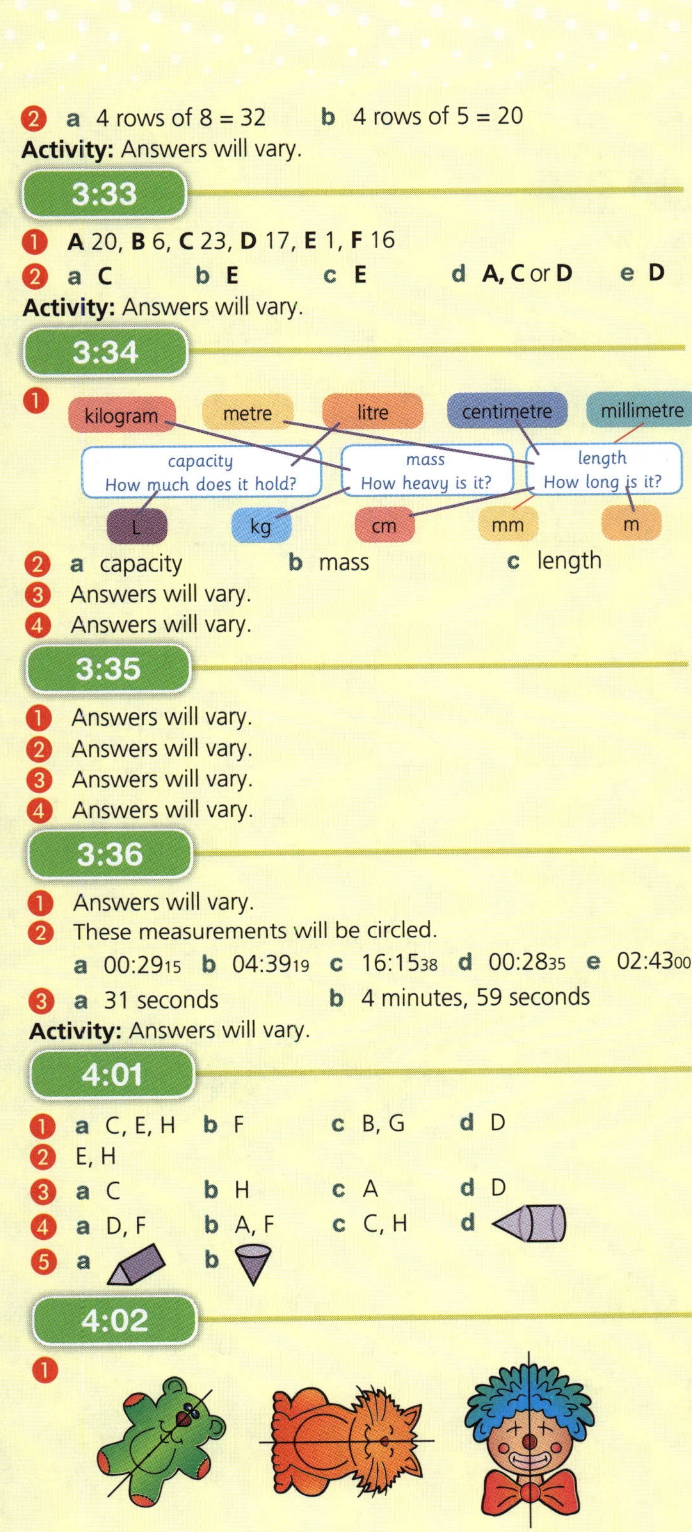

2 a 4 rows of 8 = 32 b 4 rows of 5 = 20

Activity: Answers will vary.

3:33

1 **A** 20, **B** 6, **C** 23, **D** 17, **E** 1, **F** 16

2 a **C** b **E** c **E** d **A, C** or **D** e **D**

Activity: Answers will vary.

3:34

1

2 a capacity b mass c length

3 Answers will vary.

4 Answers will vary.

3:35

1 Answers will vary.

2 Answers will vary.

3 Answers will vary.

4 Answers will vary.

3:36

1 Answers will vary.

2 These measurements will be circled.

a 00:29$_{15}$ b 04:39$_{19}$ c 16:15$_{38}$ d 00:28$_{35}$ e 02:43$_{00}$

3 a 31 seconds b 4 minutes, 59 seconds

Activity: Answers will vary.

4:01

1 a C, E, H b F c B, G d D

2 E, H

3 a C b H c A d D

4 a D, F b A, F c C, H d

5 a b

4:02

1

2

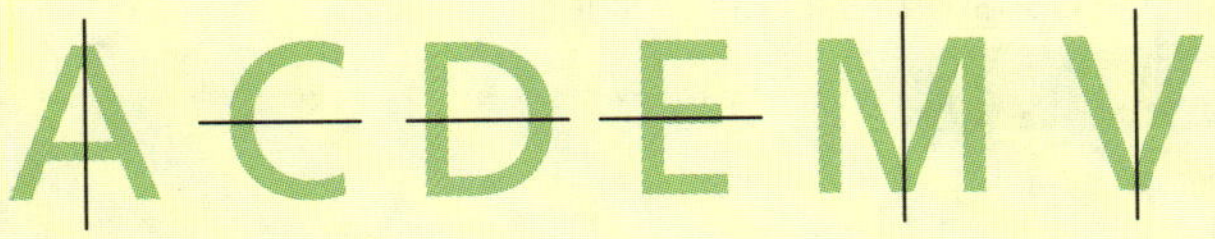

3

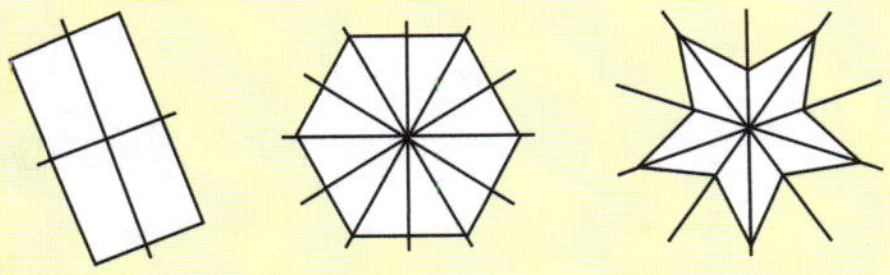

Activity: Answers will vary.

4:03

1 a 6, cube b 2, cylinder c 1, cone
d 0, sphere e 5, (triangular) prism

2 a square b circle c circle
d circle e triangle

3 a e b a c a d c e e
f e g d h b i b, c, d

4 a 2 b 1 c 3 d 4

4:04

1 Answers will vary.

2

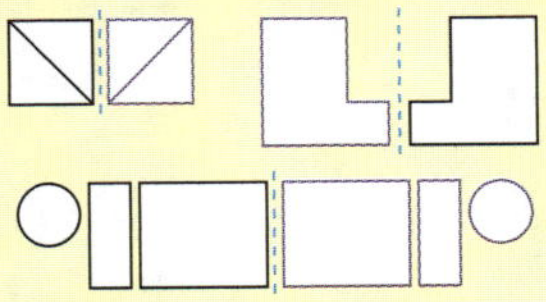

Fun spot: Answers will vary.

4:05

1 a 0 b 1 c 3 d 0 e 3 f 0 g 1 h 3

2 a, d, f. The lines are going in the same direction and will not meet.

3 Where the lines meet, a right angle (square corner) is formed.

4 square, rectangle

5 a Chen, Alan b Chen, Alan c Chen, Alan

6 a Answers will vary, e.g. railway tracks, electricity poles.

b yes, no
When things are further away they look smaller.

4:06

1 a triangle 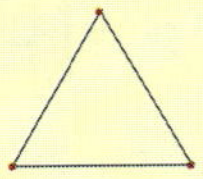 b square

c pentagon 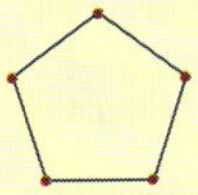 d hexagon

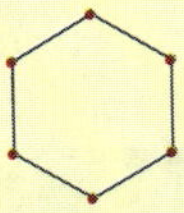

yes, yes

2 b (square), d (hexagon)

3 a triangle 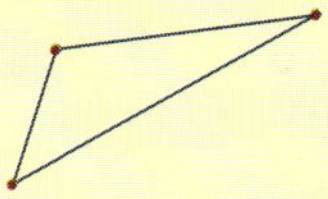 b quadrilateral

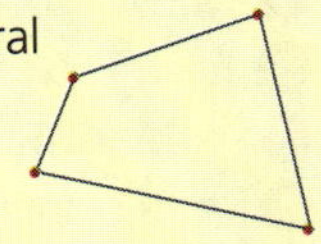

c pentagon 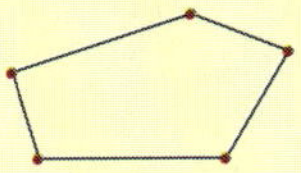 d hexagon

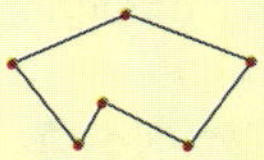

no, no

4 a 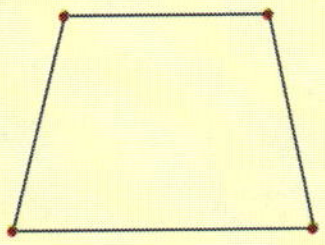 b 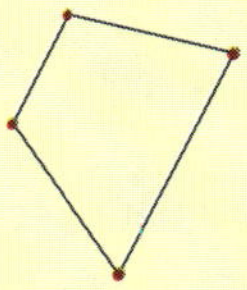 c

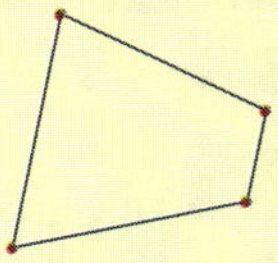

irregular

Activity:

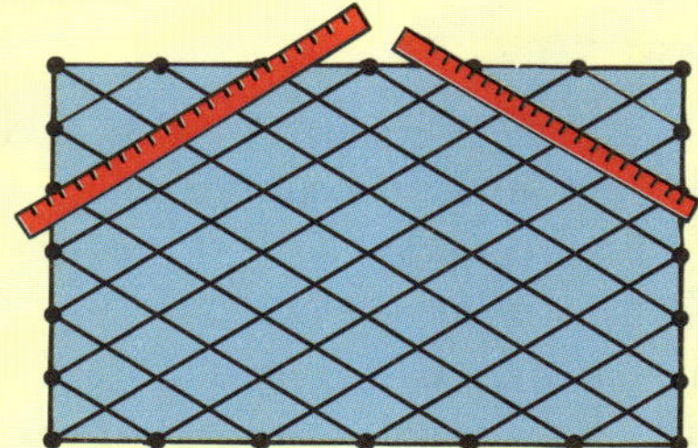

parallelogram or rhombus or diamond

The shape repeated is a parallelogram, rhombus or diamond. Rhombuses are irregular because their angles are not all equal.

4:07

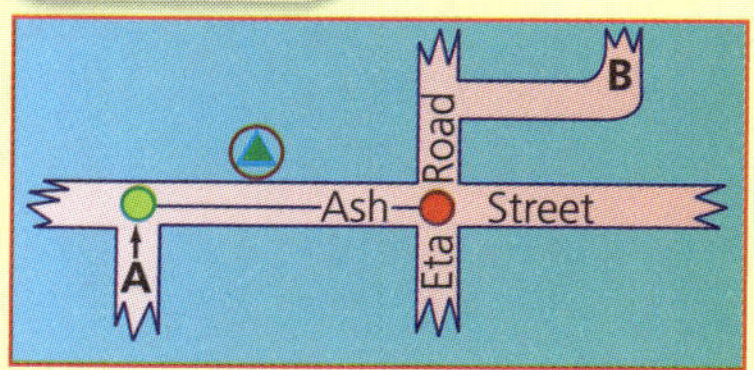

1. a turn left, then first left
   b turn right, then first left, then first right
   c turn right, then first right, then first left
   d turn right, then first right, then second right
2. a G (Post office) b H (Hospital)
3. a H b E c N d E

4:08

1. a D b A c A d C e C f F
   g Answers will vary. Example: 3 right, 7 up.
2. a 3 up, 2 right, 4 up b 2 up, 1 left, 5 up
   c 6 up, 1 left, 3 down, 1 left, 4 up
   d 5 down, 1 right, 2 down e 4 down, 2 left, 3 down
3. a 3 forwards
   b 1 forwards, turn right, 2 forwards, turn left, 4 forwards
   c 1 forwards, turn right, 6 forwards, turn right, 2 forwards
   d 2 forwards, turn left, 2 forwards, turn right, 2 forwards
   e 2 forwards, turn left, 2 forwards, turn left, 4 forwards

4:09

1. a D b A c E d C e F f B
2. a E b A, B and F c C d D
3. a A, C, F b A, B, C, F
4. a rectangle, triangle b triangle, triangle
   c hexagon, square d circle, rhombus (or diamond)
5. a 2 b 23 c 9 d 5

4:10

1. a 3, 3 b 4, 4 c 3 d 4
2. a 3
   b any quadrilateral: square, rectangle, rhombus, trapezium, parallelogram, kite
   c 5 d hexagon

Activity: Answers will vary.

4:11

1. J
2. L
3. a H, I b E, G c C d D e yes

Investigation: Answers will vary.

4:12

Header: 4, 3, 5, 8, 6

1. a

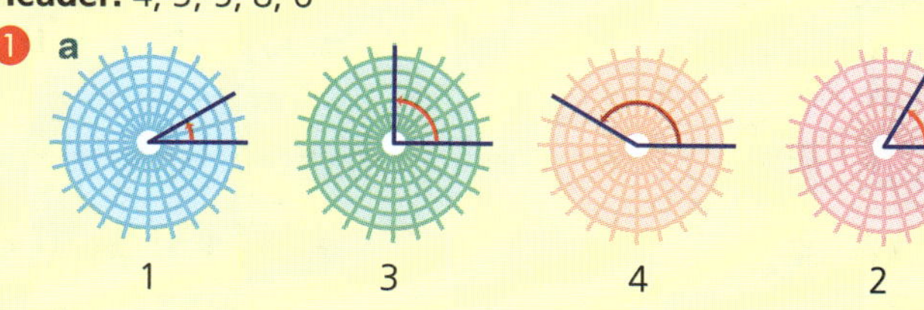

1 3 4 2

b

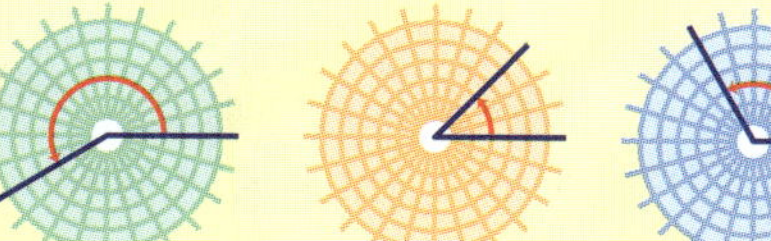

4 1 2 3

2. a

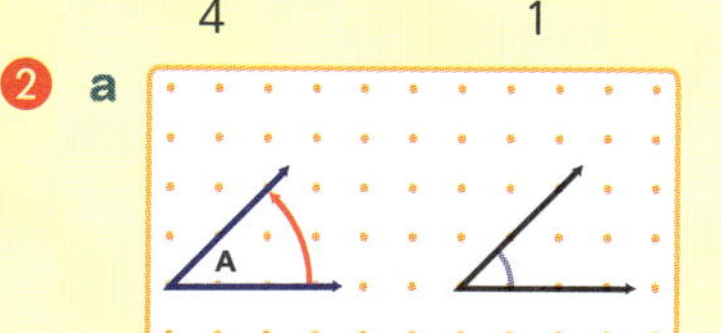

b

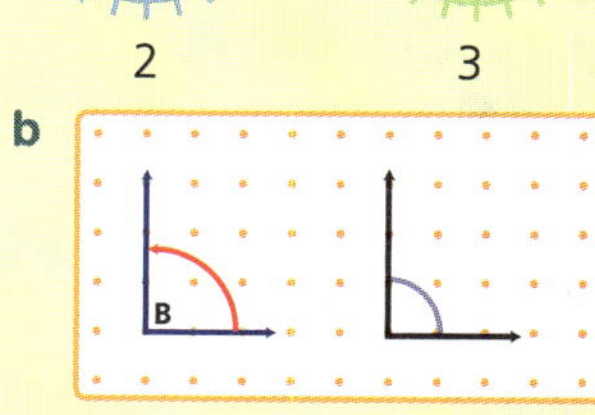

c B is a right angle because the two arms makes a square corner.

4:13

1. a C, E, F (Note: F is a parallelogram, which is a kind of trapezium.) b F
2.

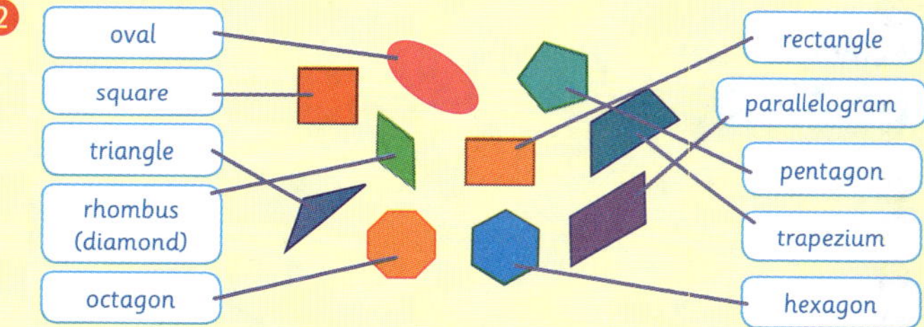

3. Answers will vary.

4:14

1. a C, G b A, B, H, J c E, I d A, C, D, E, F, J e H, I
2. a A, J b F
3. triangle (C, G)
4. a Answers will vary.
   b 8 (including 4 squares leaning at an angle)
   c 9 d 12
5. Each shape has a curved side.

4:15

1. A, D, E, G
2. B
3. yes

Investigation: Answers will vary, e.g. the corner of the page.

4:16

1. a clockwise, quarter turn b anticlockwise, half turn
   c anticlockwise, quarter turn d clockwise, half turn
   e clockwise, three-quarter turn
   f anticlockwise, three-quarter turn

 ISBN 9780655708773

2 a
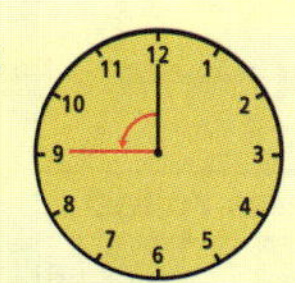
b
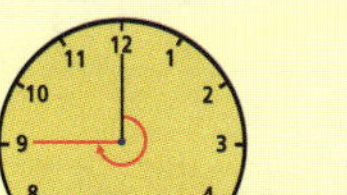
c yes

Investigation: Answers will vary.

4:17

1 a pencil b duck c doll d ball
e right side of top shelf f left side of top shelf
g middle of middle shelf

2 a saucers b plates c mugs d pots
e first on the left (or fourth from the right) on the top
f second from the right (or third from the left) on the bottom
g first on the right (or fourth from the left) on the bottom
h first on the right (or fourth from the left) on the top

3 a Tran b Sophie c Mark d Felicity
e second from the left (or fourth from the right) on the top
f fourth from the left (or second from the right) on the bottom

4:18

1 a
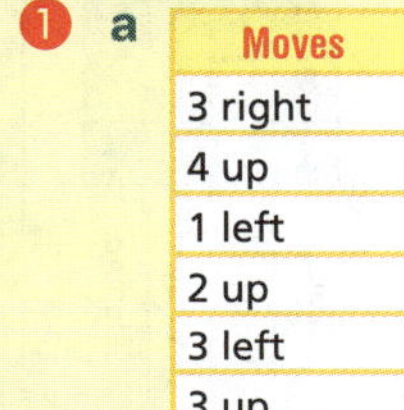

Moves
3 right
4 up
1 left
2 up
3 left
3 up
4 right
2 down

b

Moves
5 left
9 up
2 right
7 down
2 right
4 up
1 right
3 up

2 a
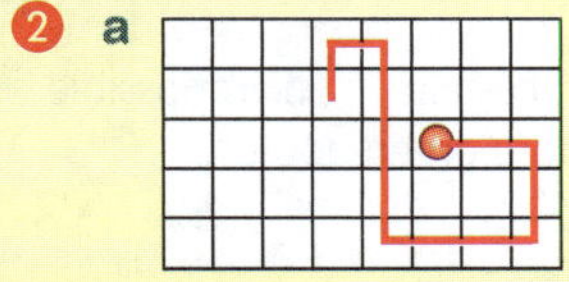
b
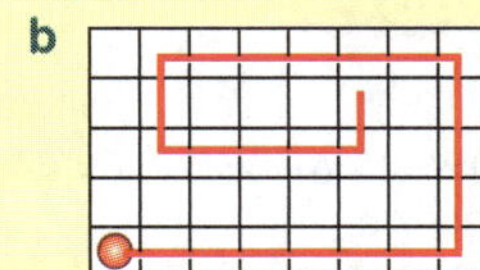

3 H C K B J F E A I D G O

Activity: Answers will vary.

4:19

1 a cylinder b neither c prism d prism e neither
f prism g cylinder h neither i prism

2 a Y b X c Z d Y

3 a 8 b 18 c 12

4
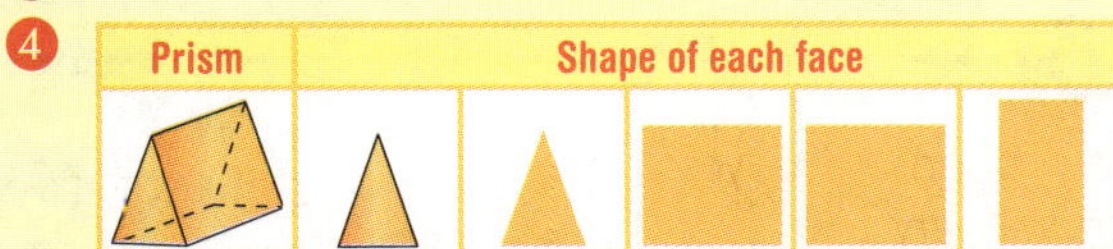

Prism	Shape of each face				

The faces are triangles and rectangles.

4:20

1 b, d, e, f, g, i

2 a A b C c A

3 a 5 b 8 c 5 d 4

4
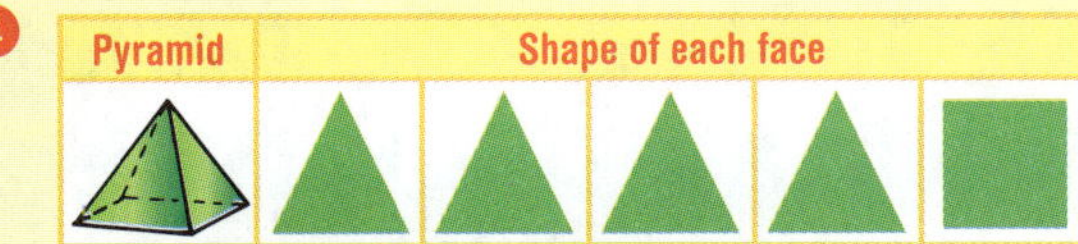

Pyramid	Shape of each face				

The faces are triangles and a square.

4:21

1 a 37 b 3 c cupboard d on the back wall

2 Answers will vary.

Investigation: Answers will vary.

4:22

1 Koala

2 Echidna

3 Platypus

4 Wallaby

Fun spot: Answers will vary.

4:23

1 a B, E, I b D, F, H c B, D, E, F, H, I

2 a false b true c false
d false e true f false

Activity: Answers will vary.

4:24

1 a pyramid b cone c cylinder d sphere
e prism f cylinder g prism h pyramid

2 a b c
d e f

4:25

1 B

2 6 faces, 8 vertices, 12 edges

Activity: A cube will be made using the net.

4:26

Header: 8, 12

1 a **A** 4 blocks, **B** 8 blocks, **C** 16 blocks, **D** 20 blocks
b The longer the base, the greater the number of blocks.

2 Answers will vary.

5:01

Students will use the language of chance to discuss the pictures.

5:02

1 a A, B, E, F, G, H, J, K, L b C, D

2 a Answers will vary, e.g. I might eat pizza for dinner.
b Answers will vary, e.g. I will turn into a frog.

3 Answers will vary.

5:03

1 a The picture on the left is more likely.
The picture on the right is less likely.
b The picture on the left is more likely.
The picture on the right is less likely.
c The picture on the left is more likely.
The picture on the right is less likely.

2. The tower is most likely to fall over.
   Answers will vary, e.g. It is impossible for the blocks in the tower to suddenly change colour.
3. red or blue

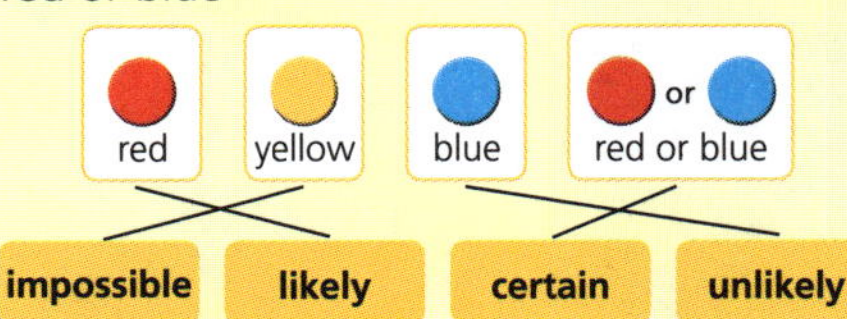

5:04

1. **a** blue **b** orange **c** 8 **d** 30
2. **a** 825 **b** 46 **c** 166 **d** 72 **e** 88
   f 201 **g** 405 **h** 193 **i** 388
3. **a** 87 **b** 27 **c** 23 **d** 0
   e Answers will vary.

Investigation: Answers will vary.

5:05

1. **a** 1 **b** 3 **c** Fish and Mice **d** Birds **e** 16
2.

Pets kept in the classroom			
Birds	Fish	Mice	Turtles
3	6	6	1

Pets kept in the classroom	
Birds	3
Fish	6
Mice	6
Turtles	1

   a 3 **b** 16 **c** Answers will vary.
   d

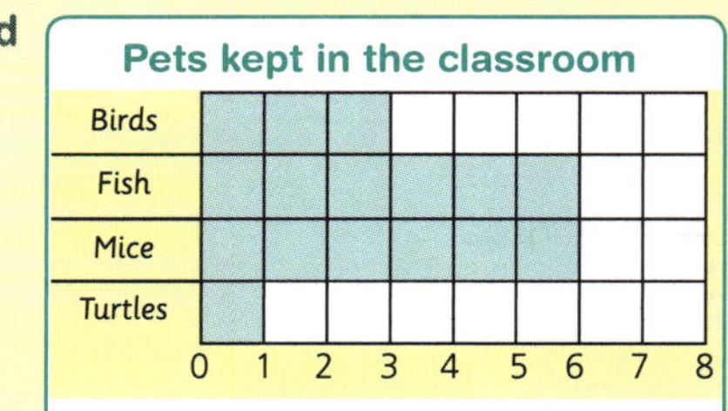

3. **a**

Youth group attendance	
Carmen	● ● ● ●
Erika	● ● ● ● ●
Holly	● ● ●
Paul	● ● ● ● ● ● ●
Yong	● ● ● ● ● ●

   b Holly **c** yes **d** 8 times
4. Answers will vary.

5:06

1. **a** 6 **b** Tuesday **c** 20 **d** 10
2. **a** 7 **b** 6 **c** 8 **d** Mandarin
3. **a** 21 **b** 15 **c** 10 **d** 47

5:07

1.

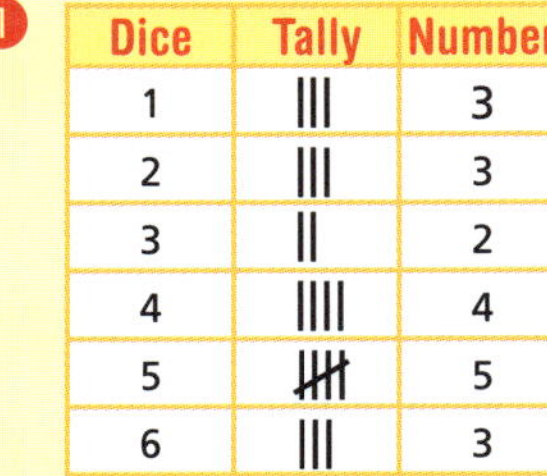

Dice	Tally	Number
1	|||	3
2	|||	3
3	||	2
4	||||	4
5	𝍸	5
6	|||	3

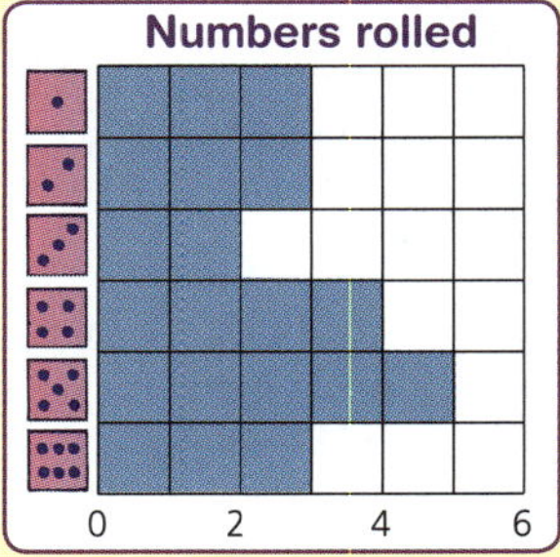

2.

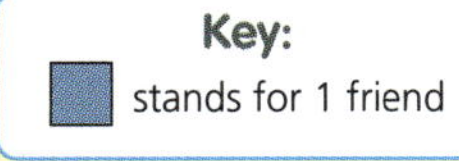

Favourite game

Handball
Hopscotch
Marbles
Skipping
0 2 4 6 8 10

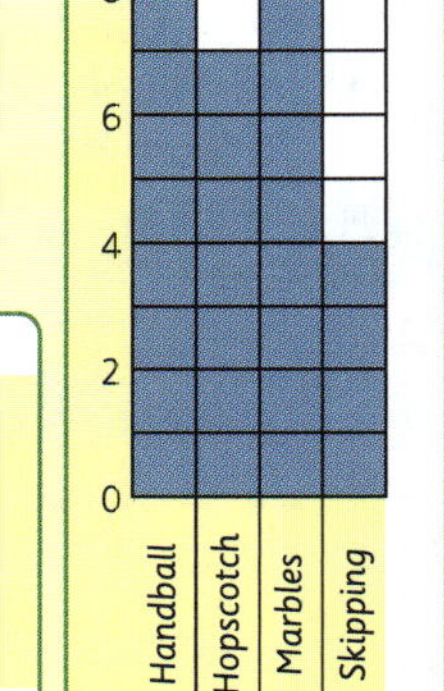

3. Answers will vary.

5:08

1. **a** likely **b** unlikely **c** certain **d** impossible
2. Answers will vary. There will be more green apples than red.
3. 1, 2, 3, 4, 5, 6
4. Answers will vary.

Investigation: a, b Answers will vary. c yes. There is only one way of throwing six 1s in a row (1, 1, 1, 1, 1, 1) which makes it very unlikely. If you think of another example like throwing two 1s out of six throws, there are lots of ways for this to happen (for example, 1, 1, 2, 5, 4, 4 or 3, 6, 1, 4, 1, 6). This means that throwing two 1s out of six throws is much more likely than throwing six 1s in a row.

5:09

1. **a** yes **b** no **c** yes
2. Answers will vary.
   a win, lose, draw
   b sunny, rainy, windy, stormy
3. **a** red, blue, green **b** red **c** green
   d no **e** yes
4. highly unlikely

Investigation: Answers will vary.

5:10

1. a no b yes
2. a yes b yes
   c no (but there is an equal chance compared to the other colours)
3. a blue b no c no
4. a C b B c A, D, E d yes
   e no f no g yes

Investigation: Answers will vary.

5:11

1. a 6 b 100 c 70 d 10 e 184 f 380
2. a Amanda b Juan c 10
   d 8 e 33 f 24
3. a 14, 18 b Tuesday and Thursday
   c 26 d 8
   e No, because some students may have practised more than once during this week.

Activity: Answers will vary.

5:12

1. a 400 b 200 c 2008 d 1400 e 50 pears
2. a 16 b 12 c Thursday d Monday and Saturday
   e 12 f 74 g The shop was closed.
3. a 20 b 2 pm to 3 pm c 4 pm to 5 pm d 125
   e That is the time when most people are driving home from work.

5:13

Investigation: Answers will vary.

5:14

Investigation: Answers will vary.
ICT: Answers will vary.

5:15

1. a red b yellow c no d yes
   e blue or yellow f blue, red or yellow
2. a red b yellow
3. a Yes. There is an even chance of spinning blue or red.
   b No. There is still an even chance of spinning a blue.
4. a yes b 2

Investigation: Answers will vary.

5:16

1. a unlikely b impossible c certain d very likely
   e very likely f very likely g unlikely h impossible
   i certain j even chance
2.

Will always happen	It can happen but not always	Will never happen
c, i	a, d, e, f, g, j	b, h

3. Answers will vary. Example: E A C D B

Fun spot: Answers will vary.

5:17

1.

Hair colour in Kai-Lin's class

Black	● ● ● ● ● ●
Blonde	● ● ● ● ●
Brown	● ●
Red	●

Key: ● stands for 2 students

   a Black b none c 6 d 28
   e To tell the value of each picture on the graph.
   f Answers will vary. Example: They are easy to draw and read and are attractive.
2. Answers will vary. Examples:
   a It is useful for recording information as it is observed.
   b It looks impressive and interesting.
   c You can compare categories at a glance. It is attractive.

ICT: Answers will vary.

5:18

1. a 13 b 10 c 1 d 23 e 29
   f before 8 pm g 30, yes
   h Answers will vary.
2. Answers will vary.

5:19

Investigation: Answers will vary.
ICT: Answers will vary.

5:20

1. a January and February b 16 days
   c Winter d April and November
   e Yes. Although the graph shows there were less days that had rain in June, there may have been some days in June with very heavy rainfall.
2. a i) March ii) August
   b Summer
   c Answers will vary.

Investigation: Answers will vary.
ICT: Answers will vary.

5:21

Concept: 6 students had no pets. 7 students had 1 pet.

1. a 2 b 3 c Monday d 13
2. a 7 b 24 c 3

3 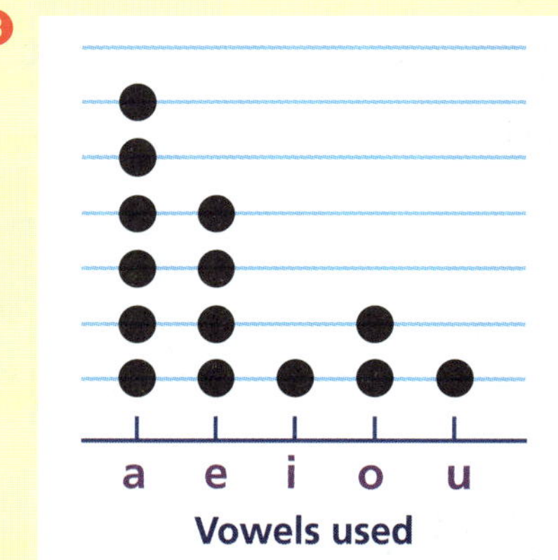

a a b i and u c 14 d 5

4 'e' is the most likely result. The more text you use, the more likely this will be.

ES 1

1 a

+	
2 + 6	1
4 + 6	7
0 + 1	8
5 + 7	9
5 + 6	10
0 + 7	11
4 + 5	12
7 + 10	15
8 + 7	17
10 + 10	18
9 + 9	20

b

+	
2 + 3	4
4 + 3	5
2 + 2	7
5 + 4	9
8 + 5	8
8 + 0	10
7 + 5	11
1 + 9	12
10 + 5	13
6 + 5	15
10 + 9	19

c

+	
3 + 6	6
2 + 8	7
4 + 2	8
5 + 2	9
4 + 7	10
3 + 5	11
9 + 6	12
6 + 6	13
8 + 8	14
7 + 6	15
10 + 4	16

d

+	
3 + 4	5
6 + 2	6
4 + 5	7
3 + 2	8
2 + 4	9
8 + 4	10
4 + 9	11
5 + 5	12
4 + 7	13
7 + 8	14
5 + 9	15

e

−	
8 − 6	1
10 − 4	0
1 − 0	2
12 − 5	4
11 − 6	6
7 − 7	5
9 − 5	7
17 − 7	8
15 − 7	10
11 − 8	9
18 − 9	3

f

−	
5 − 2	2
7 − 3	3
4 − 2	4
9 − 4	5
13 − 5	0
8 − 8	1
12 − 5	6
10 − 9	7
15 − 5	8
11 − 5	10
19 − 10	9

g

−	
6 − 4	0
5 − 2	1
10 − 9	2
7 − 7	3
9 − 3	4
7 − 3	5
10 − 3	6
14 − 5	7
9 − 4	8
18 − 8	9
10 − 2	10

h

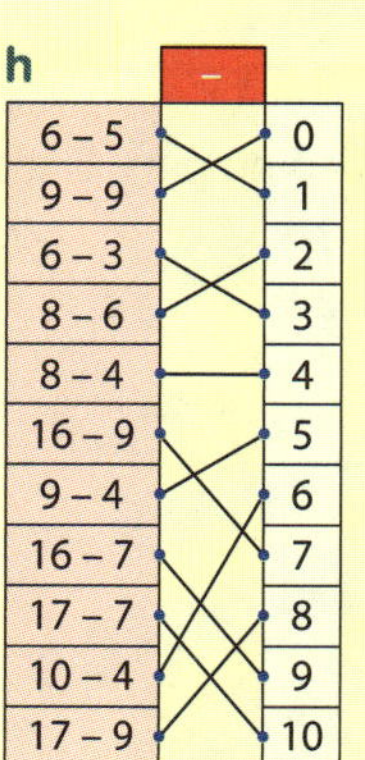

ES 2

1 A 2, 6, 6, 5, 9
B 7, 4, 4, 7, 7
C 7, 8, 4, 8, 9
D 7, 12, 9, 8, 11
E 5, 11, 5, 9, 13
F 4, 10, 9, 6, 7
G 8, 5, 10, 6, 8
H 10, 10, 10, 8, 9
I 7, 9, 10, 8, 12
J 9, 3, 7, 6, 10
K 14, 10, 11, 5, 18
L 9, 3, 12, 13, 17
M 6, 9, 16, 8, 10
N 11, 12, 11, 16, 15
O 13, 11, 11, 11, 12
P 12, 4, 16, 14, 14
Q 14, 13, 15, 13, 12
R 15, 17, 13, 15, 14

ES 3

1 A 7, 9, 5, 9
B 4, 6, 9, 8
C 1, 7, 9, 6
D 8, 9, 5, 2
E 9, 8, 4, 7
F 7, 2, 7, 3
G 8, 4, 8, 5
H 3, 9, 6, 6
I 9, 6, 5, 5
J 3, 9, 7, 6
K 8, 4, 7, 8

ES 4

There are no answers for this page.

ES 5

1 a 49 b 64 c 83
d 91 e 51 f 37

2 a 77 b 55 c 87 d 91

ES 6

1 a 154 b 117 c 108 d 283 e 790
f 388 g 516 h 510 i 428 j 331
k 514 l 733

2 Answers will vary.

ES 7

1 a 334 b 662 c 361 d 432 e 615
f 531 g 792 h 657 i 727 j 762
k 321 l 731 m 805 n 640 o 962

2 a 432 b 374 c 377 d 921

ES 8

1 a $0.78 b $1.52 c $4.73 d $5.31 e $6.69
f $8.25 g $4.70 h $8.51 i $6.43 j $7.11
k $6.08 l $6.97 m $5.40 n $6.29 o $7.14

2 a $3.79 b $5.77 c $5.68
d $8.68 e $6.49 f $8.48

3 a $9.55 b $8.20 c $8.85 d $8.70

4 a $4.88 b $8.83 c $9.37 d $9.01

ES 9

1 a 5468 b 8975 c 7588 d 3798 e 7967
f 6324 g 8600 h 7251 i 3573 j 8240

2 a 7195 b 4885 c 4343 d 8925 e 8019
f 7505 g 9281 h 4339 i 7617 j 7932

3 a $9149 b $8291 c $7909 d $6297 e $9430

ES 10

1. a 7561 b 6935 c 9818 d 7482
2. a 3904 b 5108 c 7837 d 7088
3. a $86.14 b $52.53 c $90.10 d $86.80
4. Estimates will vary.
   a A = 5495 b A = 8456 c A = $8273

ES 11

1. a 2 hundreds, 4 tens, 5 ones
   b 6 hundreds, 4 tens, 5 ones
2. a 131 b 733 c 533 d 331
   e 674 f 902 g 682 h 713
   i 362 j 129 k 123 l 443
   m 178 n 400 o 205

Fun spot: Answers will vary.

ES 12

1. a 528 b 315 c 229 d 421
   e 264 f 108 g 836 h 908
   i 711 j 315 k 248 l 628
   m 727 n 55 o 105 p 608
   q 6 r 734 s 16 t 107
2. Answers will vary.

ES 13

1. a 464 b 255 c 194 d 691
   e 376 f 255 g 594 h 40
   i 289 j 291 k 312 l 562
   m 575 n 80 o 193 p 453
   q 190 r 364 s 491

ES 14

1. a 258 b 179 c 34 d 646
   e 274 f 63 g 489 h 589
   i 138 j 177 k 659 l 567
   m 29 n 99 o 87 p 28
   q 457 r 417 s 228

ES 15

1. a $5.22 b $5.17 c $6.34 d $2.39
   e $4.17 f $1.84 g $2.77 h $6.08
   i $3.34 j $4.08 k $1.70 l $2.58
   m $3.89 n $5.45 o $2.04
2. a $2.11 b $4.98 c $5.35 d $0.05
   e $5.50 f $1.51
3. a $1.05 b $6.20 c $5.45 d $1.20
   e $3.55 f $4.95